Judy

William Hunter

Finding Free Speech

A British Soldier's Son
Who Became an Early American

Eugene A. Procknow

Gene

OXFORD SOUTHERN
an imprint of Sunbury Press, Inc.
Mechanicsburg, PA USA

OXFORD SOUTHERN

an imprint of Sunbury Press, Inc.
Mechanicsburg, PA USA

For information about special discounts for bulk purchases, please contact Sunbury Press Orders Dept. at (855) 338-8359 or orders@sunburypress.com.

To request one of our authors for speaking engagements or book signings, please contact Sunbury Press Publicity Dept. at publicity@sunburypress.com.

FIRST OXFORD SOUTHERN EDITION: January 2022

Set in Adobe Garamond | Interior design by Crystal Devine | Cover by Lawrence Knorr | Edited by Lawrence Knorr.

Publisher's Cataloging-in-Publication Data
Names: Procknow, Eugene A., author.
Title: William Hunter : finding free speech : a British soldier's son who became an early American / Eugene A. Procknow.
Description: First edition. | Mechanicsburg, PA : Oxford Southern, 2022.
Summary: William Hunter, the son of a Revolutionary War British soldier, witnessed the terrors of combat and capture and penned the only surviving Revolutionary account written by a child of a British soldier. Remarkably, Hunter immigrated to America and became a gutsy Kentucky newspaper editor and a prominent politician, businessman, and community leader.
Identifiers: ISBN : 978-1-62006-573-0 (trade paperback) | 978-1-62006-565-5 (hardcover).
Subjects: HISTORY / United States / Revolutionary Period (1775–1800) | HISTORY / United States / 19th Century | BIOGRAPHY & AUTOBIOGRAPHY / Historical.

Product of the United States of America
0 1 1 2 3 5 8 13 21 34 55

Continue the Enlightenment!

For Mary

Contents

Illustrations

Prologue

In Pre-Civil War Washington City,[1] an aging, robust man sat down to reminisce about his colorful life. He didn't know how many years he had left. Pulling out a red Moroccan leather blank book, he penned his memoir. His name was William Hunter, and his account chronicled the experiences of a child born to a British sergeant stationed in New Jersey during the Revolutionary War. Most Americans' strong anti-British sentiment had waned since the War of 1812. His neighbors and friends had no concerns over his loyalty, and he no longer wanted to obscure the past. Most of all, he wished his family to know the truth.

Hunter's memoir is an enthralling account of his first twenty-five years. William and his family suffered the horrors of war and the hardships of capture and Trans-Atlantic travel. His turbulent childhood narrative is the only known journal or diary written by the child of a British soldier during the American Revolution. It's a unique historical source filled with incisive observations and novel insights. As importantly, the journal describes the development of a child coming from a family with modest means into an adult who benefited from parents who gave him the gift of a printing apprenticeship. Living in England after the war, William recounts his development as a printer and how the trade fostered his education and intellectual development. Abiding in the hotbed of political and religious dissent, Hunter describes the nascent republican movement in Britain, his adoption of the principles of the Enlightenment, and his rejection of politics dominated by a monarchy and the upper class.

So fervent his belief in republicanism and his desire to escape British class confines, the twenty-five-year-old decided to move to America. His return ocean voyage was every bit as arduous and dangerous as the childhood situations he faced during the War for Independence. Abruptly, Hunter ends his journal upon emigrating to Philadelphia in 1793. Perhaps, Hunter believed that his family was familiar with his life events from this point forward. In addition, heirs and other interested parties could find salient records of his occupations, accomplishments, and community contributions documented in newspapers, books, and legislation. Therefore, he may not have felt the need to finish his memoir. Alternatively, an aging Hunter may not have been physically able to complete his life's story. Whatever the reason, Hunter's journal reflects his love for his father, who fought against the rebelling Americans, and his pride in becoming an American.

William Hunter lived an extraordinary life spanning the American War of Independence, through the Early Republic, and ending just a few years before the American Civil War. Residing in Britain, Canada, France, and the United States, he experienced the terrors of a soldier's family following a father in combat, arduous land and sea journeys, loss of a sibling, separation from family, and immigration to a new country. Overcoming these obstacles, he became a pioneering newspaper editor, a leading member of his community, and a watchful government official. While William did not achieve the stature of a famous founder, his fulsome life represents those who helped a struggling new nation develop during the Jacksonian period. William's life story exemplifies the major social and political changes of the period. He espoused freedom

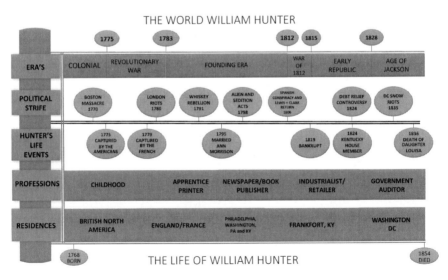

FIGURE 1. Overview of William Hunter's Life.

from state-sponsored religion, increased access to education, and the republican principles of the people versus monarchs (or despots) controlling the levers of government.

Like most Americans of the period, Hunter was torn between the aspirations and ideals of American society and the reality of its institutions. He engaged in incongruent practices and prejudices. Hunter became an owner of enslaved peoples while at the same time espousing anti-slavery views. Another significant variance, Hunter exhibited total disdain for Native Americans, calling them "vile instruments of barbarity," a view that was rife among nineteenth-century Euro-Americans. Understanding these broadly held contradictions are important for those wishing to understand the United States in the early republic period. Hunter's life is a seminal example for a discerning exploration of the prevailing eighteenth-century mores and provides provocative insights beyond the basic facts of his life. Finally, in the face of considerable personal risks, he courageously followed his political and religious convictions at key points in his life.

The late seventeenth and early eighteenth centuries produced many "William Hunters," several of which crossed paths with our journalist. Notable examples are an English physician, a Rhode Island Senator, and a Virginia printer. Additionally, there are numerous lesser-known William Hunters, including several who lived nearby who require sorting out from our protagonist. While his name was not distinctive, his experiences were. And that's our story.

Part I

Discerning Revolutionary Journalist

William's early years highlight striking dichotomies, including some which are difficult to reconcile today. Born in America, Americans regarded him as an immigrant. Raised in a family that labored with their hands, William matured into an adult who worked with his mind. Taught to support the monarchy, William became an ardent believer in democracy (a republican in his terminology). While espousing lofty egalitarian ideals, he also demonstrated the prevailing damaging prejudices against Native and African Americans. Lastly, he became an American despite accompanying a father who suffered grievous wounds fighting for King George III against the Americans.

William's journal starts with a partial recitation of his family history.[1] In 1727, William's father, John Hunter, was born in Lisburn, Ireland (today part of British Northern Ireland). Located astride the primary trade route between Belfast and Dublin, Lisburn was a market town centered in an important linen production region. Upon reaching working age, John earned a modest living in the dominant textile industry as a weaver. While the late eighteenth-century linen market experienced overall growth, the vicissitudes of increasing competitive markets, British trade barriers, and competition from other cloths caused the number of weaving opportunities to decline periodically. Perhaps during one of these declines, John Hunter sought more stable employment and enlisted in the 26th Regiment of Foot. Just as likely, he enlisted for other reasons such as interest in leading a soldier's life or seeking adventurous opportunities. In any

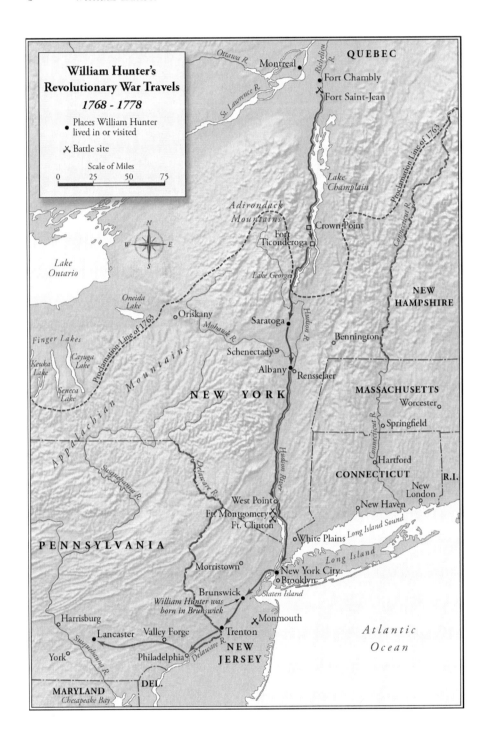

William Hunter's
Revolutionary War Travels
1768 - 1778

• Places William Hunter
  lived in or visited

✗ Battle site

Scale of Miles

0   25   50   75

event, John followed a common pattern, as textile weaving was one of the most prevalent occupations of British Army recruits during this period.

During late seventeenth century religious tumult in Scotland, radical Presbyterians known as the Cameronians formed a regiment in the lowlands to oppose the English Catholic kings. Named after Richard Cameron, a widely popular field preacher who died a martyr to his adherents, regimental officers recruited the initial complement of soldiers from the Glasgow region. With the British Army reorganization in 1750, the Cameronians became the 26th Regiment of Foot in the British establishment. However, many inside and outside the army continued to refer to the regiment as the Cameronians. Over the years, other nationalities joined the regiment, but the regiment maintained its Scottish heritage, and during the American Revolution, its ranks consisted of three-fourths Scots.

The British military command transferred the 26th Regiment to Ireland in 1751, and John Hunter enlisted as a private soldier a year after its arrival. Certainly, a Protestant, as British law prevented Catholic enlistments, the regiment's Presbyterian heritage and the opportunity for long-term employment most likely attracted John Hunter to enlist. Despite having the right religious background in a historically radical protestant regiment, it does not appear from the journal that Hunter was particularly devout. The 26th Regiment consisted of three to four hundred soldiers organized into ten companies. Components of the 26th Regiment were dispersed among several Irish towns to lessen the impact on any one location and with the military objective of keeping the peace and thwarting smuggling. After a few years, British commanders ordered the regiment to Scotland for a short period and then back to Ireland by 1754.

The 26th Regiment remained on garrison duty in Ireland during the French and Indian War (Seven Years War in Europe). However, a significant number of the regiment's soldiers were tapped to reinforce units destined for British America. In 1755, a fortunate Hunter avoided a draft of fifty-four men from the 26th Regiment to fill out the complement of the undersized 44th and 48th Regiments.[2] These two regiments were destined to join the disastrous Major General Edward Braddock's expedition to capture Fort Duquesne at modern-day Pittsburgh. Two years later, nine Gaelic-speaking non-commissioned officers were transferred to two newly formed Highland regiments, opening up advancement opportunities for Hunter. During the Irish deployment, Hunter served as a good soldier and earned several promotions achieving the rank of sergeant, a Non-Commissioned Officer.[3]

In the mid-1760s, Hunter courted and married Margaret Nance. While Nance is generally regarded as a Cornish name, some family members moved from Cornwall, resettling in Ireland. As there is no record of the 26th Regiment passing through Wales, John met the ten or more years younger Margaret either in Lisburn or at another Irish duty station of the 26th Regiment. Specifically, how or where they met is not known. What is known is that Margaret had relatives living in Lisbon, Portugal, so it is possible that her family moved several times.[4]

CHAPTER ONE

Garrison Duty in British North American Colonies

On Saturday, May 16, 1767, the 26th Regiment, along with the 16th and 18th Regiments, boarded lighters in Cork, Ireland, for transport to the city's ocean docks at Cove (now Cobh).[1] Shortly thereafter, the three regiments and their dependents loaded onto ocean transports, forming a seven-ship convoy for British North America.[2] In the 18th century, wives and children often accompanied British soldiers on lengthy foreign deployments. This was the case for the 26th Regiment as many women and children joined the regiment on the voyage.[3] While deployed overseas, the army provided half rations for duly authorized women and one-quarter rations for children. Commonly, women worked to supplement the family income and sometimes as a condition for accompanying the regiment on campaign or foreign deployment. Women serving in hospitals received full rations making nursing particularly attractive. Other military support roles open to women included laundresses, sutlers selling provisions, and seamstresses, for which soldiers paid the women a fee for their services.[4]

Consistent with the norm for sergeants, Margaret joined John for the anticipated extended North American tour of duty. Curiously, John and Margaret left a very young daughter in Ireland. Left with relatives, the daughter may not have been well enough to survive an arduous transatlantic crossing. Tragically, the parents never saw their daughter again. Further, she disappears from the family record as William never connects with her. William's older brother John was born either just before embarking for America or shortly after the couple's arrival. In his memoir, William did not recall his sister or his older brother John who died at a young age.

After a seven-week ocean passage, regimental records indicate that the unit disembarked in New Jersey and deployed to three relatively quiet locations in the increasingly unruly North American colonies. John Hunter's company received orders to proceed to Brunswick (now New Brunswick) while other components of the 26th Regiment were sent to nearby Perth Amboy and Elizabethtown. The family billeted in the town's barracks which dated back to the French and Indian War. The colonial government constructed the barracks as an alternative to quartering the troops in the homes of the local populous. William understands from his "mother that I was born at Brunswick in Jersey[5] in the year of 1768, and I believe she said, in the month of July" and "my father seemed to indicate it was in 1769." William adopted his mother's recollection of his birth year throughout his life, although some historical references cite 1770 as his birth year.[6] The birth of a child fathered by a British soldier stationed in Brunswick was not an unusual event. Remarkably the one hundred and sixty British soldiers fathered fifty children during the regiment's almost three-year stay in Brunswick.[7]

Despite the cordial relationships between British soldiers and the Brunswick citizenry, British commanders determined to move Sergeant Hunter's regiment out of Brunswick. The British government adopted a policy of rotating duty stations of its army regiments on long-term overseas deployments. The Pensacola garrison required relief due to a high death rate among the soldiers resulting from the extremely unhealthy environment for Europeans. As the Florida duty station was particularly hazardous, British commanders opted to choose between the 16th and 26th Regiments as the replacement regiment by drawing straws. The 16th Regiment drew the short straw and transferred to Pensacola.[8] In May 1770, British commanders ordered the 26th Regiment to make the short journey to New York City. By drawing the long straw, the life of William Hunter and his family avoided a potential catastrophe due to the shortened life expectancy among British soldiers and their families posted in Florida.[9]

After hearing of the 26th Regiment's re-deployment, the citizens of Brunswick sent an open letter to Major Charles Preston, the local commander, commending him for his leadership and the good behavior of the troops under his command. The town magistrates observed "a pleased reflection on the Tranquility we have enjoyed from the harmony that has uniformly subsisted between the inhabitants and the troops quartered in the Barracks under your immediate command." Remarkably, the letter concludes that the British operated with the "least infringement on our Rights and Privileges." In turn, Major

Preston responded to the citizens' address thanking the town citizens for their "friendships" and "general good dispositions." Preston remarked on the town's healthiness as only two of the one hundred and sixty-two soldiers died (one by natural death and one by accident) during the three years of the 26th's stay in Brunswick. To celebrate, the town offered Preston and his officers "genteel entertainment" at White Hall tavern.[10]

While amicable relationships existed between the soldiers of the 26th Regiment and New Jersey residents, the British garrison just a few miles away experienced a hostile reception from an increasingly divisive populous. Signifying civil discontent, New Yorkers raised a succession of mast-like logs, dubbed liberty poles in City Hall Park to protest British legislative acts obnoxious to the colonialists. Each time, British soldiers cut down the dissent symbols leading to increasing tensions and, heretofore, minor violence. On January 19, 1770, a riotous clash erupted between New York protesters called the Sons of Liberty and the British Army. The Sons of Liberty detained several British soldiers who were posting hand bills criticizing them as "real enemies of the state" and brought them before the mayor.[11] Hoping to diffuse the situation, the mayor ordered the soldiers back to their barracks. However, the Sons of Liberty followed the British soldiers, and a scuffle erupted. British officers intervened to calm the situation but not before each side suffered minor injuries. Proclaimed by rebellious media as the Battle of Golden Hill, tensions heightened between the city residents and the occupying soldiers.[12] Only six weeks later, the killing of five Boston residents by British soldiers from the 29th Regiment, referred to as the Boston Massacre, further exacerbated the already inflamed situation in New York City but did not demonstrably change the situation in Brunswick. Facing an untenable situation in revengeful Boston necessitated removing the offending 29th Regiment to the relative quiet of the Jersey posts.

While William was too young to discern the broader geopolitical situation and looming rebellion, Sergeant Hunter and the regiment's move to New York City temporarily calmed an increasingly divisive populous. While not the ease of friendly garrisoning as experienced in New Jersey, duty in New York City was not yet hazardous, and on balance, the population supported King George III. In the weeks after the Golden Hill melee, physical conflicts between the Sons of Liberty and the British Army dissipated. As a measure of how much things had calmed, the city hosted a robust celebration of the King's birthday. City residents gathered at Fort George for drinking of toasts and to hear the discharge of cannons. Ships in the harbor responded with their own twenty-one-gun salutes to the King's health. The 26th Regiment paraded under arms

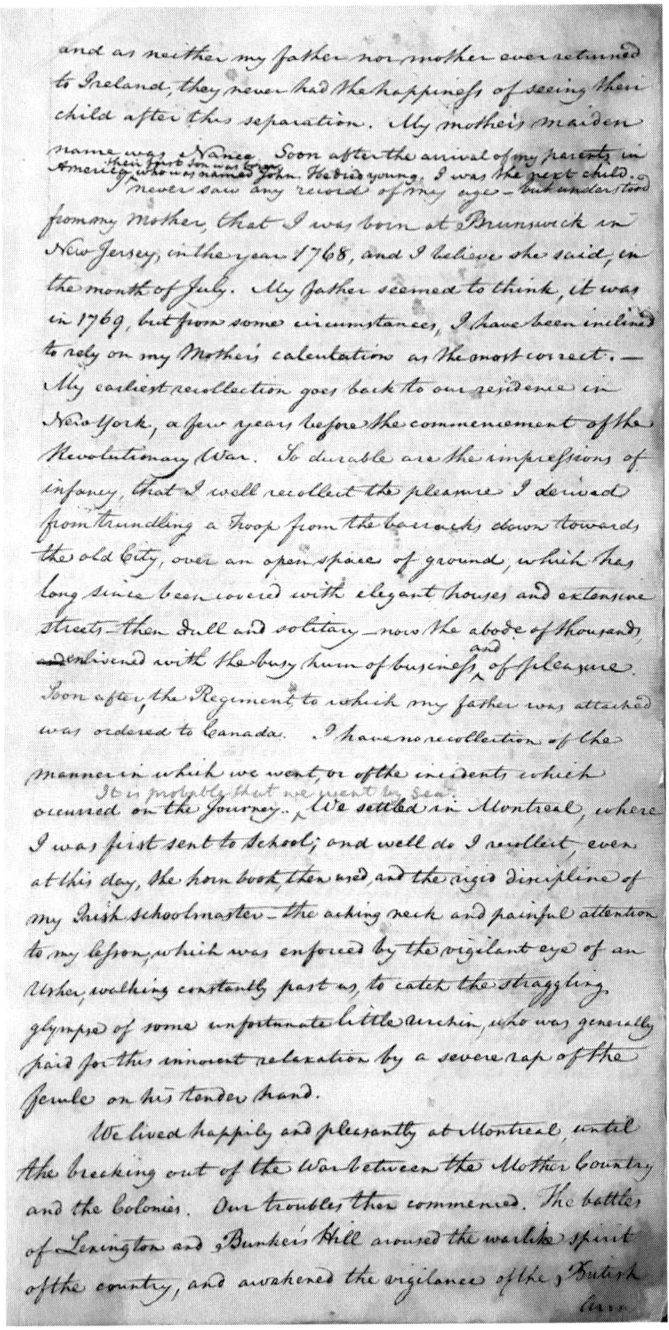

and as neither my father nor mother ever returned
to Ireland, they never had the happiness of seeing their
child after this separation. My mother's maiden
name was Nancy. Soon after the arrival of my parents in
America, their first son was named John. He died young, I was the next child.
I never saw any record of my age – but understood
from my mother, that I was born at Brunswick in
New Jersey, in the year 1768, and I believe she said, in
the month of July. My father seemed to think, it was
in 1769, but from some circumstances, I have been inclined
to rely on my Mother's calculation as the most correct. –
My earliest recollection goes back to our residence in
New York, a few years before the commencement of the
Revolutionary War. So durable are the impressions of
infancy, that I well recollect the pleasure I derived
from trundling a Hoop from the barracks down towards
the old City, over an open space of ground, which has
long since been covered with elegant houses and extensive
streets, then dull and solitary – now the abode of thousands,
and enlivened with the busy hum of business, and of pleasure.
Soon after, the Regiment, to which my father was attached
was ordered to Canada. I have no recollection of the
manner in which we went, or of the incidents which
occurred on the journey. It is probably that we went by Sea. We settled in Montreal, where
I was first sent to School; and well do I recollect, even
at this day, the horn book, then used, and the rigid discipline of
my Irish schoolmaster – the aching neck and painful attention
to my lesson, which was enforced by the vigilant eye of an
Usher, walking constantly past us, to catch the straggling
glimpse of some unfortunate little urchin, who was generally
paid for this innocent relaxation by a severe rap of the
ferule on his tender hand.

We lived happily and pleasantly at Montreal, until
the breaking out of the War between the Mother Country
and the Colonies. Our troubles then commenced. The battles
of Lexington and Bunker's Hill aroused the warlike spirit
of the country, and awakened the vigilance of the British
Arr.

*FIGURE 2. First surviving page of the Diary. Note impressive
handwriting characteristic of the 18th century.*

and performed manual exercises and volleys of small arms for the celebrating crowds. The festivities were capped with a night of fireworks, which William remembered were "handsomely illuminated."[13]

In the early 1770s, over twenty thousand inhabitants lived within the bounds of modern-day New York City. First arriving, William describes the city as "dull and solitary," which had been transformed by the time of his journal composition fifty years later to "elegant and extensive" houses and streets. The officers and soldiers of the 26th Regiment resided in three Manhattan locations, Fort George Barracks, Battery Barracks, and Upper Barracks. Exacerbated by many wives and children, the three barracks did not contain enough space to house the entire regiment. As a result, commanding officer Lieutenant Colonel Dudley Templer and six other officers (about twenty-five percent of the total officers) procured lodging in the homes of locals. The dispersed quarters created daily close contact between soldiers and residents. For the most part, the military and civilians each went about their business harmoniously without conflict.

While open hostility between the residents and the British Army led to explosive issues in Boston and other locations, crime and desertion were typical of the 26th Regiment officers and New Yorkers. For example, thieves pilfered Private James Browne's quarters, making off with twelve pounds in Jersey money, one half Johannes (a Portuguese gold coin), silver, beaver hat, and shoe buckles. British officers placed an advertisement in the newspaper offering a five-dollar reward for their return.[14] Although desertions from the 26th Regiment were fewer than other regiments posted in North America, soldiers occasionally deserted. Officers vigorously pursued the deserters and posted advertisements in local papers offering cash rewards for their apprehension. The British Army continued to hunt down deserters even years after their abscondment. An advertisement in the *Pennsylvania Journal or Weekly Advertiser* announced a forty-shilling apiece reward for capturing several deserters, including Robert Mitchell and Mark Jordan, who left the 26th regiment three years and one year ago, respectively. Both soldiers enlisted in Ireland. Prior to the army, Jordan worked as a weaver, and Mitchell toiled as a common laborer. Reportedly, the deserters found employment in Pennsylvania iron works.[15]

After a two-year stay in New York City, the British Commander Thomas Gage announced the transfer of the 26th Regiment to Montreal to relieve the first battalion of the Royal American Regiment (60th Regiment of Foot), which he relocated to the Caribbean as part of a general redeployment of North American troops.[16] To assess fitness before the Canadian deployment, General Gage ordered a comprehensive military review of the 26th Regiment ending with a public parade. Newspapers reported that "The Officers and Soldiers made an elegant appearance and went thro' the Exercise, and a variety of evolutions with the utmost exactness."[17] Just as in their last posting in Brunswick, men of the 26th Regiment received high marks from the citizens of New York City upon their departure. "To do Justice to the Officers and private Men of this Regiment, we can affirm, that during their residence in this City, they have behaved with such Order and Decorum, as gave universal Satisfaction to the inhabitants."[18]

While British Colonial Office records indicate the unit marched by foot to Montreal,[19] local newspapers reported the 26th Regiment embarked on boats to sail up the Hudson River to Albany. Despite William having "no recollection of the manner in which we went or of the incidents which occurred along the way," boats provided transportation for at least a portion of the journey. While sailing the Hudson River, a horrible tragedy occurred. James Lipseed, a soldier standing on the gunwale, fell overboard holding his child. "He kept the child above the water and swam a great way, but his strength failing, he let the child go, and immediately sunk." A passing canoe rescued the child who, "having blood let, perfectly recovered."[20] From Albany, the regiment began its journey on foot to Montreal. It is possible that transport boats on Lakes George and Champlain facilitated the journey. In any event, on its journey, the unit passed Fort Ticonderoga, Crown Point, and Fort Saint-Jean, three locations that elements of the 26th Regiment would eventually occupy during the Revolution.

The decision to send the 26th Regiment to the overwhelming French Catholic Montreal further exemplifies the regiment's secularization and the dissipation of its founding anti-Catholicism. During the French and Indian War, the British wrestled control of Montreal and the entire colony of Quebec from French occupation. After the conquest, the British government garrisoned troops in the major cities and other strategic locations to guard against any local rebellion contesting sovereignty and authority. The city of Montreal consisted of more than one thousand homes sheltering approximately five thousand citizens, mostly French Canadians with only a few recent anglophone immigrants. The British upgraded a French-built small barracks in the center city for housing its soldiers. However, most British soldiers were quartered in private homes hired under annual contracts to the army.[21] Just as in Brunswick and New York City, the 26th Regiment made a good impression on the local populous. In June 1773, a stable and house fire erupted at Mr. Lawrence Ermshinger's. The fire quickly spread to a second home. Eighteenth-century urban fires were difficult to control and could quickly engulf entire towns. Soldiers from the 26th

Regiment turned out to help the Montrealer's fight the fire. After successfully extinguishing the flames and preventing further damage, local newspapers expressed that citizens were "much indebted to the 26th Regiment for their agility and ingenuity in playing the engines," which avoided "greater disaster."[22]

A few months later, Montrealers, with the assistance of the 26th Regiment, conducted an installation ceremony for a bust of King George III. The Regiment's elite grenadier company provided an honor guard to transport the statue from the Recollect Convent to its center city display site on the Place d'Armes facing the Notre Dame Church. The bust commemorates the British relief contributions to the Montrealer's after another more disastrous conflagration in 1765 that destroyed most of the city. In addition to a substantial amount of money, the British had sent over two fire engines, which ably assisted the soldiers of the 26th Regiment in fighting the 1773 fire. After extinguishing t the fire, the Regiment fired three musket discharges and robustly shouted three cheers. Following the military display, residents tapped a hogshead of wine for the enjoyment of all. Similar to the celebrations between the 26th Regiment and the residents of Brunswick, an elegant dinner in Montreal concluded the day's festivities.

The passage by Parliament of the Quebec Act of 1774 interrupted the calm garrison duty by changing the balance of power between the majority French and small minority British populations. The Quebec Act formalized the French Canadians' rights to use the French Civil legal system, the freedom to practice Catholicism, and the restoration of the Catholic Church's right to enforce tithes. With these defining cultural practices protected, the predominant French Canadians became compliant with British rule. However, a small minority of British residents expressed their unhappiness with the Quebec Act by vandalizing the center-city bust of King George III. The Quebec Act drove a wedge between British and French heritage citizens in Montreal and inflamed the colonists south of Quebec.

The increasingly stormy geopolitical situation failed to captivate the adolescent William. In his journal, he turned to more typical issues of childhood. He commented on the rigors of his first years of formal education and the constraints of proper discipline.

> We settled in Montreal, where I was first sent to school, and well do I
> recollect, even at this day, the horn book, then used, and the rigid discipline
> of my Irish schoolmaster—the aching neck and painful attention to
> my lessons, which was enforced by the vigilant eye of an usher, walking

constantly past us to catch the straggling glimpse of some unfortunate little urchin, who was generally paid for thus innocent relaxation by a severe rap of the ferule [broad, flat ruler] on his tender hand.

Contrary to commonly held misconceptions, Revolutionary Era British soldiers held high regard for education. Upwards of fifty percent of the soldiers were literate, so it is little surprise William's parents provided William educational opportunities even in foreign locations.[23] Other than a stern schoolmaster, William lived the care-free existence of a young child of a soldier on quiet and peaceful garrison duty. However, the outbreak of the American War of Independence immensely altered the Hunter family's lives. Ominously, William wrote, "Our troubles then commenced."

CHAPTER TWO

Defense of Canada in the War for American Independence

Separated by hundreds of miles, the outbreak of hostilities between the colonialists and the British Army shocked William and his family. He reported, "The battles of Lexington and Bunker's Hill aroused the warlike spirit of the country and awakened the vigilance of the British Army." Uncharacteristically for a child whose father will be in harm's way, but believable when later written in a different situation, the author sided with the Americans who vociferously protested, then violently resisted British rule. Immediately upon hearing of the hostilities, the British Governor Sir Guy Carleton and his military commanders commenced preparations to defend Canada against the Bostonians as Americans were called in Quebec. Notably, William described British efforts to enlist Native Americans to fight on their side. Presaging future depictions and racist views, William characterized Native Americans as "vile instruments of barbarity" that from the effects of too much alcohol wallow "in the mire and filth of the streets from these effects of their debauch."[1] Consistent with most Colonial Americans, the journalist regarded Indians as inherently inferior, uncultured, uneducated, and savage.

William claimed to have witnessed one of the opening skirmishes of the Rebel invasion of Canada in the Longueuil area, a few miles outside of Montreal. Attempting to replicate his vaunted capture of Fort Ticonderoga, the famous Vermonter Ethan Allen led a few dozen American and Canadian volunteers in a rash assault on Montreal in advance of the main Rebel army. British commanders received intelligence of Allen's surprise attack and sallied forth from Montreal to ambush the Vermonter's advancing force. In a short battle,

the British overwhelmed Allen's command, which suffered from disorganiza-
tion and desertion. Seeing no chance of success, Allen and the remnants of his
small force surrendered. British captors ignominiously marched him through
the streets of Montreal and incarcerated the heretofore war hero in chains on
a ship for transport to London as a traitor. A seven-year-old William indicated
that he observed the Longueuil battle, a claim that is highly suspect. While
William may have seen Ethan Allen in Montreal, the running, chaotic battle
was actually fought several miles north of Montreal in a wooded area. However,
it is highly likely that an impressionable young boy heard stories from soldiers,
as the capture of the "hero of Fort Ticonderoga" became blockbuster news and
a boost in morale for the few British soldiers expecting an attack from a much
larger Rebel army.

While the British soldiers' families remained in Montreal, Major Charles
Preston, commander of the 26th Regiment, forward-deployed units of his
command to deter an expected Rebel attack into Canada from Lake Champlain. Along with a cobbled-together force of elements of the 26th and 7th
Regiments, militias, and naval units, William's father moved south to confront
the Rebels. Major Preston fortified a small outpost at the village of Saint-Jean,
a strategic location for the defense of Montreal and the St. Lawrence River Valley. At the head of navigation from Lake Champlain, the hastily strengthened
fortifications sat aside the west bank of the Richelieu River, which connected
Lake Champlain and the St. Lawrence River. The defensive positions consisted
of two earthen walled enclosures (redoubts in military language) six hundred
feet apart. A large stone house built by the absentee seigneur British Lieutenant
Colonel Gabriel Christie anchored the southern redoubt consisting of six buildings, including the bake house, magazine, and storage house. The area within
the southern redoubt measured two-hundred and fifty feet by two hundred feet.
Slightly larger, the northern redoubt enclosed the two-story home of Moses
Hazen, a native to Massachusetts who immigrated to Canada after the French
and Indian War and who sided with the Rebels.[2] A seven-foot covered trench
connected the two redoubts allowing movement of troops and supplies shielded
from enemy fire. Surrounding the fortifications, the British constructed a
wooden palisade with an exterior trench and moat.[3] In addition, a sloop and a
row galley stationed on the river between the two redoubts provided artillery
support for the British garrison. Laying siege, a larger and better-supplied Rebel
force surrounded the fortifications and cut off any means of rescue by relieving
British forces. Inside the fort, conditions were miserable, with limited shelter
and few dry places. Exuding pride in his father's service, William reported that

"after a gallant defense of several weeks, the fort surrendered, and the garrison became prisoners of war." When surrendering, Major Preston and Sergeant Hunter must have wistfully recalled the friendly days just five short years ago in Brunswick when the Americans lauded rather than attacked British soldiers.

Despite fifty-three days of furious and incessant Rebel bombardments, British casualties were relatively light, and the garrison surrendered principally due to lack of food and ammunition. Unfortunately, Sergeant Hunter suffered debilitating wounds.

> My father was severely wounded during the siege having been blown up
> by the explosion of a large keg of gunpowder, into which a spark or part of
> a shell had fallen, while a hot cannonade was going on. He suffered much
> having lost the skin off his face, hands and several parts of his body.[4]

Consistent with the customs of eighteenth-century warfare, the soldiers' wives and children accompanied the prisoners into captivity. The Rebel commander, Brigadier General Richard Montgomery, sent British Lieutenant John Andre under a parole agreement to Montreal to escort the soldiers' families to Fort Saint-Jean. In snowy, wet, and miserable conditions, the soldiers' families traveled twenty-six miles by foot and arrived at Saint-Jean on November 10, 1775. While William's journal is silent on the harshness of the weather and the travails of the families, a Connecticut officer describes them as, ". . . in a miserable Plight, Women badly clothed, Children bare foot and almost naked & covered with Mud and Water. My Heart pitied them."[5] Fortunately for William and his family, the American officers received orders to "offer the least insult to any of the gentlemen, their soldiers, their wives or children" and to treat the captives according to the "principles of Englishmen" with the "utmost attention and politeness."[6]

On the same day, all British regulars fit for travel and their families were sent south towards intended incarceration in southern New England. En route, the Continental Congress intervened and changed the place of confinement to Lancaster, Pennsylvania. Still recovering from severe burns and lacerations, John Hunter could not travel. Therefore, Rebel guards transported John Hunter, his family, and other incapacitated soldiers twelve miles[7] north to Fort Chambly, at the foot of the Chambly rapids on the Richelieu River. American forces captured the largely intact British fortress three weeks before Major Preston's surrender at Fort Saint-Jean. Fort Chambly's twenty-five-foot-high stone and masonry curtains (walls) were built to repel Native American attacks but proved highly vulnerable to modern artillery. After two days of light skirmishing, the Americans rolled three nine-pounder cannons into place.[8] Anticipating the futility of withstanding a sustained bombardment, Major Joseph Stopford, the British commander, surrendered the archaic masonry fortress. Major Stopford received significant criticism for surrendering the post and its valuable supplies after such as short period of resistance. As a result of the light physical damage, the masonry structure offered better wintertime shelter than the largely destroyed housing stock at Saint-Jean.[9]

William and his family spent the winter of 1775-6 housed with other prisoners within the confines of the sturdily built fort. Constructed in 1711 by the French to guard against Iroquois attacks, the 168-foot square stronghold occupied a strategic transit location at the foot of the Richelieu rapids, the furthest point of navigation on the Richelieu River southward from the Saint Lawrence River and Montreal. The square stone fort with four thirty-foot bastions and stone walls evoked a medieval castle rather than an 18th-century frontier fortification designed to withstand modern artillery and siege tactics. Although showing some evidence of the Rebel cannonade, its largely intact four-foot-thick walls provided a modicum of comfort from the harsh wind and cold.[10] The fort's interior consisted of a central courtyard, with accommodation quarters, storerooms, and two bakeries built into the outside walls. Given its substantial inner courtyard and buildings nestled within the walls, the American Rebels converted the outdated fortress into a supply depot and transit point for soldiers and families traveling to and from the front lines in Quebec. In addition to housing wounded British prisoners, the outdated fort served as a jail for Canadians deemed dangerous to their cause.

After a few weeks of captivity in Chambly, William demonstrated an unnatural equanimity for his father's enemy a second time. In his diary, he recounted that the captured British soldiers lamented the death of Rebel Major General Richard Montgomery in leading the failed New Year's Eve assault on Quebec City. The loss of the general was "regretted by all." After their surrender at Fort Saint-Jean, the British prisoners remembered Montgomery's "amiable and gentlemanly deportment." Further, Montgomery's willingness to unite the soldiers with their families and offering to care for the soldier in the vicinity rather than sending them on an arduous journey southward enhanced the prisoners' view of his character.

In early spring, the tide of the Canadian invasion turned on the Rebels forcing them to rapidly retreat down the St. Lawrence River Valley, pressured by a powerful British Army. Prudently, the Americans protected their captives from recapture by moving them south. The Fort Chambly prisoners prepared for the journey to join their comrades in Lancaster, Pennsylvania, prisoner camps. Fortunately, the early spring timing permitted sleigh travel on the frozen surfaces of Lake Champlain while being warm enough not to suffer terribly from wintry exposure. Upon reaching Fort Ticonderoga, the group followed the portage trail to Lake George and another portage trail at the south end of the lake to the Hudson River. This mainly water route served as the superhighway of north-south travel during the pre-industrial times. The prisoner convoy traveled in horse-drawn sleighs over the lake ice with furs and each other to stay warm. However opportune the timing, the travelers still had to overcome dangers and obstacles.

> Frequently, in the course of the day we had to pass large cracks in the ice, which was done by the foremost sleigh throwing over it some loose planks, which they carried for that purpose, to form a kind of temporary bridge. From the advanced state of the season, the ice was becoming rotten near the shores of the lakes, to which we had to go in the evening for the purpose of making large fires. It sometimes happened that in the evening, as we approached the shore, some of the horses would break-in. The dexterity of the Canadian drivers, however, was great. They soon released them by means of ropes, with which they hauled out the horses. We saw the remains of many horses who had perished with the cold, after they had been taken out of the water.

Upon reaching the south end of Lake George, the prisoners entered the Hudson Valley at Saratoga, the site where British General John Burgoyne surrendered his army two years later. Further evidence that William wrote the journal much later in life, he noted that the Saratoga area sported a "fashionable resort on the account of numerous medical springs." Traveling a few miles further south, the party reached Albany, New York. Stopping in the first town of any size, William remarked upon the Dutch architectural practice to site the houses' gabled end to the street. After a short rest stop, the prisoner convoy loaded on transport boats to sail the Hudson River to New York City.

William witnessed the new Continental Army's massive preparations to defend against an expected British attack in the militarized port city. The metropolis teamed with twenty thousand Continental Army soldiers drilling and preparing fortifications. The Rebel army officers most impressed the young author who described them as "tall, handsome men, clothed in blue uniforms and making all together a great military display." During the Revolution, there weren't many instances in which people were impressed with the Continental Army's appearance but more impressive to an eight-year-old who had never seen such a large group of officers and soldiers.

Leaving Manhattan before the one-sided battles in which the British captured New York City, the prisoners and their families traveled through New Jersey to Southeastern Pennsylvania. Traveling by foot through a fertile agricultural region, William and his family reached the "regular and pretty" Lancaster. Laid out in squares, the multi-ethnic immigrant town boasted a courthouse, a market house, and several churches.[11]

The newly arrived prisoners and their families rejoined their fellow 26th Regiment comrades at the internment camp located within the city grid on Saturday, May 25th.[12] Remote from navigable waters and boasting barracks leftover from the French and Indian War made this western Pennsylvania town ideal for housing upwards of one thousand captives and their families. Further, the area's predominately German-speaking immigrants produced surplus foodstuffs to feed the prisoners and, as a bonus, could profitably put the prisoners to work in agricultural and home industries.

While the town residents were wary of their new charges, they obeyed the Continental Congress and set up a governing committee to oversee the prisoners. The committee placed prisoners and their families in the old three-story, "U" shaped barracks and stables occupying nearly a square city block on Walnut and Duke Streets' northwest corner. A high wooden stockade fence enclosed the barracks for physical security guarded by the town's militia. To enhance security for the townspeople and discourage a prisoner uprising, the Rebel jailors separated officers from the enlisted soldiers sending the officers to outlying towns on parole. The committee rules allowed women and children free passage to town and provided, on occasion, passes for captives to leave the prison enclosure. Prisoners received food rations similar to those on active duty, with family members each receiving half rations.

William reported that "every necessary being regularly supplied." This almost idyllic description of living conditions is inconsistent with the general treatment given prisoners of war on either side during the war. However, William cited an interesting and plausible rationale that other observers and historians have overlooked.

> The particular good treatment which the prisoners received at Lancaster was attributed at the time in a great measure to the circumstances of their having been sent from Europe before the commencement of hostilities, not for

the purpose of butchering or enslaving the Americans, but to defend them against the encroachments of the French and Indians. Be that as it may, no men in their situation, could have had less reason to complain, and none I believe were better satisfied with their lot to which they had been consigned by the fortunes of war.

Several British regulars found the town environment especially blissful. A few days after William's arrival, James McCarty of the 26th Regiment married a woman from the local community.[13] Remarkably, marriages between prisoners and local women became common, with at least twenty prisoners, including eleven 26th Regiment soldiers tying the knot. Reverend Thomas Barton, the long-serving and erstwhile highly respected rector of the Lancaster Episcopal Church, performed the marriage ceremonies. However, Rebel authorities closed the church when learning that the matrimonial ceremonies included a prayer for the King. After committing to omit the King's prayer, the Lancaster Committee permitted Rev. Barton to resume prisoner marriages.[14] More weighty, other matters considered by the Lancaster Committee focused on citizen safety and prisoner security. Upon receiving a report from Lebanon, Pennsylvania, of British prisoners using a fishing excursion ruse to escape, the Committee put out an alarm and notified the prisoner oversight committees in York and Cumberland.[15]

Many Lancaster area men were absent serving in the Continental Army or state militias deployed to the front lines. To alleviate labor shortages, Lancaster prisoners enjoyed opportunities to earn wages utilizing their skills in civilian trades. Philadelphia Executive Council authorized iron works forging much-needed cannons to employ prisoners from Lancaster and Reading, and local committees expanded the number of employment openings.[16] Several 26th Regiment privates took advantage of job opportunities, including John Smith, a shoemaker, and John Gostitch, a skin dresser. Additionally, two 26th Regiment soldiers trained as weavers worked for Lancaster tailor Michael Shirdle. Upwards of one hundred captive soldiers found gainful employment in the summer and fall of 1776, "commanding handsome wages."[17] Even though there were opportunities for weavers, there is no record of Sergeant Hunter hiring out. More likely, Margaret Hunter sought employment to better provide for the family's food and clothing. However, the large number of captive wives created a highly competitive environment, and therefore, Margaret likely generated modest and infrequent employment earnings.

William may have supplemented family finances in an unusual occupation. Prisoners in close confinement created the right conditions for outbreaks of the dreaded and deadly smallpox. The disease ravaged the British prisoners in

York a few weeks before William arrived. The closeness of the smallpox threat motivated the Hunter family to receive disease-sparing but still dangerous inoculation. Fortunately, Dr. Hammond Beaumont, the 26th Regiment's surgeon and fellow captive, was an experienced smallpox inoculator.

The doctor practiced the highly successful Suttonian method of inoculation, which featured a minute puncture of the skin to admit a small amount of the disease-ridden pus into the wound.[18] While in Lancaster, William received the inoculation and swiftly recovered with minimal disease. Given his mild reaction, William traveled with Dr. Beaumont to remote prison sites and towns to inoculate other captives and their families. The standard charge for a patient's inoculation was one guinea. William would have received minor compensation from Dr. Beaumont for his services as the provider of the infected pus.[19]

Despite the cooperative work arrangements, not all relations between the prisoners and the Lancaster community were amiable. Some prisoners evaded guards and left the stockade to simply experience a modicum of freedom, while others sought to escape to British lines or harass residents. During the second half of 1776, guards caught at least forty-eight offenders and committed them to the county jail. Offenses included insulting the sentries, stealing wine, and attempting to escape. Cash rewards incented Pennsylvanians to return offending prisoners to Lancaster for incarceration or return to the stockade.[20] Sergeant Hunter mediated with local authorities on behalf of his troops sent to the local jail.

William and his family endured one tense and scary incident during their captivity. In early August 1776, Lancaster residents received a report of a Rebel unit planning to travel through Lancaster to a new post in New Jersey. Per these preliminary accounts, this unit attacked prisoners while passing through Carlisle, Pennsylvania, in retaliatory attacks for purported British atrocities. Reportedly, an enraged Rebel force wantonly fired on unarmed prisoners and even slightly wounded John Andre, the officer later made famous for his association with Benedict Arnold's treason. Upon hearing these alarming rumors, the Lancaster Committee warned the prisoners to remain in their barracks and attempted to allay their fears by committing that the prison guards would protect them. The journalist states:

> Such was the clamor which it excited and so firmly believed was the report, that every soldier armed himself with a bullet of wood (the only weapon they could get), seemingly determined to defend themselves to the last extremity. The whole night was spent in great anxiety, expecting every moment the attack, but the return of the day light restored confidence.

Leadership elements of the Lancaster militia intercepted the purportedly out-of-control Rebel unit on the town outskirts and queried their intentions. After receiving satisfactory answers, the transiting Rebels under the command of Captain Thomas Clark entered the town and peaceably dispersed to local homes and buildings for shelter. The next day, the Committee held an inquiry into the rumors and purported charges of murdering innocent prisoners. Captain George Hubley, a well-known Lancaster resident recently returned from Carlisle, and he witnessed no evidence of butchery or foul play but heard a couple of random shots. After hearing testimony, the Committee concluded that aimless muskets discharges might have been the cause of the alarm and no foul play occurred. Alternatively, William believed that the story was "the mere fabrication of some mischievous person." Whatever the reason, nothing came of the incident, and the Rebel unit continued on their deployment to New Jersey, and prison life returned to normal.[21]

While the prisoners perceived reasons to worry about their safety and security, the local citizens were also worried about prisoner uprisings and criminal behaviors. To better control the enlisted soldiers, prisoner movements took place in groups of less than one hundred, and officers quartered physically separated from their troops. Additionally, the Rebels separated enlisted soldiers from officers to aid prisoner recruitment into their army. Despite protests from captive officers and the British army high command, approximately eight percent of the soldiers switched sides and enlisted in the Continental Army. None of the turncoat Lancaster soldiers were married.[22] As a thoroughly loyal sergeant, William's father actively sought to keep his unit together and prevent desertions.

In November 1776, word arrived from Congress to ready the prisoners and their families for transport to Fort Lee, New Jersey, in anticipation of exchange for Rebel soldiers captured in Canada. The prisoner movement required a substantial logistical effort and coordination with residents on the route for food and shelter. Nearly sixty wagons carried the prisoners' effects and transported members of their families.[23] The British prisoners marched through Trenton and across New Jersey, escorted by a contingent of Lancaster militia. As a result of the numerous prisoner marriages, the number of people to be transported increased as the prisoners' new wives followed their new husbands. By early December, William and his family were back again within British lines in New York.[24] For Sergeant Hunter, freedom from Rebel captivity meant he resumed dangerous wartime service. British commanders refitted the 26th Regiment with arms and prepared the unit for combat operations.

CHAPTER THREE

War Through the Eyes of a Child
With a Father in Combat

While most Revolutionary War accounts describe the privations suffered by the Rebels, William confirmed that the British soldiers and their families also suffered greatly during the harsh, bitter Revolutionary winters. After the Rebel retreat in 1776, fires destroyed one thousand private houses representing approximately a quarter of the city's homes.[1] A depleted housing stock, the lack of fuel to burn for heat, and inadequate food supplies converged to make the winter of 1777 especially severe for the British soldiers and families. Initially, the soldiers and their families were quartered in public buildings, warehouses, churches, and private homes. However, the close living arrangements caused considerable conflict with the local population. As a result, British commanders ordered several regiments, including the 26th, to construct crude huts for shelter outside the center city.[2]

Despite the bad weather and a year away from active duty, the newly exchanged soldiers did not have much time to regroup as the British command immediately thrust the 26th Regiment back into combat. The astonishing Rebel victory at Trenton forced the British commanders to reposition their forces to better defend New York and to maintain control over valuable New Jersey farmlands. William stated in his journal, "The British, roused from their torpor, immediately commenced active operations against a foe which they had till now considered as nearly vanquished." The British launched a "predatory and skirmishing kind of warfare" from their bases in and around New York City. British Army units ventured into the New Jersey farmlands more than twenty times to glean from residents' food supplies and forage for their horses to alleviate acute supply shortages.[3] Rebels vigorously challenged these raids causing British commanders to send out large covering forces of at least five hundred and sometimes two thousand soldiers for protection. Numerous well-contested, deadly clashes ensued with heavy casualties on each side, a highly kinetic type of warfare unaccustomed to by the British during the normally quiet months of winter quarters.[4] The 26th Regiment took part in many of these battles and skirmishes, including one in William's hometown of Brunswick. For the eight-year-old boy, this high level of military activity created "great fears for his [father's] safety and anxiety for his return."

However, the raids did not garner sufficient fresh provisions beyond those allocated to the hospitals. Therefore, the British Army and dependents relied upon uncertain but vital supply ships (victuallers in eighteenth-century parlance), making the treacherous transatlantic crossing.[5] On several occasions, the British Army went to great lengths to rescue supply ships wrecked on the New Jersey coast and open to plunder by Rebel forces. Elements of the 26th Regiment, led by the recently freed Major Andrew Gordon, conducted one such recovery mission. On February 13, 1777, a detachment of one hundred and seventy soldiers from the 26th Regiment supplemented by a regiment of American Tories marched from Richmond to Cole's Ferry on the northeastern shore of Staten Island just above The Narrows of New York harbor and embarked on the warship *Syren*. After being stalled in a violent storm of three days, the British waded ashore on Sandy Hook at the southernmost entrance to New York harbor after just a seventeen-mile voyage. Quickly moving inland, the attackers surprised New Jersey militia units from Monmouth County in the Battle of Navesink (sometimes Neversink) Highlands.[6] While the British regulars engaged the militia, the Tory regiment and Marines from the *Syren* secured the foodstuffs from the shipwrecked victualler. After killing several rebels, the British returned to their ships, capturing over seventy prisoners and highly valued food supplies. The extent to which the British and the Rebels went to recover the foodstuffs demonstrates the scarcity of provisions and privations suffered on both sides.[7]

However, William's most notable entry during the winter of 1777 involved possible Rebel intrigue in recapturing the quixotic Major General Charles Lee, unreported by other contemporary sources. Officers on both sides thought Lee, a former British Army major, to be the most able and experienced Rebel general and should have been named over Washington as the supreme Rebel commander. During early December 1776, after Washington's disastrous defeat and loss of New York City, Lee cautiously moved his army through western

New Jersey in the general direction of combining forces with Washington to protect Philadelphia. Recklessly, Lee decided to stay the night in a comfortable house, remote from the protection of his command. While scouting for the movements of Lee's army, the Queen's Light Dragoons under Colonel William Harcourt garnered excellent intelligence from a captured messenger about Lee's weakly guarded location. The soon to be infamous Cornet Banastre Tarleton led the advance guard to attack the Rebel sentries, forcing them to retreat into the house. The main British force surrounded the house and easily captured Lee, which officers on both sides thought was momentous and game-changing. Tarleton prematurely bragged to his mother, ". . . this coup de main has put an end to this campaign."[8] Another British officer pronounced the capture of Lee "Glorious." [9]

After a month moving among Royal forces in New Jersey, the British held Lee a "close prisoner" in relative comfort at New York's City Hall, "a few doors away" from William's accommodations. Hearing scuttlebutt from his father or men in his father's unit, William reported a nocturnal disturbance.

> The sentry at his door was stabbed one night by some person, who was never discovered. It was supposed that an attempt to rescue the General was intended—but failed from some cause not understood. After this event, the sentries were doubled.

Neither British nor Rebel sources offer corroborating evidence of either plans or attempts to rescue Lee. However, given the high value placed on Lee's leadership and command capabilities, a covert liberating mission is plausible. In any event, the British did transfer Major General Lee to the warship *Centurion* for "greater security."[10]

While the 26th Regiment stayed safe in winter quarters with no other notable events, the harsh weather and living conditions brought happiness and tragedy to the Hunter family. William gained a sister but tragically lost a second brother (the first died soon after his parents arrived in America). Busy with childbirth, the mother ". . . was unable to procure the necessary assistance, the little fellow was neglected and fell victim to the effects of exposure in the inclement season." Certainly, a lack of firewood and poor housing accentuated the harsh winter conditions. More likely, a rampant disease caused his brother's death. However, traumatized by losing a second sibling, a young boy believed his parents could have done more to save his brother. His sister would be the last child born to his parents. Perhaps due to the large age gap, William and his sister did not enjoy a close relationship, and he never again mentioned her in the journal.

While in Manhattan, the impressionable youth witnessed the miserable and wretched incarceration of Rebel prisoners confined near to one of his father's posts, including those that capitulated in Fort Washington's fall. William's statement that most of the three-thousand-member garrison perished during British captivity is consistent with modern assessments.[11] Distressingly, William portrayed the prisoners' plight:

> Well do I recollect these unfortunate victims of British cruelty. They perished of cold hunger and disease and after being collected from the cold, damp Churches[12] in which they had been confined, until death that "Friend to the Wretch" whom every friend forsakes, "relieved them from their miseries, they were taken by cartloads to large holes into which they were thrown in one promiscuous heap without a coffin or a sheet to cover them. These scenes I saw, and still remember with horror and disgust.

The supportive Rebel prisoner views are oddly out of character for a child of a British soldier but consistent with prisoner accounts Rebel authors. By regulation, British jailors allocated two-thirds rations of active-duty British soldiers to Rebel prisoners. British officers believed a partial ration was more than sufficient, as the prisoners did not perform the manual labor and maneuvering of soldiers at the front.[13] Further, the British had trouble just feeding their own soldiers and dependents. More damaging than the lack of food was replacing worn-out clothing with warm garments to withstand the winter temperatures. Under generally accepted prisoner of war standards of the period, the Rebels, not the British, were responsible for providing clothing to the captives. William's account of British cruelty is consistent with other prisoners' accounts, but as a young child, William lacked insights into the limited British resources on hand and food shortages for their own troops exacerbated by supply lines stretching across the Atlantic. Further, he would not have known that the Continental Army needed to provide the Rebel captives with proper clothing under the customary rules of war.

Spring and summer 1777 brought new assignments for the 26th Regiment, necessitating several venue changes for William and his family. British commanders ordered his father's regiment transferred from New York City to Staten Island. On September 11, William's father and the 26th Regiment participated in a large, well-planned raid with two objectives. First, General

Henry Clinton sought to support General Howe in his advance towards Philadelphia by diverting Rebel forces and, secondly, to gather much-needed food and forage from New Jersey farms. Under Lieutenant General Henry Clinton's command, British expeditionary forces crossed the waters from New York and landed in New Jersey at four locations. The 26th Regiment, along with the 52nd Regiment, several Hessian units and loyalist militia came ashore unopposed at Elizabeth Point, New Jersey, and marched to the town of Elizabeth. After leaving Elizabeth, a Rebel force of three to four thousand militia and two battalions of Continental soldiers under the command of Major General Israel Putnam blocked the British advance. After a "prolonged attack," the Rebels retreated, which allowed the British to continue their mission to commandeer food and forage. The British continued onto Newark, a small town to rest and recover. While the Rebels continued to offer sporadic resistance, the expedition achieved its mission by garnering a much-needed five hundred cattle and fifteen hundred sheep with minimal losses. General Clinton ordered his soldiers to Paulus Hook with the confiscated livestock for transport across the Hudson (North) River. Due to the overwhelming success, each private on the raid were rewarded with a Spanish dollar.[14] Initially, the 26th Regiment bivouacked in the Bloomingdale section of northwestern Manhattan Island and then redeployed south back to New York City.

The fall of 1777 brought more combat for Sergeant Hunter, leading to high anxiety for his family. General John Burgoyne led a British Army south from Fort Saint-Jean, Canada, into Rebel territory. After a quick and overwhelming victory at Fort Ticonderoga, it appeared that Burgoyne would quickly march down the Hudson Valley and link up with British General Henry Clinton in New York City. However, Rebel resistance stiffened just north of Albany, and now the tables seemed to be turning, and Burgoyne faced increasing numbers of hostile forces and diminishing supplies. To relieve pressure on Burgoyne, Clinton launched a strike up the Hudson River. Initially, he sought to capture the mutually supporting Rebel Forts Clinton and Montgomery, which prevented British water navigation from New York City to Albany. Astride the Popolopen Creek just south of the unfortified West Point, the recently constructed forts commanded the Hudson River with high caliber cannon and guarded a heavy link chain across the river blocking ship passage.

After defending a fort in Canada, William's father turned to the more dangerous attack. The 26th Regiment and other assault forces totaling three thousand soldiers sailed up the river to a point ten miles south of the fort. After outmaneuvering the Continental Army forces by faking an assault on the east side, the British landed on the river's west side below the twin forts. With the aid of Loyalist Colonel Beverly Robinson's local knowledge, the British launched a two-prong attack against the forts' weaker rear defenses. William possessed a remarkably accurate memory, but his description of the assault on the Hudson Highland forts contained the most lapses in recollection. First, he reported, "My father was with the detachment and aided in the storming Fort Montgomery . . ." However, Sergeant John Hunter and the 26th Regiment were part of the twelve hundred soldier force which assaulted Fort Clinton. Perhaps with a bit of pride, William incorrectly cites his aging father as serving in the Grenadier Company, the most elite and fit company within the Regiment. Finally, he mistakenly stated that "The celebrated, but unfortunate Andre served, I believe as a Lieutenant in that company in the attack on Fort Montgomery." At this time, Andre ranked a Captain and served several hundred miles south as aide-de-camp to Major General Charles Grey.

While getting some of the details wrong, no one can fault the son's worry for the father's safe return.

> I well recollect seeing the wounded carried on biers to the hospital the day they were landed from the shipping, at New York, a few days after the battle. Ignorant of the fate of my father, and fearing that he might be amongst them, I was struck with horror at the sight of the pale and deathlike countenances of the unfortunate victims of the bloody contest, as they passed along upon the shoulders of their comrades. It was an awful sight and to a young mind, excited like mine then was by the most anxious apprehensions for the fate of a beloved parent and indescribably shocking.

Fiercely contested, the intense combat produced substantial casualties on both sides. The British particularly suffered heavy losses while conducting a bayonet-only charge into Fort Clinton, an attack in which William's father participated. Storming Fort Clinton particularly devastated the 26th Regiment's officers. William had good reason to be concerned for his father's safety as Lieutenants Donald McDonell and Lawrence Delhuntry suffered wounds, and Captain Francis Stewart (sometimes Stuart) and Lieutenant James Gordon died. Not mentioned in William's journal, Stewart and Gordon were the only two officers in the 26th Regiment to lose their lives in combat during the Revolutionary War. Recognizing the British victory, New York and Philadelphia papers noted the "extreme ardour" of the British soldiers and cited Clinton's second in command, Major General John Vaughn's "spirited behaviour" and "good conduct."[15]

After the forts' capture, British forces continued up the Hudson River to link up with Burgoyne's army. The northern most British units under the command of Major General Vaughan "burnt the beautiful village of Esopus[16] [*sic*]," approximately one hundred miles south of General Burgoyne's army. The British strike up the Hudson transpired "too little, too late." Failing to receive relief in time, Burgoyne surrendered his entire army, providing the Rebels their largest victory to date. General Clinton ordered General Vaughn and all British regiments to return down the Hudson River to the security of fortified New York City. Sergeant Hunter re-united with his family after participating in his only victorious, though costly battle. A relieved William stated, "My father's return, uninjured and in fine health, gave us indescribable (great) pleasure. Those only can conceive it, who have been placed in a similar situation."

"But our joy was short lived!" he wrote. With little rest and recovery time, British commanders sent Sergeant John Hunter on a several hundred-mile sea voyage and back into active combat. Howe captured Philadelphia in a methodical, tactically brilliant fall campaign, decisively defeating George Washington in several land battles. However, the British could not deliver a knockout blow and achieve total victory. As winter set in, the Rebels held forts along the Delaware River, preventing British resupply of their forces. General Howe ordered the 26th Regiment to reduce the riverside forts and open the Delaware River to British shipping, an urgent and critical assignment. If the Rebels prevented shipping access, the British Army would be left without a dependable supply line and would have to abandon Philadelphia. After securing riverine supply and communication routes, British strategists planned to deploy the regiment to reinforce defensive positions in and around Philadelphia. In New York harbor, the 26th Regiment loaded onto transport ships for the passage into Delaware Bay below Philadelphia. Signaling a long campaign and occupation, spouses and children joined them on the voyage.

The nine-year-old child's first time at sea must have been quite an adventure. However, William does not mention any thrills of watching the ship's operations and sailors with their duties or viewing porpoises or other fish congregating around ocean-going ships. Equally missing are the most dangerous and distressing nature of life aboard 18th-century sailing ships. Packed into tight quarters with little privacy, the enlisted soldiers and their families slept in uncomfortable hammocks or rough berths. The passengers endured noxious smells, bothersome rats, and unappetizing and frequently rancid foods. Typically, British soldiers were issued two-thirds rations of salted meats and hardtack biscuits or flour while shipboard. Soldiers' families received one-half of these reduced rations.

Late fall sailing along the North American coast presented especially dangerous weather conditions. Consistent with these weather norms, the forty-sail British fleet with reinforcements for General Howe encountered several violent storms followed by calm weather during the voyage[17]. Even in relatively tranquil waters, the constant wave motion caused most passengers to experience long bouts of seasickness. Either William had strong "sea legs," or through the passage time, he overlooked and neglected to mention sea sickness, the lack of food, or illnesses that afflict most passengers, especially during gales and stormy weather. Interestingly, William did not mention these deleterious physical privations on any of his youthful sea voyages. Perhaps as a young boy, the adventure outweighed the hardships, but hardships were common in the eighteenth century and were not worth describing in his diary.

After weathering the storms, the final days of William's first ocean voyage proved unremarkable. However, signs of war and associated dangers emerged immediately upon entering Delaware Bay, the ocean gateway to Philadelphia.

> When we entered the Delaware, the difficulty was to ascend it without striking on some of the Chevaux de freeze, which the Americans had sunk in the channel to obstruct the passage of the British vessels. We escaped but near Mud Island, I saw a transport loaded with Hessians strike on one, which sunk her. We took a part of the men on board our vessel.

Two independent, credible accounts confirm William's report. British Captain Sir James Wallace observed in the ship's log that the troop transport *Crawford* became entangled in the Chevaux-de-frise, took on water, and had to be towed to shore. In his diary, Hessian soldier Johann Dohla noted that one ship ran aground while attempting to circumvent the iron and wood water barrier on November 22, 1777, consistent with the timing in William's diary.[18]

The 26th Regiment landed at Chester, Pennsylvania, and then crossed the river to join a planned assault on the Rebel fort at Red Bank, New Jersey, the last obstacle preventing safe river passage to Philadelphia. Lord Charles Cornwallis commanded the multi-regiment expedition to reduce the rebel fortress. Upon viewing the superior force, the Rebels abandoned the stronghold and fled into the New Jersey countryside. A relief to William and his mother, Cornwallis captured the fort without bloodshed. As a result, on November 23rd, the transports with the families on-board made their way through the weakened Chevaux-de-frise and landed at the docks in Philadelphia.

Bustling with people and military activity, William and his family stepped off the transport into a much different city than their last duty station. Unlike New Yorkers, Philadelphians did not endure deadly combat nor suffer fires. However, a Hessian officer described the city as "desolate" and questioned the ability of the British to properly defend and supply their army within its boundaries.[19] Most concerning to William, his father's regiment left Philadelphia on December 4th as part of the main British assault force led by British General William Howe, who sought to defeat Washington in a general engagement. The 26th Regiment formed with the 7th Regiment and the 3rd Brigade under the immediate command of Hessian Major General Wilhelm von Knyphausen and marched northwest of the city to confront Washington's entrenched forces. The resulting Battle of Whitemarsh consisted of a series of small but bloody skirmishes and an unsuccessful British attempt to flank the Continental Army. Running out of supplies and having no shelter, General Howe decided to break off the battle and return to the city for winter quarters.

Howe ordered the British Barracksmaster to find protective winter quarters in Philadelphia for his army of thirty thousand soldiers with twenty-two hundred dependents. Most of the city's twenty-four thousand inhabitants stayed in their homes under British occupation. Loyalist Joseph Galloway estimated that there were almost six hundred empty and houses and two hundred and twenty-four empty stores that could house soldiers. However, empty buildings and only one city military barracks were insufficient to house all of the soldiers and their dependents. Many officers quartered with private citizens and soldiers billeted in other public buildings and warehouses. The need for hospitals and jails further overburdened the city's building infrastructure. British commanders converted the churches into hospitals for the thirty-five hundred sick and wounded soldiers. The British re-purposed existing jails and other government buildings to house the two to three thousand Rebel prisoners. While better housing existed in Philadelphia than New York, accommodations were uncomfortably tight. Pre-war Philadelphia swelled from twenty-four thousand to approximately sixty thousand inhabitants by the end of the British occupation.[20]

Sergeant Hunter's regiment billeted within the city center while the other reinforcing units were sent to garrison the well-designed ring of stoutly constructed battlements on the urban outskirts. Stretching from the Delaware to the Schuylkill Rivers, a line of ten well-fortified redoubts guarded the northern approaches, the only land access to the city. Demonstrating military science prowess, British chief engineer John Montresor strengthened the redoubts by placing a demilune, a crescent-shaped fortification between redoubts seven and eight, and a ravelin, a triangle fighting position designed to split attacking forces between redoubts five and six. Additionally, to provide warning and to control city access, the British established advance redoubts on two major roads into the city. Commanded by a Captain with the assistance of two subalterns, fifty soldiers manned each redoubt for a watch period of twelve hours. The units on the front lines served for forty-eight hours, after which a new unit assumed responsibility.[21] Possibly, the 26th Regiment took its turn in manning the redoubts. But, more likely, British planners relegated the increasingly combat-ineffective unit to occupation duties within the city[22]. Further, when the British Army sortied outside of Philadelphia in an attempt to capture a small Rebel force under the command of Marquis de Lafayette at Barren Hill, the 26th Regiment remained in the city on guard duty. After two-and-a-half years of active combat, many long marches in harsh conditions, and just recently receiving two hundred recruits, British commanders recognized that Sergeant Hunter's unit lost much of its functional combat effectiveness.

William recorded little of note about the initial stages of his stay in Philadelphia. Other diarists noted that the winter of 1778 started more comfortable than the previous one in New York City with better housing and more plentiful food.[23] Garrison life appeared calm with "tolerable plenty" to eat and relative safety behind strong fortifications and waters protected by the Royal Navy.[24] Unlike the experiences around New York City, the early winter foraging expeditions outside of Philadelphia met little resistance with few casualties. However, as the winter passed, weather conditions worsened, and the Rebels more hotly contested the foraging patrols. As a result, Philadelphia food prices dramatically increased.[25] For example, later in the occupation, one quarter of mutton sold for one guinea, a slab of butter for six to eight shillings, and ships biscuit regularly substituted for fresh bread.[26] Each Wednesday, Sergeant Hunter visited the market to procure food and necessities to augment the weekly issue of standard rations. As in Lancaster, Margaret performed what domestic work she could find to supplement the oft poor-quality and many times inadequate army rations. The crowded conditions led to concerns over sanitation and safety. British commanders ordered those residents with sooty chimneys to be fined twenty shillings and that all trash and rubbish be placed in receptacles on the street for pick up the fourth week of the month.[27]

William's journal does not mention that his father participated in any foraging expeditions outside the city. However, British forces embarked on large-scale foraging missions to supplement commissary rations shipped from Britain.

Initially, the British generally succeeded in bringing fresh food and livestock into the city. Later on, Rebel forces heavily resisted the supply forays, limiting the garrison's flow of fresh provisions. While British willingness to pay in specie greatly increased their foodstuffs, individual soldiers often stole food and wood and plundered homes for valuable items. As the food supplies diminished, army discipline became a significant problem for the British commanders. Soldiers' wives and families also engaged in theft and committed criminal acts. Sergeant Hunter spent considerable time enforcing order within his company and meting out punishments.

Officers led a considerably more comfortable existence than enlisted soldiers and families. The British officers organized many festivities in Philadelphia, including gambling, theatrical performances, and lavish parties. Nearing the end of Philadelphia's British occupation, the British officer corps planned a magnificent pageant called a Mischianza consisting of a medley of festivities celebrating the generalship of General William Howe in leading British forces in putting down the American Rebellion. The British government recalled Howe and replaced him with Henry Clinton as Supreme Commander to defeat the rebels and return the Royal government to the American colonies. Taking place on Joseph Wharton's lawn overlooking the Delaware River, the grand party occurred on May 18, 1778, lasting into the wee hours of the next morning. Festivities consisted of a costume ball, feast, a grand procession of the honored guests in boats and on the shore, music including trumpeters, and a salute of cannons from nearby warships. Fireworks amazed the assembled British officers and over seven hundred and fifty American Loyalists. Captain John Andre played a large role in planning the extravaganza, including designing the tickets and painting several decorations. Our journalist offered a vivid description of the night's pageantry,

> A great military display was made the whole ended with a Spectacle after the manner of the ancient tournament. Officers, dressed like knights with horses gaily cassarisoned [?], and attended by faithful squire, entered the lists, in honor of their favorite damsels—shivered a lance with their antagonists, and went through all the ceremonies and numeracies of these exhibitions. Splendid fireworks concluded the entertainment. The whole was termed a Mischeanza [*sic*]. A singular employment for an army to be engaged in, who had so vigilant a foe to watch them as General Washington!

Most assuredly, as a young boy, William did not attend the event, but his father may have provided event security or served as one of the ceremonial escorts. However, given the city's close confines, the fireworks, pomp, and parades would be hard to miss for a nine-year-old child.

A few days after the Mischianza, General Howe departed Philadelphia for London, replaced by General Henry Clinton, an able but reluctant military commander. Having signed a *Treaty of Amity and Commerce* with the United States, France entered the war immediately, challenging British naval superiority in the Americas. Clinton received orders to send five thousand troops to St. Lucia in the West Indies, three thousand to Florida, and six hundred Marines to Halifax and transfer the bulk of his army to the more defensible New York City to counter the French threat. Ordered to move his forces by ship to New York City, Clinton decided that the French fleet provided too significant of a threat to his army. Overruling his London instructions, Clinton ordered an overland march of most of his fighting units through New Jersey. Naval transports would be waiting off the coast for the short ferry to New York City across the harbor. Only baggage, heavy stores, the sick and wounded, and some families voyaged by ship down the Delaware River and by sea to New York. The ten-year-old boy loaded onto a transport ship with his mother and sister to return to New York City.

Under General Clinton's command, William's father crossed the Delaware River on the 18th of June and commenced marching through New Jersey to New York City. John and the 26th Regiment were assigned to the 5th Brigade in Clinton's 1st division under General Alexander Leslie's command. Washington's forces shadowed the British columns while attempting to disrupt the march by tearing up bridges and destroying roads. Finally, Washington decided to attack the British 1st division that contained most of his army's combat power near Monmouth, New Jersey. Washington ordered his advance corps under the exchanged General Charles Lee to attack the British rear guard. Clinton, who wished for an opportunity to engage the Rebels, struck back hard and forced Lee to retreat. Famously, Washington arrived on the battlefield with the main Rebel army, encountering the retreating Lee. A bitter quarrel between the two Rebel generals ensued, with Washington relieving Lee of his command on the spot and ordering a counterattack against the advancing British forces.

On a brutally hot, humid June day, both sides immensely suffered. While Sergeant Hunter's unit remained in reserve to protect the strategically important crossroads at Monmouth Court House, William's father remarked that "he has never experienced such excessive heat nor suffered so much from fatigue and thirst." William continues, describing the impact of battle and oppressive heat, reporting that ". . . hundreds died, without being touched by a ball or any weapon whatsoever. Numbers, it is said of the British Army literally dropped down dead in the ranks." Officially, General Clinton reported fifty-nine British soldiers expiring from heat prostration.[28]

After a day of intense fighting, nightfall brought relief and an end to the combat. Remaining on the battlefield, Washington planned to attack the British again in the morning. However, Clinton had other intentions. His forces stole away during the night, redeploying towards the New Jersey coast near the protective cover of British warships. Clinton led his troops to the same highlands at Navesink, where William's father skirmished with the Rebels a year ago. Planners moved the army to Sandy Hook's safety from the well-protected coastal highlands and then onto transports to New York City. By July 6th, all troops were securely back in New York. The 26th Regiment traveled to Long Island and encamped in modern-day Queens. Safe again in New York City, William's father prepared for what turned out to be the last battle in his military career.

William's sea voyage to New York turned out to be equally as dangerous as he reported,

> We had just time to clear the Capes when the French fleet hove in sight, and chased us into New York harbor, which they blockaded for some time, but attempted nothing more.

Not citing a harrowing chase into the harbor, other diarists noted the lightly guarded four hundred transport ships arrived without incident on July 1, 1778.[29] In any event, William's safe arrival in New York harbor avoided the powerful French battle fleet under the command of Admiral Charles Henri Hector d'Estaing, which could have wreaked havoc among the largely unprotected transports. Only sluggish progress against strong headwinds from Toulon, the French naval base in the Mediterranean Sea, prevented the French fleet from beating the British to New York and blocking the harbor. Fortuitous for the Hunter family, this slow start allowed the English to complete its Philadelphia evacuation safely.

While the French admiral considered potential avenues of attack, "The French fleet lay off Sandy Hook, it was frequently seen from our encampment in clear weather." While not mentioned and unknown to William, the British garrison possessed only three weeks of food supply on hand. The British forces faced a significant risk of starving or surrendering if the French blockade continued.[30] Although outnumbering the British 830 to 534 guns, the French fleet remained on station outside the inner harbor for a few weeks without engaging in any hostile actions.[31] Admiral d'Estaing concluded that he could not navigate his heavy ships over the sand bar at the harbor entrance and sailed away on July 22nd, removing any blockade threat to the city. While the French retreat ended seaborne threats, the garrison and their families faced privations.

For the remainder of the summer, Sergeant Hunter remained on New York area garrison duty. "That part of the Army to which my father belonged, having been ordered to encamp on Long Island, we accompanied him as usual." William and his family settled in, safe from naval attack, but the entire British Army remained dangerously short on provisions. The standard half rations for wives and quarter rations for children were further reduced to stretch the garrison's food supplies. Fortunately, a few days later, six victualler (supply) ships from Britain entered New York harbor, eliminating the food shortage for a short time.

Even though food shortages and enemy attacks subsided, other issues, including crime and misbehavior, plagued the 26th Regiment while stationary on garrison duty. Excessive drinking of rum and spruce beer constituted a common pastime for soldiers. Especially while in garrison, drunkenness often led to many alcohol-infused crimes and disobedience. When identified, harsh discipline ensued, including regular floggings for large and small military regulations violations. The harshness of the British Army disciplinary regime must have been apparent to William, but he chose to omit any mention in his journal. Like its pre-war tour of duty in New York City, thievery plagued the officers and men of the 26th Regiment. Thieves stole Captain Gordon's fourteen-hand, a light bay horse from his quarters on Laurel Hill (modern-day southwest Queens). Other thieves made off with a young dark brown stallion with cropped ears stabled at the regiment's hospital on McGowan Hill (Modern Day Central Park, Manhattan). The British officer offered a twenty-dollar reward for intelligence as to the horse's whereabouts or its return.

At the end of November, the 26th Regiment moved to Staten Island and occupied huts recently vacated by the 7th Regiment, redeployed to Manhattan.[32] Remarkably, William does not complain about the constant relocations and the temporary camp's harsh, primitive conditions. Perhaps the persistent army moves and new locations fascinated the young boy. As fall turned to winter, the Rebels quartered in Jockey Hollow, New Jersey, experienced continual food and supply shortages. British soldiers also suffered from a lack of sustenance. British provisions again became scarce, relying on uncertain re-supply across a three-thousand-mile ocean. Going into the winter of 1778-9, the commissary reduced food rations for both British soldiers and dependents.[33] However uncertain and uncomfortable the situation in New York, William's life would become more fraught with danger and adventure.

> About the latter part of September, I believe, we removed to New York, where we remained until a fleet of transports sailed for England about Christmas, on board of one of which my father was permitted to take a passage, accompanied by his family. The cause of his return to Europe, I do not precisely recollect, but have a faint idea that it was in consequence of having lent some money to an officer, who had sailed for England without paying him, and upon complaint made to the General in command, he granted permission to my father to follow the officer. [34]

Plausibly, an officer returning to England might have owed the sergeant money but, more probable, the real reason for Sergeant Hunter's recall had nothing to do with money. After twenty-seven years of active duty, including the last three years of highly kinetic combat and suffering debilitating wounds, John's health no longer permitted active campaigning and combat. The regimental command recognized Sergeant Hunter as a good soldier but worn out and deemed a recruiting assignment in England his highest and best use to the army. The 26th Regiment needed his help to recruit new soldiers to re-fill its ranks depleted by continual combat and active campaigning in Canada, New York, New Jersey, and Philadelphia.

CHAPTER FOUR

Captive Again!

William and his family sailed on the *Henry & Ann* transport ship to Britain as part of a large convoy of troopships. Typically, empty supply (victualler) and troop transport ships from various British posts along the North American coast gathered in New York harbor to assemble for safer passage to Britain. Often, convoys returning to Britain stopped at Halifax, Nova Scotia, to pick up ships from Canadian ports, but the convoy upon which William sailed directly to Britain.

Unrealistically, William's journal omits any mention of the crowded, unsanitary conditions, poor food, rampant illness, and many deaths which characterized Eighteenth-century North Atlantic crossings. Converted privately-owned merchantmen served as British troop transports. Regulations allowed the typical ship of two to three hundred tons to carry one soldier for every two tons of weight for a total capacity of one hundred to one hundred and fifty soldiers. The Navy Transport Board retrofitted the ship's cargo spaces with small cabins and added several cannons for defense. The soldiers and their families resided on wooden berths built into each cabin, typically housing six people with four places to sleep. Often, low ceilings inhibited occupants from standing up straight.[1] Bedding consisted of straw, though sometimes soldiers could improve their comfort by bringing their barracks bedding. Candles provided the only light.[2]

Onboard, food rations were set at two-thirds the standard Army rate by The Navy's Victualler Board which refused to reimburse the transport owners for any amounts in excess. Provisions consisted of old salted beef or pork and poor-quality flour and biscuits supplemented with a gill of rum. Many times,

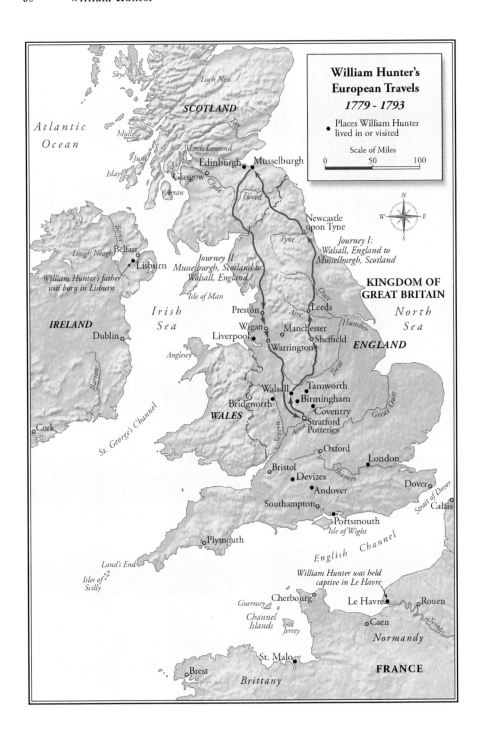

**William Hunter's
European Travels
*1779 - 1793***

● Places William Hunter
  lived in or visited

Scale of Miles

0   50   100

during a voyage, food became rotten and inedible. At sea, women received the same food ration but no alcohol. The lack of vitamin C in the shipboard diet, putrid water, and heavily salted foods frequently led to scurvy outbreaks and other malnutrition diseases.

Indications of seasickness, particularly rampant among children, were even more of an omission in the journal. Seasickness became more acute as ships entered the rough, open Atlantic waters, and ships became buffeted by strong winds and storms. In the eighteenth century, there were no effective counter-measures for seasickness. As a result, those afflicted became dehydrated and more susceptible to other shipborne illnesses such as dysentery, typhus (called malignant jail fever in the eighteenth century), and scurvy. Commonly, non-en-slaved passengers arrived at their destinations with a three to five percent mor-tality rate. Death rates widely varied for Atlantic crossings and could be very high in a few cases. The unpredictable nature of mortality caused high anxiety and constant dread for the passengers. Upon arrival, sick soldiers required time to recover from shipborne illness and would have been immediately available for duty. In all cases, the soldiers needed sufficient rest time on land with full rations to regain their strength before engaging in campaigns or combat.[3]

Perhaps, a contemporaneously written account would have recounted these severe privations. However, William vividly described the meteoritical and sail-ing dangers of transatlantic voyages, commonly encountered in the dead of winter. This crossing became no exception, and the transport fleet confronted a "succession of stormy weather." During one of these tempests, the need to trim sails led to,

> . . . the loss of a very worthy man one blustery night, who fell into the sea
> from the shrouds, as he was ascending to regulate something aloft. As soon
> as the alarm was given by the watch upon deck, great exertion was made
> and much confusion took place. The hencoops were all thrown overboard,
> in hopes that he might catch hold of some of them, to enable him to float
> while a boat was hoisted out. But while some fastened ropes to them, others
> cut them loose, in the confusion and all were lost. We distinctly heard him
> cry out several times—but the night being very dark and stormy, it was
> impossible to save him. He was an active, well disposed man, who had
> agreed to work his passage as were much in want of sailors.

Cramped below decks with little light, no ventilation, and water leak-ing into the sleeping quarters, the passengers endured particularly horrific conditions during windy tempests. The succession of violent squalls left the ship, the *Henry & Ann*, damaged and barely seaworthy. Compounding the situation, a troubled William characterized the captain as "insane" and the crew as "poorly functioning." With tattered sails and tangled rigging, the weakened ship proved challenging to sail with an undersized crew and could not keep up with the transport fleet. Separated from the protective convoy, the *Henry & Ann* entered the English Channel after a five-week passage. Not even a fully functioning transport would be safe so near hostile French territory without warship protection. Sure enough, by the light of the moon, a lurking French privateer spotted the lone transport and began to give chase. Rigged for speed, the French warship quickly overtook the ponderously slow *Henry & Ann*. Upon reaching hailing distance of the troop carrier, the ninety-two-ton French corsair *Normande* with its sixteen cannons and eighty crew lobbed a broadside into the poorly armed transport followed by a volley of brisk musketry.[4] Having escaped the French in New York harbor, William's luck ran out in the English Channel. The British vessel struck its colors and dropped sail as the captain sensed further resistance futile. Frightened, William described the battle's aftermath.

> I well recollect to see the Frenchman boarding us. Armed with cutlasses, and pistols in their girdles, etc. added to their blustering and violent gestures, they made a most terrific appearance. The ship being large and scarce of men, but few were hurt. A British officer received a cannon ball through his thigh, of which he died in a few days. Some others were slightly wounded. The privateer being crowded with men, it was said, that several were killed and wounded by our fire.

With this short naval battle, the impressionable young William witnessed bloody horrors, just as his father did many times. This brief but impactful brush with combat further disabused William of any future interest in military life. After capitulating to the French privateer, he and his family faced a second round of indefinite internment, this time on the other side of the Atlantic. Louis Hamel, the privateer captain, placed a prize crew on the *Henry & Ann* and sailed to Le Havre de Grace (today Le Havre).[5] Similarly sized as 1779 New York City, Le Havre de Grace boasted a population of fifteen thousand inhabitants occupying over thirteen hundred houses and buildings. Built in the sixteenth century as a walled city at the Seine River's mouth, Le Havre de Grace served as a vital conduit for Atlantic trade with Paris and Rouen. A bustling harbor, its large inner anchorages could hold fifteen to thirty ships with over three hundred in the outer harbor. France's second-largest seaport hosted the arrival of ten to twelve ships each day.

France's entry into the American War for Independence significantly disrupted the city's thriving commercial shipping, and many merchant businesses floundered. However, astute French ship owners adapted to wartime opportunities. Enterprising owners contracted with King Louis XVI's government to use their ships to supply overseas French colonies and military forces. Alternatively, military-minded owners sought governmental *letters de marques* that provided legal authority to engage in the dangerous but lucrative privateering practice. Under these legalized piracy terms, J. Papillon, the corsair *Normande* owner, sold the captured ship and its contents and divided the proceeds with the government, captain and crew. Papillon turned over the British army soldiers, families, and *Henry & Ann*'s crew to the French government for incarceration.

Even in this large, cosmopolitan city, the British prisoners evoked considerable curiosity among the residents. The privateer crew paraded ten-year-old William and his family through the streets to the police station amid the curious Havre de Grace's citizens who sought to catch a glimpse of the British. While the British may have been a spectacle for the French, the unfamiliar sound of "clattering of wooden shoes" on cobblestone streets served as William's first impression of the French town. In Brittany, wooden shoes or sabots were typical in the sixteenth to nineteenth centuries, especially among the lower classes. Leather had replaced wood in most of the British Atlantic world. Similar to his prisoner experience in Lancaster, favorable treatment by the French captors impressed William. His father required medical attention as he was not well and feeling "somewhat indisposed," reminiscent of the aftermath of the Fort Saint-Jean siege in Canada. Typically, a small percentage of soldiers on Atlantic crossing transport ships required medical care upon arrival. French authorities sent William's father and the other sick soldiers further inland to a well-run hospital attached to a nunnery for treatment. Rather than going to prison with the others, the supervisors of prisoners permitted William to accompany his father to the hospital. William did not mention his mother or sister, but they also resided near the hospital.

> The good nuns were indefatigable in their executions to extend every comfort in their power to such as stood in need of their kind offices. It was truly a most gratifying spectacle to see with what steady and unremitting attention these excellent women attended to everything calculated to

promote comfort of the distressed objects committed to their charge. Young as I was, I noticed with great pleasure the cleanliness, order and decorum which prevailed under their benevolent superintendence.

William and his debilitated father lodged in the hospital's large communal prison ward. Requiring constant care, William ran errands for his convalescing father and assisted with the sergeant's personal care. While his father required an extended stay to recover, William enjoyed being with his father and the other recuperating soldiers. One of the most remarkable passages written by William was a description of the soldiers' amusement while convalescing. Typically, Revolutionary-era journalists focused on descriptions of battles, campaigns, and rigors of daily life and omitted accounts of their leisure time activities. William's journal was one of the few accounts of soldiers' entertainment.[6]

> Locked up at an early hour in the evening, our only amusement was storytelling, which was generally kept up until a late hour of the night by some of the prisoners, several of whom distinguished themselves by this talent. But I recollect more particularly, an old soldier who was preeminent in his line. Indeed, he exceeded any person I have ever heard. No sooner had the prisoners retired to bed, but by general consent he was called upon for a story, and well he repaid the attention that we bestowed upon him. He appeared to have gotten the whole of Arabian Tales by heart, and could relate them as circumstantially as if he had the book before him. This pleasantly passed our time until my father recovered his health and was liberated from the hospital upon his parole, and the security of the Owner of the Privateer, who captured us.

More accurately entitled *A Thousand and One Nights*, the Arabian tales were relatively novel to English-speaking audiences, translated from French (originally Arabic) by an anonymous London writer in the early eighteenth century. Readily available cheap booklet versions appeared in bookstores and on street corners. Widely spread by word of mouth, the mysterious Middle Eastern stories captivated British audiences with tales of magical flying characters, exotic cultures, and eroticized subjects. The stimulating descriptions of striking colors, clothes, and perfume reconnected Europeans with medieval times.[7] As soldiers, the prisoners related to the magical stories of courage, a curiosity of foreign lands, and acquisitive desires. The colorful tales provided enthralling respites from drab prison life with nightly renditions of a new Arabian legend. William's journal provides unique evidence of British soldiers' non-military interests, including reading, literature, and education.

Gradually, the sergeant recovered his health and received parole to live with his family within the vicinity of Le Havre de Grace. With the worldwide conflict between Britain and France intensifying, both sides held thousands of prisoners, which were costly to incarcerate. William and his family hoped for a general prisoner exchange allowing a return to Britain. In the interim, the sergeant developed a friendly relationship with J. Papillon, the owner of the privateer who captured him. Papillon, a "wealthy and generous man," owned at least two privateering ships.[8] "Having been a prisoner himself in England during the former war and well used as he said, he was exceedingly kind to all that fell into his power . . ." Papillon invited the sergeant and his family to his "country seat" where "we met a handsome company of gentlemen captains of vessels and others who he had hailed—and truly he gave us a most sumptuous entertainment." Other than his prisoner experience at the hands of the British, it's not clear why Papillon treated William and his family so well. Shortly after the country seat visit, the sergeant received limited parole and relocated with his family to a small town. William recalled the town's name as Balbec, a small village a few miles from Le Havre de Grace. Perhaps, the countryside or Papillon's businesses needed labor, similar to the American held prisoners in Lancaster who gained employment in nearby farms and businesses.

In France, William continued his education at a local school and quickly learned to "jabber the language of the Country with my play fellows." Perhaps his prior experiences in Montreal assisted in the quick assimilation of the French language. The ten or eleven-year-old boy relished his stay in the Normandy countryside, stating . . .

> This, I have considered as the happiest period of my life. Delights with the Country and its inhabitants—blessed with fine health, and the society of my parents and sister, and captivated with the manners of the French people, I had nothing to desire, but a continuance of these blessings. Contrasted with the dangerous and troublesome events through which I had passed, it was Heaven itself.

However, bucolic William's time in Normandy, the global reach of the American War for Independence continued to affect his life greatly. In the summer of 1779, the French government assembled troops in the Le Havre de Grace area for a large-scale invasion of Britain. King Louis XVI named Lieutenant

General Comte de Vaux as supreme commander of the invasion forces in Brittany and Normandy. Over a fifty-year career, the aging military commander fought in nineteen sieges, ten small and four large battles. Compatriots viewed him as a simple but excellent character.[9] He later rose to be Marshall of France.

In the Le Havre de Grace area, de Vaux began training the thirty-thousand-soldier French assault force for a challenging England invasion. Not planning to overrun the entire British Isle, French military planners sought to inhibit British sea power projection to overseas theaters of war. To support this initial objective, de Vaux targeted capturing the largest British naval base at Portsmouth. William and the other captives could not avoid seeing such a large military force in rural Normandy. The French military took no actions to keep the prisoners and their families from observing the invasion preparations. William watched a large military training exercise, stating, "They had a grand field day—went through a sham fight of a variety of other military maneuvers, exhibiting the finest discipline. Truly they made a beautiful display." Displaying a condescendingly British bias, William opined that the military exercises were "a post of scarecrow with which the French are always in the habit of using to frighten the English whenever a war exists between the nations."[10] In July 1779, Marquis de Lafayette traveled to Normandy to train the invasion force and attend this military display. With youthful vanity, he hoped to be named the overall commander of the French invasion forces. Officially, in the French military, Lafayette merely held a minor post in a single Dragoon unit. However, given his experience in large-scale, hotly contested American Revolutionary War battles, he lobbied the Royal government to be named to command the French invasion force. However, trusted and experienced senior military leaders were already in place. The King, still furious with Lafayette for serving in the Continental Army without his consent, only offered Lafayette the *aide-marechal de logis* to Monsieur de Jaucourt, one of three quartermaster generals in the invasion force. Clearly, in late 1770s France, Lafayette did not enjoy the prominence he possessed as one of George Washington's most trusted and valued major generals.

William did not meet the Marquis de la Lafayette. However, he wrote, "My mother afterward dined in company with him [Lafayette] at the house of an English gentleman in the vicinity, where she was in the habit of spending part of her time as a companion for his Lady." From time to time, members of the English upper class retired to France to benefit from a lower cost of living. Logically, a transplanted English gentleman would gravitate to any British prisoners on parole in the area. Most probable, the lady of the house invited Margaret to a large dinner gathering.[11] Lafayette may have referenced the same dinner in a letter to Comte de Vergennes, the French Minister of Foreign Affairs. Lafayette wrote to the minister that he gathered valuable intelligence while dining with several British officers in the Le Havre de Grace area. In any event, Lafayette's intelligence on the political and military situations in New York and Halifax gleaned from the low-level British officers turned out not to be especially valuable.[12]

Later, William reported that the relationship between his mother and the wife of the English gentleman increased when "his only son (a beautiful child of four years old) was scalded to death by falling into a pot of hot water. This unfortunate accident caused my mother's company to be the more necessary at the seat of this gentleman, to alleviate the sorrows of his amiable and distressed wife." Margaret helped nurse John back to health after being burned in the Fort Saint-Jean siege. Perhaps, she leveraged this burn care experience to save the toddler. A precocious William accompanied his mother and unexpectedly received permission to use the library on several occasions.

> I was frequently there myself and was, at all times, much delighted with the reception that I received. There it was, perhaps, I embibed [*sic*] my first taste for reading. Indulged in the use of a fine Library, I read Don Quixote, Gil Blas[13], and several other works of that description, with great pleasure and some profit. They made an indelible impression on my memory, and excited such a desire for further information as has never been extinguished, and in the lapse of so many years is but little abated.

In the fall, orders arrived from Paris to abandon the invasion plans and redeploy the French forces to other strategic war objectives. With this change in plans, Lafayette left Le Havre in September and returned to America, where he eventually led an important independent command of Continental Army forces in Virginia leading up to Yorktown.

Most importantly for William and his family, with no imminent invasion threat, British and French commissioners of prisoners agreed upon a prisoner exchange clearing a path to complete the family's travels to Britain.

Despite the good news, returning to Britain required more travel time than a short channel crossing from Le Havre de Grace. To board the ship designated to transport prisoners to England, William and his family traveled one hundred and seventy miles southward.

> Early in the spring, we set out for St. Malo[14], to embark for England. We passed through Havre de Grace, where we spent one night, and were locked

up in prison. Crossing the Seine next day, we resumed our journey through Normandy and Brittany to our destined port. When we entered the latter province (the theater of the Lechouan War[15] in the late Revolutionary contest), my attention was forcibly arrested by the great difference in the habits, manners and appearance of the people. We met women, coarsely appareled, riding astride on horseback, like men. The country too, had a very different appearance. It was badly cultivated, hilly and poor.

After this seemingly unnecessary detour and delay, the authorities concluded the prisoner exchange mechanics negotiations, which permitted the Hunters to leave France. Relieved, the family received orders to proceed to England. While moving to a locale under the British government's control, the Hunter family did not return to their Irish homeland nor an area familiar to them. England represented just another in a long string of isolated military posts in which the Hunters lived without the benefit of long-term friends or relatives. England appeared foreign to William. Having never lived anywhere in the British Isles, William would have to learn new customs and complete an education that had been interrupted so many times in his early youth. At least he took comfort from being released from captivity and in the move to a more physically secure environment. While the prospect of a more peaceful life loomed in the future, William and his family still faced one life-threatening wartime danger.

CHAPTER FIVE

Gaining an Education and Trade in Britain

U pon arriving at the granite island port of St. Malo, William and his family embarked upon a ship for the one hundred and fifty nautical mile passage across the English Channel to Britain. Designated as a cartel or prisoner exchange vessel, the ship sailed from the ancient walled city with non-belligerent papers to ensure safe passage. However, the French hand-off to the English crew did not go smoothly, and new dangers emerged.

> Scarcely had we left the port before the English sailors took possession of the ship and soon after had nearly run her unintelligible upon the rocks of Guernsey. With the aid of the French crew (who were called up for that purpose) we escaped, however, very narrowly, having approached so near the rocks as to be considered by all on board in the most imminent danger—Apprehensive of being pressed if the vessel was remitted to Portsmouth harbor (to which place, I believe, she was destined) the sailors ran her into a small inlet below Portsmouth, where we landed with some difficulty. The bar was dangerous to cross with the vessel, and the surge nearly swamped the boats before we reached the shore. With a little wetting, however, we got in safe, and consoled ourselves with some good English beer. As soon as we landed, the Sailors scattered in all directions, to avoid the press gangs.

Naval press gangs were not idle threats. Chronically experiencing manpower shortages, the naval press gangs scoured seaport taverns, inns other public places to impress anyone that they could deem a sailor. In the same timeframe as William's crossing, another cartel ship carrying three hundred and fifty British parolees arrived near the English seaport of Swansea from Nantz, France. A British naval vessel spied the men coming ashore in boats and sought to press them into service. However, when the former prisoners of the French refused to be pressed, the crew of an armed ship *Mackworth* opened fire, killing several returning soldiers and sailors. Recently contracted for use by the British Navy, the *Mackworth* patrolled the coast of southern England with the primary mission of protecting trading ships from French privateers. In this instance, the former merchant ship also provided an impressment mechanism to compel sailors into British naval service.

Amid the attack, an eleven-year-old boy among the returning prisoners said, "We have been 22 months in a French prison and refused to serve the French or Americans on any terms, now we are come here to be murdered by own countrymen."[1] As William substantiates, free sailors desperately sought to remain employed in private shipping and assiduously avoided the naval press gangs.

Fortunately, William's ship landed safely without incident. "From the West of England, we proceeded to London, where my father waited on his Colonel to report himself and receive his orders for the future Destination." As customary in the British Army, the commanding officer of the 26th Regiment, Colonel Lord Adam Gordon, remained in England and did not accompany the regiment on its tours of duty in North America. A member of Parliament and a titled man, the colonel sought firsthand information on French invasion preparations. Newspapers reported that "the French are hard a work in building flat bottomed boats that upwards of fifty are finished, which are laid under the guns of the fort for fear any of the English cruisers should go in to destroy them."[2] Further, the prisoners' eyewitness accounts of Lafayette's activities and the training of French troops would be valuable intelligence. However interesting the information provided by the former prisoners, orders for the sergeant's next duty station were not immediately forthcoming. A five-week delay in receiving orders afforded time for a precocious child to explore the city streets of London and acquaint himself with English customs. Even though William had lived in three major North American cities, London's population and urban institutions were an order of magnitude larger, providing fascinating new attractions for the colonial-born pre-teen.

While in London, Sergeant Hunter learned that British Army ordered its American Commander, General Henry Clinton, to disperse the remaining enlisted men of the 26th Regiment as replacements soldiers to other units in New York City. Typically, when a regiment's combat effectiveness fell too low, British military leaders redistributed or "drafted" enlisted soldiers to other regiments. To ease the transition, drafted soldiers received a bounty of one and one-half guineas. The drafting process prevented Sergeant Hunter from reuniting with his former comrades in arms who remained in North America. Likewise, William lost contact with many friends and playmates. To make things even more new and uncertain, a new complement of officers led the regiment. Of the fifteen officers at the siege at Fort Saint-Jean four years ago, only Major Andrew Gordon and Captain William Borough remained assigned to the 26th Regiment.

In December 1779, Clinton reserved a cadre of the officers, non-commissioned officers, drummers, and a few privates of the 26th Regiment for a recruiting mission in Britain to reconstitute the enlisted ranks. Embracing the new recruiting assignment, the officers set up regimental headquarters in Tamworth, a market town in the English West Midlands. Receiving orders, the sergeant and his family left London not for regimental headquarters in Tamworth but a recruiting assignment in Devizes, a town built around a mostly destroyed 11th century Norman castle. Located in southwest England ninety-three miles west of London and one hundred and twenty miles south of Tamworth, the ups and downs of the area's textile and corn (grains) industries promised good recruiting prospects. The town is best known for a famous smuggling tale in which locals late one night outwitted the Crown's revenue agents by pretending to rake in round cheese rather than bootleg French brandy. From then on, town residents enjoyed the moniker of moonrakers.

A typical recruiting mission consisted of a commissioned officer, a sergeant, a corporal, a drummer, and two privates. Strict rules prohibited military recruiters from signing up "vagabonds, tinkers, chimney sweepers, colliers or sailors." Generally, to be eligible for the service, recruits had to be between five feet six- and one-half inches and six feet tall and less than thirty years in age. The men had to be in good health with no injuries or impediments to their knees as attested to by a surgeon. Nineteenth-century soldiers marched long distances at high rates of speed which necessitated strong legs and fully functioning knees. To maintain quality and military effectiveness, the officers and Non-commissioned officers (NCOs) were libel to court-martial if recruits did not meet these minimum standards.

Enlistment and recruiting could be lucrative for both the recruits and the recruiting officers and NCOs. The lead recruiting officer received a five-guinea fee for each abled-body man who enlisted. The fee funded recruiting expenses, including inducements such as food and drinks. Also deducted from the recruiting fee was a bounty not to exceed two- and one-half guineas paid to the recruits, which represented approximately three months' pay.[3] Enlisting was euphemistically referred to as "taking the King's Shilling." Any remaining funds accrued to the lead recruiting officer who could (and likely did) share a portion of the profits with the other recruiting team members. Likewise, the entire bounty was not available to the newly enlisted soldier, as regulations required the purchase of shirts, shoes, and socks with their bounty money.[4]

Military recruiters sought the voluntary enlistment of men seeking a better or more stable profession or who wanted the adventure of military life. Similar to Sergeant Hunter, cloth weavers displaced by industrialization were key recruiting targets and represented one of the largest trades in the army.[5] In some cases, criminals and debtors could enlist to avoid jail terms. After the repeal of portions of the Recruiting Acts of 1778 and 1779, British Army recruiters could no longer forcibly impress men and were required to entice recruits voluntarily. As inducements to volunteer, the new recruiting acts exempted recruits from Statue (highway) duty and permitted them to serve as a parish officer. As a final incentive, retiring soldiers enjoyed the legal right to trade in any town without guild or governmental approval. The ability to practice a restricted trade in any location induced many recruits.

Quickly exhausting the number of potential recruits in the Devizes area, the sergeant and his family moved thirty miles to the town of Andover, in Hampshire, "where we resided at the time of the great riots in London in the summer of 1780." The London riots started as a peaceful protest against the Papist Act of 1778, which increased legal standing for British citizens of the Catholic faith. Crowds gathered to protest the end of legal restrictions and penalties on the practice of Catholicism. Incensed with parliament's debate to further legitimize Catholic worship, the crowds grew to massive proportions. The unhappy London throngs quickly got out of hand. A week-long rampage ensued, killing hundreds of innocent Catholics and destroying numerous Catholic churches and homes. The unrest became known as the Gordon Riots after the protestant Member of the Scottish Parliament and chief instigator of the intended peaceful protests, Lord George Gordon (no relation to the officers of the 26th Regiment with the same surname). The London riots were the "biggest, deadliest and most protracted urban riots in British history."[6] Important for the sergeant's recruiting mission, a provision of the 1778 Papist act permitted the British Army to enlist Catholic soldiers without taking an oath of faith to the Anglican Church. The end of the religious oath increased the potential army recruiting pool during the rising unpopularity of the American War of Independence.

In the fall of 1780, Sergeant Hunter received orders to report to the Tamworth Headquarters in Warwickshire, 124 miles north of Andover. On the way to Tamworth, William witnessed a hotly contested parliamentary election while passing through the city of Coventry. Featuring one of the largest borough electorates (though far from universal suffrage), the turbulent political campaign for two seats in the House of Commons pitted candidates from the Corporation and Independent parties. Charging a "self-perpetuating oligarchy," the Corporation Party opposed Prime Minister Frederick, Lord North's government while the Independent Party consisted of supporters of the Tory government.[7] Like the Gordon riots, the Coventry political contest highlighted religious differences as Protestant dissenters supported the Corporation party while Anglicans backed the Independents.

The vitriolic Coventry political contest keenly interested the precocious twelve-year-old.

> Some idea of its violence may be gathered from the following circumstance, to which I was an eye witness. Passing along a street one day, I met a large assemblage of persons consisting of several thousands, designated with cockades of ribbons and bearing several standards descriptive of the party to which they belonged. Presently appeared in sight from the opposite direction, an immense number of their opponents decorated and distinguished in a similar manner. Each of the parties were armed with clubs and other weapons, which they made a liberal use of as soon as they met. Thousands were instantly engaged and before the combat was over, many were severely wounded, and a few killed. It was, indeed, a dreadful fray, and alarmed one much, as I was in a situation to see it distinctly without the opportunity of escaping until it was over, being hemmed in between the parties. By climbing upon a frame before a house, I got out of the way of the belligerents, and had a pretty fair view of the battle.

Interestingly, William did not take sides in the election but noted the dozens of broadsides and newspapers to sway public opinion. Bitter disputes over polling procedures and disruptive mob violence led the sheriff to close the polls for several weeks. The British government brought in troops to restore. Although passing through the area, military leaders did not call upon John Hunter's unit for assistance. After election officials reopened the polls a few months later, the Corporation declared its candidates as the winners by a few votes. However, upon petition to the friendly Parliament, the House of Commons overturned the election results, and the anti-Corporation, Independent Party candidates, were seated due to polling irregularities and support for the incumbent North government. The Coventry election campaign sparked William's lifelong interest in politics and illuminated the growing importance of printed media.

Especially attention-grabbing to an almost teenager, William noted the Coventry town legend of a thirteenth-century Lady Godiva riding the city's

streets covered only with her long, flowing hair. While William did not personally witness one of the annual reenactments, he recounted the tale as told to him
while visiting Coventry.

> At the annual fair, a female is dressed in fleche colored silk, so tightly made
> as to represent a naked woman. She's mounted on horseback, and followed
> by the Corporation and thousands of the populous, passes in procession
> through the streets of the City. The custom originates, it is said, from a heavy
> fine imposed upon the inhabitants by the Lord of the place, and which he
> refused to remit unless his Lady (the fair Godiva) would agree to ride naked
> through the City. Moved by the distressing entreaties of the people, she
> consented to do so, much to the astonishment of the husband, who then
> ordered every house to be shut up, and that no person, on pain of death
> should look at her. Tradition says, all observed the injunction except a poor
> Taylor [*sic*] name of Tom, whose curiosity induced him to take a peek, for
> which he lost his eyes. I saw a representation of him, made of wood and
> handsomely painted placed in an obscure garret window, and in the act
> of peering upon her ladyship. He is regularly put in trim for the annual
> exhibition.

After a short stay, the family left Coventry and completed the journey to
Tamworth. Sergeant Hunter reported to Captain William Myers, who commanded the recruiting detachment at regimental headquarters.[8] The family did
not stay but a few weeks before receiving orders on a new recruiting mission.
They moved a short distance to Walsall in Staffordshire, a large manufacturing
center in the English Midlands, about ten miles from Birmingham and seventeen miles west of Tamworth.

> At Walsall, I spent many years of my early Life. It was there that my
> habits and principles were chiefly formed, and took that shade and cast
> of character, which is a great degree, influenced my future destiny. There
> I went to School, there is served an apprenticeship to the business which
> furnished me the means of support and there it was I imbibed my religious
> and political principles and a knowledge of my moral duties. In short, it was
> there I learnt nearly all that stamped a character on my after life.

Much larger than Tamworth, Walsall would become a more permanent
home for the heretofore peripatetic sergeant and his family. Eighteenth-century
Walsall surrounded an ancient town centered on a limestone hill. The Anglican

Church of St. Matthews stood on the hill's apex, dominating the skyline. In keeping with the increasing religious diversity of the times, four meeting houses for non-conforming or non-Church of England faiths served dissenting residents. With a population nearing ten thousand, Walsall provided many of the opportunities found in the larger cities in which William had resided, such as Philadelphia and New York. During the late 18th century, the West Midlands town boasted numerous manufacturing industries, including metalworking, tinning, horse furniture workshops, tanning, saddlery, and woolen mills. Industrialists operated extraction enterprises, including mining coal, clay (for bricks), limestone, and iron. Market days were Tuesdays, and the city hosted three major fairs a year for the selling of horses, cattle, sheep, and other animal and agricultural products. A horse racing track and associated events drew spectators into Walsall from the surrounding areas for recreation.

While William and his family remained in Walsall, the British army transferred the 26th Regiment of Foot headquarters to Shrewsbury about fifty miles from Tamworth and forty miles from Walsall. At this new post, a regimental inspection concluded that the regiment was in poor shape and significantly understrength. Army leadership lamented the officer's youth and inexperience. Further, the inspection report determined that the NCOs were old and worn out, and the new enlisted soldiers required two years of intense training to be ready for active duty. The British high command assigned the 26th Regiment to oversee two hundred captured Dutch soldiers. Happy with their food, lodging, and the terms of their captivity, guarding the Dutch soldiers proved to be easy duty. While the Dutch wished to return home as soon as possible, they represented no physical threats or violence towards the soldiers or the civilian population.[9]

Under the direction of the newly promoted Major William Myers,[10] the recruiting stations began to turn things around and produce promising recruits. An extra bounty funded by local towns and publicized in local newspapers greatly assisted the recruiting efforts. The town of Newcastle upon Tyne offered a bounty of two guineas over and above all other bounties to the first fifty men who enlisted in the 26th Regiment with the approval of the Tynemouth Barracks commanding officer.[11] Although still understrength, regimental muster rolls indicate a complement of thirty-six officers and three hundred and seventh-eight enlisted soldiers, an increase of over one hundred and twenty when drafted in New York. A year later, a second inspection noted service readiness improvements, and the number of regulars increased to four hundred and twenty-four.[12]

Settling in, William attended an unnamed "English" school for three years prosecuting "my studies with much success. In that time, I had learnt to write a pretty good hand (which hard work and little practice afterwards spoiled) became a ready accountant, and acquired a tolerable smattering of the English grammar." Although modern sources indicate the first subscription library wasn't established until 1800, William reported that he augmented his formal education as a voracious reader of books from the local library.[13] Quite possibly, a shopkeeper or a bibliophile operated a small lending library that William frequented.

> In lieu of the dead language, my mind was stored with information derived from a miscellaneous course of reading at a circulating library, to which my father had the kindness to subscribe for my benefit and amusement. This was to me a source of great delight, and had I been furnished with suitable books, and my course of reading properly directed, I should have derived a tenfold advantage from his kind indulgence. But left to myself, I read without method or system, and wasted too much time in the perusal of Novels and other ephemeral publications of the day.

William continued in his education until the spring of 1783, when army command ordered the 26th Regiment to a new billeting station in Musselburgh, Scotland.[14] Wishing to see the countryside, the not-yet fifteen-year-old boy walked the three hundred miles with the corporal and privates while his father rode in a stagecoach. His father's deteriorating physical condition prevented him from walking long distances. Initially, William and his father traveled to the eastern side of the British Isles, then north through Sheffield, Leeds, Newcastle upon Tyne, and Berwick. The walking party made fifteen to twenty-five miles per day, depending on weather, while the stagecoach zoomed ahead.

> In passing along, we frequently gratified our curiosity by viewing a Nobleman's Country Seat, or in examing [sic] an old Castle, which had been the scene of many a battle during the conflicts of the Barons, or [in] the civil war of Charles and Cromwell. Now and then we saw a Roman road, or the remains of some ancient fortification of that warlike people and sometimes we treated ourselves with a sight of some of the interesting manufacturing establishments in the towns throughout which we passed. In short, the journey was to me a rich treat, and added considerably to my stock of information, correcting by personal observation many prejudices and erroneous views which fasten on the mind from reading alone.

After a safe journey, father and son reunited in Musselburgh. Known as the "Honest Toun," Musselburgh sat on the southern coast of the Firth of Forth on the east bank of the Esk River. The ancient town of Musselburgh's name derived from an Old English name for shellfish. At this site, occupying Romans built a fort and an arched stone bridge connecting the Esk River's east and west banks. A sixteen-century three arched, reconstructed bridge evoked images of the town's Roman past. Smaller than the recent 26th Regiment of Foot posts, the local economy consisted of fishing and manufacturing items supporting the fishing industry. Town industries included the manufacture of sailcloth, fishing nets, hats, leather works, bricks, tiles, and pottery.

American War veteran and recently appointed Colonel of the 26th Regiment, Sir William Erskine ordered the move to Musselburgh, reconnecting the regiment with its Scottish heritage. Additionally, Colonel Erskine sought to increase the proportion of Scotsmen in the unit. In Erskine's previous command, he prided himself on raising an entire regiment without enlisting one Englishman.[15] To increase the attractiveness of the military unit to Scotsmen, Colonel Erskine petitioned King George III to officially change the regiment's name to the Cameronians, its unofficial moniker since inception. Not all soldiers found the 26th Regiments move to Scotland to their liking. The 26th Regiment experienced a raft of desertions, primarily by teenaged recruits seeking escape from army life. The regiment's commander offered an additional two guineas reward over and above the parliament set reward. While common throughout the regiment's history, desertions particularly plagued the regiment in Musselburgh.[16]

After settling into new quarters, Sergeant Hunter found that for the first time since 1775, he had free time on his hands. Refreshingly, he could engage in leisure activities with his son without the threat of war or capture. Taking advantage of the opportunity, William and his father visited the historical sights and city attractions of the nearby Scottish capital.

> After spending a few weeks there, I went with him to Edinburgh, distant about six miles. We remained but two or three days during which time I was gratified with a sight of the old Castle, Holyrood House (the residence of the ancient Kings of Scotland and lately the abode of the deposed King of France[17]) and generally saw all that was remarkable in old and new Town. The contrast in their appearance was very great. In the New Town, the eye is delighted with fine broad streets, built up with houses in the handsomest state of modern architecture having beautiful marble fronts and generally uniform in size and appearance—While the Old Town exhibits only narrow, crooked and dirty streets, crowded with houses of all sizes and descriptions— the stories of many of them low and numerous, and inhabited by families

who in many cases, no more knowledge of each other than if they lived a hundred miles apart.

However, Sergeant Hunter and the 26th Regiment's stay in Musselburgh would be brief. The regiment discharged Sergeant Hunter, and he returned to Walsall. A few months later, in October 1783, the British command transferred the 26th Regiment to Dublin, Ireland.

Sergeant Hunter left his wife and daughter in Walsall, knowing that his army career was ending and he would not be crossing the Irish Sea with the 26th Regiment. Without an army-provided coach for transportation, father and son walked the three hundred miles back to Walsall. The fifty-six-year-old father slowed the pace. The return journey required three times the outbound trip due to the sergeant's declining fitness. However, a different route back to Walsall provided new sightseeing opportunities. Father and son traveled on the western rather than the eastern side of the British Isles through Preston, Wigan, Warrington, and the region of the renowned Staffordshire Potteries.[18]

Once back in Walsall, an impending career decision loomed over William and his parents. The fifteen-year-old needed to gain a trade, earn an independent living, and end financial reliance on his family. As might be expected, his father wished him to enlist in the Army as an honorable profession, especially in economically rocky times. Perhaps this is why Sergeant Hunter brought William along to Musselburgh. Having experienced firsthand the toll that soldiering and combat took on his father and family, William did not share his father's desire for a military career. Fortunately, after enduring two captivities, his mother nursing a wounded husband and suffering through years of wartime stresses had different ideas. She prevailed upon her husband to find a civilian profession for their son. In the late eighteenth century, Britain's market economy began transforming from an agrarian society into an industrial powerhouse. While emergent industries provided new employment opportunities, labor strife gripped the nation due to the rising population and workers' inability to transition into new jobs. Escalating food prices further fueled unrest with urban rioting and frequent mob attacks on market traders and food mills. However, industrialization brought opportunities for educated workers, especially those who could apprentice in budding industries. As an expanding industrial town of ten thousand inhabitants, more apprenticeship opportunities existed in Walsall than many other places in Britain.[19] While disjointed, William's schooling and understanding of the world beyond Walsall placed him in a good position to gain a knowledge-based apprenticeship. The prospect of apprenticing led to William's mother winning out over his father's desire for him to enlist in the military.

"In a few weeks, after my return to Walsall, my father placed me with a Mr. Frederick Milward,[20] to learn the business of a bookbinder and stationer." The choice of apprenticeships proved prescient as the printing and stationer (a bookseller and purveyor of writing materials) businesses boomed in the late eighteenth century.[21] Once limited to London, the publishing industry decentralized into mid-sized British towns as demand soared for locally published books. Additionally, emerging manufacturing regions like Walsall experienced surging demand for commercial printing. New, larger, and more complex firms needed increasing numbers of business forms such as ledgers, advertisements, coupons, and invoices to market, manage, and control their operations. Looking back, John and Margaret Hunter made a wise choice of advocations for their son.

In industrializing England, apprenticing a son indicated that the family had sufficient financial resources to forgo the value of the child's labor and to pay a premium to the master for taking on the new apprentice. In William's case, the funds to pay the premium came from a modest accumulation of savings over and above Sergeant Hunter's base pay generated by successful recruiting in the last two to three years. Typically, apprentices received no compensation for the first several years other than room and board. Therefore, William enjoyed very little income for any other necessities of life. While William's parents were relieved of providing him lodging and sustenance, Sergeant Hunter and his wife and daughter could expect little support from their son.

Exacerbating the strain on the family's financial resources, after over thirty-one years of continual military service, John suffered from debilitating rheumatism and became worn out. His commanding captain recommended John for a military pension, denoting that he was a good soldier with an exemplary service record. At the time, only ten to twenty percent of soldiers discharged were recommended for pensions.[22] Sergeant Hunter traveled to the Royal Hospital of Chelsea in London to confirm the captain's judgment for an in-person medical examination of his fitness for duty. The medical examination board found him too disabled for active service. Finding a high level of infirmity, the examiners determined that Sergeant Hunter could not serve in an Invalid Regiment for garrison and other light duties. The examination board recommended that he be placed under the supervision of the Royal Hospital of Chelsea and on its outpension list (non-resident pensioner). On August 15th, army examiners recorded the final decision, approved a sergeant's standard pension, and discharged him from the regiment.

On the one hand, Sergeant Hunter was fortunate as almost all other professions lacked retirement payments. While better than other occupations, the sergeant's legal rate of nine pence a day did not permit the retiree, especially one with a family, to live a comfortable existence solely on the military pension. If able, most retirees and members of their families worked to supplement their pensions. Free to pursue additional income in retirement, John settled in Walsall with his family as a civilian. As customary, the army furnished John with clothing for the journey home and a small allowance for lodging and subsistence for the trip to and from Chelsea Hospital.

The sergeant may have tried resuming work as a weaver, his occupation before his military service. To the extent physically possible, he toiled part-time as a laborer, and his wife and daughter worked in a domestic role. John Hunter probably earned very little, and he steadily declined in health. Shortly after retirement, William's father passed away. Military pension payments ended with the death of the retired soldier with no survivor or spousal benefits. Left with no substantial means of support, Margaret and her daughter moved to Lisbon, Portugal, to live with her family. From this point onward, William regarded himself as an orphan. With a strong note of melancholy and loss, William's printing apprenticeship started with "gloom and despondency." Over the years, William sporadically corresponds with his mother but gives no account of her or his sister's life in Portugal. Both emotionally and physically, William entered into adulthood and a career entirely on his own. He had to look out for himself and make his way.

Fortunately, he embarked upon an apprenticeship in a growing industry that provided new and exciting opportunities. His first boss, a former apprentice himself, Frederick Milward, operated a stationary, bookbinding, bookshop, and paper warehouse on High Street in central Walsall.[23] Although William said that "No business could better suit my taste . . ." he worked long hours starting before first light and ending at nine or ten at night, six days a week. William's benefits included access to a circulating library housed in Milward's business. Further fueling his voracious reading, the extensive book shop received twice monthly shipments of new volumes from London publishing houses. Working with Mr. Milward provided the additional benefit of meeting notable authors and scientists. Further, townspeople gathered in Milward's book shop to exchange news and gossip. A precocious self-learner, William enjoyed the opportunity to interact with the many educated customers who came to Milward's store in search of books and conversation.

One renowned visitor, Doctor Erasmus Darwin, profoundly affected William's spiritual and intellectual life. An accomplished Enlightenment thinker and the grandfather of the more famous evolutionist Charles Darwin, Erasmus Darwin published works on botany and, most controversially, a poem on evolution. Darwin lived in the English Midlands town of Derby. Starting in the early 1780s, Darwin spent seven years translating a four-volume botanical work by Carl Linnaeus from Swedish to English. According to the journal, Darwin made the forty-mile journey to Walsall to meet with Mr. Milward to publish another book that he was writing entitled *On the Fall of Man and Origin of Evil*. Reading the finished sections of Darwin's radical draft changed William's spiritual and religious beliefs.

> His views on that subject (which he appeared to have investigated with great labor and effort) were different from those of any other man whose writings and opinions I have every read or heard of—and if he had lived to finish the work, he contemplated giving to the public on the subject, it would doubtless have excited much attention, and very probably changed the opinions of thousands of persons who now firmly believe the popular doctrine as it is literally detailed in the Bible . . . he evidently intended to prove that the Fall of Man, as related in the Bible, was a mere allegorical description of Man's transition from a state of nature into that of artificial society—in which the vices of the latter are contrasted with the virtues and simplicity of the former: and these constitute the ground work of the whole theory on which so much superstition has been built. A delusion by which Priests __[?] has, in all ages, enabled to lead the minds of men astray, and to bewilder their judgment in the mazy labyrinth of artificial systems of Religion, in which forms and ceremonies are substituted for the more doctrines of the Creator, as taught in his Works.

Darwin espoused provocative views on human evolution, significantly at odds with the established Church of England's literal biblical doctrines. Concerned with the commercial viability of his works, Dr. Darwin sought the advice of both English and American sources to assess the size of the purchasing public.[24] As a prominent printer and bookseller in the West Midlands, Mr. Milward would be a credible source better to understand the sales prospects of such a controversial book. William hinted that the feasibility inquiry expanded to more extensive thoughts of a comprehensive publishing project.

> From a synopsis of the work (which I have in a printed proposal for publishing it by subscription), and from other writings of Mr. Milward, which his son shewed [*sic*] me, I saw, what appeared to me evidently the commencement of a fair copy for the press of this highly interesting work, but as no trace could be found of his notes, or rough draft, it is to be feared they fell into the hands of some bigot, who committed them to the flames,

where doubtless, he would have put the author too, had it been in his power. So perished the labors of a long life, devoted to the enlightenment of the human race on a subject of the deepest interest to all lovers of truth.

Despite Hunter possessing the subscription proposal, there is no evidence that Milward or any other printer published a book or pamphlet by this title. Joseph Johnson, a prominent London book publisher specializing in radical authors, regularly published first editions of Darwin's books. Over many years, Darwin enjoyed a close and productive relationship with Johnson, who warned against using "country printers" such as Milward as they use inferior paper, incur larger transportation costs, and are not in the center of substantial book buyer demand. While the Milward publishing project referenced by William never came to fruition, Darwin's deist religious and evolutionary views were published in pieces over the next twenty years culminating in a book posthumously published in 1803, entitled *The Temple of Nature: or The Origin of Society.*

While evolutionary scientists' visits captivated William, Mr. Milward kept him busy composing and printing religious texts and sermons authored by conforming Anglican clergy. Before this time, London publishers held a monopoly on book printing.[25] On the cutting edge of publishing books outside London, Milward identified prominent local writers overlooked by the big London publishers for his first publishing opportunities. In one early publishing project, he printed in book form various sermons delivered by John Darwall, the longtime vicar of Walsall's St. Michaels Church.[26] Poetry books were also good sellers, and Milward published a book of poetry by the talented Mary Whateley Darwall, the vicar's second wife. Combined with portions originally published in 1764, the two-volume set also included poems by two of their daughters.[27] In addition, he reprinted religious texts, dramatic plays, novels, and political tracts previously published in London.[28] Learning from Milward's experience of printing popular religious texts, William followed his master's lead and pursued promising markets for religious texts throughout his publishing career.

While working as Milward's apprentice, William met George, the first of his close friendships while living in Walsall.[29] Older than William and likely Frederick Milward's younger brother, George apprenticed in the wholesale factor business and assumed the operation when the master factor died. A wholesale factor purchased goods from the area's manufacturers for resale to outlying retail stores and traveling salesmen. He described George as a challenger of both political and religious orthodoxy.

He was an ardent lover of truth—a Republican in politics, and a Free
Thinker in Religion. No man had in him, more of the mild of human
kindness—nor was nay more esteemed by his acquaintances for his
many good qualities. We became greatly attached to each other, and were
inseparable when business and other engagements did not keep us apart.
Our Sundays were always spent in each others company. We read the same
books, and conversed freely in our walks upon what we had read. In short,
he was my Mentor—for being older than me, and having read more, I
profited much from his conversation and instruction.

In an interesting vignette, William described George's father as a "man
of profound talents." Unnamed, the father received a top education at the
Universities of Oxford and Cambridge in Ancient Mythology and religion. In
line with other Enlightenment thinkers, the father dismissed organized religion as another "superstition of man." As the father did not "subscribe to the
thirty-nine articles of the Church of England,"[30] he was ineligible to work in
the church, academia, or any learned profession befitting a university graduate.
As a result, he moved to a country village and lived off a small bequest from
his mother's side. However, the inheritance barely met his living needs and, at
his death, "left his children (Clearly George but also likely Frederick Milward)
to their own executions for support." This is why George and Frederick were
apprenticed in professions to earn a living. Calling Christianity "superstitious,"
this vignette and the passage on Dr. Darwin are the only written inklings of
William's religious beliefs. Despite living in areas of intense religiosity, William
espouses enlightenment views that emphasize a natural god. William looked
to nature for spiritual guidance throughout his life and did not practice organized religion. William devoted Sundays to engaging with George, his only
day off. The pair engaged in active, probing intellectual discussions as well
as physical exercise and other outdoor leisure activities. The long, twelve to
fifteen-hour work days and stress of the business did not inordinately bother
the young apprentice as he enjoyed living with the Milward family and "felt
amply rewarded for my toils, and in some degree reconciled to the separation
from my friends."

Capitalizing on the trend to expand printing beyond the traditional London
center, William's master, Frederick Milward, added a printing press to his stationery and book-selling businesses. Milward employed an additional apprentice,
William Maurice, born on June 16, 1772, in Bridgnorth, a nearby town, to
assist in operating the expanded business. Maurice's father preached one of the

eighteen or more Protestant dissenting religions in England. Both official and societal discrimination against the non-Anglican sects generated considerable religious upheaval. Often the rift between Anglicans and the dissenters led to violence and destruction. Especially in the high-profile publishing business, Milward's hiring a son of a non-conformist courageously demonstrates the unusual intellectual openness within which William lived. William expressed both respect for and admiration of the new apprentice.

> He as a well educated youth, of pure morals and fine disposition, and whithal [sic] possessed of good natural abilities. His letters to his parents, which he generally shewed [sic] me, were fine specimens of Epistolary Correspondence for a youth of his age. [Cut out section] . . . himself and his friends. He had, besides a fine for drawing and as a self taught genius, his performances were very respectable. In short, he was an excellent young man, and added much to my happiness. We worked and slept together for years—enjoyed each others amusements, and never had an angry word or felling for each other. No brothers could have been more attached.

Frederick Milward officially apprenticed William Maurice as a bookseller. Milward paid the required apprenticeship tax upon Maurice's completion of the apprenticeship period on March 20, 1789. Typically, due to the high tax, the master only officially recorded the apprenticeship when the apprentice continued to work in his establishment. Unlike Maurice, Hunter did not continue with Milward as a journeyman. There are no indications that Milward and Hunter had any fallout, and the lack of official apprenticeship papers did not impair William's future employment prospects.

William's budding social circle added Hill Cox, a High Street grocer and druggist, three years younger than William.[31] "With these two youths and my friend George Milward,[32] warmly and sincerely attached as we were to each other, my time passed happily away, and I may add, very profitably too—for from their conversation and example, I derived much useful information and instruction."

While initially focusing on literature and academic subjects, the quartets' conversations turned to the period's most significant political issue. In 1789, an armed revolt broke out against King Louis XVI, and the French people replaced the failed monarchy with a populist Republic. The French Revolution stirred considerable political agitation in Britain, and a vocal minority advocated abolishing the British monarchy and implementing a more representative government. Espousing anti-nobility sentiments, British republicans threatened the British crown's rule and the supremacy of the prevailing political orthodoxy. The government responded with crackdowns on political dissenters. Adding to the discord, rising numbers of artisanal and knowledge workers such as William and his friends fueled "discontent over food, labor conditions and taxation."[33] The intense political controversy dominated the early 1790s political environment and became a lively part of the conversations between the foursome.

> Prepared as our minds were, but a course of free enquiry with Religious and political subjects, we all became ardent Republicans, and warmly attached to the principles of Reform. These principles I have continually cherished through the whole of my eventful life and doubtless, they will remain with me to the last moment of my existence. Founded in truth, and firm fixed in the mind at an early age, when no selfishness could interfere to mislead the judgment, they must continue to guide and stay of my mind and actions for the remainder of my days . . .

Like-minded in politics and religion, George, Hill, and the two Williams remained friends throughout their lives and exchanged letters after going their separate ways. Unfortunately, none of their correspondence survives.

Leaving the employ of Milward, William moved ten miles to Birmingham. The much larger city afforded a burgeoning economy based upon innovative manufacturing industries.[34] While new employment prospects were important to William, the intellectually vibrant city provided expanded opportunities for interaction with learned thinkers. Late eighteenth-century Birmingham hosted an eminent coterie of Enlightenment thinkers who called themselves the Lunar Society. The dinner club and informal society of scholarly men and influential thinkers met once a month during the full moon to discuss scientific, philosophical pursuits as well as political and religious activism. Between meetings, members swapped ideas and facilitated each other's intellectual development.

William attended public philosophical lectures delivered by Dr. Joseph Priestley, a leading member of the Lunar Society. Dr. Priestley is best known for the co-discovery of oxygen and the invention of soda water. The scientifically minded and highly religious Priestley also served as minister at Birmingham's New Meeting Unitarian church. Unitarianism is a Protestant Christian sect that emphasizes reason in interpreting the bible and believes in one God versus the trinity (God, Jesus, the son of God, and the Holy Spirit) as espoused in other Christian religions. The state-supported Anglican Church represented itself as

English religious orthodoxy and claimed England's vast proportion of believers. As a group, non-Anglicans were known as dissenters. In politics, Priestley ardently believed in republics as the best form of government (a republican in the language of William's era) and was a staunch supporter of the French Revolution.

While not drawn to Priestley's religious doctrine, William ardently supported the scientist's radical political views. Nevertheless, most of all, William craved intellectual discourse with like-minded individuals. He observed, "never did I see anywhere, either before or since, so intelligent an assemblage of young persons, of both sexes . . ."

Both Priestley's dissenting religious beliefs and republican politics represented an existential threat to the status quo. William left Birmingham in July 1791. A few days later, an incensed mob, angry at Priestley's written reply to Edmund Burke's *Reflections on the Revolution in France*, confronted the unwanted dissenters and burned three of their churches. Unconstrained by local constables, the rioters gutted Priestley's home and destroyed many valuable papers and scientific apparatus.[35] The contagion spread throughout the region targeting at least twenty-seven houses occupied by other religious dissenters. With the benefit of hindsight and additional perspective, William averred a prescient observation. "Had he [Priestley] been a Deist in the former, like Bolingbroke, Shaftesbury, Hume or Hobbes, &c,[36] he might have escaped prosecution; but the unyielding advocate of Equal Rights could not be forgiven." The four philosophers cited by William disputed orthodox religious beliefs but did not challenge the Church of England's authority or seek to set up competing churches. On the other hand, Priestley directly challenged church leadership. He advocated for the repeal of the Test and Corporation Acts of Parliament, which gave special privileges to the Church of England, including the right to tax and receive public funds, restrict dissenters from public office, and precluded dissenters from enrolling in universities. William concluded that Priestley advocated equal rights for all Britons, regardless of religious beliefs, and to permit membership in the church of their choice. Further threatening to the Church of England, Priestley and Unitarians rejected fundamental Anglican theology such as the concepts of original sin, predestination, and the infallibility of the bible. In direct competition to Anglicanism, Unitarians established formal churches and proselytized converts. William respected Priestley as a learned member of the eighteenth-century Enlightenment who taught him the value of religious and political freedoms. While he embraced Priestley's ardent republican political views and freedom of religion beliefs, William did not become a Unitarian adherent as a formal religious practice did not become a big part of his life.

Attempting to find physical security, Priestley first moved to the more cosmopolitan London, then fled England for the United States. He settled with his extended family in Sunbury, located in rural northeast Pennsylvania. Now safe to publicly express his thoughts, Priestley started a Unitarian Church and continued his scientific research and religious writing. Generally, scientists and the Pennsylvania citizenry openly accepted and embraced Priestley. However, declining health limited his intellectual productivity, and he quietly passed away in 1804. Priestley's near miss with mob destruction illustrated that disputing political, social, and religious orthodoxy takes gutsy fortitude and can be personally and professionally dangerous. Following Priestley's example, later in life, William would take courageous stands on several controversial, high-profile issues and, as many enlightenment thinkers of the period, would compromise his ideals on others.

William departed Birmingham for an employment opportunity with George Gitton, a stationer, bookseller, postmaster, and one of the earliest printers in Bridgnorth, a town thirty miles away. With a population of less than four thousand, Bridgnorth typified the emerging small-town markets for printers and their journeymen in the fast-growing manufacturing areas in the Midlands. The ancient borough town is situated on the River Severn with a lower part riverside ("low town") and another portion perched on a hill overlooking the river ("high town"). One of two printers in town, Gitton sought help expanding his bookbindery and book shop into a more significant printing business. While only three years older than William, Gitton offered an attractive employment opportunity. William received a salary expressed in guineas, the mark of gentlemanly employment as customers commonly paid tradespeople and laborers in pounds. William's salary of one guinea per week (one pound and one shilling or twenty-one shillings) approximated three times the amount his father received in base pay as a British Army sergeant.[37] In addition to attractive compensation, William could count on full employment for twelve months and learn how to manage and grow a vertically integrated printing and publishing businesses. But at the same time, his experience with Gitton may have soured his taste for working under the direction of an owner. While William stated, "Their attention to me were at all times kind and polite," he noted that Mr. Gitton exhibited "occasional fits of melancholy" especially when "business became slack." Over the long run, George Gitton's printing business endured. When he died in 1823, the elder Gitton left his printing establishment and equipment to his son, George Robert Gitton.[38] On balance Gitton's business insecurities did not interfere with William's contentment in Bridgnorth, concluding, "however, upon the whole, I had great reason to be satisfied with my lot." He had come a long way from a rough, dangerous, and desolate life in a soldier's family.

Socially, William discovered a personally warm, intellectually engaging relationship to ease his transition to an unfamiliar town. William's friend, William Maurice, provided an introduction to his parents, who lived in Bridgnorth. William Maurice, the Senior, served as a long-time minister to a well-established dissenting congregation. Reverend Maurice led worship services at the historic Stoneway Chapel, initially constructed in 1709. In addition, to William Junior, the Maurice family included a daughter and another son. Finding common intellectual interests and shared opposition to the orthodox Church of England theology, William enjoyed visiting the Maurice family.

> When I chose to call upon the parents of my friend Maurice, I always received a hearty welcome, and came away improved and delighted with the conversation of his Reverend Father and most amiable Mother. She was, indeed, a woman of great intelligence, and possessed a happy mode of communicating what she knew. With such advantages I could not be surprised at the solid sense and acquirements of my young friend.

Consistent with the era's practices of keeping women in the private sphere, William did not identify the name of Maurice's wife, but unlike many other period observers, he extolled her intellectual and discursive abilities. Certainly, William missed his mother and father and enjoyed the company of Maurice's parents.

Despite long hours at work, William enjoyed socializing with a next-door neighbor.

> In addition to the society of this worthy couple, I had the happiness of a familiar intimacy with the family of a Mrs. Bache, a most respectable old Lady, who lived next door to Mr. Gitton. She had a Son about my age and two daughters. Becoming attached to the Son, who with the rest of the family treated me with great kindness, I most generally spent my evenings in their society, until bedtime, and at their house frequently met others, their relations and friends, which greatly extended my acquaintance. Among the rest, a female Cousin, about 17 years of age, possessed an agreeable voice, and very pleasing manners. There was a pensive melancholy in her manner,

which could not fail to call forth the sympathy of her acquaintances, and made her an object of peculiar interest to those who knew her story. She had, unfortunately formed an attachment for a young man, a musician in a Regiment of the British army, that had sometime stationed in Bridgnorth, but had removed therefrom a short time before I went there to reside. Her parents, from prudential motives, refused their consent to marriage. Her lover, however, contrived to carry her off from her father's home, but before a marriage could be effected, she was discovered and brought back. The young man, who was highly honorable in his principles, and . . .

William may have been attracted to Mrs. Bache's female cousin as she is the only woman of similar age he mentions during this period. Perhaps providing further romantic hints, there are missing pages at this point that may have expunged any tender love interests which subsequent family members did not want to be recorded for posterity.

Uneventfully, William's one-year contract with George Gitton expired with no impetus from either party to renew. Entering 1793, William could freely pursue a radically new course for his life and career. Contemplating prospects and advancement opportunities as a journeyman printer, stationer, and book-seller in the English Midlands, William decided to make a significant change in direction. William formed many of his lifelong social, religious, and political beliefs during his apprenticeship. Greatly influenced by Erasmus Darwin and Joseph Priestley, he became an ardent adherent to Enlightenment thinking. William lost respect for the British monarchy, class distinctions, and inherited privileges. Instead, he advocated for individual freedom and liberty, a representative government, and universal religious tolerance. He also adopted the Enlightenment view that one, if given the opportunity, could make the world a better place. William concluded that living in England was incompatible with these views. As with most Enlightenment thinkers of the day, future events would test his thinking's consistency and result in less than the entire achievement of the sweeping goals. However, he decided on a risky new course with youthful courage and enthusiasm and re-crossed the Atlantic.

CHAPTER SIX

Returning to America

William Hunter made the intrepid decision to emigrate to the United States. On the surface, the decision to move to the United States appeared perplexing due to good career prospects. The British printing business grew substantially during the 1790s, generating a burgeoning demand for journeyman printers. The printing business especially thrived in the English countryside outside London, where William lived and worked.

Making his decision harder, moving to the United States would cut off his close, personal friendships and physically separate him from his entire social and professional networks. Further, given his evident love for his family, why did he leave his parents and sister and sail to American and never return to Britain or Portugal? William does not directly state his reasons for immigrating to the United States. Perhaps, dissatisfaction with working as a journeyman printer and limited upward mobility available in class-conscious England led to his emigration decision. In his journal, William wrote about his career advancement aspirations,

> Stimulated too by an ardent desire to rise in society by my own personal exertions and acquaintances, I diligently applied myself to the acquisition of knowledge at every leisure moment I could command—taking care at the same time not to neglect the means of strengthening my constitution by suitable exercise and temperate habits.

Additionally, William may have professed too vociferously his considerable dissatisfaction with the British monarchy and political institutions. In his journal,

A self-declared republican seeking a more democratic form of government, William may have been out of step with Britain's royalty and upper class-dominated political climate. During the 1790s, the British government enforced widespread repression of dissonant voices with republican views due to the perceived threat of a "French-like" revolution toppling the British monarchy and displacing the entrenched ruling political class. In addition, the prevailing societal norms stressed attachment to monarchy, the importance of empire, value of military achievement, and desirability of government run by elites. Hunter rejected all these norms, which facilitated severing his ties with Britain.

Finally, the lack of family ties in England sealed his decision to leave Britain and move to the United States. With his father's death and his mother and sister moving to Lisbon, Portugal, no family ties kept him in Britain. Alternatively, William's meager income and prospects were insufficient to bring them back to England to support them.

Throughout his life, William referred to himself as becoming an orphan as a young man. With no family left in Britain, limited career advancement prospects, and more welcoming social and political environments, returning to American appeared to be an excellent opportunity. Sealing the deal, William remembered pleasant thoughts of America from his time before and during the American Revolution.

A governmental crackdown on Enlightenment thinkers advocating religious freedom and a republican form of government spurred a surge of British emigration to the United States during the 1790s. Joseph Priestley reported that "such as the spirit of bigotry . . . that great numbers are going to America."[1] William's leaving proved none too soon. Within a year of his departure, the government would suspend the writ of *habeas corpus* and sentence many religious and political dissidents to brutal transportation to overseas penal colonies. Any advancement in the printing industry to a position of prominence would have exposed William to similar penalties.

Exploding opportunities for printers in America eased his decision, especially apprentices trained in Britain. Further reducing his risk, English language publishing and printing expertise were highly transferable skills. High literacy rates in America drove an unprecedented increase in demand for books and newspapers. From 1700 to 1749, there were sixty-seven printers in the United States. Over the next fifty years, the number of printers exploded to five hundred and eight. In the first four decades of the 19th Century, the count of printers multiplied over five times to twenty-eight hundred and sixty-three.[2] Whether or not he remained in the publishing industry or sought a new career,

William grasped the potential in America to exploit this unprecedented rise in economic and career opportunities.

In preparation for sailing to America, William journeyed roughly eighty miles northwest from Bridgnorth to the bustling port city of Liverpool. As the major English port of entry on the Irish Sea, Liverpool reaped enormous profits from the Atlantic trade in enslaved people and operated substantially more slave ships than any other British port. In addition, Liverpool merchants sent ships to trade in most parts of the Western and Mediterranean worlds, including the United States. Bi-laterally, many American ships docked in Liverpool, delivering cotton, timber, and other goods imported in Britain. On one of these transatlantic merchant ships, William hoped to secure safe passage to the United States.

Upon arrival in Liverpool, William checked into one of the many dockside inns serving transients. Short of funds and realizing that finding the best ship to travel to the United States would take some time, William moved from the inn to a lower-cost boarding house. While in the boarding house, he met a former apprentice to a London merchant who took him "into Partnership and gave him the chief management of the concern . . . as his conduct and gratifications for business had been so acceptable to his employer." He suggested to William that he was "desirous to extend their operations in trade to the United States, he generously offered me a Consignment of such articles as I might find suitable to the wants of the market to which it was going—consisting of Liverpool ware, and the cotton and other manufactures of Manchester." By reselling British goods, William could finance his journey to America, a standard business proposition offered to immigrants. Unfortunately, for the most part, there was little profit to be made by reselling items in America, and many times, these types of business propositions were merely scams.

It is unclear how many items William purchased to sell in America, but similar to others, this proposition turned out not to be a profitable and sustainable business opportunity. William may have been scammed, but he offers excuses for why he did not reap profits and enter the import business. It "would have enabled me to commence business in Philadelphia on a respectable scale— and but for the unfortunate state of things which if found on my arrival and caused me to abandon the flattering prospect before me, I should, probably, have made a handsome fortune, as an importing Merchant in Philadelphia like many others who had commenced that business with the means at their command." Importing goods to American would prove to be the first of several partnerships that would sour for William.

By "strolling about the docks of Liverpool," William sought to procure transit on a ship sailing to America. His choices were highly constrained, required significant research and negotiations, and came with unique risks and dangers. Motivated but possessing a low budget led William to take risks by securing passage on what he perceived a barely seaworthy ship. "A few days after my arrival. . . I discovered a Brig from Kennebeck [sic] River, which was about to return home as soon as the wind would permit." He "did not like the appearance of the vessel" but described his decision-making as a "*Hobson's choice*"— the Kennebec brig or nothing. With his sailing experience limited to only one trans-Atlantic voyage, William's nautical judgments are a bit suspect. Not recognizing sea-worthiness, he, fortunately, selected the American ship *Diana*, a newly constructed copper bottom brig.[3] Distinguished as a hermaphrodite brig, the two-masted *Diana* sported a square-rigged sail on the foremast and fore-and-aft-rigged sail on the mainmast providing improved maneuverability and increased sailing speeds. Perhaps the relatively small size of a brig intimidated William versus the larger size of the Royal Navy ships he had transited during the American War of Independence. Although good-sized for a brig, the *Diana* measured seventy-three feet in length and almost twenty-three feet in width with a draft of only eleven feet.[4] A prominent mariner from Portland, Maine, Elisha Turner captained the one hundred- and sixty-two-ton ship. *Diana's* principal cargo consisted of Liverpool fine salt and house coal, two high-demand commodities in Philadelphia. In addition to commodities, the captain offered passage in cabins and more spartan steering class transit to paying travelers.

Unmentioned by William, the outbreak of war between Britain and Revolutionary France made the choice of a ship and its flag a perilous decision. Numerous British ships sailing to and from the port of Liverpool had fallen prey to French privateers, and William did not want to risk capture for the third time in his life. Even traveling on a non-belligerent American ship represented personal risks as both British and French warships preyed on neutral shipping. British warships and privateers had captured hundreds of American ships and impressed many crew members into the Royal Navy. William's concern proved prescient as a British privateer captured the American vessel *Aerial*. The British government detained the ship for three months before permitting its voyage to Philadelphia.[5] Maybe more by chance than nautical knowledge, William selected a ship that would best secure passage through the raging conflict on the Atlantic. However, William's prior sea voyage experience served him well in making the trip as comfortable as possible. Despite meager financial resources, William wished not to return across the Atlantic in steerage class as he did on the British troop transport fifteen years earlier. For this voyage, "I engaged a cabin passage for twelve guineas." At the low end of transatlantic fares, William did not travel in luxury. Still, he was vastly more comfortable than most passengers as only a tiny fraction of immigrants could afford a cabin. On the newly constructed, fast sailing Kennebec brig, William should have a much more pleasant crossing on his return trip to America. However, things did not go as planned.

At the Liverpool boarding house, William met a fellow traveler by the name of Larned (likely his last name), a professed gentleman from Liverpool "bred in the life of luxury, and desirous to see the world." While Larned may have lived in a seaport, he did not understand the necessary preparatory steps for a trans-Atlantic Ocean journey. Veteran transatlantic passengers knew not to rely on the poor quality of the passengers' food on sailing ships. On William's vessel, "These consisted of lean, tough beef—a little pork once a week—hard biscuit and bad water." Anticipating the need, William supplemented the ship's provisions by bringing onboard food and drink, which he called "small stores." However, Larned recounted to William that he thought he could purchase these sustenance items at sea on the ship. More plausible, Larned hastily boarded the ship just before sailing after a night of drink and merriment, bringing on board a single bottle of brandy and no food. This irresponsible omission would cause William considerable distress on the voyage.

Wind direction and tides, not pre-posted sailing schedules, dictated the date and time of sailing. Providing no further opportunity for provisioning, the captain immediately decided to hoist the sails and head out to sea. "The wind, which had been foul for three weeks, became favorable for leaving the port." The winds shifted from the west to the south or southwest, allowing a sailing ship to negotiate the northwesterly exit of Liverpool harbor. "The Captain availed himself of the change, by getting clear of the rock before day . . ." The rock is at the mouth of the River Mersey on the tip of the Wirral Peninsula and is marked today by the New Brighton Lighthouse. Favorable winds were not William's only good fortune. Within a few short months, the British-French Republic wars disrupted transatlantic trade, leading to a United States' trade embargo on shipping to and from Britain.[6]

"Happily, we cleared the land and got into the open sea before the Equinoxial [sic] gale overtook us." William's reference to an equinoctial gale was a mistaken eighteenth-century belief that more frequent tempests occurred during the two equinoxes (March 20th and September 23rd) when the plane of the Earth's equator passes through the center of the sun. Perhaps contributing to this misperception, the North American hurricane season coincides with the fall equinox, and possibly William's ship encountered a tropical storm. William recounted that the howling winds continued "with great fury for three days." After the raging winds and rains subsided, William professed a different view of the ship's resilience and now assessed "the vessel being strong, we sustained no injury—and proceeded on our voyage in high spirits—anticipating, as is usual, a pleasant trip across the ocean in which we were most woefully disappointed."

The shortest transatlantic course navigated ships north through the Irish Sea and around Ireland's northern shore before turning west to the North American coast. Ships regularly sailed this route along the Gulf Stream's northern edge to take advantage of the favorable currents and winds. Typically, this route required the least sailing time, which netted more profit for the shipowners. Icebergs represented the major drawback of this route, but this risk lessened in the fall. While icebergs did not deter William's ship, other problems emerged.

> A few days after our departure, I found my young friend and fellow passenger had taken to his berth, which at first I attributed to the strain of parting from his friends, but apprehensive that he might possibly be indisposed, I questioned him about his situation. He told me that his low spirits were the consequence of his ignorance and folly in coming onboard without those comforts which he saw I had provided myself—and that he was unable to exist on the Ship's provisions, such as they were. Knowing the necessity of estimating the duration of the passages, I had amply provided myself for eight weeks, instead of six, which the Captain affirmed us would be the extent of a trip across the Atlantic.

> Incapable of seeing my only fellow passenger in the Cabin suffering for want of comfortable food of which I had plenty—I desired him to partake with me as long as it might last—which, with reasonable economy, we hoped would serve until we approached the end of our voyage.

Uneventful, the second half of the voyage became a "dreary and monotonous" routine with "few incidents worth relating."

> Not a vessel had we seen during the whole voyage from the time we parted with those of the British Channel, and sailed with us from Liverpool, until we reached soundings on the Coast of America—when we spoke of a small vessel just out from port.

The weather cooperated with "boisterous" winds propelling the ship. Despite favorable breezes, the promised voyage of six weeks extended to ten weeks which William attributed to "our reckoning not very accurately kept." Not being a trained navigator, it is not clear how William knew that the captain did not plot the best course. Further, eighteenth-century Atlantic crossings could widely differ in durations and ten weeks was not outside of reasonable expectations. In any event, the unexpectedly extended duration caused William and Larned to run out of supplemental provisions mid-voyage.

> Not a particle of Tea, Coffee, Sugar Biscuit, or butter had I for near half the voyage—none a drop of Liquor to revive our spirits, or relieve indisposition, where it might have been useful. Yankee parsimony had compelled us to exist upon the tough Beef, hard Biscuit, and Water, which was either sour or had a stench like bilch [sic] water, and when boiled frothed up like soap suds.

As the voyage extended well beyond the expected passage, even the ship stores began to run out, triggering even more misery for the crew and passengers. Adding to the monotony of consuming the same bad food each day, the *Diana* did not encounter other ships until reaching the coast of America.

> Under these circumstances, joyful was the shout of the Cabin Boy from the mast head, when he announced at early dawn, the sight of "Land"—(Those who only have been in a similar situation can judge the effect of this welcome sound to the ear of the wearied passenger at the termination of a long voyage—who for weeks past had been deprived of every article in his small stores.

However, the sight of land did not end the voyage and provide immediate relief to passengers suffering from dwindling food and water supplies.

> For a want of the observation of the Sun for three or four days, the Captain was afraid of approaching too near the land, after it was discovered. We kept off and on therefore, until mid day—when Quadrant showed us the latitude of the Capes of the Chesapeake, instead of the Delaware, to which we were bound. Giving the Coast a good berth (as the phrase is)—we took our course for the latter—a sight of which we were favored with in the afternoon of the next day.

Entering Delaware Bay, "we saw two pilot boats" approach to guide the ship into Philadelphia Harbor.

> They commenced a beautiful race to reach our vessel, which has closely contested for sometime, but another vessel approaching in the offing, they separated. We were then quickly boarded by one of the pilots—who instantly took the command of the Brig, and brought us up to Reedy Island, where we anchored early the next day.

Located in the middle of the Delaware River, sixty miles south of Philadelphia, one mile from Port Penn on the Delaware shore and five miles southwest of Salem, New Jersey on the north shore, the long, narrow fifty-acre, low lying island served as a customs station. Routinely, ships stopped at the island while United States Customs officials overseeing the harbor's shipping activity inspected the ship's contents and passengers. Although uninhabited, the island offered a safe anchorage where ships congregated before and after sailing to Philadelphia.

"In the afternoon of the day of our arrival at Reedy Island, the Captain had a boat prepared to pay a visit to the Port Penn—a small village—nearly opposite to where we lay at anchor." Originally laid out by Dr. David Stewart in 1764, the eight-block town served as a commercial center along the lower Delaware River. During the Revolutionary War, the strategically located town served as a Rebel lookout location and witnessed a naval skirmish just three months before William and his family transited the area on their June 1778 voyage to New York from Philadelphia. Captain John Barry of the Continental Navy engaged several British warships and captured two armed transport ships and a schooner providing prize money and needed supplies to the Continental Army.[7] When William arrived in 1793, the two-hundred-and-fifty-person town served as a small port for the shipment of the area's agricultural products, a home base for fisherman, and a harbor for a small fleet of coastal traders.

After being a sea for ten weeks, William jumped at the opportunity to get off the ship and consume fresh food and strong drink at the local Port Penn bar. "Larned, myself and a young Irishman (a steerage passenger) accompanied him. Eager to gratify our appetites, which had been so long suffering at Sea . . ." However, the chance to heartily satisfy their cravings turned into the most harrowing experience on the return voyage to America. The danger started on the south side of Market Street between Stewart and Congress Streets at the Port Penn Tavern.

We indulged ourselves, perhaps, too lavishly—for when we left the Tavern, near the close of evening to return to the vessel, there were but few of the party who did not feel rather too top heavy—as the Sailors phrase is—"carrying more sail than Ballast." Several of the party fell before they reached the boat—showing how unfit they were to navigate it, so as to get to the vessel in safety—which lay off two or three miles from shore—and that too in a night destitute of moonlight, and scarcely enlightened by the twinkling of a star. We set out in high glee, the Captain taking the helm, and directly the course. But, in little more than half an hour found ourselves near the shore having, doubtless, worse round for want of some object on which to fix the eye. We set out again, and in a short time discovered that we were near the point from which we started. I then began to apprehend the danger of the attempt we were making—and my apprehensions were much increased by the rising of the wind, which greatly agitated the water. But the worst of all was yet to come—scarcely had we got out of sight of the land the third time, when a violent dispute arose between the Captain and the young Irishman about the course we were steering. Greatly irritated, they jumped up to grapple each other—which would inevitably have overset the boat, and doubtless Drowned the whole of the party, but for the prompt interference of the rest on board in keeping them down and at the same time warning them of the fatal consequences that must ensue should they persevere in the struggle. Gradually their anger subsided, and they became sensible of their folly.

Indeed, serious apprehensions began to be felt that we should not find the vessel at all, and might be lost in the gale of wind which seemed to be rising, before we could reach the shore—even if we made the attempt to get back—and of which we had but faint hopes, as we know not in what direction it lay. However, after three hours struggling with the wind and waves (which ran very high) a light was discovered, which we believed, which we believed was the vessel. Our exertions were doubled to reach it—and to our great joy, it proved to be the fact—thanks to the sound judgment and prudence of he good old Mate. He began alarmed at our detention and suspected the cause. He ordered a light to be placed in the shrouds, as a guide by which to shape our course.

This adventure I always believed was among the most perilous of my life. And truly it seemed to be a very silly affair, to expose ourselves to such imminent danger uselessly, after having passed safely through many heavy storms at sea, in the course of a long voyage of weeks.

A few days after this adventure we had a storm indeed. It was so violent as to cause our vessel to drag her anchor a considerable distance, and throw many small craft ashore. Had is occurred while we were off the Capes, it would probably have driven us far out to sea, and much increased our sufferings. So far, then we had a fortunate escape.

Informed by the Pilot of the dreadful pestilence which had broken out in Philadelphia, in the month of August, and still continued, we were in no hurry to approach the city. But finding our position off Reedy Island was too much exposed to storms of the Ocean, we slowly ascended the Delaware . . .

Leaving Port Penn and traveling up the Delaware River certainly evoked bittersweet memories for William of his 1778 voyage with his family and the 26th Regiment from New York City to British-occupied Philadelphia. Although the passage proved uneventful in 1793 as there were no navigation obstructions or threats from enemy warships, he experienced a bit of melancholy at the loss of his father and felt heart tugs for his far-off mother and sister. The excitement of starting a new life in America tempered these familial feelings. His ship "dropt [sic] our anchor opposite the City on the 9th of November 1793—the day on which the public authorities invited the citizens to return to their homes." After receiving clearance, the Diana docked in Philadelphia at the "large and capacious" Hamilton's wharf, and William disembarked.[8]

William arrived in a disease devastated city. Swampy areas around the Federal Capital bred swarms of mosquitos which spread a virulent, ghastly yellow fever in Philadelphia during the late summer and fall of 1793. The fast spreading, uncurable disease caused as many as twenty thousand of the fifty thousand terrified city residents to flee the city, including President Washington and most federal officials, wealthy citizens, and civic leaders. Unfortunately, however, four to five thousand remaining citizens succumbed to the horrible disease. Prudently, the captain of William's ship waited for the epidemic to take its course before continuing up the Delaware River to land at the Philadelphia docks.

One or two slight frosts had destroyed the contagion—but many were still sick with the fever; and several died of it after we entered the City—although no new cases occurred. Had we arrived sooner, and landed, it is very probable, that several of us might have fallen victim to the fever which the unusual length of our passage prevented. How often it happens in the affairs on man, that what he deplores as a misfortune turns out to be his greatest benefit—so inscrutable are the ways of that Being who governs the Universe!

Ten years of peace had transformed the desolate, cramped military city into a major commercial and governmental center for the United States. Since the end of the War of Independence, many immigrants from both the British Isles and Europe flocked to the city, making Philadelphia the new country's largest city.[9] Adding to the diversity, French settler refugees from Saint-Domingue (Haiti) and African Americans seeking freedom from slavery in abolitionist Pennsylvania congregated in the city. For William, the city's citizens represented the most ethnically diverse population he encountered in one city. However, his experience living in Scotland, England, and France and spending his formative years in the United States well prepared William to navigate this complex, culturally diverse and multi-linguistic environment successfully.

In addition to increasing diversity of backgrounds, Philadelphia hosted the nascent but growing United States federal government. Under a 1787 constitution, President George Washington presided over the executive branch of government, and Congress convened adjacent to Independence Hall in Congress Hall. The initial stirrings of party politics presaged the upcoming formation of the rival Federalist and Democratic-Republican parties. Moreover, most federal government senior members were only beginning to return from Trenton, New Jersey, where they had sought refuge from the yellow fever outbreak.

The deleterious effects of the 1793 yellow fever contagion ravaged the city's population and once-thriving businesses. William walked into a shaken city and an economy with a stunted level of commercial activity.

> As soon as Larned and I landed, we passed up Market Street to the Black Horse Tavern[10]—where falling in with some company, we asked their assistance to find us a good Boarding House and particularly to avoid such houses were the Yellow Fever had prevailed. One of the company kindly offered his services to accompany us to a house at the corner of Walnut and Water streets, kept by a Mrs. Slade[11] of whom he spoke highly—and where several young men who had lately arrived from Europe, had taken up their abode.[12]

Listed in the 1795 Philadelphia Directory, Anne Slade operated a boarding house at 34 Arch Street at the corner of Chancery Lane. Her home was dangerously close to 77 N. Water Street, the perceived epicenter of the yellow fever outbreak.

> . . . we were tolerably well accommodated—but in a few days discovered that we had settled down within a few hundred yards of Mr. Lemaigre's [sic] dwelling[13]—the very spot where the first cases of the fever appeared. His wife, and others of the family fell victims to it—and even our land lady and a female boarder in her house, lost their husbands by the fever. Indeed, we had some reason to apprehend, that we might be reposing on the beds, which the sick had occupied but a few weeks before. However, we sustained no injury—and soon became reconciled to our situation. Our fellow boarders were set of happy mortals—full of fun and frolic—and troubled themselves but little about the future.
>
> At this time the City presented a most melancholy appearance. With very few exceptions, all business had been suspended for many weeks. Upwards of 4000 of the inhabitants had died of the fever—most of whom were buried in Potter's field—now the site of Washington Square, one of the greatest ornaments of the City.

Washington Square had long been an internment location. Revolutionary War commanders buried soldiers on both sides of the conflict in the area known as Southeast Square. During the 1793 yellow fever epidemic, residents interred indigents in the square, hence the colloquial name Potter's Field. In 1825, the city renamed the space Washington Square, and today signs and monuments recognize the thousands of unnamed people buried there.

The smallpox devastation caused Philadelphia's economy to suffer much. Many businesses collapsed, and others required long periods to recover to pre-epidemic activity levels. For an immigrant without contacts and a support network, it was an inauspicious time to be looking for employment in a devastated city. William began searching for a livelihood in the career of his first choice.

> No Counting houses were open, many of the Merchants had died—and the families of all had removed to the Country. Hence I found that so much of my original plan of getting employment in a Counting House was, for the present, totally defeated.

Counting houses keep accounts and manage funds for merchants and trading companies. Clerks keep ledgers, prepare correspondence and communicate instructions on depositing and receiving monies between banks and their clients. Counting houses are analogous to the modern business process outsourcing of in-house accounting departments. It is not clear why William sought this profession as all of his previous occupational experiences were in the printing industry. Perhaps, he wanted to improve his career prospects in a new field and use his education to provide higher-value employment. A printer's life consisted of hard, dirty physical work, and maybe he sought a cleaner, less physically demanding career. However, the yellow fever epidemic drastically reduced business and commercial shipping activity, and there were few job prospects in Philadelphia counting offices. As a result, William could not find employment in his preferred profession. Facing uncertain prospects, he lamented,

> Business, but slowly revived, and consulting my purse, saw myself reduced to the last guinea—and as I was totally unacquainted with any person from whom I could hope for assistance, should I stand in need of it, I thought it high time to look out for some sort of employment. And here I felt the value of having been provided by my parents, with a good Mechanical Business, without which, in all probability, I should have experienced much difficulty in supporting myself.

Given the imperative to gain immediate employment and to capitalize on his British printing experience, William accepted a printing firm job.

> In a few days I called the Office of Mr. Andrew Brown, who was then publishing the Philadelphia Gazette—the only Newspaper which the pestilence had not stopped. I stated my wishes to be employed. He questioned me about my qualifications as a Printer, and asked me where I had served my apprenticeship? Understanding that it was in England, he required no more. "Turn in tomorrow morning. In that country," says he, "make people learn their trades—but here I am daily plagued with a parcel of bunglers, who are only half taught." I thanked him for the compliment—and commenced work the next day, at eight dollars per week which was the highest price then given to Compositors.[14]

The relatively high-paying "starter job" in a booming American newspaper eased William's initial transition to America. Although he would have preferred a position that exclusively used his mind, a compositor's manual labor provided living expenses and eventually opened new vocations and business opportunities. A compositor arranged the individual printing types, a higher-level position requiring skill and education. Although tedious work and similar to his apprenticeship in England, William expanded his publishing experience beyond books and broadsides that he printed in Europe to the burgeoning business of newspaper publishing in the United States. Fortunate to find work among the many competing immigrants, William joined a successful printer's office, albeit one with a checkered past, including differing public and private reputations. While other newspapers ceased operation, Brown earned the community's enduring support for being the only newspaper to continue publication during last summer's yellow fever epidemic. Brown reported Dr. Benjamin Rush's controversial views on how best to treat patients suffering from yellow fever. While not altogether altruistic, Philadelphians rewarded Brown's courage with readership, and his newspaper prospered.

Hunter and Brown possessed more in common than just printing business proficiency. Both immigrated to America and suffered through prior British Army associations. Born in Ireland, Andrew Brown relocated to America and enlisted in the British Army in 1774. While Brown's unit, the 47th Regiment of Foot, quartered in New Jersey before Revolution, his tenure did not overlap with William's father, who was garrisoning Montreal by the time Brown enlisted. Later, the 47th Regiment transferred to Boston to help quell the increasingly rebellious city.[15] Just before the outbreak of hostilities, Brown deserted. Surprisingly for a recent turncoat, he enjoyed a high-profile reputation as an ardent Patriot among the Rebel leadership. Samuel Adams reported that Brown eagerly fought against his former comrades in the battles of Lexington and Bunker's Hill and served in a militia unit stationed at Fort Ticonderoga under the overall command of General Horatio Gates. Whether or not Brown participated in all these battles, he developed a strong reputation for military leadership and patriotic reliability. In April of the next year, the Continental Congress appointed Brown as Deputy Mustermaster of the Continental Army's Eastern Department. Brown held this post until the close of the war[16]. In his most important assignment, Brown commanded the housing and feeding of General John Burgoyne's army, which surrendered at the Battle of Saratoga. Ironically, the prisoners included Brown's old outfit, the 47th Regiment. Many British officers and soldiers exhibited consternation and dismay at being forced to submit to Deputy Mustermaster Brown's immediate supervision.

After his Continental Army service, Brown first moved to New York City and then Philadelphia to enter the newspaper and printing businesses. Brown commenced publishing the *Federal Gazette* in 1788, implementing several innovative newspaper publishing practices that fueled rapid subscriber and advertising growth. He deployed reporters down the Delaware River in small boats to gather the most exciting and pertinent European, Caribbean, and American news from arriving vessels waiting for customs and immigration clearance before passage to the Philadelphia dockyards.

Scooping his competitors with the latest news from these reporters increased subscriber demand for the *Federal Gazette*, particularly among the merchant houses and other business establishments. Another of Brown's innovative newspaper practices, the *Federal Gazette*, became the first newspaper to employ a dedicated reporter to record and publish the Federal Congressional debates and proceedings. Further leveraging his political contacts, Brown received government contracts in January 1791 from Secretary of State Thomas Jefferson to publish Congressional laws.

In an era in which newspapers commonly represented a political party's partisan views, Brown initially attempted to espouse a neutral editorial policy and publish "unvarnished" information. However, by 1791 it became untenable to record political events impartially, and to survive, economic necessity compelled Brown to select a political constituency to represent. Taking sides with the anti-Federalists, Brown engaged with heated editorial fights with *Publicola*, pseudonym of John Quincy Adams. In a July 1791 editorial, Brown wrote, "A host of enlightened writers have arisen, in every part of the United States, to oppose the abominable heresies of Publicola."[17] As the political environment increasingly devolved into two-party factions, Brown changed the paper's name in 1793 to the *Philadelphia Gazette* to better represent the paper's editorial slant and distance himself from the emerging Federalist Party. With these reporting innovations and its expanding Jeffersonian leaning subscriber base, the *Philadelphia Gazette* continued as a successful business providing much for William to learn about running a successful newspaper.

Consistent with the experiences of many of the *Philadelphia Gazette*'s employees, William's association with the newspaper lasted only a few months. Brown's apprentices and journeymen viewed him as an extremely difficult, harsh, and overly demanding employer. One apprentice characterized Brown as acting with "villainy, wickedness and cruelty."[18] Reportedly, Brown physically struck his employees when unhappy with their performance. He burned through journeymen at a remarkably high rate, and only one of his sixteen apprentices completed their terms of service.[19] Given this rapid personnel turn-over, Brown did not truly value William's British-based printing experiences, as William bragged at the end of the journal. It's more probable that Brown paid William the generous rate of eight dollars a day due to others shying away from his reputation as an abusive employer and for William's willingness to work on the Sabbath, which, although necessary in newspaper publishing, many journeymen found sacrilegious. William does not characterize his relationship with Brown or describe why he left Brown's employment; however, he did learn valuable lessons about the promising but highly risky publishing business. A publisher needed to vertically integrate into providing stationary, publishing books and broadsides, and operate bookshops to sell their and others wares. Even with these profit-producing diversifications, the most successful printers obtained publishing contracts with the government to print legislative proceedings and enacted laws to earn a modest profit. Lastly, he learned the mechanics of the labor-intensive printing business and appreciated the need to treat employees well as they can easily "jump ship" due to the burgeoning demand for experienced publishing and printing workers.

Brown continued to operate a successful paper after William left his employment. Tragically, Andrew Brown and his family perished in a house fire in 1797. Ironically, one of Brown's greatest political enemies, President-elect John Adams, personally passed buckets of water as a volunteer in the fire brigade to quell the printing house fire.[20]

After boasting about above-market wages, William's journal abruptly ended mid-story and mid-page. William left many subsequent blank pages in the leather-bound journal, which could have contained accounts of the rest of his life. Descendants kept the journal's binding intact and did not rip out or destroy the latter portions. Perhaps William only wanted to communicate his Revolutionary War experiences to his family, which he downplayed during his life, and his heirs might not have well understood. Alternatively, he may have chronicled his most adventuresome years, safely knowing that published records and newspapers adequately memorialized the rest of his life. With a fulsome account of his childhood and time in Britain, William fully disclosed the secrets of his past, at least to the journal's readers. The rest of his story reveals why he kept such secrets.

Part II

Reporting the Peoples' News

In 1790s America, the printing business boomed. High literacy rates mixed with spectacular growth in party politics and economic activity resulted in burgeoning demand for newspapers, pamphlets, and broadsides. Traditional barriers to entry were no longer limiting. Only recently did American manufacturers begin to make newsprint, ink, printing presses, and type. Not importing production means lowered costs offering new opportunities for enterprising apprentices to open their printing businesses. To William's credit, he seized the opportunity. He started small and with a partner to share the upfront investment costs. William brought his education and apprenticeship knowledge to the partnership venture to most efficiently manage business operations. In the new role as an editor and owner, William needed a grasp of local, state, and national politics and the emerging American societal norms. Always a quick learner, William moved from employee to entrepreneur over a short few months. As with any new business venture, some aspects proved unprofitable. But, learning on the fly, he adapted and rapidly shifted to new products and markets.

CHAPTER SEVEN

Nascent Printers

America's largest city, Philadelphia, functioned as the national center for publishing, law, education, and scientific research. Although silent on the reasons for selecting the Federal capital to start a new life, Philadelphia's pre-yellow fever commercial, political, and intellectual vibrancy attracted William. His initial foray into the American publishing industry with Andrew Brown opened new ideas and expanded business prospects for him to pursue. Similar to a co-worker at Brown's *Philadelphia Gazette*, William found "the printing business . . . is the genteelest and most flourishing in the country."[1] Unique among the industrial occupations in the Revolutionary era, printers exhibited the combined characteristics of both laboring and educated classes. While printers toiled long hours in backbreaking, smelly, and dirty manual labor, most vital to their success proved to be a high literacy level and extensive classical knowledge. The most successful printers regularly interacted with the learned lawyers, politicians, physicians, and educators. Through peddling advertising, printers also developed a wide range of business acumen. As a result, printers developed commercial and personal relationships with business leaders, including prosperous merchants and ship owners. In addition, the opportunity to expand his knowledge and interact with leading men of intellect certainly attracted William to the business. Working in printing and publishing provided a stepping stone from his lower-class background.

Ambitious, Hunter soon realized that there were limited advancement prospects for a journeyman printer in America, just as in Britain. Hunter faced significant competition from at least forty other Philadelphia-based journeymen, many seeking to start their own businesses.[2] To escape the economic confines of a journeyman printer, William established a promising publishing partnership. A couple of months after starting with Brown, William met John Colerick, a Scots-Irish immigrant who recently landed in Philadelphia. Similar to Hunter's association with Brown, Colerick initially worked as a journeyman for a famed and successful publisher, Matthew Carey. Also, an Irish immigrant, Carey published a newspaper in the 1780s. However, by Colerick's and Hunter's arrival, Carey had become a nationally known, full-time book publisher. Notably, his business thrived by offering Catholic and Protestant versions of the Holy Bible. Carey established a national bookseller network to promote sales based upon wholesale and itinerant distribution. Carey often outsourced the book printing and binding. Later, this contractual production relationship proved fruitful for Colerick, who periodically engaged in printing for Carey.[3] Colerick introduced Hunter to Carey, creating a life-long friendship.

Partnering, Hunter and Colerick commenced a printing business at 23 Union Street (present-day Delancey Street), two blocks from the waterfront in the heart of the city.[4] Setting up a printing office required considerable capital, and William claimed to have little money when he landed in Philadelphia. As Colerick's name is listed first, perhaps he provided most of the seed money. The cost to fully equip a single press shop could range from three hundred dollars for second-hand or estate sale equipment to over one thousand dollars for imported new presses and types. Costing seventy-five dollars and up, printing presses consisted of a large iron screw and a wooden frame generally fashioned from mahogany. Most offices operated one or two hand presses. The lead printing types were the costliest print shop investment. Printers could locally source for the least expensive typeset options. However, many printers sought imported types to produce the highest quality pages, impressing readers and spurring sales. In addition to equipment, the partners required reliable and low-cost sources of paper and ink. Fortunately, Pennsylvania was the center of American paper making, and several mills were located in nearby Germantown. Made from readily available varnish and lampblack, ink could be sourced locally or imported. A few printers manufactured a surplus of ink to sell to fellow printers to augment their incomes.[5]

To assist with the heavy manual labor of the printing business, the partners ran an August 6, 1794 advertisement in Andrew Brown's newspaper, the *Philadelphia Gazette* offering to hire a compositor and an apprentice. A few weeks later, the new duo ran a promotional advertisement stating, "Colerick & Hunter, truly grateful for the liberal encouragement they have already experienced, sincerely thank their friends, respectfully soliciting a continuance of the same, and the commands of the citizens in general—their types having been carefully selected from the first foundaries [*sic*] in Europe, they hope, to execute printing with elegance, Accuracy, punctuality, and dispatch with also claim their particular attention."[6] Fierce competition for workers with printing experience forced Hunter and Colerick to re-run the job opening advertisement a few months later, "A youth, with tolerable education is wanted as a compositor, and a stout lad for Press."[7]

In May 1795, the Hunter and Colerick partnership produced their first book, entitled the *New Spanish Grammar*. The idea for publishing the Spanish language volume emanated from John Peter Davancens, a Spanish teacher who shared a room with Hunter at 53 Walnut Street, a couple of blocks from the printing office. In the late eighteenth century, the few North American universities did not teach the Spanish language. Tutors such as Davancens provided the only available instruction for those who needed the Spanish language for commercial trading relationships or those who were personally interested in Spanish culture. A Spanish professor would not join a university faculty (Harvard) until 1817.[8] Although the second Spanish grammar book published in the United States, the *New Spanish Grammar* served as a staple of Spanish language education for English speakers, first published in London in 1763 with a second edition in 1777 and a third in 1787.[9] Hunter and Colerick perceived a ready-made market for the book with Davancens' students. The partners prognosticated that the increasing merchant trade with Spanish America and the growing cosmopolitan Philadelphia would increase demand for Spanish language skills. Promoting their business, partners advertised the upcoming book in the *Philadelphia Gazette* on April 15 and 24, 1795. Selling points included a convenient size sold at one dollar, half the price of the London edition. Due to the lack of international copyright laws, North American printers regularly republished foreign published works with legal impunity. Despite initial success with Davancens' students, other early nineteenth-century Spanish grammar books quickly eclipsed Colerick and Hunter's book sales, and the co-venture with the tutor ceased. The printing partnership moved on to other publishing ventures.[10]

Future family members and friends indicated that Hunter published a French-language newspaper in the city. A surge of newly arrived French colonial refugees from the Caribbean Island of Saint Domingue provided increasing demand for French publications. Adding some plausibility, Hunter did learn conversational French during his year as a prisoner of war in France and certainly remembered a few words from his brief stay in Montreal. Hunter and

Colerick could have seen this as a way to differentiate themselves in an increasingly crowded Philadelphia publishing market by exploiting a new profitable niche. However, native-speaking refugees from Saint Domingue published eight French-language and bilingual newspapers. Expatriate Pierre Parent published the *Courier Francais*, the most prominent paper.[11] Casting considerable doubt, there are no surviving references to or copies of a French-language newspaper published by Hunter and Colerick. Colerick and Hunter may have printed one of the French papers under a contract with its publisher/editor. Alternatively, a friend and colleague, Matthew Carey, published several French-language books during this period, none of which became widely popular. Perhaps, Hunter assisted Carey, his lifelong friend, with several French language titles, which led to the family's confusion.[12]

Operating a new publishing and printing business in Philadelphia proved to be unfertile grounds for the partnership. Fiercely competitive, the local marketplace swarmed with forty-two newspapers in the 1790s.[13] Larger, established publishers such as Matthew Carey commanded the most lucrative portions of the publishing market, and other printers such as Benjamin Franklin Bache possessed valuable government printing contracts. Like many enterprising immigrants of Early America, the partners decided to seek improved opportunities by moving west to find less crowded but emergent marketplaces. On May 25, 1795, the partners placed an ad in the *Philadelphia Gazette* to sell a portion of their valuable print types. The advertisement offered one font each in the following sizes Paragon (19.4), English (13.5), Small Pica (10.4), Brevier (7.9) which are arrayed from largest to smallest. As the print types came from European foundries, most likely Hunter brought print types with him from England.[14] The print-type sale helped fund the partners' move into the western country.

CHAPTER EIGHT

Impartial Printers

A few weeks later, the partners initiated a new publishing venture in Washington, a rapidly growing town in southwestern Pennsylvania. On the west side of the Allegheny Mountains, Washington served as the commercial center of Washington County and southwestern Pennsylvania. The area boasted a settler population of almost twenty-four thousand in 1790, growing to over twenty-eight thousand in 1800. Mostly white, the population included a few enslaved people and free blacks in the area. Recently, violent conflicts between Euro-Americans and native peoples ended with most surviving Native Americans fleeing the region. As a result, European culture dominated the new residential and commercial development. A western traveler noted that Washington's impressive public buildings and "handsomely built dwelling-houses, give this town a very reasonable appearance. It seems to be a place of considerable business and of thriving manufacturers and trade."[1]

While the partners' rationale for selecting southwestern Pennsylvania was not documented, the Trans-Appalachian area offered an expanding, untapped market for a publishing and printing business. Washington sat astride the main route for people traveling to and from the west via the Ohio River. Surging travelers were both a source of demand for newspapers and could provide exciting and informative news for the partners' readers. Essential for receiving newsworthy information from the east and disseminating newspapers and other publications to subscribers, a postal route operated to and from the town, a critical requirement for any western press's success. There was another reason that Colerick and Hunter felt more comfortable with the area. The predominately Scots-Irish residents made up the largest ethnic group in Washington County. While Hunter never lived among the Scots-Irish, he experienced a

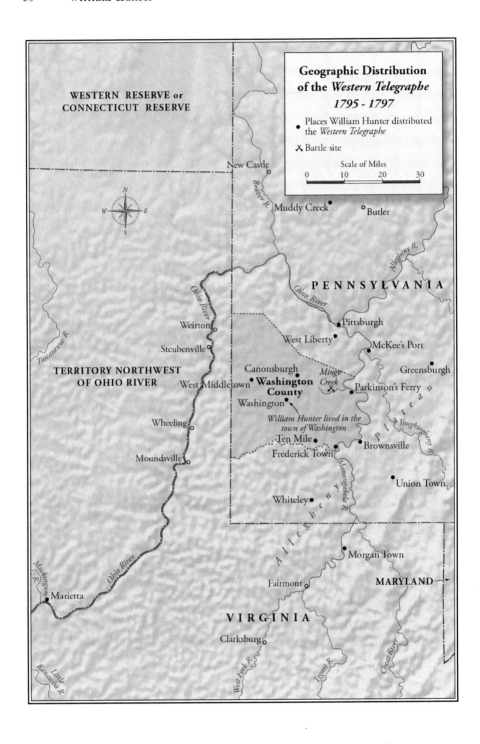

WESTERN RESERVE or
CONNECTICUT RESERVE

Geographic Distribution
of the *Western Telegraphe*
1795 - 1797

• Places William Hunter distributed
the *Western Telegraphe*

✗ Battle site

Scale of Miles

0   10   20   30

New Castle

Beaver R.

Muddy Creek   ○ Butler

Allegheny R.

N
W   E
S

PENNSYLVANIA

Ohio River

Ohio River

Pittsburgh

Weirton

West Liberty

McKee's Port

Steubenville

Greensburgh

Tuscarawas R.

TERRITORY NORTHWEST
OF OHIO RIVER

Canonsburgh

Mingo Creek

West Middletown   • **Washington County**   ✗ Parkinson's Ferry

Washington

Plateau

Youghiogheny R.

William Hunter lived in the
town of Washington

Wheeling

Ten Mile •

Brownsville

Moundsville

Frederick Town

Union Town

Whiteley •

Allegheny

Monongahela R.

Ohio River

Morgan Town

Muskingum R.

MARYLAND →

Marietta

Fairmont ○

VIRGINIA

Clarksburg ○

West Fork R.

Tigart R.

Cheat River

Little Kanawha R.

connection to his parents and felt more comfortable with people who share their ethnic heritage. Additionally, no printing and newspaper competition existed in southwestern Pennsylvania. The only other Pennsylvania newspaper west of the Alleghenies operated thirty miles away in Pittsburgh. Perhaps most importantly, area residents highly valued literacy and believed that having a newspaper "put your town on the map" and provided strong local press support. All these factors seemed to point to Washington to be a good bet for launching a printing business to sell books and publish newspapers.[2]

Immediately before Hunter and Colerick set up shop, the southwestern Pennsylvania region experienced violent social and political unrest. A year before, anti-Federal government riots and agitation associated with the Whiskey Rebellion engulfed Washington and the surrounding Washington County. To fund its growing operations, the Federalist-dominated Federal Government passed a tax on the sale of whiskey. A critical component of the frontier economy, southwestern Pennsylvanians believed the tax placed a more considerable burden on its small-scale whiskey distillers and favored larger producers in the country's eastern areas. An armed insurrection broke out to oppose the perceived unfair tax, and insurgents prevented Federal revenue agents from collecting the tax. In response, President Washington called out the militia of surrounding states to put down the insurrection and re-establish tax collections. A massive, imposing militia army marched across the Alleghenies and quickly put down the rebellion. The army arrested twenty leaders of the insurrection and transported the prisoners to Philadelphia, parading the prisoners down Broad Street to the assembled crowds' jeers. Possibly, Hunter and Colerick witnessed the prisoner parade sparking their interest in southwestern Pennsylvania's political environment. While a few insurgents fled the area, including some of Washington's leading citizens, hundreds signed amnesty agreements and returned to their regular occupations and peaceful living.

Exacerbated by the political insurrection and societal unrest, Hunter and Colerick arrived in Washington amidst an intense and burgeoning Christian Protestant religious revival. "The Great Revival of the West" brought together thousands in open fields for communal sacraments. Surges in religious fervor resulted in spiritual rebirths and piety among older and newer immigrants. Particularly affected, Scotch Irish citizens dramatically increased their membership in the Presbyterian church. Political fault lines followed religious beliefs. The revival Presbyterian congregations tended to support the Democratic-Republican party and oppose the area's Federalist leaders.[3] Certainly for Hunter, living among a rebellious political and religious unrest seemed similar to the situation in the British Midlands from which he fled.

With the intense political debates and religious awakening, Washington County became fertile ground for a new printing and publishing operation, especially since the partners were free of the stifling competition in Philadelphia. Perhaps seeking knowledge of the local community and its unique politics and culture, Colerick and Hunter added a partner, William Henry Beaumont, to help set up their printing business. Two years younger than Hunter, Beaumont moved to the frontier town of Pittsburgh after emigrating from England in 1789. Beaumont's self-taught education proved sufficient to land a job performing secretarial and clerical duties in the law office of prominent Pittsburgh lawyer Hugh Henry Brackenridge. In addition to being a highly successful lawyer, Brackenridge actively engaged in local politics. Beaumont advocated his employer's anti-Federalist and Democratic-Republican views and followed him into politics. In 1794, residents of the newly incorporated borough of Pittsburgh elected Beaumont to a town regulator (surveyor) position, a post responsible for street improvements, including sidewalks and curbs.

Embroiling himself in the western Pennsylvania maelstrom over the Federal whiskey tax, Beaumont attended the fateful July 23, 1794 meeting of the insurrectionists at Mingo Creek, approximately twenty-five miles south of Pittsburgh and fifteen miles east of Washington. Beaumont supported two leaders of the moderate faction attending the meeting, Hugh Henry Brackenridge and Albert Gallatin, who merely protested the unfairness of the whiskey tax. The moderates sought redress by the repeal of the tax and did not side with the radical insurrectionists who advocated armed rebellion and the formation of a separate political state. However, extremists overwhelmed the crowd. Militant leaders advocated organizing militia resistance and setting up a competing government. After the Federal government reasserted in authority, Federal officials investigated Brackenridge and other leaders of the Mingo Creek mass meeting for alleged treasonous behaviors. Brackenridge selected Beaumont as one of five witnesses to testify to his meeting participation to ensure a fair representation of his moderate views.[4] Beaumont quickly signed an amnesty pledge and testified in the legal proceeding supporting Brackenridge. Eventually, both Brackenridge and Gallatin re-joined the country's accepted political structure, with Brackenridge becoming a state judge and Gallatin serving two presidents as Secretary of the United States Treasury. Beaumont cultivated a friendly personal relationship with Gallatin by campaigning for his election to Congress. Despite receiving amnesty and participating in national elections, Beaumont and the moderates would vociferously complain that Federalist judges hounded them for their democratic and republican views for many years.[5]

Before the arrival of the printing partners, Beaumont relocated from Pittsburgh to the Washington, Pennsylvania area to live among like-minded citizens and escape persecution by the Federalists. His literary capabilities and knowledge of western politics caught the new arrivals' eye, and Colerick and Hunter offered Beaumont a share of the printing partnership. As his foray into radical politics dimmed other possibilities, Beaumont accepted the offer and joined the publishing duo. Further planting his roots, in May 1794, Beaumont married Elizabeth Duncan-Cooper. Born in the Germantown section of Philadelphia in 1765, Elizabeth most recently hailed from Westmoreland County, Pennsylvania. Elizabeth entered the marriage with three children from her first marriage to Jacob Cooper.

With the closest newspaper published in Pittsburgh, the rising population of southwestern Pennsylvania needed a local newspaper and a printing establishment. Newspapers were burgeoning businesses in the Early Republic. High rates of literacy in rural America placed "the common people are on a footing, in point of literature, with the middle ranks in Europe; they all read and write, and understand arithmetick [*sic*]."[6] To support the dissemination of enacted legislation and promote political discourse, the government subsidized the distribution of newspapers through the operation of the Post Office Department, which offered low rates or free mailings for newspapers. Congress established a discounted newspaper rate of one cent for transits less than one hundred miles and one and a half cents over one hundred miles making the United States mail an affordable distribution method. Most importantly, editors and printers could send one free copy to any editor, thereby papers even from the remotest regions traveled throughout the country. With free distribution, newspapers became vital publicity organs for political parties seeking to increase their voter bases.

Colerick, Hunter, and Beaumont recognized this market opportunity and commenced publishing the first newspaper in Washington County, Pennsylvania, and the second paper west of the Alleghenies in Pennsylvania. The partners published the inaugural issue of *The Western Telegraphe and Washington Advertiser* on August 17, 1795. The French spelling of telegraph suggests the partners sought to evoke the newly invented semaphore non-electronic telegraphic system designed by Claude Chappe and three of his brothers, which relayed critical and time-sensitive messages for the French military over long distances. While most readers would not be familiar with a semaphore system's operations, the association with the newly invented communications system lends the paper a modern, high technology image. Of course, the *Washington Advertiser* portion of the name signifies the practical reason why residents should purchase a copy of the paper.

Like other period papers, the weekly newspaper consisted of a single sheet folded in half and printed on both sides to produce four pages. Each page had four columns with a limited number of pictures or drawings. The old English style with a long "f" ("f with a crossbar) for "s" denoted the partners' use of old, but still commonly used, typefaces. Initially published on Mondays, the publication date moved to Tuesday as Pittsburgh's mail schedule changed, and the partners endeavored to include the latest news. The paper circulated by post rider east and south through Frederick town, Brownsville, Union Town, Whitely, Muddy Creek, and Ten Mile settlements. Post riders also sent copies north to Cannonsburgh, Pittsburgh, McKee's Port, and Parkinson's Ferry (see Map 2 on page 90).

Consistent with prevailing rural newspaper rates in other western regions, the partners established a subscription rate of two dollars per annum, with one dollar due upfront and one dollar every six months for local delivery. If delivered by a post rider, the partners added fifty cents each six months to the subscription cost. Advertising revenues were the engine that created profitability for the enterprise. The partners set advertising rates for a square (column width times column height) at one dollar for three insertions and twenty cents thereafter. Advertising rates rose in proportion for larger insertions.

The three editors described their editorial policy as "making it useful and entertaining, and uniformly spurned at every attempt to make it the vehicle of party spirit."[7] The partners embraced the role of a newspaper as a neutral reporter of the news as espoused by Benjamin Franklin and many other colonial printers. However, with the rise of party politics in the late 1790s, attempted neutral news reporting diminished, except on the western edges of European settlement with isolated newspapers. Increasingly newspaper editors chose to support either Federalist-leaning (supporting Washington, Hamilton, and Adams) or Democratic-Republican-leaning (supporting Jefferson, Madison, and Monroe) political parties. However, with only one newspaper in southwestern Pennsylvania, the partners attempted to take a neutral stance on national politics. Staying balanced proved a daunting task as the three editors espoused widely differing political views.

The partners designed a masthead with the motto, "Free but not Licentious," which suggests a free press without legal or political constraints. The motto's origin is unclear.[8] Later newspapers in the Ohio Valley and other western areas adopted the same motto for their mastheads.[9] Despite the partners' attempt to offer a neutral editorial policy, readers might interpret the motto based upon their political affiliations. Federalists viewed the motto as a fair representation of their views, while Jeffersonian Democratic-Republicans felt that the motto connoted antagonism towards them. As a Federalist supporter, Colerick's views conflicted with his two partners' Jeffersonian or Democratic-Republican views. Later observers would even go so far as to call the newspaper "ultra-Federalist."[10]

Federalist leaning Colerick appeared to be the first of the three equals, having his name listed first, followed by Hunter and then Beaumont. Unusually, the partners' names appeared at the bottom of the last page. The prominent banner at the top of the first page often paraded the editor's names. Capitalizing on the recent political turmoil, each partner contributing articles and balancing editorial content sold more papers in a one-paper town. As the Federalists prevailed in the Whiskey Rebellion controversy, many area residents supported the Jeffersonians as an alternative to separation from the United States. These opposition readers related to the subject matter provided by Hunter and Beaumont. Often, the trio did not compose the editorial content but merely reprinted articles from other newspapers. Discerning readers knew the political biases of prominent eastern papers and thus perceived a local newspaper's party affiliations.

Western newspapers carried few local news items. In small towns, people had little need for news of their community as word of mouth efficiently spread most news. People did not need to wait for a weekly newspaper to learn of notable local events. However, residents in isolated towns such as Washington highly valued newspapers for regional, national and international news. Typically, the editors devoted over one-third of an issue to international news as western readers had an unusual thirst for reporting on wars, trade politics, and other global events. Western economic interests depended upon access to global markets despite geographic isolation, heightening interest in international affairs. For example, the relative demand for Western agricultural products increased and decreased due to European wars and trade embargoes.

Further, the Revolutionary and Napoleonic era conflicts between Republican France and its monarchist neighbor greatly interested American readers and embroiled the two-party factions in advocacy and controversy. Generally, the western Pennsylvanians who supported the Federalists also supported Britain. More numerous, the area residents who supported the Jeffersonian Democratic-Republicans supported the French Revolution and the French Republic's formation.

The editors' first issue was an excellent example of the newsworthiness of European affairs. On the first column of the first page, the inaugural edition of *The Western Telegraphe* led with an article on a French victory over the Spanish during the War of the Pyrenees. As typical with eighteenth-century news delays, a peace treaty signing occurred almost a month before this article ran in *The Western Telegraphe*. Another article described the successful eleven-month siege and capture of the Luxembourg Fortress by French Revolutionary forces. Related international news included the impressment of American sailors and interference with American commerce by the British Navy and the report that South Carolinian Thomas Pinckney concluded treaty negotiations with Spain for free navigation of the Mississippi River. However, other news reports contained new hazards to western access to foreign markets. The *Western Telegraphe* reported the Spanish building a menacing fort at Chickasaw Bluff on the Mississippi River, threatening free trade. Vitally important, westerners relied on the Mississippi's free navigation to send agricultural products to international markets through New Orleans. Typical of ninteenth-century newspapers, *The Western Telegraphe* prematurely reported the successful conclusions of treaty negotiations for access to the Mississippi. Treaty negotiators signed the actual agreement with Spain a few months later.

While large-scale conflicts had ended in the region, Native American affairs were highly newsworthy. The first issue reported the end of armed resistance by the Iroquois Nation to American settlers' encroachment. Typically, period newspapers cited the information source as word of mouth. In this case, *The Western Telegraphe* reported that a "Gentlemen arrives in town with information on treaty negotiations with Six Nations (Iroquois Confederacy or Haudenosaunee)" and proceeded to recite rumored, not actual events. Although still a rumor, the source reported the conclusion of a momentous treaty. Led by Chief Red Jacket and over five hundred Indians, the Iroquois Nation ceded much of their land in modern-day New York and Pennsylvania by the *Treaty of Canandaigua*. Demonstrating the periods time delays, a second news story reported ongoing, though promising treaty negotiations with northwest Indians in the Ohio town of Greenville. Actually, the commissioners signed a definitive treaty two weeks before the publication of the partners' first issue. The August 3, 1795 *Treaty of Greenville* ended the Euro-American wars with a coalition of Great Lakes Native Americans, opened up much of Ohio to American settlement, and brought relative peace to the western frontier.

The partners also featured commercial news, including an article describing the business venture of another Scottish immigrant. They reported that a Judge Charles Williamson at Great Soda (Sodus Bay on Lake Ontario between present-day Rochester and Oswego, New York) is building two schooners for packets to Niagara and importing English horses for resale. Williamson served as lead agent for the two million-acre Genesee Tract land development association in central New York State. As a former British Army officer at the time of the American Revolution, Williamson raised the eyebrows of some *Western Telegraphe* readers by establishing communications with Fort Niagara, a post the British military refused to relinquish at the end of the war.[11] British furnished military supplies to Native Americans opened westerners to possible attacks. Likewise, Williamson caused the British Army considerable consternation. His settlements around Sodus Bay rattled the military, who considered the new American settlements a threat to the fort's security.[12] Nothing came of this controversy as Williamson's patron in Britain caused diplomatic orders to Canada's governor not to oppose the new settlement. While the Sodus Bay incident peaceably concluded, Williamson's name would re-emerge during a later treason controversy reported by Hunter and which involved his friends.

Turning to local events of prime economic importance, the partners noted completing a market house in Washington that townspeople funded by a voluntary subscription. Waxing positively on these civic and commercial endeavors, the partners concluded, "Thus we see the spirit of enterprise is busy on the great Western theatre, which contrasted with the apathy which generally pervades the old settlements, produces a distinction highly favorably to this vast Western Country." The partners heartily welcomed the market house, which provided spaces for the sale of local agricultural and other products as it stimulated additional advertisements and subscribers.

Highly relevant to the partners' interests, the first issue featured an article on the aftermath of last year's insurrection disputing the new Federal Whiskey tax. A few weeks earlier, President George Washington issued a blanket pardon for most rebels in exchange for sworn assurances of submission to the United States laws. A beneficiary of Washington's actions, William Beaumont signed a pardon and reaffirmed his allegiance to the Federal Government. However, the political divide instigated by the tax and the resulting insurrection transformed a brief armed conflict into a long-term divisive political dispute. As Washington's pardon only extended to Federal crimes, Beaumont and many western Pennsylvania insurrectionists lived under the threat of criminal and civil prosecution in state courts. The aftermath of the Whiskey Rebellion would not be wholly negative for Beaumont and his partners, as within a year, Federal tax collectors would become paying customers of *The Western Telegraphe* by placing public notices on due dates for excise duty on southwestern Pennsylvania stills.[13]

Rounding out the editorial portions of the first edition, the partners featured a "Parnassian Corner" on the back page, featuring poetry selections from various European, American, and local writers. One issue featured the works of a local poet only identified as "A Reader," which commemorated George Washington's presidency. The author laments, "As I have seen nothing in the Poetic way on the retiring of the beloved Washington, that it may not be said the Muses were intirely [*sic*] silent on the great Occasion, I send you the following lines." The thirty-five-line, ten verse poem ends with "A friend of PEACE and Man."[14]

Disappointing from a commercial perspective, the first edition contained a mere seven advertisements. The partners would have to significantly increase the ad sales to establish a commercially viable newspaper. However, the attention-grabbing editorial content provided a good start, bringing blockbuster news of international wars and Native American treaties to a frontier town. Exuding a zest for the opportunity in America, William Hunter took pride in establishing a newspaper in his new country within two short years. In his old home town of Walsall, England, residents would not read a local newspaper until 1855.[15]

Over the next year, the first contested presidential election emerged as the biggest news story but received little notice in *The Western Telegraphe*. After two terms, President Washington announced that he would not be seeking reelection. The two leading candidates to replace him were John Adams and Thomas Jefferson. Most Federalists supported Adams, with Jefferson receiving support from the Democratic-Republican faction. Consistent with the editors' desire to avoid being a party mouthpiece, *Western Telegraphe's* pages contained muted election coverage. In one of the few articles on the election, lists of electors for Federalist and Democratic-Republican parties were inserted in the October 25, 1796 edition. While the Federalist electors were enumerated without comment, Hunter and Beaumont inserted a message from the Democratic-Republican members of the Pennsylvania state legislature and Congress with their party's electors. The circular describes Jefferson as a "uniform advocate of equal rights" and a "steady supporter of the present form of republican government." Adams is charged with being a "champion of rank, titles and hereditary distinctions" as well as the "warm panegyrist of the British Monarchial form of Government." On election day, the town of Washington residents voted overwhelmingly for Jefferson. His slate of state electors received six hundred and eleven votes to seventeen for the Adams ticket.[16] However, Adams prevailed nationally and became America's second president.

Presaging upcoming controversies, the partners turned to the issue of slavery a few months after moving to Washington. First, a strikingly stark anti-slavery poem appeared in the *Parnassian Corner*.[17] Following a short while later, the partners reprinted an article decrying the slave trade. The page-one article concluded, "The eye of reason cannot distinguish between the criminality of the buyer and the seller."[18] While the slave trade did not operate in Washington, slavery existed but was not prevalent throughout southwestern Pennsylvania. In 1780, the Pennsylvania legislature was the first state to pass a gradual emancipation act that prohibited the importation of enslaved people and freed children born into slavery. However, the new act maintained the lifetime bondage of existing enslaved persons. Additional provisions enacted in the 1780s further restricted the legal protections of slave owners and reduced the number of legally enslaved people in the state. Members of Congress, then under the Articles of Confederation, were exempted. The Pennsylvania law caused difficulties for the fledgling Federal government, then in Philadelphia, as many Southern officials were slaveholders.

While on the decline, slavery remained an important moral issue for the readers of *The Western Telegraphe*. After the presidential election, the partners reprinted verbatim a New York paper's editorial about the African Free School in New York City. The article stated that "the African is capable of the same intellectual improvement as the European" and goes onto conclude, "How pleasing to a virtuous mind is the prospect of seeing so many human beings rendered capable of discharging the duties of Citizens, and of being useful to themselves and society." Signaling the editors' support for ending slavery, *The Western Telegraphe* was one of only a handful of papers that reprinted the African Free School story. The anti-slavery editorial stance was not particularly courageous as gradual emancipation had been Pennsylvania law for almost two decades. However, distinct from the ethics of enslaving people, the view that African Americans were equal to whites in terms of intellect and abilities was unique even among abolitionists. Despite strong views on the pages of *The Western Telegraphe*, the debate over racial equality and slavery did not captivate southwestern Pennsylvanians as slavery was relatively unimportant to the local economy. Under Pennsylvania's gradual emancipation laws, only a few hundred persons remained in bondage among the newspaper's readership.

While the issues of slavery and racial equality may have faded from *The Western Telegraphe*'s pages, stories about African Americans and advertisements for runaway enslaved peoples continued. The partners ran articles about criminal actions committed by blacks, such as murder, theft, and other heinous crimes. However, the partners also published positive articles, including blacks saving white people from fires and other courageous acts. The partners' readers chimed in with a poem published in the *Parnassian Corner* sympathetic to the plight of enslaved African Americans. The verse resonated with both local and national readers. Several papers, including two in Philadelphia and one in Vermont, reprinted the poem.[19] Uniquely among the press of the day, the partners printed a roughly equal number of positive and negative articles on slavery. Consistent with many white Early Americans, pecuniary interests often trumped personal views on slavery. The partners were no exception as they accepted at least nine advertisements offering rewards for the capture of absconding enslaved people and for the sales of African Americans due to the death of their masters. Representing a tiny fraction of total ads, the slavery ads could have been rejected without impairing the financial viability of the paper. Perhaps the partners rationalized the inconsistencies with their editorial policies as all of the ads out of staters or residents on the border with the slave state of Maryland placed the ads. In the ads, slave owners warned sympathetic residents to not harbor the escapees or assist them in any way. Whether for pecuniary interests or not, Hunter's *The Western Telegraphe* editorial days represented the first instance of Hunter's compromising his Enlightenment and egalitarian views developed during his formative years.

Although changing his views on slavery, Hunter continued to revere Dr. Joseph Priestley's lectures in Birmingham, guiding his personal republican philosophies. Hunter reprinted a famous Priestley quote on magnanimously treating one's enemies. After the mob destroyed Priestley's library and laboratory in England, Priestley responded, "I should have read my books to little purpose if they had not taught me to bear the loss of them with composure and resignation."[20] Perhaps Hunter inserted the Dr. Priestley quote to help his readers recover civility and heal after the conflict over the whiskey tax and the hard-fought 1796 presidential election.

The partners located their newspaper and printing business on the northeast corner of the town's public square. This central location placed the editors at the hub of the town's information flow. Both subscribers and casual readers dropped by the print shop to exchange local news and to read eastern newspapers delivered to the editors per the gratis mail policy. Capitalizing on the "foot traffic," the partners soon offered books published by the trio and from national and international publishers for sale. A prominent ad boasted a "well-chosen assortment" comprising books on divinity, philosophy, history, travels, novels, as well as educational and children's books. With tensions from the Whiskey Rebellion still raw, the printers featured Hugh Henry Brackenridge's account of the Federal excise tax maelstrom, which vindicated William Beaumont's association with the rebellion.[21] In addition to books, the partners offered maps and prints for sale and advertised proposals for printing books by subscriptions for eastern publishers.[22] Denoting Colerick's and Hunter's continued relationship with Matthew Carey, the November 24, 1795 issue of *The Western Telegraphe* contained an ad proposal to publish a French grammar textbook by Nicholas Gouin Duffief. While there was probably little demand for a French grammar book in western Pennsylvania and sufficient demand did not materialize in other locales, Matthew Carey scrapped the project.[23] Expanding their business further, the partners acquired bookbinding equipment. With this new capability, the partners could offer standard and customized ledgers, journals, and day books for merchants, manufacturers, government officials, and tradesmen. Additionally, storekeepers in nearby towns could purchase standardized blank books at wholesale prices and resell them in their retail shops.

Printers and newspaper publishers often opened book stores and binderies to augment their incomes. The three partners especially needed this vertical business expansion to support their livelihoods. Having three partners in a newspaper business was extremely rare in the United States, especially in the smaller western town markets. The three partners began to publish books and pamphlets to generate additional income. First, the trio published a reprint of a June 6th, 1795 article in the *Philadelphia Gazette* entitled *An Address to the Citizens of Philadelphia Respecting the Better Government of Youth* by Matthew Clarkson, Mayor. Offered for sale at six and one-half cents, the twenty-four-page volume featured parental advice to "restrain children from engaging in sports and trenching on laws and morals."[24] Printed sextodecimo (a sheet of paper folded into sixteenths), the article was reprinted in book form "by the desire of some gentlemen in Washington [PA], and earnestly recommended to the attention of all parents, masters, guardians, and others."[25] The partners offered the book for sale in out-of-town bookstores, including Pittsburgh and McKee's Port.[26] Six months later, the number of out-of-town sellers offering the partners' books mushroomed to eleven. The expanded sales network included a New Geneva, New York shop operated by Beaumont's political ally and fellow moderate during the Whiskey Rebellion, Albert Gallatin.[27]

Consistent with the practices of many printers of the era, the partners published an annual almanac with the imposing title *Alamanck for the year of 1796 being Bissextile or Leap Year*. Announcing the book's availability, the partners proclaimed, "We now present you with an Almanac, the first, we presume, ever printed on this side of the Appalachian Hills, and trust it will be found correct, and replete with useful matter as any other published in the United States." While rare, the partners incorrectly attributed their edition as the first locally published almanacs west of the Appalachians.[28] Traditionally, the partners' almanac started with astronomical information, including daily sun rises and sets, planets' positions, and monthly moon phases. Other useful information includes a brief history of each state in the union, local and appeals court calendars, currency conversion tables, and a list of government officers. The almanac concludes with an essay on the *Art of Health* by "the celebrated Dr. Cheyne," several items of practical advice, and a few pieces of poetry. Generally, printers experienced good demand for almanacs as they contained both pertinent and interesting reference information that the printers could easily glean from materials published in other locations. Other factors suggesting a promising market for the partners' almanac included increasing literacy and little local area competition (a Pittsburgh publisher printed the only almanac in western Pennsylvania). Almanacs were cheap to produce, therefore affordable by most households.

The partners published four books targeting Washington County's children's education and an updated Almanac the following year. All four scholastic volumes were reprints of previously published books free of American copyright restrictions. Thomas Dilworth, an English cleric, penned the first book, *Dilworth's Spelling Book, Improved. A Book Well Adapted to the Forwarding of Youth in the English Language.* The trio's edition joined many others, including at least seventy-six editions published since the first edition in 1740. The partners republished *Mrs. Barbauld's Lessons* by British poet Anna Laetitia Barbauld, a four-part reading primer designed to help children read. Initially published in 1778, the primer espoused a republican notion of mothers educating the nation's youth. Barbauld's book gained widespread use in both Britain and America. The partners advertised *Mrs. Barbauld's Lessons* at the attractive price of one-eighth of a dollar.

At midyear, the editors reprinted a new spelling book from uncertain sources for the higher price of one-quarter of a dollar. The fourth educational book published in 1796 is most puzzling due to his religious provenance. In the fall, the partners republished *The New England Primer,* a religious-based reading text written by unknown authors. First published in 1727 (at least the first surviving copy), *The New England Primer* contained authorized catechism and other theological writings of the Anglican Church. New Protestant sects modified the text generating over one hundred editions through the years. The partners decided to republish this already widespread text due to the increasing religiosity of the surrounding community.

After a spate of book printing, publishing activity diminished in 1797 with the publication of just two books, both in the first half of the year—*Beveridge's*

ALMANACK

FOR

THE YEAR 1796,

BEING

Biſſextile, or Leap Year:

CONTAINING

The uſual ASTRONOMICAL CALCULATIONS, a brief Account of the UNITED STATES, abſtract from the CONSTITUTION of PENNSYLVANIA, COURTS of LAW, Rates of POSTAGE throughout the UNION, LISTS of the CONGRESS of the UNITED STATES, and of the OFFICERS of the FEDERAL GOVERNMENT, &c. &c.

ALSO

Plain and eaſy Rules for the attainment and preſervation of HEALTH, curious Receipts, Anecdotes, Poetry, a remarkable inſtance of Affection between Br s, Aphoriſms on Man, and ſeveral uſeful Tables of Intereſt, Coins, &c.

WASHINGTON :

PRINTED BY COLERICK, HUNTER & BEAUMONT,

PRINTERS AND BOOKSELLERS.

1795.

FIGURE 3. First Washington, Pennsylvania Almanac.

Private Thoughts and *The Gentleman's Pocket Farrier*, priced at twenty cents."[29] In addition to publishing newspapers and books, the partners' print shop produced forms, legal documents, contracts, and other printed items for the businesses in the growing community. Further expanding their money-making ventures, Beaumont and then Colerick rented a portion of their residences near the Washington Market House to Alton Pemberton to "open a most elegant, extensive and well-chosen assortment of Dry Goods, &c. as they were all imported immediately under his inspection from the first manufactories in Europe."[30] The combination of printing and retail sales would continue to be important in Hunter's and his partners' future.

The partners started or expanded their families during the period, making increased profits imperative. Colerick supported a particularly large family. By 1800, his household consisted of seventeen persons, including his wife Ann, two elderly relations, four teenagers, and six children under age ten.[31] The total included three apprentices or journeymen who worked in the publishing business. While not on the same size and scale, the families of the other two partners enlarged during this period. In a ceremony conducted in Washington, Pennsylvania, William Hunter married Ann Morrison of Bedford, Pennsylvania (or Anne in some accounts). In Washington, Elizabeth Beaumont gave birth to two daughters, Matilda (March 19, 1795) and Louisa (August 29, 1797).

As relative newcomers to Washington County, Colerick and Beaumont joined the local Masonic Lodge. Masonic membership provided new avenues to develop business and personal relationships for the partners. Further, membership signaled a commitment to the community to influential town leaders. Lodge officers included judges, state representatives, business owners, and other civic leaders. Colerick attained his master mason certificate on July 27, 1795. Speeding through the process a year later, Beaumont achieved his Apprentice followed in two months with elevation to Master Mason. Curiously, Hunter did not join the Masons, perhaps due to his lack of formal religiosity.

While the masonic lodge membership may have aided Beaumont and Colerick in integrating into the community, the publishing business remained challenging for the partners. The partners were pleased with the number of subscribers at the one-year mark, but the considerable non-payment of subscription fees greatly troubled the partners. "We once more intimate to our patronizers [*sic*] the punctuality in payment of the small annual sum is absolutely necessary to the carrying on of the business." To offset the bad debts, the partners attempted to receive payment upfront. However, new subscribers found this policy to be "objectionable."[32] Unhappiness in the print shop further stressed the business.

An experienced apprentice, John Sharp, absconded from Washington. Nearly 17 years of age, Sharp entered into an apprenticeship with Hunter in Philadelphia and continued when the partners moved their business to Washington. Hunter surmised that the teenager made for Philadelphia to be with his family. Apparently, Sharp had intimated a strong desire to return to his parents. Hunter advertised in *The Western Telegraphe* offering a reward for Sharp's return. However, the partners probably did not want him back as they only offered a five-dollar reward (plus reasonable expenses). The ad's true intent warned future employers of Sharp's unreliability and inhibited Sharp from entering into employment with other printers. The loss of an experienced worker created more manual work for the remainder of the staff, especially during tight weekly deadlines to issue the newspaper.[33] However, Hunter's contemplated plans also factored into the lack of interest in Sharp returning to his employ.

Within two years, advertisement volumes in *The Western Telegraphe* had grown from seven in the inaugural issue to thirty paid ads, two public notices, and only one internal ad in the May 16, 1797 issue. Ad sizes also increased, with one-quarter of page three and the entirety of page four devoted to paid advertisements. Space in *The Western Telegraphe* devoted to advertisements approximated the amounts in successful newspapers in other parts of the country. Despite apparent commercial success, this issue announced the termination of the printing partnership. Colerick purchased the partnership interests of Hunter and Beaumont and informed readers that he would continue to publish the paper. As political factions hardened and newspapers had to choose sides, the trio could not agree upon editorial policies, especially the ardently held political differences between Beaumont and Colerick. Even newspapers in towns with only one newspaper could not remain neutral and aligned with either the Federalist or the Jeffersonian parties. After Hunter and Beaumont departed, *The Western Telegraphe*'s editorial policy took a sharp turn to the Federalist positions. A competitor newspaper alleged that John Colerick served as a puppet of the Federalists and merely prints what the party demands.[34] Principally referring to the period after the partnership with Hunter and Beaumont ended, historians of the era characterize Colerick's paper as "ultra-Federalist." However, Hunter and Beaumont touted their "independent press" as they left *The Western Telegraphe,* providing a hint that Colerick overtly promoted Federalist policies during their tenure. On the other hand, Colerick defended his editorial policy as "uninfluenced by party attachment or party views, and a firm friend to Order, he is determined to be solely directed by the great principle of PUBLIC UTILITY." Naturally, each side claimed non-partisanship and unattachment to political parties to widely promote their views among subscribers and read-ers.[35] Several weeks later, Hunter and Beaumont announced their plans for a newspaper based in Washington, Kentucky, in *The Western Telegraphe*. The new partners also promoted their new publishing venture in *The PittsburghGazette*. Pittsburgh served as a gateway to migrants and travelers journeying to Wash-ington, Kentucky.[36]

Diverging political opinions and insufficient profits factored into the breakup as the economic potential of a small-town printing office proved inadequate to support the three partners' sizable families. Even in the largest cities, almost all printers worked independently or with one other partner. Only a tiny fraction of printing partnerships involved three partners, especially in firms located in frontier areas. Additionally, Beaumont continued to feel threatened by the Pennsylvania authorities for his participation in the Whiskey Rebellion, albeit a bit part. He complained to others about being persecuted by Federalist-leaning Judge Alexander Addison, the presiding judge of Pennsylvania's fifth Federal cir-cuit court. Noted for his vociferous prosecution of anyone associated with the whiskey rebels, Addison lived a few blocks away from the Beaumont. Politically affiliated with moderate protest leaders, Beaumont felt hounded by Addison for his republican views, stating, ". . . I refused to become a tool in his nefarious pursuits, exerted himself to the utmost to accomplish my ruin."[37] Another reason Beaumont might have sought to leave is to escape several lawsuits. Numerous people filed civil suits seeking damages over land sale disputes with Beaumont, including Richard Potter and John McKee, two prominent landowners in Wash-ington County.[38] In a letter to Thomas Jefferson seeking Federal employment, Beaumont lamented that he "removed to Kentucky to escape persecution."[39]

While William Beaumont may have felt hounded by the judge, Alexander Addison may have provided substantial financial benefits to the two departing partners. In 1800, an anonymous article in a Democratic-Republican leading paper alleges that Judge Addison purchased Hunter's and Beaumont's share of the printing partnership for five hundred dollars. Further, Addison is alleged to have used public funds to provide payment to the departing partners. The allegations of using public funds were never proved, but Addison providing the funds for Colerick to buy out his partners is entirely plausible, and five-hun-dred dollars is a reasonable value that approximates the partners' investment. Beaumont would continue to cite his troubles with Judge Addison for political gain in any event.[40]

Whatever the specific reasons, the partnership breakup was less than amica-ble. Colerick believed that Hunter and Beaumont left the partnership without fulfilling their obligations to him. Several weeks after the breakup, Colerick advertised in this paper that Hunter and Beaumont departed town without finishing printing a book entitled, *An Historical and Geographic Account of the Country West of the Allegheny Mountains*. Over the past year, the erstwhile partners had widely advertised for subscribers to fund the western America geographical account in Pittsburgh, Philadelphia, and other Pennsylvania newspapers.[41] While the first portions of the book went to press, the partners garnered insufficient paid subscribers to fund the remaining portions of the book. Colerick announced that the departing partners had only completed a quarter of the book, and Colerick would not be completing the volume. Colerick announced his intent to sue his former partners for damages and refund subscribers' deposits in several months. It's unclear whether Colerick ever sued Hunter and Beaumont or received compensation from the erstwhile partners for the unfinished volume. The conflict over the unfinished book provided Colerick with a graceful cover to close down the unprofitable publishing project. Other disputes arose, and Colerick sued Hunter and Beaumont over collecting partnership debts. Colerick believed that Hunter and Beaumont were responsible for collecting a two-hundred-dollar debt from David Duncan. As this is an unusually large amount, it is unlikely that the debt was related to disputes over newspaper operations, subscription amounts, or advertising revenues. An amount of this size suggests a land sale as Hunter became a part-time land speculator later in life. After waiting a sufficient period, Colerick sued to collect.[42] This lawsuit dragged on until at least 1800 when Thomas Marshall (brother of U.S. Supreme Court Chief Justice John Marshall) recorded a deposition by William Beaumont. Beaumont stated for the record that the Duncan debt was included in the allowance for bad debts at the time of the dissolution of the partnership, and William Hunter only agreed to make an honest effort to collect. Neither side was happy with the partnership dissolution, but all parties moved on to successful printing businesses.

While Hunter and Beaumont sought more profitable undertakings in Kentucky, *The Western Telegraphe* flourished under Colerick's sole leadership until he died in 1804 from natural causes. Originally printed in the Philadelphia press and reprinted in numerous eastern papers, an obituary lauded Colerick for his "gentle, charitable and friendly disposition."[43] Colerick's wife, assisted by journeymen, continued to publish the paper and operate the publishing business for several years.

CHAPTER NINE

Republican Printers

The move to Kentucky proved fortuitous. In the rapidly growing Blue Grass state, the son of a British soldier and recent immigrant became a courageous and highly respected newspaper editor, a prominent civic leader, and an enterprising business owner. Espousing the differing economic interests of the "western states, Hunter gained a distinguished political reputation which sustained him through the vicissitudes of the economic booms and busts of the early nineteenth century. However, participating in the Kentucky economy meant compromising his "republican" values that he espoused as a young adult in Britain by operating businesses using enslaved people. For the first time in his life, stability replaced itinerancy, and contented family life dulled the pain of being an orphan without connections to his biological family.

In the summer of 1797, the Hunter and Beaumont families moved three hundred miles west to Washington, Kentucky, where "they were invited by the most flattering prospects of success" to establish a printing business. In the July 4, 1797, edition of *The Western Telegraphe*, Hunter and Beaumont advertised the new business. "Their intention is to commence a Newspaper on a Royal Sheet in Folio, a size much larger than any Kentucky Papers are at present printed on, and equal to many of the Philadelphia Papers, which will enable them to give the Public the whole of interesting intelligence, and leave ample room for Advertisements."[1] While unrecognized by most readers, the boast about offering the largest-sized newspaper turned out to be not entirely accurate. Ending the ad, the new partners thanked their Washington, Pennsylvania, readers and wished them "every blessing that men of independent principles and virtuous citizens they deserve to enjoy."[2]

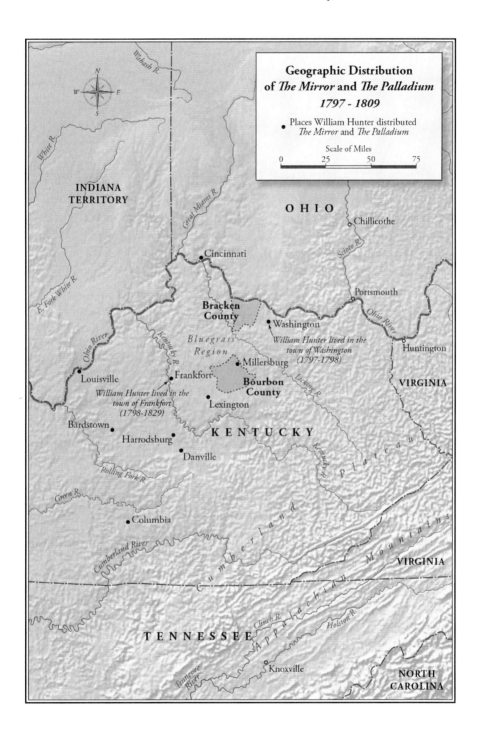

**Geographic Distribution
of *The Mirror* and *The Palladium*
1797 - 1809**

• Places William Hunter distributed
The Mirror and *The Palladium*

Scale of Miles

0   25   50   75

Wabash R.

N
W   E
S

White R.

**INDIANA
TERRITORY**

Great Miami R.

O H I O

○ Chillicothe

Scioto R.

Cincinnati

Portsmouth

E. Fork White R.

**Bracken
County**

Washington

*Bluegrass
Region*

*William Hunter lived in the
town of Washington
(1797-1798)*

Ohio River

Huntington

Ohio River

Kentucky R.

Millersburg

Licking R.

Louisville

Frankfort

**Bourbon
County**

VIRGINIA

*William Hunter lived in the
town of Frankfort
(1798-1829)*

Lexington

Bardstown

K E N T U C K Y

Harrodsburg

Danville

Kentucky R.

Rolling Fork R.

Plateau

Green R.

Columbia

Cumberland River

Cumberland

Mountains

VIRGINIA

Cumberland

T E N N E S S E E

Clinch R.

Appalachian

Holston R.

**NORTH
CAROLINA**

Tennessee River

Knoxville ○

The partners followed the lead of several leading British enlightenment thinkers who believed that Kentucky represented the best place in America to immigrate.[3] The British proponents of Kentucky cited the inhabitants' fiercely independent thinking, lack of religious conformity, and the existence of a more egalitarian society. The vast, open spaces that were recently free of Native American attacks and open to mass settlement provided perceived opportunities to shape a new polity around enlightened ideals. Kentucky was especially attractive to Baptists and other Christian sects for the opportunity to practice their faith without discrimination and the freedom to build new communities centered around their churches. While Beaumont and Hunter did not select Kentucky for religious reasons, the individualistic nature of the culture appealed to their political views, and economically, they perceived an opening to get in "on the ground floor" in shaping and building a new community.

Experiencing rapid growth due to its location on key water and land transportation routes, Washington, Kentucky, appeared to be a promising location for a new press. Located four hundred and five miles downstream from Pittsburgh and sixty-five miles east of Cincinnati on the Kentucky side of the river, the frontier town of Washington served as an entry point from the Ohio River into central Blue Grass Kentucky.[4] A former buffalo trace, later named by Europeans, the Maysville Road linked Washington with Lexington, Kentucky's largest city. Characterized by travelers as the "Athens of the west," Lexington stood fifty-five miles to the southwest. All imported goods and settlers from the east and all goods from the west going to eastern markets traveled through Washington. In addition, the surrounding countrywide offered important natural resources for settler sustenance. An English dissenting minister and early traveler to the area, described in a published 1792 handbook aimed at other potential immigrates that in the Washington area, "everything assumes a dignity and splendor I have never seen in any other part of the world." The emigration-booster minister goes on to laud the surrounding land's agricultural potential as "produces prolific soil" and is "truly astonishing."[5] In addition to fertile, phosphorus-rich limestone soil, early travelers noted a type of native bamboo (*arundinaria gigantea*) referred to as cane by Europeans flourishing in the Washington area. Cane provided early settlers with ready-made, natural feed for cattle. An early historian of Kentucky, John Filson, described forests of six- to twenty-foot-high cane called cane brakes, which are "so thick and tall that it is difficult to pass through them."[6] The area's agricultural resources and geographic advantages were a big draw for the partners seeking a new place to start a newspaper and printing business.

Capitalizing on these natural advantages, the rapidly growing, economically prosperous town of Washington boasted five hundred and seventy people (1800 census), the second-largest Kentucky town after Lexington. The seven-hundred-acre town consisted of over one hundred primarily wooden houses arranged along a grid street pattern. Despite a few brick houses, a courthouse, and several well-appointed retail establishments, Washington appeared to a visiting Frenchman as having a "dull sameness."[7] Town residents operated seventeen businesses that offered good advertising and print business prospects. Washington's location provided additional natural advantages to the eighteenth-century newspapermen. Astride travel routes into Kentucky's interior from the Ohio River, the town received many business travelers and migrating European settlers who provided word of mouth reports and out-of-area newspapers for the latest news. Critical to the newspaper business, the town boasted a large, established post office that served as a distribution point for the entire Northwest Territory (the area north of the Ohio River). As customary on the western frontier, the mail arrived once a week, and the editors had the opportunity to glean the most important and exciting news for their latest edition. The town's postal service offered the editors efficient and timely dissemination of their weekly papers to eastern and western locales. The central Kentucky mail delivery left Washington at 8:00 am, traveled as far west as Danville, Virginia (one hundred and ten miles southwest of Washington, Kentucky) before returning on Thursday evening. Mail destined for the Northwest Territories continued down the Ohio River before transiting to points north and west.

Most important for the partners' success, printing office competition appeared negligible with only two other newspapers in the entire state. Encouraged by the earliest settlers and enticed with the promise of government printing contracts in 1787, John Bradford, a Revolutionary War veteran, started the first newspaper in Kentucky. For many years, Bradford operated the only newspaper and printing shop for hundreds of miles around. Untrained in the printing business, Bradford's *Kentucke Gazette* (later the *Kentucky Gazette* after the state's name change) commenced as a primitive paper but by 1796 grew to have the most considerable influence and readership in the state. Bradford's printing press operated out of Lexington, Kentucky's largest town with over two thousand people. As the state's commercial center, Lexington proved the best local market for advertising and readership.

Pioneering, but "not a brilliant editor," John Bradford gradually improved the *Kentucky Gazette* into a well-established paper.[8] As typical of the only newspaper in a remote location, Bradford espoused an open forum to discuss politics. He proudly asserted his politically neutral editorial policy by stating, "More than nine years' experience has convinced me that *Impartiality* forms one of the most valuable traits in the character of a News Paper Printer."[9] Although he assiduously provided space for opposing views without journalistic comment, the citizens of Lexington highly respected Bradford. Residents widely respected his mechanical ingenuity, astronomical understanding, philosophical knowledge, and mathematical abilities. Given this broad range of knowledge, some residents referred to him as "Old Wisdom" or the "Kentucky Franklin."[10] Outspoken on slavery, Bradford advocated the emancipation of the enslaved peoples. Finding ways to vie with Bradford's widespread reputation and proven business skills, Hunter and Beaumont engaged in intense and spirited competition with John and his sons for the entire lengths of their printing careers.

James H. Steward operated the second, albeit less influential, paper entitled *Stewart's Kentucky Herald.* Steward printed his weekly newspaper also in Lexington. In 1802, Bradford purchased the *Herald* and merged it into the *Gazette.* By setting up shop at the first eastern mail stop in Kentucky, Hunter and Beaumont received global and national news in advance of the Lexington papers, creating a competitive advantage. Bradford and his sons proved to be durable competitors leveraging Lexington's prosperity and statewide prominence. Despite the intense competition with the Bradford's, the partners landed in a promising business environment to launch a paper. At least three years passed before another Kentucky newspaper appeared.[11]

The partners established their printing business at the corner of Main Street and D Street (2014 Old Main Street today), next to the town's post office with a tavern on the other side.[12] Located on a three-quarter-acre lot, the first floor of the two-story log house served as a printing office, and William Hunter's family lived on the second story. A post and rail fence ringed the lot, including several out-buildings for necessaries and business storage. William Hunter also owned two five-acre parcels of land outside of town, on which he grew produce and food for the family.[13]

A few weeks after the partners traveled the three hundred miles from Washington, Pennsylvania, Hunter and Beaumont set up shop and readied their first newspaper edition. The partners named their new paper *The Mirror.* In the inaugural September 9, 1797, issue, the new Kentucky publishers rolled out an utterly re-designed colophon (masthead on top of the first page). A banner adorned with leaves and acorns from a Laurel Oak tree indigenous to Northeastern Kentucky trimmed the top of page one. A new motto below the Laurel Oak announced to readers a newspaper editorial policy that is "Firm, free and temperate." Like *The Western Telegraphe*, the editors' names appeared at the bottom of the last page and local contacts to purchase the paper in nearby towns. The duo decided to price an annual subscription at three dollars, increasing one dollar over the price commanded by *The Western Telegraphe*. In line with other western newspapers, the higher price helped startup costs and the higher newsprint and other publishing costs of operating in the remote western frontier. To reduce the typical problem of non-payment by subscribers among newspapers of the era and further minimize the partners' investment, the partners collected one-half of the subscription rate in advance. On their first anniversary, the partners placed an advertisement in *The Mirror* thanking its subscriber base and announcing similar pricing of three dollars. Recognizing Kentucky's multi-currency economy, the ad also expressed the subscription price in British shillings. During the 1790s, prices were often stated in British or Spanish currency as American dollars were in short supply. For ease of conversion, the editorial stated the subscription price at eighteen shillings per year, one-half payable in advance. The partners set this price to be competitive with the more established *Kentucky Gazette,* which commanded a price of twenty-one shillings per year.[14]

Hunter and Beaumont continued to employ the old type (even for its period) with the long "f" used for "s." The partners offered a standard four-page, four-column paper organized into five news sections. Page one, the top left column, featured a lead article. The lead article's sources included letters written to the editors, information from other papers, governmental news, or sometimes editorial content provided by Hunter and Beaumont. Following the lead article, a section labeled Foreign Intelligence consisted of articles reprinted from the eastern and foreign press. The Napoleonic Wars captivated Kentuckians who named Louisville, Fayette, Bourbon, and many other towns and counties after French allies and revolutionists. Next, a section on Domestic Intelligence featured reprints of eastern and western papers. A section entitled *The Mirror* contained local Mason County and other Kentucky news curated by the editors. In most issues, news items in *The Mirror* section represented the only portion of the newspaper written by Hunter and Beaumont, with the rest of the copy reproduced from other newspapers. Following *The Mirror* section, a Postscript column provided space for late-arriving news. The partners organized to typeset most of the paper in advance and saved some space in this section for late-breaking news from the mails. On the top left column on page four, the partners usually printed a poem under the heading of The Parnassiad (poet), slightly modified from *The Western Telegraphe*'s Parnassian (poetry) Corner. The volume of advertisements and interesting news sometimes crowded out this literary feature. In the second year of operation, the editor omitted the Parnassian section in favor of revenue-producing advertisements.

Revenue-generating advertisements appeared on pages two and three, primarily on the interior columns (columns three and four of page two and columns one and two on page three). Ads dominated all four columns of page four. For the next issue, the deadline for accepting new advertisements closed two days before publication. Not surprising given its outsized contributions to the Kentucky economy, land sales dominated ad placements. However, ads for the partners' publications commanded an entire column or more of most editions and, in many cases, were more extensive than the ads of paying customers. Frequent advertisers included purveyors of merchandise, horses, and farm supplies.

In addition to ads for goods and services, notices appeared, such as announcing that one spouse will no longer be responsible for the other spouse's debts, rewards for runaway enslaved people, or lost or stolen items. The number of paying ads grew over time and represented vital financial support for the newspaper. In addition, advertisers were more likely to pay cash upfront than subscribers, who often merely promised to pay in arrears.

Initially, the partners selected to publish *The Mirror* on Saturday to coincide with the scheduled mail delivery. Upon receiving the incoming mail, the partners feverously incorporated the latest news from out-of-town newspapers and other material from personal letters that came to the editors' attention. The editors had a short publication window to ready *The Mirror* for distribution in the outgoing mail. By publishing as close to the receipt of incoming mails and before the outgoing mail, the partners hoped to gain a competitive advantage by offering the most up-to-date news. Eastern mail came first to Washington, giving the partners an advantage over his Lexington Competitors. John Bradford printed two weekly editions of the *Kentucky Gazette* Lexington on Wednesday and Saturday. The *Stewart's Kentucky Herald* came out on Tuesdays. Changes in the postal schedule necessitated continual switching the publication dates for *The Mirror* to retain a competitive advantage as possible. As a result of these changes, the partners moved the publication date to Friday, starting with the November 30, 1797 edition. Mysteriously, "Fryday" prominently appeared in the masthead, and the mis-spelling or colloquial form continued for about six months. The normally proficient editors were playing a pun, or the partners lost the 'i' of the masthead types. Such a prominent typo would not have continued during such a lengthy period. Typically, the partners and employees were careful typesetters and effective proofreaders producing a high-quality paper with few typos and errors. Eventually, the partners corrected the spelling of Friday, and several months later, a postal schedule change required switching the publication day to Wednesday.[15]

Following their multi-media business model in Washington, Pennsylvania, the partners offered the same book genres to the public as those published with John Colerick. On October 28, 1797, the partners advertised the publication of *A Sermon on Sacred Music Preached in Washington* by Reverend John Campbell, priced at twenty-five cents and available by subscription. The partners first promoted a *Kentucky Primer* on March 10, 1798. Continuing to offer books aimed at children›s education, on May 26, 1798, the partners announced publishing a *Kentucky Spelling Book* priced at one shilling and ten pence (1s, 10d) or roughly eleven dollars in today's currency. In addition, the partners offered discounts to schoolmasters and booksellers to entice bulk purchases.

In addition to religious and educational books, the partners launched a significant new monograph that provided invaluable navigation information to assist western river voyagers. On March 24, 1797, the partners announced a concise travel handbook entitled The Ohio Navigator. The twenty-eight-page river guide's provenance is uncertain, but the contents were extracted from the contemplated more extensive but unfinished geographical guide to the country west of the Allegheny Mountains planned during the last months of the partners' time in the business with Colerick. Perhaps, the river guides anticipated sizable commercial value led to Colerick's unhappiness with Hunter and Beaumont skipping town without finishing the committed work. Further evidence points to Zadok Cramer, an apprentice in *The Western Telegraphe* office, as the primary source or at least a significant participant in collecting information on the Ohio River. In 1800, the New Jersey-born but Washington, Pennsylvania reared Cramer completed his apprenticeship with Colerick, Hunter, and Beaumont, and left town for Pittsburgh where he opened a bookbinding business and a book shop named "Sign of the Franklin Head."[16] The next year he published a volume entitled the *Ohio Navigator*. Hunter and Beaumont caught wind of Cramer's publishing plans, as they registered a copyright on the *Ohio Navigator* with the Clerk of the Kentucky District Federal Court nine months after their initial publication. The legal maneuver asserting ownership failed as Cramer updated his work, including a major expansion covering the Mississippi River.

Adding a bit of intrigue, in November 1800, a manuscript describing the navigation of the Mississippi River disappeared from Hunter's printing office. After a few weeks of being unable to locate the manuscript, Hunter advertised in his paper for its recovery, stating, "There are several thousand dollars subscribed to a commercial plan, which it contains."[17] It's unknown what happened to the lost or purloined draft, but Hunter never recovered the Mississippi River manuscript. The lack of a description of the Mississippi River portended the demise of Hunter's *Ohio Navigator* as travel down the Mississippi became increasingly important to potential book purchasers. Cramer's book outcompeted the partner's limited version despite selling at four times the price. As a result, Hunter ceased advertising the sale of the *Ohio Navigator* in late 1800 and issued no new editions.

Unfortunately, there are no known copies of either the partners' or Cramer's first two river navigation editions to compare content. Cramer's book garnered a growing regional and national audience. Continued high levels of customer demand spawned over one dozen editions into the mid-1820s, and several of these later editions are available for sale today. Contrary to the assertions of notable historians and booksellers who cite Zadok Cramer's volume, Hunter and Beaumont should be credited with publishing the first navigation guide to the Ohio River though the content may have come from Cramer under their employment.[18] In any event, the partners did not keep up with changing customer needs and lost the business to Cramer. With an eye on making a mark in a different arena, the Washington publishers turned to an emerging political crisis.

The Kentucky partners published their most important and courageous editorial in July 1798, taking an outspoken stance on an emerging national crisis. With the real prospect of a Franco-American war erupting, the Federalist dominated Congress passed, and President John Adams signed into law the Sedition Act.[19] This act made it a Federal crime to agitate against government policies or even criticize officials in the administration. The hastily passed law targeted Democratic-Republican newspaper editors and politicians who disagreed with the Federalist Party's foreign policies and its government leaders. Ostensibly, the United States government declared the country neutral in the ongoing conflict between France and Britain. However, the ruling Federalists instituted trade and commercial policies which supported the British. The Democratic-Republicans favored republican France and opposed aligning the United States with autocratic Britain. Unable to remain neutral, the Federalist policies favoring British commercial interests led to an undeclared naval conflict with France in the Atlantic and Caribbean waters termed the Quasi-War. Given perceived threats of French subterfuge of the United States political processes, Congress narrowly passed the Sedition Act, making it a crime to criticize the government. The infamous law intended to silence the political opposition and target Democratic-Republican newspapers and editors. Even before passage, efforts were underway to use existing libel laws to quell dissent. In a high-profile case, a Federalist prosecutor brought common law charges against the outspoken administration critic Benjamin Franklin Bache. Ominously, these libel suits and the new Sedition Law portended trouble for *The Mirror*'s editors.

The new sedition law is the second time Hunter experienced an act outlawing criticism of the government. While a young adult, he witnessed King George III issue a Royal proclamation against publishing seditious writings. Hunter fled Britain to escape such autocratic laws and now faced a similar situation in America. However, he unflinchingly opposed stifling free speech and suppressing the press. Less than one week after the enactment of the infamous Sedition Act, an editorial appeared in *The Mirror* under the pseudonym of Aristides decrying the law's severe restrictions on the free press.[20] To American newspaper readers, Aristides evoked the image of a well-known ancient Greek politician and military general known for meting out fair justice and for personifying public and private integrity. In post-Revolution political discourse, a newspaper article was written under the pseudonym Aristides connoted a writer who supported the Jeffersonian Democratic-Republican faction. Major political figures who used the Aristides pseudonym include Alexander Contee Hanson, an out-spoken anti-Federalist Maryland judge and delegate to the 1787 Constitutional Convention, and Washington's Attorney General Edmund Randolph, who defended Thomas Jefferson from attacks by Alexander Hamilton. Closer to home, the *Kentucky Gazette* published a series of five essays under the authorship of Aristides, which described the irreconcilable differences between the interests of the seaboard states and the western territories. The *Kentucky Gazette* essay concluded that the eastern states were "foul nests of inequity" and "had uniformly and invariably adopted the British systems of government" in detriment to the economic interests of the Kentuckians.[21] In a letter to Abigail Adams, nephew William Cranch identifies Aristides as Dr. Samuel Brown. Brother to Kentucky's Senator John Brown and Professor at Transylvania University, Dr. Brown most likely wrote both *The Mirror* and the *Kentucky Gazette* articles. His use of the pseudonym Aristides invoked the aura of a higher authority rather than mere party politics in the highly critical attack on the Sedition law and the Adams administration. Despite the cover of a pseudonym and not being the authors, the courageous partners could be prosecuted just for publishing an article deemed subversive. The expansive law permitted Federal prosecutors to charge newspapers owners and editors with sedition even if they did not write offending articles. The partners faced severe penalties if found guilty, including up to two years in jail and a two-thousand dollar fine. Any prosecution could destroy their commercial prospects and put their paper out of business.[22]

Immediately upon the law's enactment, Secretary of State Timothy Pickering organized a systematic scan of newspapers to detect Sedition Act violations. If found, the cases were referred to the United States district attorney with local jurisdiction for enforcement. Within days, *The Mirror*'s Aristides article came to the attention of William Rawle and Parker Campbell, the United States attorneys for the districts of Pennsylvania and Kentucky, respectively. Beaumont had particular reason to fear, as Rawle aggressively prosecuted the high-profile cases against the Whiskey Rebellion rebels a few years earlier. Rawle also prosecuted the most Sedition Act cases of any district attorney.[23] Fortunately for Hunter and Beaumont, Pickering decided against prosecution. Finding better opportunities, Secretary Pickering identified a plethora of notable test cases in other venues. In these cases, he could establish clear authorship and anticipate Federalist leaning juries. Concerning Hunter's and Beaumont's article, Pickering chose not to prosecute over concerns that an anti-Federalist Kentucky jury would not vote to convict the newspaper owners. While Hunter and Beaumont escaped prosecution, fines, and jail time, an unquestionable, sizeable threat existed as the Adams administration prosecuted twenty-six people, aggressively targeting Democratic-Republican leaning newspapers and their editors.[24] Federal prosecutors obtained most of the Sedition Act convictions in heavily Federalist New England. At the time of the partners' Aristides article, the threat of prosecution appeared to Hunter and Beaumont more dangerous than looking at the situation in hindsight. However, they unflinchingly opposed stifling free speech and suppressing the press. Nipping at the partners' heels, Federal prosecutors attempted to indict an editor in their most recent hometown for printing a poem mocking President Adams just a few months later. Fortunately, for John Israel, the *Herald of Liberty*'s editor, two Washington, Pennsylvania grand juries refused to indict him.[25] Demonstrating that it is easier to enact rather than enforce laws, the Adams administration convicted no one of seditious actions in the country's western regions.

Aggressive prosecution of political opponents in eastern jurisdictions created considerable controversy in all corners of the nation. Secretary Pickering even considered deporting the politically-quiet scientist Dr. Joseph Priestley until President Adams' cooler head prevailed.[26] These overreaches of governmental power appalled Hunter, who fled Britain as a result of similar oppression only five years prior. Most Kentuckians agreed with Hunter and the state became a hotbed of opposition to the Alien and Sedition Acts. Engendered by the covert urgings of Vice President Thomas Jefferson, Kentucky residents convened a series of public meetings protesting the Federalist use of these laws to outlaw dissent. First in Clarke County, then in other counties, Kentuckians held mass protest meetings chaired by prominent local leaders. The partners advertised such a meeting in their home county of Mason "at the Baptist church at 12 noon on August 27 for people with republican views" in the August 18, 1798 edition of *The Mirror*. The advertisement had its intended effect as the September 1st edition of *The Mirror* reported that an estimated fifteen hundred to two thousand people attended the county meeting. The assembly selected as chairman General Henry Lee (no relationship to Virginia's Light-Horse Harry Lee). The assembled citizens easily passed a resolution condemning the Alien and Sedition Acts and named five representatives to present the protest resolution to the Kentucky governor. In the same September 1st issue, the editors reprinted an article from the *New Windsor* (NY) *Gazette* that authorities arrested the editor of the *Mt. Pleasant Register* on charges of libeling the president. The editor, William Durrell, caught the ire of federal prosecutors by comparing the conduct of President John Adams to that of the infamous traitor and Revolutionary War Major General Benedict Arnold. Although a Sedition Act conviction could result in a maximum of two years in jail and a $2000 fine, prosecutors set an outrageous bail for Durrell at $4000, ensuring that the editor remained in jail.

During the fall, The Mirror reported that Fayette, Mercer, Bourbon, Lincoln, and Madison Counties all held similar mass citizen meetings which approved resolutions almost verbatim, as adopted in Mason County. Each county selected a small group of representatives to personally transmit the resolves to the governor. The large and growing citizen unrest became too large for the Kentucky State government to ignore. Upon convening in early November, the Kentucky Legislature immediately considered and debated a unified, statewide response to the Sedition Act and the three Alien acts, allowing the president to arrest and deport foreign visitors and residents and inhibit recent immigrants from citizenship and voting. Enacted November 10, 1798, the result is a proclamation commonly referred to as the Kentucky Resolutions. At the time, most observers attributed authorship to the widely respected John Breckenridge, Speaker of the Kentucky House, who introduced the resolutions and led the floor debate. Later historians have concluded that Thomas Jefferson authored the document which Breckenridge made a few edits to tone down too radical provisions. Safer from Federal prosecution, Kentucky politicians agreed to take up the mantle and shield Jefferson's authorship of a possible "treasonous" and "seditious" document to preserve his presidential candidacy in 1800. The Kentucky Legislature ordered the public printer to strike eight hundred copies and send two copies to each state government.

The controversy surrounding the Kentucky Resolutions burgeoned into a national issue. A month later, Virginia passed a similar resolution written by James Madison. The Virginia Resolutions went further, asserting that states have the right to determine if Federal laws are unconstitutional. Both resolutions became core beliefs of the Jefferson-led Democratic-Republican party. To gain national consensus, the resolutions were sent to the legislatures in other states for consideration. In the end, the other thirteen states either formally rejected, expressed disapproval, or ignored the Kentucky and Virginia resolutions. While dissent over the Alien and Sedition Acts disappeared from the pages of *The Mirror*, Hunter's brave, unequivocal public opposition to the Alien and Sedition Acts served as a lifelong source of immense pride. Decades later, in a public letter, he wrote under his signature, "A Republican of 1798."[27] Fortunately for newspaper sales, new and more intense political controversies emerged. But first, the partners needed to buttress their finances and counter competitor moves.

In addition to steadfast republican views, Kentuckians believed they, along with others who lived west of the Appalachians, had unique commercial interests apart from the seaboard states. Free and open navigation of the Ohio and Mississippi Rivers was a principal concern of *The Mirror* readers as the waterways provided a vital economic trade link to the outside world. Through its staunch advocacy of western concerns, *The Mirror* gained readership and advertising listings. Taking advantage of the increasing demand in surrounding areas, the partners established new delivery routes extending the newspaper's reach throughout the state and into parts of the Ohio Territory. Their biggest instate rival, John Bradford and his adult son, opened a competitive newspaper to counter this impressive growth. They began publishing *The Guardian of Freedom* in Frankfort, Kentucky's current, but not necessarily permanent capital city. Located forty-five miles from Washington, Kentucky, the growing, five-hundred-person town offered close proximity to the increasingly active legislature and the promise of government printing contracts.[28] Hunter and Beaumont decided to establish printing operations and commence a weekly newspaper in the capital city a few months later, not to be outflanked. In preparation, "Hunter the practical printer of the combination" traveled to Philadelphia to procure type, printing presses, and other materials to start up the second newspaper.[29] Entitled *The Palladium* and published under the banner of "A Literary and Political Weekly Repository," the partners' second newspaper featured a clean, brighter style but continued many of the features of *The Mirror*. "It shall be printed on a plan similar to the Mirror, and on paper of the same size and quality."[30] Given *The Mirror*'s apparent commercial success, the partners decided to keep publishing the Washington (Kentucky) paper and divided their efforts between the two papers. William Beaumont remained in Washington and exerted primary editorial control over *The Mirror* as he participated in community activities such as managing a lottery to build a town water system.[31] William Hunter moved to Frankfort and managed the new paper.

Beaumont's impact on *The Mirror*'s editorial policy is best evidenced by his continual obsession with the Federal Pennsylvania judge Alexander Addison who prosecuted the Whiskey Rebels and denounced him and other Republican-leaning politicians well after the end of the Whiskey Rebellion. The Kentucky county meetings protesting the Alien and Sedition Acts reignited the past enmity between Addison and Beaumont. In the wake of the new laws, Addison restated his disdain for newspapers and their editors, "Nothing is more dangerous and detestable than such printers and newspapers . . . they are public nuisances [and] ought to be rejected, and such printers punished."[32] On December 7, 1798, the editors reprinted the extract of a September 21, 1798, letter between two unnamed Pittsburgh gentlemen originally printed in the Reading, Pennsylvania, *The Weekly Advertiser* and the November 28, 1798, edition of the *Kentucky Gazette*. The letter from "a gentleman of respectability" reports "commotions in Kentucky," including "seditious speeches delivered, violent resolutions entered into, and a flame everywhere kindled. The letter's author identifies Beaumont as one of the Whiskey Rebellion rebels who is one of the leaders of the inflammatory Kentucky county meetings. The letter derisively described Beaumont as having "a long jaw" and one of the principal speakers at the Lexington meeting, George Nicholas, as "a little indolent, drunken lawyer, of some talents, but not principle . . ." One of the most prominent public figures in Kentucky, Nicholas is credited as "the person most responsible for the first Constitution of Kentucky in 1792" and the state's first attorney general. As a popular advocate for the interests of the western states and a virulent anti-Federalist, Nicholas's views on other matters would be prominently featured in the upcoming pages of *The Mirror*. Addison aimed his most incendiary comments at the alleged Whiskey rebel William Beaumont. However, vitriolic the personal attacks, Addison penned one of the most intellectually coherent and persuasive essays supporting the Sedition Act.[33]

Calling the letter "scurrility and personal invective," Beaumont could not let this article go without a full-fledged rebuttal, stating, "Would they reflect, they would not bring into view so strong an instance of the infringement of the Constitution of the United States and of the wanton exertion of lawless power."[34] In addition to an assault on civil liberties, Beaumont interpreted the letter as further proof of "the unmerited, the inhuman treatment he (Beaumont) then met with . . ." and boastfully continues, he "still refuses to bow the knee to the Baal [owner or lord] of the day."

The letter from "a gentleman of respectability" had a different effect on William Hunter. The Pittsburgh gentleman named Hunter's friend Harry Toulmin as a key instigator of the Lexington protest. The Pittsburgh letter cites Toulmin as a follower of the English dissident and famed scientist Doctor Joseph Priestley who accompanied the doctor on his journey to America. While Priestley and Toulmin did not sail together, both Toulmin and Hunter interacted with the politically active scientist who first identified oxygen in their formative years in England.[35] As cited in his journal, Hunter attended lectures given by Priestley in Birmingham, England and Toulmin received instruction from Priestley at his father's school in Taunton, England. Toulmin immigrated to the United States a year before Hunter. Unlike Hunter, who arrived without contacts, Toulmin landed in Norfolk, Virginia, with influential letters of introduction to Thomas Jefferson and James Madison. Leveraging these connections, Toulmin moved to Lexington to become President of the growing Transylvania Seminary (now University). However, Toulmin's Unitarian religious views clashed with the Presbyterian dominated Board of Trustees. After two years, Toulmin left the university and moved to the state capital. Toulmin quickly gained the confidence of Governor James Garrard, who named him Secretary of State.

Hunter and Toulmin instantly became friends, political allies, and professional associates, recognizing their common intellectual and national heritage. Toulmin stirred Hunter's memories of his young adult days in England, and their similar backgrounds and Enlightenment views fostered a common bond and friendship. Further, the raging conflict over the Alien and Section Acts and the bitter dispute between Jeffersonian republicanism and Hamiltonian federalism brought Hunter and Toulmin together politically. The clash between Jeffersonians and Federalists harkened back to the conflict observed by Hunter and Toulmin as young adults associated with the English dissenter and republican movements which supported the French Revolution. In both cases, heavy-handed governmental authority sought to stamp out political opposition and engender mob action to silence dissident views. Nevertheless, during the tumultuous debates over the Alien and Sedition Acts, a flourishing business relationship emerged, with Hunter becoming the publisher and printer of Toulmin's compilation of Kentucky's legal statutes.

As a further rebuttal to the "gentleman of respectability" a month later, Beaumont ran two prominently featured page one articles denouncing the activities of Judge Addison.[36] The *Kentucky Gazette* previously published the articles signed "a lawyer who does not want to be a judge." Most readers would have attributed the article to George Nicholas, and subsequently, both Bradford and Hunter and Beaumont would publish this letter and others in pamphlet form, citing George Nicholas as the author. Consistent with John Bradford's neutral editorial policy, he also published an article from an unidentified pro-Alien and Sedition Act author with Federalist leanings. Typical of Hunter and Beaumont, they did not provide space for the Federalist point of view in their paper. The planned third installment never appeared in *The Mirror*. Perhaps reader feedback signaled disinterest in the Federalist Pennsylvania state judge's opinions. A sympathetic Kentucky legal environment protected *The Mirror's* Republican-leaning readers. In any event, another explosive political issue, one with critical import to Kentucky's economy, emerged to dominate *The Mirror's* pages.

Late in 1798, the Kentucky legislature passed an act calling for a convention to consider a new state constitution in the following summer. With the electorate's increasingly republican bent, the impetus for a convention emanated from a desire to increase the power of a more inclusive electorate and reduce the control of the politically connected elite. For example, citizens clamored for changing the indirect elector system for governor and state senator elections to direct elections by the voters. An emotionally charged, high-profile second issue would sweep the dispute with Judge Addison from the pages of *The Mirror*. Started by religious leaders and recent immigrants, increasingly a tiny subset of the electorate demanded an end to Kentucky's constitutional protections for slavery. The partners responded to this controversy with a series of front-page articles for and against enslaved peoples' emancipation.

With a gradual emancipation law passing in New York State in 1799, eight of the seventeen states either ended or embarked on a course to end slavery. Many of the first European settlers in Kentucky emigrated from Virginia and brought their enslaved peoples. Other settlers came from Pennsylvania, which had a history of slavery emancipation for the last twenty years. Former Virginians and other wealthy landowners dominated the first Kentucky constitutional convention in 1792. With a closer than expected vote of 26 to 16, the convention adopted "Article VII Concerning Slaves," which read, "The Legislature shall have no power to pass laws for the emancipation of slaves without the consent of their owners or without paying their owners previous to such emancipation a full equivalent in money, for the slaves so emancipated."

Seven years later, most Kentuckians became economically dependent on slavery. Over forty thousand enslaved residents worked in agricultural, manufacturing, and domestic roles. Slave ownership represented the second most extensive use of wealth in the state, only exceeded by capital invested in land. The wealthy Blue Grass planters with fertile lands sought to preserve the constitutional protections of their enslaved "property." In contrast, smaller farmers on the edges of the most fertile regions favored ending slavery. At the same time, increasing religiosity swept over the state. Newly prominent clerical leaders fostered a movement for the emancipation of enslaved African Americans. Hunter and Beaumont printed a precursor to future coverage in issue number thirteen, an anti-slavery article written by an abolitionist Quaker adherent. The report called for the immediate end of slavery, "let us restore the negroes to that liberty, which man should never take from man."[37]

The new constitutional convention reignited the potential for state-mandated emancipation of enslaved persons. The key to how the constitution would deal with the slavery issue lay in selecting the fifty-eight delegates to the Frankfort-based convention, including three from Mason County. Voters would choose among delegate candidates during the regular election for state and federal offices in May. To obtain the best possible outcome, anti-slavery advocates wrote articles intended to influence public opinion by damning the institution of slavery. Hunter and Beaumont readily provided prominent space to those who decried the institution of slavery.

The first of these articles appeared under the pen name EMANCIPO which featured a withering attack on the immorality of slavery. Powerfully, EMANCIPO opens by stating, "The subject of Negro slavery deservedly claims the attention of every benevolent mind; and if the whisper of reason and humanity could be heard amidst the clamour of self interest and prejudice, few arguments in favour of a gradual emancipation would be necessary, as, on the scale of justice and humanity, the measure would have few opponents." Hunter and Beaumont continued to feature EMANCIPO's advocacy of emancipation by publishing five additional articles under the pseudonym over the next two months. Although the authorship of the EMANCIPO letters is unknown, they fit the pattern of abolitionist Presbyterian church leaders. Adding to EMANCIPO's voice, Hunter and Beaumont published more pro-emancipation articles under the pseudonyms Wilberforce, Franklin, and Hurly Burly.

After a few weeks without any pro-slavery rebuttal, the editors published a testy subscriber letter in the April 5, 1799 edition of *The Mirror* expressing a financial threat to the publishers, "I now begin to fear you have not only joined a combination against the Government, but you have formed a design to rob our citizens of their property . . ." The writer continues, "And now you and your Emancipos, Philanthropos, Wilberforce, etc have laid you heads together to take away our negros, or least to free them to . . ." Clearly written by a Federalist, the letter signed MASSA SAMMY ended with a play on the newspaper's name. "But in the first place, and as an omen of the evils which are to follow the propagation of such erronious [*sic*] principles, your MIRROR, which has already received a flight shock, may possibly be broken to pieces if you countenance such bad practices." Hunter and Beaumont could not let this moment go by and inserted a footnote to MASSA SAMMY's letter. *"To shew VICE, her own image, VIRTUE her own likeness, are the inherent qualities of a true mirror: but a little anger from the Deformed Lady, a seeing the reflection of her resemblance, is a thing naturally expected, nor is it to be wondered at, if she even throws dirt at the glass; but it does not adhere long to polished surfaces—The Mirror will always recoil from the burnish of Truth."*

This spirited back and forth between supporters and opponents of slavery continued up to a few weeks after the May 3rd election. While *The Mirror* displayed a strong pro-emancipation bias, the electorate thought otherwise and sent fifty-seven slave-owning delegates out of a total of fifty-eight delegates to the Frankfort Constitutional Convention. Almost half of the delegates owned ten or more enslaved people. As the deck was stacked against emancipation, the summer's convention would keep the 1792 constitutional protections for slavery. The new constitution went even further by statutorily disenfranchising "Indians, Negros and Mulattos," adding to the people of color's distress. After a promising start, the slave owners prevailed and dealt a complete and bitter defeat for the opponents of slavery.

Although anti-climactic with respect to emancipation, the constitutional convention commenced on July 22 to consider other important governance questions. Delegates elected Alexander S. Bullitt, one of the first constitution drafters, to preside over the convention. Bullitt owned a prosperous plantation near Louisville using enslaved labor. As he did for the first constitution, future United States Supreme Court, Justice Thomas Todd served as clerk. John Breckenridge, the legislator who introduced the Kentucky Resolutions, provided the intellectual and political leadership to the conservative convention without a formal position.[38] *The Mirror* did not cover the almost month-long convention proceedings extensively, only reprinting one set of interim resolutions adopted early in the deliberations. The interim resolutions provided for a Lieutenant Governor and direct voter election of the Governor, Lieutenant Governor, and State Senators. The draft resolutions were silent on the slavery provisions in the new constitution. Given the pre-convention anxiety over emancipation, the Convention delegates produced a broadside announcing the re-adoption of the 1792 Articles establishing slavery before the new constitution's completion.

After the convention's conclusion, *The Mirror* printed a final set of constitutional resolutions, relegated to page three. In these final resolutions, the constitutional convention proceedings included no mention of slavery; only that "Article VII was adopted." The lack of discourse signaled a complete failure for the anti-slavery faction. As the editors had prognosticated, the "die had been cast" by the selection of convention delegates. Only the delegate from Harden County, Patrick Brown, a former slave owner, advocated for emancipation. With slavery firmly embedded in the new Kentucky Constitution, the editors dropped coverage of abolition and slavery issues. The editors returned to reporting on the political disputes between the Federalists and the Democratic-Republicans.

Despite *The Mirror*'s admirable editorial policy advocating emancipation and racial equality, Hunter and Beaumont engaged in actions that are hypocritical in today's society but prevailing comportment in eighteenth-century Kentucky. Both partners leased enslaved men and boys' services to staff their printing office cheaply and regularly received revenues from ads for the return of runaway slaves. Hunter's friend, Harry Toulmin, first arrived in Kentucky advocating for the complete and immediate abolition of slavery. Like Hunter's eventual ownership of slaves, Toulmin later compromised his ethics by owning a cotton plantation in Alabama that enslaved people. Such were the moral inconsistencies that characterized the region and the period. In many cases, even the most strident proponents of Enlightenment ideals held views that egregiously conflicted with their actions condoning racial injustice.

On a lighter, personal note, the partners continued their practices in Pennsylvania of advertising for their lost items or stolen possessions. Examples of the editors' personal ads include Hunter dropping a pocketbook while traveling by horseback and Beaumont mislaid or had stolen farm items, including a dung fork, two stray cows, and a missing horse. While these items seem insignificant, they were necessary as the partner's financial situation became progressively stressed, requiring raising cash by all means.

The Mirror's circulation exceeded five hundred subscribers, a large subscription list for a frontier paper.[39] With rising readership and increasing advertisements, the partners should have enjoyed a financially successful enterprise. However seemingly prosperous, Hunter and Beaumont experienced the same pervasive financial problems as many eighteenth-century newspaper owners. The printers committed large sums of capital for purchasing paper, ink, and equipment in advance. Also, upfront, they paid wages for printing and distributing newspapers to a widely dispersed subscriber base. However, customers signed a promissory agreement to initiate subscriptions, which called for the first payment after six months of service. Further damaging the partners' cash flow, subscribers often failed to pay the subscription fees when due. The partners issued numerous strident pleas for payment from delinquent subscribers and advertisers. In addition to normal reminders that subscription fees were due every six months, the partners added special requests for payment. For example, the partners reminded readers that it would be convenient to pay for their subscriptions when they came to town to vote. To foster payment in a cash-poor economy, the partners proposed that "we are ready to receive the following articles at cash prices, well cured bacon, flour, Indian meal, corn, tallow, sugar and country linen."[40] Using all efforts to raise money, the partners offered books for auction as well as cows and calves for sale to supplement their incomes.

After one hundred and nineteen issues, the partners decided to consolidate their printing business in Frankfort and discontinue publishing the financially marginal *The Mirror*. After the December 19, 1799, final issue, Hunter and Beaumont sold *The Mirror*'s entire shop, including the printing press and all printing materials, to Francis Taylor.[41] A clerk of the district state court of Mason County, it is not known what Taylor did with the print shop, but he did not start a competitive paper.

CHAPTER TEN

Government Printers

As two recent English immigrants, Hunter and Beaumont entered the vastly different and personally challenging social, economic, and political environment of Frankfort, Kentucky. After the Revolutionary War, thousands of veterans migrated to Kentucky seeking land and fortunes. War veterans dominated not only the state's civic, business, and political leadership but that of Frankfort and the surrounding Franklin County.[1] Several decades of fighting generated a marshal military spirit among the male citizens who relished victories over the British Empire and the extermination and removal of Native Americans from Kentucky. Both men and women exhibited an intense hostility towards Native Americans and slightly less hatred of the British. More than one-half of the area's families owned enslaved people, firmly ensconcing the institution of slavery throughout Kentucky. Upon the partners' arrival, few churches and organized religious institutions existed. Contrary to several other states, Kentucky's constitution did not authorize a state-established religion. Instead, supporting a more egalitarian view of their fellow Euro-American citizens, Kentuckians recognized fewer class distinctions with more mixing of people with different economic means.

Although less prosperous than the Blue Grass region, Frankfort residents, similar to all Kentuckians, sold their surplus of agricultural and manufactured goods on the world markets. Frankfort residents even constructed ocean-going ships to transport goods from Frankfort directly to foreign markets. Kentucky's citizens supported Federal tariffs to reduce competition from foreign manufacturing but, first and foremost, sought free and unfettered international access for their agricultural products.

Kentuckians thirsted for global news to stay abreast of developments that impacted their manufacturing and agricultural goods supply and demand. As a result, the partners printed all news associated with keeping the vital connection along the Mississippi River open to navigation and free trade.

While not Kentucky's business center, as the capital, Frankfort provided the partners a firsthand view of the state's political debates. Kentucky's political environment featured several unique practices and events. As contrasted with the New England town meeting, Kentuckians conducted countywide, mass public gatherings in open fields to debate and offer position papers on serious political issues. Broad white male suffrage gave gravitas to the large assemblies. As distinct from the eastern states North versus South split, Kentuckians strongly advocated for the commercial interests of westerners and supported increasing the number of western states. In general, they believed that Federal power should be limited in favor of state laws. Although there were a few western Federalists, the predominance of the populous supported Thomas Jefferson and the Democratic-Republicans. As former Englishmen who did not serve in the American Army or fight Indians, Hunter and Beaumont's backgrounds could raise suspicions from time to time. However, their fervent republican political beliefs, outgoing personalities, and journalistic skills helped them assimilate into the community.

On August 9, 1798, the partners commenced publishing *The Palladium*, which an observer declared "a newspaper of some importance in the state capital."[2] The masthead prominently boasted an ambitious dual purpose, "A Literary and Political Weekly Repository." Similar to *The Mirror*, *The Palladium* consisted of a single sheet of paper printed on both sides and folded to create a four-page newspaper. In a change to the layout of *The Mirror*, the partners prominently printed their names on the masthead. Unlike *The Mirror*, the partners omitted the subscription rate from the masthead nor any other place in *The Palladium*. Initially, a subscription costs three dollars per year. Learning from their experiences with *The Mirror*, the partners' demanded advance payment with half paid at the time of subscription and the remainder in six months. Ads in the size of a column square cost one dollar for three insertions and twenty-five cents for each subsequent insertion. Later, the printers lowered the subscription price to two dollars and included the price in the redesigned masthead. To increase the number of subscribers and advertisers, the partners hired Isaac Collett to deliver *The Palladium* to Shelbyville and Middletown, twenty and forty miles west of Frankfort, respectively. Out-of-town subscribers paid an extra fifty cents to support the cost of the post rider. Often, Collett had trouble

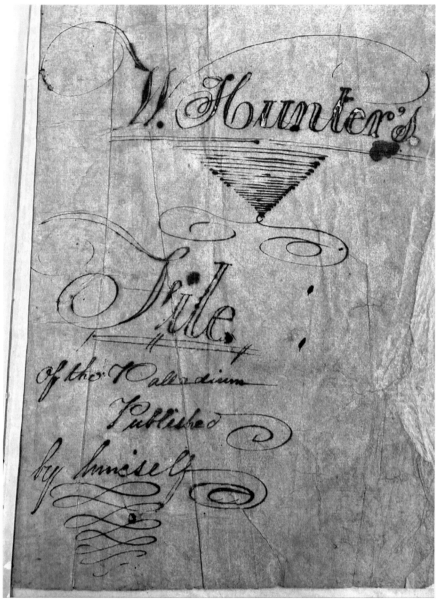

FIGURE 4. *First page of William Hunter's personal bound copy of the* Palladium *newspaper file, University of Chicago Library.*

collecting this supplement and advertised the need for subscribers to pay for his services. Further expanding *The Palladium's* weekly reach, copies were available post-paid at regional post offices with postmasters handling payments.

Later the partners completely redesigned the paper's masthead. They inserted a bold, new motto, "Let it be impressed upon your minds, let it be instilled into your children, that the Liberty of the Press is the Palladium of all the Civil, Political, and Religious Rights of Freemen." Hunter gleaned this quote from the introductory dedication chapter of a book containing a compendium of well-known British letters initially printed under the pseudonym Junius. The highly politically charged opposition letters appeared as a series of articles in the *London Public Advertiser* from 1769 to 1772. To make it applicable to the United States, Hunter and Beaumont substituted "Freemen" for "Englishmen" as the last word of the quote. In another interesting connection, Junius goes on to "chasten from licentiousness" the liberty of the press, which harkens back to the motto of their first newspaper, *The Western Telegraphe*.[3] During his formative days in England, Hunter became familiar with the *Letters of Junius*, given the writer's similar republican leanings and support for French revolutionary doctrine. Junius as a pen name is thought to evoke the image of Lucius Junius Brutus, who led the overthrow of the Roman dictatorship to re-establish the Roman Republic. Unknown at the time, twentieth-century linguistic investigators linked the Junius pseudonym to Sir Philip Francis (22 October 1740—23 December 1818). An Irish-born British Whig politician, Francis served as a clerk in the foreign and war offices, a member of parliament for almost twenty years, and a pamphleteer who was highly critical of King George III and the British monarchy as a governmental system.[4]

Focusing on governmental affairs, *The Palladium* became the go-to source for politically aware citizens to follow partisan debates and other political developments. "The satisfaction which a number of our subscribers have expressed at the attention we have paid to the business of the Legislature (a subject scarcely noticed before by any other print) is particularly grateful to our feelings."[5] Receiving positive feedback and giving a knock to their competitors reinforced the partners' editorial policy of extensively covering governmental activities. While readership interest in *The Palladium*'s coverage of the Kentucky legislative activities heightened, advertising revenues grew slowly, presenting a vexing financial concern for the partners. After almost three months of printing *The Palladium*, there were only one-third the number of paying ads as in *The Mirror*.[6]

Exacerbating the weak advertising revenues, the partners bungled the initial subscription process and had to appeal to readers for help. "Subscription papers for the publication of *The Palladium* having been scattered through the country in such a manner as to render it impossible to ascertain in whose hands they have fallen, the Editors entreat those Gentlemen who have them in possession to forward them to the Office as speedily as possible."[7] The partners moved quickly to rectify the distribution problems by appointing individuals to authorize subscriptions and collect associated fees. John McGaghey performed these services in Shelbyville and Major James Leon, and Captain John Hunter in Georgetown.[8] In addition to named contacts, the editors arranged for all state postmasters to accept subscriptions and receive payments. Having dedicated distribution and points of contact in surrounding counties alleviated advertiser pressure for wider distribution. However, even with well-known points of contact, maintaining subscription lists and collecting fees from remote subscribers would continue to vex the partners and place a considerable drag on profitability.

As a result of prevalent non-payment of subscription fees, the financial viability of eighteenth-century newspapers and printers heavily rested on receiving stable revenues from lucrative government contracts. State and Federal governments outsourced the publishing of newly enacted laws, legislative debates, and legal notices to private printers. John Bradford held the Kentucky state printing contract for most of the commonwealth's history. As the state's first printer and newspaper publisher, Bradford possessed prodigious reputational and economic advantages over newcomers. He printed two newspapers, operated larger production facilities, and enjoyed a solid, state-wide standing. However, Bradford continued an assiduously impartial editorial policy in an increasingly polarized political environment. Even though Bradford's personal views were decidedly Republican, this lack of an unambiguous editorial policy created an opening for Hunter and Beaumont. Hunter and Beaumont began issuing one-page, high-profile broadsides for Frankfort residents and politicians to demonstrate their capabilities. For example, on November 10, 1798, the partners published the "Kentucky Resolutions adopted in General Assembly" in broadside form.[9] These broadsides demonstrated the partner's printing abilities and their proven support for the prevailing political sentiments of the Kentucky governor and legislature.

The partners ardent Republican editorial policies provided a more attractive mouthpiece for the increasingly Republican-dominated legislature. The opposition Federalist faction did not share a positive view of Hunter's and Beaumont's editorial perspectives. The leading Federalist and one of Kentucky's Senators, Humphrey Marshall, derisively referred to *The Palladium* as a "so called" paper.[10] At the beginning of each annual session, the general assembly elected its officers and made several appointments, including a state printer. During the early years, the legislative selection represented a pro forma vote with John Bradford, first, as the only Kentucky printer and later, the most established printer in the state. This year, the partners' political allies forced the legislature to accept competing proposals from the Bradford family and the team of Hunter and Beaumont. On Thursday, December 6, 1798, William Hunter and William H. Beaumont were elected printers to the Commonwealth on the narrowest margins. A joint vote of the House of Representatives and the Senate favored the partners by the razor-thin margin of 34 to 32. The Bradford's suffered a bitter defeat as the father had been elected state printer for all but one year of Kentucky's statehood.[11] Falling back on a large subscriber base, Bradford continued to operate the *Kentucky Gazette* in Lexington while scaling back expectations for his much smaller Frankfort paper.

The state printer assignment provided a meaningful boost in economic viability for the partners' newspapers and printing businesses. Each year the legislator required the public printer to publish and print three separate volumes; Acts of the Legislature, Journal of the Senate, and Journal of the House. In addition, the legislature regularly placed orders with the state's printer for the production of bills in process, broadsides, and pamphlets. These government contracts increased in the winter months after the annual legislative session adjourned in late January or early February. As a public printer, *The Palladium* became an official outlet for public notices, court orders, and notices of legal proceedings. While other papers in the state were authorized to publish the notices, Hunter's location in the capital city and nearness to the courthouse allowed him to solicit and engender many new printing assignments. In addition, the state printer enjoyed the perk of a dedicated office within the capitol building, located next to the state auditor's office. Hunter took advantage of "walking the halls of power to develop deep personal relationships with the commonwealth's politicians. These relationships helped lobby for special printing projects and protected his continuing role as the state printer.

While the state printing contract shored up *The Palladium*'s finances, Beaumont sank deeply into debt. Correspondents ascribed his financial difficulties to the economic demands of a large family. However, other unknown factors contributed to Beaumont's financial distress. To help satisfy creditors, Hunter purchased Beaumont's share of the printing partnership. Beaumont remained in the Washington, Kentucky area to "institute an academy on a different plan from the generality of schools in the state."[12] The academy never reached high levels of success and eventually faded from the scene. Although there would be inklings of Beaumont's desire to return to the printing business, the association with Hunter would be his last publishing venture.

With the dissolution of the partnership with Beaumont, *The Palladium*'s editorial slant continued tilting towards Kentucky's mainstream Democratic-Republican politics and was supportive of President Thomas Jefferson's administration. Hunter's partisan reputation expanded beyond the boundaries of Kentucky into nearby states catching the attention of the Democratic-Republican party's national leader. To better understand the political winds in Kentucky and the western states, Thomas Jefferson purchased a paid subscription to *The Palladium*. True to Jefferson's lifelong penchant for borrowing, he paid two dollars and fifty cents in arrears for an annual subscription which costs two dollars when paid in advance.[13] In addition, *The Palladium*'s prominence with national Republican leaders brought Federal government printing contracts. While not nearly as lucrative as the Kentucky government contracts, Congress passed a law that new Federal acts were to be published in two papers in each state. Secretary of State James Madison selected *The Palladium* and the *Kentucky Gazette* as the two Kentucky newspapers. However, prestigious this selection, the annual payments from the Federal government amounted to less than one hundred dollars per year.[14] While small, the certainty of collecting outstanding amounts critically aided printing businesses that provided services in advance and experienced problems collecting in arrears. Further, Hunter could headline "By Authority" above the newly enacted laws, conferring a lustrously reliable aura.

Another benefit of his election to state public printer is that court clerks were authorized to post notices in Hunter's newspaper to record public legal actions required by state statute. Local, state, and Federal jurisdictions mandated public notices to be published up to twelve weeks in a row. As Frankfort housed a United States Federal District Court and the Kentucky Court of Appeals, the number of Orders of the Court ballooned and, in some editions, wholly covered the last paper of the paper (page 4). In addition to specific lawsuits, the clerks regularly published lists of lands owned by non-residents who were delinquent on their property taxes. After a notification period, the county sheriff sold these lands by auction under court supervision to recover the unpaid taxes. In addition to unpaid state taxes, the Federal government required an annual listing of Federal direct property taxes and associated land values to be published. These listings usually covered the entire first and most of the paper's last pages for several weeks.

Another class of legally required notices drove additional revenue opportunities for Hunter. Commonly, Blue Grass landowners discovered unclaimed horses which had strayed on their property. Kentucky enacted strict laws which governed the disposition of these roaming horses. State law required finders of a stray horse first to obtain an independent appraisal of the horse's value. Within two months of appraisal, the new caregiver must place an ad in a designated newspaper which included both *The Mirror* (until its demise) and *The Palladium*, as well as several competitive papers. The law required advertising a fulsome description of the horse and the finder's place of residence for three consecutive weeks. The previous owner could prove ownership during the advertisement period and claim the horse after paying expenses. Hunter received the legally mandated rate of two shillings (approximately 26 cents) for the first insertion and then one shilling after that as recompense. The stray horse statutory rate yielded roughly one-half of Hunter's standard advertising rates but had the significant benefit of requiring immediate cash payment. Demonstrating the importance of chattel slavery, another category of legally mandated paid advertising included a public notification associated with runaway enslaved people. Upon incarceration of a runaway, the county sheriff advertised the legally mandated three months to allow the owner to come forward to claim and pay expenses. During the first decade of the eighteenth-century, more advertisements appeared for stray horses than runaway enslaved people.

While not legally required, subscribers also placed various ads in *The Palladium* to limit their liabilities and protect their financial interests. Often, women preferred to leave their homes and husbands rather than go through complex, one-sided divorce proceedings. To warn others that they would not be legally responsible for any future debts of an estranged wife, men regularly placed ads in the paper to announce their separation. Occasionally, wives also placed ads disputing the facts provided by their husbands. In one example, Mary Harbold responded by ad to her husband's ad warning others not to give credit to her. With a firm resolve and a hint of sarcasm, she stated, ". . . a man who is destitute of principle and honour, not to provide for his family, but is rambling about in this country from one place to another, will not have so much credit that I could get the value of a single cent upon his account."[15] Owners of escaped enslaved people and apprentice masters also placed ads to either recovery their "property" or to disclaim financial responsibility. If an owner or master wanted the escapee back, a reward of ten to fifty dollars enticed their capture and return. However, if a one-cent or other de minimis reward amount appeared in the ad, the master did not desire a return of his "property." The advertisement served to absolve the owner of any future debts incurred by the runaway.

In addition to the profitable government printing contracts and public notices, Hunter eagerly sought to exploit the printing opportunities emanating from the expanding commercial and financial opportunities in Frankfort and throughout Kentucky. Hunter boasted, "No paper in the state is better calculated to serve them than *The Palladium*. It circulates extensively through every county in the state where the mail passes, and is sent to printers in all the principal towns of the Union."[16] Frankfort's location on the navigable Kentucky River and at the edge of an agriculturally productive region spawned manufacturing industries and new potential advertisers. The four-hundred-foot-wide river provided power for various water-powered mills to grind locally produced flour and spin hemp into yarn. One mile above the city, a large rope walk wove locally grown hemp into ropes. Numerous flour mills sprung up on tributaries with sufficient drop and water flow. Several large warehouses received tobacco, hemp, and flour for transshipment down the Kentucky River to the Ohio River within the city limits. State-sponsored navigational improvements and locks supported cheap transportation of goods to eastern and western markets. Further supporting local commerce, a bridge commission started in 1799 to span the Kentucky river connecting its northern and southern banks. While Lexington represented the largest commercial center of the state, Frankfort offered Hunter a growing, prosperous commercial environment to support his newspaper and printing businesses.

Further committing to Frankfort, Hunter placed his Washington home and out lots on the market for sale, signaling that publication of *The Mirror* would not be resumed. Selling the Washington property proved not to be easy. Hunter continued to periodically offer its sale for at least five subsequent years. Desperate, Hunter advertised, "I will give a liberal credit for the greater part of the purchase money or take in payment tobacco, flour, hemp . . ." Demonstrating his eagerness to sell and move on, he even offered to trade the property for making and laying a quantity of bricks. All around, his Washington experiences were not profitable, demonstrating the commercial benefits of the move to Frankfort.[17]

Before coming to Frankfort, Ann gave birth to at least two children. To house a growing family, Hunter purchased a home in the city center and an eight-acre out lot for food production and for grazing his horse. In 1802, Dr. Isaac E. Gano inoculated, along with several other residents, Hunter's two children to prevent smallpox.[18] Unlike the Suttonian method that William endured, Dr. Gano employed the newly discovered technique of using the safer cowpox virus for inoculation. Whether successful or not, these two children disappear from the historical record. All too common, Kentucky couples lost newborn and young children to illness and accident. Unfortunately, William and Ann Hunter did not escape this horrible reality of eighteenth-century life. Despite these setbacks, Ann continued to work in the printing business and bear children with enslaved servants performing cooking duties and household chores. Town tax and census records reveal that two or more enslaved persons lived with the Hunters. Hunter could have either owned or, more likely, rented the enslaved people. Increasingly common, about five to ten percent of enslaved people were rented out by owners as the agricultural demand for labor declined in the first decade of the nineteenth century in Kentucky. In addition to household slaves, Hunter employed enslaved people in his printing establishment. The use of slave labor reduced his costs and allowed him to fluctuate the number of workers based on the availability of apprentices and the demand for printing. In several instances, when demand decreased, Hunter advertised the sale of enslaved workers.

While continuing to benefit from the work of enslaved people, Hunter published articles deploring the purchase and sale of people. Since American independence, the Barbary Coast states had captured American merchant ships and sold sailors into captivity. Upon becoming President, Thomas Jefferson ended the practice of paying tribute and sought the enslaved white captives' return through military force. Hunter ran an article decrying the duplicity of the American outrage. "What a great uproar was made about the 300 Americans retained in Tripoli" versus the "no less than *two thousand and fifty-eight* HUMAN BEINGS torn from their country and everything they held dear. Exposed to sale in the public market of a chief city [Charleston, South Carolina] in one of the FREE *republics* in America" on a single day. Further, American slavery proponents were likened to the alleged cruelty of the Tripoli bashaw (pasha). Presciently concluding, "How unfortunate that this stain should be suffered to remain upon the character of our nation! The day will perhaps speedily arrive, when, instead of being stained, we shall be robed with blood, for this infernal traffic." Unsaid was the hypocrisy of using enslaved labor to print this article.[19]

Even with the added security of state and Federal printing contracts and employing enslaved labor, aggressive competitors continued to threaten Hunter's printing enterprise. On December 11, 1801, James M. Bradford assumed sole responsibility from his father for the Frankfort *Guardian of Freedom*. Operating at the corner of Montgomery and St. Clair Streets in the heart of Frankfort, Bradford engaged in fierce competition for readership, advertisers, and, most importantly, the support of Kentucky legislators and politicians. He lowered his paper's price below that of *The Palladium* to one dollar and fifty cents paid in advance, two dollars if paid in produce, and two dollars if paid with a cash note payable after one year. For ads of equal length and width, the Guardian's owner set a going rate of one dollar for an insertion printed three times and twenty-five cents for each subsequent insertion. Bradford and his father continued to publish several new books each year. Genres included religious, literary, political volumes. The father-son partnership published several legal volumes which directly competed with those published by Hunter. While intensely commercially competitive, Bradford eagerly sought the state public printer's appointment during the annual appointment process. However, a legislative selection remained elusive as Bradford never received more than a third of the total votes. In frustration, he sold the *Guardian of Freedom* to Elijah Conway (typically written E. C.) Berry in 1804 and moved to New Orleans. After failing to land a government job as secretary of the Territory of Louisiana, he started a newspaper *Orleans Gazette* in 1804.[20] With the departure of Bradford and the security of government contracts, Hunter's printing business thrived. In 1804, he upgraded his printing press, purchased a new long primer print type, and added a journeyman printer to be well paid at "Philadelphia prices." Confidently, he sold his old printing equipment regardless if it fostered new competition.[21]

As government printing volumes increased, Hunter narrowed the focus of his book publishing business. He published his last almanac and school textbook, the *Kentucky Primer*, in 1800. His future imprints consisted of legal and political monographs with only a few exceptions. A publishing partnership with Kentucky Secretary of State Harry Toulmin anchored this new market niche. Consistent with the experiences of innovative entrepreneurs, the publishing duo's first undertaking did not pan out. Toulmin advertised in *The Mirror* and *The Palladium* for over two months to sell by subscription a report of the debates and proceedings in the 1799 State Constitutional Convention. Planned to be published in small type, Toulmin offered the convention debate transcripts at nine shillings ($1.17) or three shillings ($0.39) per one-hundred pages. As the convention turned out to be less controversial and less groundbreaking than anticipated, a sufficient number of subscribers did not come forward, and the proposed volume never went to press.

Continuing to partner, Hunter printed three legal books compiled by Secretary Toulmin. Hunter and Toulmin first published a much-needed codification of the Kentucky statutory acts currently in force. The second and third books unraveled the complex criminal law statutes. A prominently placed page-one ad in *The Palladium* boasted that the law books enjoyed a wide audience with only a few copies remaining.[22] The prolific publishing partnership ended at the expiration of Toulmin's Secretary of State appointment in 1804. Toulmin received a strong recommendation of "a gentleman of talents and integrity" and 'acknowledged abilities in the knowledge of Laws" from Governor James Garrard. President Thomas Jefferson appointed Toulmin a Mississippi Territorial judge.[23] Before moving, Hunter printed Toulmin's most significant and long-lasting volume, *The American Public Prosecutor's Assistant.* Toulmin's scholarship served as a popular and enduring template for a new genre of legal volumes aimed at assisting prosecutors and judges carry out their responsibilities. Hunter did not have the reputation or distribution channels to capitalize on the guidebook's widespread demand, and the opportunity passed on to other publishers for successor editions. Subsequently, prominent publishers such as Matthew Carey printed and distributed this widely acclaimed work. For his work codifying laws in Kentucky and later in Alabama, historians have promoted Toulmin as the "frontier Justinian."[24] Even though separated by thousands of miles, Hunter's and Toulmin's personal lives would unusually intersect in the future.

Succeeding Toulmin in the Kentucky legal space, Hunter partnered with an eccentric practicing attorney but talented independent legal scholar William Littell to publish a series of updated statute law books as well as other scholarly legal books. Since its separation from Virginia, Kentucky's statutes evolved piecemeal. Moving to Frankfort in May 1805, Littell developed an overarching structure organizing the controlling statutes, expertly cross-referenced and supported by a comprehensive index. The complete eleven-hundred-page edition in two large octavo volumes sold for eight dollars, a handsome sum indicating its high value to the legal profession. The Littell and Hunter publishing relationship produced the most successful books printed by Hunter and served as a steady income source during many lean times.

In addition to publishing and printing, Hunter assisted in Frankfort's commercial development and corrected predatory undeveloped land speculation. Revolutionary War veterans' overlapping and disputed land grants, as well as rapacious speculators, plagued Kentucky real estate markets. Hunter stated, "To such an extent, the hateful spirit of inordinate speculation . . . had corrupted the fountains of legislation and the courts of justice, as well as the body politic."[25] Along with other town leaders, Hunter served as a trustee to establish clear titles for the war veterans to make the lands salable. Once legally established with confirmed titles, the trustees advertised the lands for sale. Hunter, along with other prominent members of the Frankfort community, served as a reference for Achilles Sneed, who brokered payments from out-of-state landowners to pay their Kentucky real estate taxes.[26] Lastly, as an adjunct to his businesses, Hunter acted as a real estate agent to sell developed property and town lots for others. Hunter gained valuable knowledge of Kentucky real estate markets by selling both developed and undeveloped lands, which would become an important investment for him later in life.[27] Hunter sat on a committee to develop a reliable and plentiful water supply for Frankfort on a volunteer basis. The committee planned to tap a spring outside of town, pipe the water into a series of reservoirs, and distribute water to various parts of town. The committee provided oversight to the construction contractor.[28] These economic development activities fostered personal relationships with community leaders, politicians, and business owners.

Hunter's family life also began to flourish. Ann and William were blessed with three children in rapid succession, Lavinia (1803), William Morrison (1804), and Louisa Mary Ann (1807). All three children lived into their adult years. Although there are no tutor ads in *The Palladium*, William highly valued education and most certainly provided educational opportunities to all three children. Also, Hunter's household expanded with the addition of new apprentices. Customarily, apprentices received room and board in their master's household. While living together could create strong personal relationships, industrious apprentices could become threatening competitors with inside knowledge. Two Hunter-trained apprentices who became locally prominent were E. C. Berry and George Washington Pleasants (also many times abbreviated and first apprenticed at age 16). Entering the market, Berry bought out James M. Bradford's ownership and published the Guardian of Freedom for a brief period.[29] Subsequently, both Berry and Pleasants worked as journeymen for competing Frankfort papers.

Hunter fended off competitors by reminding readers of his resolute and courageous service. In an editorial, Hunter promised to "be found at his post . . . a faithful Centinel [*sic*] to warn his fellow citizens of the approach of danger, either from foreign or domestic foes."[30] Fulfilling Hunter's promise, a steady stream of national and international events critical to Kentuckians and their economic fortunes filled *The Palladium's* pages. Hunter issued an extra edition announcing that American negotiators had completed an agreement to purchase Louisiana from Napoleon's French government. As a result, farmers and traders would enjoy secure and unfettered access to New Orleans and international markets for the first time. Kentuckians greeted the news with joy and celebrations. Many Kentuckians felt betrayed by Federalists' *Jay Treaty* and the Easterners' disinterest in Mississippi navigation and export rights. With the

Louisiana Purchase, Kentuckians now believed that the Federal government served their interests. While always high, support for Jefferson strengthened, and the small Kentucky Federalist party further diminished in stature and followers. The massive trans-Mississippi River land purchase ended any talk of succession from the union and alliances with France or Spain. However, past dalliances by prominent Kentucky politicians with Spanish officials would become major imbroglios fomented by the Federalist factions. Further, Hunter would have to address rumors that he harbored secret support for the British given his family background. Attempting to dismiss the innuendos on the pages of *The Palladium*, Hunter stated, "But, sensible that the public will form their judgment from a view of his labours, and not from the knowledge of the country he came from, he has never thought it necessary or expedient to refute, or even notice the whispers of Prejudice on this point."[31]

The unexpected appearance in Frankfort of two eastern travelers dredged up sensational allegations of a long-forgotten 1790s conspiracy by leading Kentucky politicians to create a separate county allied with Spain. The ensuing sensational newspaper expose would roil Kentucky and national politics and challenge William Hunter's reputation and livelihood. In 1805, John Wood and Joseph Montfort Street arrived in Frankfort, purportedly a short rest stop while on a mission to locate land to purchase for an eastern investment consortium. A recent émigré from Scotland, Wood initially tutored Vice President Aaron Burr's daughter in New York and penned articles as a radical Republican writer for hire. Wood learned of Burr's penchant for intrigue and quest to regain political power after dueling with Alexander Hamilton in these roles. Moving to Richmond, Virginia, and switching political allegiances, Wood gained a modicum of newspaper experience working for the Federalist-leaning *Virginia Gazette and General Advertiser*. Also, while in Richmond, the city government appointed Wood its official surveyor, giving him *bona fide* skills to serve the local consortium seeking western lands. The younger Street, who grew up in a nearby rural area, met Wood in Richmond while working as a counting-house clerk. Street and Wood developed a close personal relationship and decided to venture west together.

Stopping at the Kentucky capital, the duo learned the nuances of western state politics, found gainful employment, and unexpectedly abandoned their western land purchase plans. The older Wood painted portraits for wealthy patrons and taught at a nearby academy. The twenty-two-year-old Street served as an assistant clerk at the Federal court and in the state auditor's office in Frankfort. In these roles, Wood and Street interacted with Kentucky's political elite. Leveraging his *Virginia Gazette* credentials, Wood developed connections with leading Kentucky Federalists, including Humphrey Marshall and United States District Attorney James Hamilton Daveiss. Wood combined his knowledge of Aaron Burr's western plans to cleave off the west into an independent country with what he learned about Kentuckians'1790s negotiations with Spanish authorities to construct a blockbuster news story.

The partners commenced publishing Frankfort's second newspaper, *The Western World*, to gain maximum publicity and monetize their treasonous assertions. Since the demise of *The Guardian of Freedom* a year earlier, *The Palladium* faced no local competition. In their inaugural issue, Wood and Street claimed that they operated an "independent" paper "disclaiming all party principles, rigidly pursue the path of truth regardless of the anathemas of political maniacs or the extorted denunciations of the servile followers of faction."[32] However, rumors swirled that Federalist Humphrey Marshall and James Hamilton Daveiss funded the paper's startup operating costs.[33] As Wood and Street had little capital to purchase a printing press and type, Hunter agreed to print the *Western World* for the partners to aid a speedy entry into the Frankfort market. Later, Wood declared that he and Street contributed fifty dollars each to start the paper with an agreement to divide the profits equally.[34] Motivated to accept the new printing assignment to improve his print shop's profitability, the eager Hunter underestimated the new paper's competitive potential. This misjudgment would lead to dangerous competitors and place Hunter's reputation for political reliability among the state's political leaders at risk.

On July 7, 1806, Wood and Street published their first edition, and instantly, the inaugural issue created a political firestorm locally and, soon after that, nationally. The lead article entitled "The Kentucky Spanish Association, Blount's Conspiracy, and General Miranda's Expedition" implicated Kentucky's leading politicians in a plot with Spain to separate the commonwealth from the United States. Purportedly led by James Wilkerson, founder of Frankfort and current commander-in-chief of the US Army, Wood and Street alleged that high profile Kentucky leaders including Federal District Court Judge Harry Innes, Kentucky Court of Appeals Justice Benjamin Sebastian, and US Attorney General John Breckenridge, and United States Senator John Brown plotted with Spanish authorities to remove Kentucky from the Union during the 1790s. Two weeks later, the Western World editors singled out the highly respected Sen. John Brown for leading the Spanish negotiations and asserted his "dark and traitorous conspiracy rivaled Benedict Arnold's.[35] This group's alleged treachery even extended to conspiring with a visiting South

American revolutionary, Francisco de Miranda, who never set foot in Frankfort or Kentucky.

With just enough facts to be plausible, the alleged conspiracy exploded into a statewide and national sensation over the next several weeks. Lingering from the 1790s and adding to the intrigue, many Kentuckians believed that the Federal government did not represent their interests, which added credibility to the allegations. While the purported treasonous activities with Spanish officials occurred over ten years ago, disclosure that such prominent politicians had entertained disunion discussions with a foreign power created a stain on the participants' reputations and a threat to their current political offices. The few but vocal Federalist leaders in Kentucky used the treasonous allegations to vociferously attack Kentucky's current state and Federal Republican leadership. Republican politicians not specified in the Spanish plot distanced themselves from the named conspirators, creating disunity for the first time in the Republican political environment.

The burgeoning scandal created dangerous risks for William Hunter and his publishing business. Wood and Street opined in their first issue, "Had he [Hunter] been raised in France instead of England, I should conclude he had been in the habit of disclosing his crimes to a Father Confessor, who on his departure was accustomed to say go my son and sin again." Further mocking Hunter, the new editors refer to Hunter as "Billy Lampblack," who labors to deceive the people.[36] Street and Wood firmly conflated Hunter with the traitorous Kentuckians a few weeks later, "Mr. Hunter and his political friends may be reduced to the Spanish Associates."[37] Although discerning friends knew he merely printed *The Western World* for its editors, Hunter quickly distanced himself from *The Western World*, sensing personal risk. In *The Palladium's* next edition, Hunter unequivocally emphasized that he had no editorial voice in *The Western World's* content. However, news of the purported Spanish Conspiracy was too big for Hunter to ignore. Mounting subscriber demand forced Hunter to reprint Wood's and Street's articles in the *Palladium*. In successive weeks, Wood and Street published additional articles stoking the controversy. New revelations continued throughout the summer and into the late fall. *The Western World's* subscriber base grew to a prodigious twelve hundred, providing a welcome revenue spike for Hunter's print shop. While Hunter financially benefited from sales of *The Western World* newspaper, Wood and Street bragged that Hunter's paper only attracted seven hundred and fifty subscribers.[38] While Hunter made money from each copy of *The Western World*, the editors paid for every issue to be printed and only received cash when readers paid for their subscriptions. As a result, *The Western World* editors set their subscription rate at three dollars per year, one dollar higher than the cost of *The Palladium*.[39] In the fall, Wood and Street procured their own printing press, advertised for an apprentice, and began self-printing starting with their twenty-first issue.

Too large a public outcry to ignore, Kentucky's leading Republican politicians responded to the treasonous conduct allegations. Hurriedly, the alleged conspirators wrote letters to state and national leaders and spoke with colleagues, friends, and family to disavow any separatist plot. To document just what happened (at least from the Kentuckian's point of view), William Littell drafted a full-length history of the early stages of political development to create the state of Kentucky, *Political Transactions in and Concerning Kentucky from the First Settlement Thereof Until It Became an Independent State in July 1792*. Hunter published Littell's title for a fee, which became highly sought after by Kentucky leaders to explain their past behavior and prove their innocence.

Using his editorial pen to aid Kentucky political leadership, Hunter mounted his counter-attack in the pages of *The Palladium* seeking to discredit both the allegations as well as to impinge the reputations and motives of Wood and Street. On September 11, 1806, Hunter published a warning to Wood and Street, "The citizens of Frankfort perceive that they have been cherishing a viper, and that you have been merited with contempt."[40] Under a pseudonym, he printed an implausible tale describing Wood as a British spy in France. When French authorities caught Wood, he turned coat and then, when freed, resumed being a British spy. Even more personally vicious and inappropriate to our ears today, Hunter warned readers of Wood's "eccentricity of morals," alluding to a homosexual relationship with Street. Street fought back on the pages of *The Western World*, calling Hunter and Littell "the two constellations of prostitution." Street taunted Hunter and Littell to sue for libel. Wood warned that he had few assets to pay any court judgment. In reality, if Hunter sued, he would lose the business of printing Wood's controversial but widely read newspaper. Therefore, Street felt safe in making slanderous statements with impunity. Further, Street knew that Hunter never sued anyone for slander.[41]

The purported Spanish Conspiracy entered a new, even more sensational phase. Wood and Street alleged that former Vice President Aaron Burr and prominent Kentucky leaders are preparing to attack Spanish territories and create a separate nation on the Mississippi frontier. Attempting to reinvigorate his political prospects after he killed Alexander Hamilton in a duel, Burr vociferously advocated obtaining free navigation of the Mississippi River and New Orleans export rights by any means possible. Aligning with Western economic interests made Burr widely popular in Kentucky. Hunter reported in *The Palladium*, "The public sentiment which had all along been strongly in favor of Colonel Burr now burst forth without disguise."[42]

Suspicious that Burr sought to align Kentucky with Spain to open the trade route, Federal District Attorney James Hamilton Daveiss's leaders convened a grand jury to investigate treason charges against Burr. Sensing the need to confront the serious charges, Burr traveled to Frankfort and retained Henry Clay and John Allen to defend him. Federal Judge Harry Innes seated a grand jury to consider the treason charges. Not able to sustain the prosecution, Daveiss withdrew the charges, and Burr went free. However, Daveiss convened a second grand jury in early December. This time the jury delivered a "not true bill" partially based upon the unequivocal defense by the highly respected Sen. Henry Clay.[43] Hunter's *Palladium* proclaimed, "It appeared clearly on the examination that the rumour circulated throughout the U. States that Colonel Burr's object was to divide the union, and to separate the eastern from the western states is totally and groundless."[44] On the night of Burr's acquittal, Governor Christopher Greenup held a sumptuous dinner feting the former vice president. Numerous toasts were drunk in his honor and to the leading Kentucky politicians. Not to be outdone, James Hamilton Daveiss' supporters held a similar celebratory dinner in his honor, attracting several notable Republican politicians. The Spanish Conspiracy opened cracks among the State Republican politicians presaging splintered factions for Hunter to navigate.[45]

Although Aaron Burr escaped conviction, the controversy over the alleged Spanish Conspiracy exposed the guilt of one participant. In the current session of the Kentucky House of Representatives, a legislative inquiry established Kentucky State Court of Appeals Judge Benjamin Sebastian as a pensioner of the Spanish government. Sebastian resigned but was not prosecuted after an impeachment trial in the Kentucky legislature. To re-affirm their allegiances and to support Kentucky's Federally elected representatives, the legislature passed a resolution to quell any hints of disloyalty to the union. The reaffirming declaration stated, "the people of Kentucky, feel the strongest attachment to the federal government and consider a dismemberment of the union as the greatest evil which could befall them, and would view with abhorrence any individual or set of individuals who should attempt to separate us from those whose interests are so intimately connected with our own . . ."[46] The legislature ordered Street, not Hunter, to publish the report on Judge Sebastian and its loyalty resolution along with other supporting documentation. Street printed twelve hundred copies for circulation within and beyond the state.[47] Benjamin Sebastian proved to be the only Kentucky politician who suffered from *The Western World*'s sensational reporting of the 1790s negotiations with Spain. The other high-profile Kentucky participants in the Spanish Conspiracy continued in their current roles but, deserved or not, lived with clouds over their reputations.[48]

At the height of the Burr and Spanish Controversies in Frankfort, *The Western World* editors had a professional and personal falling out and abruptly ended their newspaper partnership. Wood characterized his rapport with Street as "more hostile to each other than Street and the editor of *The Palladium*." Wood left Kentucky for Washington City, where he started another newspaper entitled the *Atlantic World*. Flip-flopping again, the "mercenary penman" wrote in the paper's prospectus "that he now feels convinced that Burr's plan is not against the interests of the Union."[49] Street continued to publish *The Western World* and operate a print shop competing with Hunter's for commercial printing business. Street received laudatory acclaim for his investigatory journalism. "The Western World has risen very much in public estimation since the impeachment of Sebastian. This paper has certainly been productive of much good"[50] Even William Hunter admitted that *The Western World* editors had "undoubtedly rendered their country some service."[51]

Street and *The Western World*'s rise in public stature became an immediate concern, as the state printing contract, so critical to Hunter's financial condition, expired in a few weeks. Street engaged in a concerted and bitter campaign to win the upcoming election for state printer. He wrote a mocking editorial deriding William Hunter as a Billy Lampblack and a lacky of the Spanish Conspirators to convince the legislature not to renew Hunter's contract. The vituperate editorial called Hunter a "toad-eater" and "lick-spittle."[52] While the bids and evaluation records have been lost, the legislature, unconvinced of any malfeasance, overwhelmingly re-elected Hunter as the State Printer with fifty-six votes for Hunter and twenty-four for Street.[53] The lopsided vote confirmed that Hunter retained strong support from Governor Greenup and other Jeffersonian republican politicians who did not want to pursue the Spanish matter further.

While Burr's Kentucky prosecutions ended without convictions, President Thomas Jefferson and other national leaders continued to harbor doubts of Burr's loyalties. After receiving reports of Burr's nefarious and possibly treasonous activities on the Mississippi, President Jefferson informed Congress of Burr's activities and ordered his arrest.[54] By chance, a district land office official recognized Burr and informed the commander of Fort Stoddard, who effected his arrest. Worried that the nearby Spanish might attempt a rescue, the army commander sent a small detachment to escort Burr to Washington.

Upon reaching Virginia, government officials ordered the army detachment to remand Aaron Burr to Richmond for trial.

Burr's Richmond treason trial, which lasted between mid-March and mid-October 1807, renewed the spirited newspaper war between *The Palladium* and *The Western World* included *ad hominin* attacks by the rival editors. Calling Hunter his "unprovoked, malignant enemy," Street continued to condemn Hunter's character as "pusillanimous" and a "doughty" printer" with a "polluted heart" and "destitute of integrity and truth." Further damning, Hunter protects those disloyal to the union.[55] "Is this [William Hunter] the man who was born in the land of freedom? Is this the champion who was born in the tented field while his father was waging war against the rebellious Americans?" They further assert that Hunter's father "labored to extinguish" in the "Americans' bosoms" the "spark of liberty."[56] Again, Street challenged Hunter for the state printing contract. In a broadside to the people of Franklin County, he exhorted, "Rise FREEMEN of Franklin, and trample the ALTAR OF TREASON and CONSPIRACY beneath your feet, and spurn from your bosom the man who has presumed to direct your votes, with a view to his election as public printer."[57] And again, Hunter retained the contract. While Street may have exposed the participants in the Spanish Conspiracy, the state legislature deemed Hunter a more reliable supporter.

With the end of the Burr treason trials, the Spanish Conspiracy faded from the pages of the Frankfort newspapers. With no new *cause celebre, The Western World* readership dropped precipitously, and in 1809, Street sold the newspaper. Adding to his financial difficulties, Street lost a defamation suit brought by Federal Judge Harry Innes, and after violating the terms of a settlement agreement, the court ordered monetary damages. Unable to pay, Street skipped town to the Illinois territory and had a successful career as an Indian agent.[58]

Decades later, in 1854, additional information surfaced, which shed some new light on the Spanish and Burr Conspiracies. The Spanish historian Charles Gayarre uncovered evidence that General and Frankfort founder James Wilkerson served as a paid spy for the Spanish government. During the Burr controversy, Wilkerson did a masterful job in deflecting scrutiny off himself to Burr. Whether Burr had treasonous designs is still open for debate.[59] Despite no smoking gun, Burr's secretive and nefarious activities coupled with his murder of Alexander Hamilton lead to a modern-day reputation as one of the most villainous characters in American history. However, for most of 1806, Burr enjoyed a durably positive reputation with William Hunter and most Kentuckian Republicans.

Amidst the controversy over the Spanish Conspiracy, William Hunter scooped his newspaper rivals and published his most widely read news article outside of Kentucky. In the October 2, 1806 edition of *The Palladium*, Hunter wrote, "We stop the press to announce with sincere pleasure, the following highly interesting intelligence." Under this tantalizing by-line, Hunter reprinted a letter from St. Louis by John Mullanphy, a former Frankfort shopkeeper, announcing that "Captains Lewis and Clark just arrived, all in good health." Mullanphy reported that Lewis and Clark found the resident Indians "peaceful" and "as numerous on the Columbia as Whites, in any part of the United States."

The Corps of Discovery generated a high level of interest among Kentuckians for two major reasons. Economically, citizens in the western country sought to understand better the commercial prospects of the lands beyond the Mississippi River and put to rest a long-festering racial controversy. Secretary Harry Toulmin wrote in *The Palladium*, "No circumstance relating to the history of the western country, probably, has excited, at different times, more general attention and anxious curiosity, than the opinion that a nation of white men, speaking the Welch language, reside high up the Missouri."[60] Capitalizing on this intense fascination, within a few days after receiving the Mullanphy correspondence, Hunter acquired a letter written by co-leader William Clark to his brother George Rogers Clark in Louisville on the day of his return to St. Louis. Hunter wrote in the next edition of *The Palladium*, "Captain Clark, did not perhaps intend it for publication, but to gratify in some measure, the impatient wishes of his countrymen, the general was prevailed upon to permit its appearance in our paper of to-day." Hunter added a congratulatory preamble noting the "courage, perseverance, and prudent deportment displayed by this adventuresome party. They are entitled to, and will receive the plaudits of their countrymen."[61] Following Hunter's editorial comments, he reprinted William Clark's captivating letter in its entirety. Clark narrated an overview of the trip to his brother, noting both significant geographical features and many encounters with Native Americans. Debunking long-held views, nowhere did the explorers find any trace of Welsh-speaking Indians.[62]

Hunter published his editorial and Clark's letter on October 9, 1806. Over the next six weeks, dozens of local and national papers reprinted *The Palladium's* story. Becoming the authoritative account, city papers such as the *New York Herald* and smaller town papers such as *The Reporter* in Brattleboro, Vermont, picked up Hunter's preamble and Clark's letter. Most newspapers, copied from *The Palladium* verbatim under a Frankfort byline without attribution. However, roughly a third of the papers cited *The Palladium* as the source for their article. None of the papers identified William Hunter as the author of the preamble.

During this period, newspapers printed official confirmation of the successful expedition from Washington City. However, more and more papers continued to reprint Hunter's editorial and copy of Clark's letter. While Hunter did not receive personal acclaim for breaking the story, he could take pride in seeing his work reprinted in the country's largest and most influential news publications.

The public uproar over Burr and the Spanish Conspiracy and the public fascination with the Lewis and Clark story proved the high points of Hunter's newspaper publishing career. With *The Western World* as an impetus and a foil, newspaper sales and readership soared. For the first time in his publishing career, Hunter could not, at the same time, meet both the demands of his public office as well as his commercial business. "The great quantity of business to which the Editor has to attend at the close of the session and the numerous engagements of the hands in his office at that time, he hopes will induce his subscribers to extend their indulgence to him for the present."[63]

To meet the burgeoning demand, Hunter added printing capacity. The easiest way to increase output involved taking on additional teenaged men into three- or four-year apprenticeships. A father or guardian signed a legal agreement for the son to learn the printing trade, work under the supervision of the master in exchange for a low wage. Additionally, the apprentice received room and board in the master's house. Hunter also hired journeymen workers who had completed an apprenticeship either with him or another paper in several cases. However, Hunter most frequently advertised in his newspapers for apprentices, seeking boys fourteen to sixteen years of age. Apprentices worked in all facets of the printing and publishing business. They composed type from manuscripts, operated the press, and recorded transactions in accounting records. These activities provided insights into the printing business. With this newly gained knowledge, there were risks for the master printers at the end of an apprenticeship as the newly trained printers could join a competitor or begin their newspapers or print shops. Five out of the six known apprentices employed by Hunter opened their print shops or started competitor newspapers. Several of these Hunter-trained newspaper editors became fierce and effective competitors. Thus, while apprentices were sources of cheap and reliable labor, masters often created a threatening source of competition.

Two such enterprising apprentices will engender a scandal that will end Hunter's ten-year reign as the State Printer and eventually cause Hunter to sell *The Palladium*. Within a year of finishing a four-year apprenticeship, a savvy beyond his years, twenty-two-year-old William Gerard started a rival Frankfort newspaper, *The Argus of Western America*. The inaugural number appeared on

January 27, 1808. It featured an innovative format including an easy-to-read, large print-type, two-columns divided by a line, and sixteen pages. The masthead featured a quote from Horace's poems—"Quid verum atque decens, curo et rego, et omnis in hoc sum" or "My cares and my inquiries are for decency and truth, and in this, I am wholly occupied." Gerard offered *The Argus* at the higher price of three dollars in advance and four dollars if paid at the end of six months. Within a year, Gerard lowered the subscription price to a competitive two dollars in advance and three dollars at six months, and *The Argus* converted to the traditional four columns, four-page format.

After the August gubernatorial elections, Gerard sensed an opportunity to unseat Hunter as the state printer. Charles Scott, a Revolutionary War hero and the newly elected governor named Jesse Bledsoe, his campaign manager, to the powerful post of Secretary of State and provided him unusual leeway in running the state. In the November 16th issue of *The Argus*, Gerard announced a partner joined his newspaper and printing business. Gerard added Moses Owsley Bledsoe, the nephew of both the new Secretary of State and several legislators, hoping to capitalize upon powerful family connections. Gerard and Bledsoe developed a strong personal relationship while serving apprenticeships in Hunter's business. With inside knowledge and newly minted political connections, the new partners directly challenged Hunter's state printer reappointment. "We think proper thus explicitly to inform the members of the legislature that we are candidates for the public printer of this state for the ensuing year." Bolstering their case, the insurgent printers proclaimed that they were "raised in your country," an obvious knock-on Hunter's formative years in Britain.[64]

Since first winning the state contract in 1798, Hunter faced minimal competition in the annual state printer elections. Only four times competitors contested the annual election, including the Bradford family's initial competition, one by former apprentice E. C. Berry and two by James M. Street. Hunter won each of the contract's re-competitions by overwhelming margins. Over the years, the legislature established a more robust evaluation process for interested printers to submit proposals to the legislature during its winter term. Comprising members of the House and Senate, a joint committee gathered and reviewed printer proposals before presenting a recommendation to the full assembly for a final vote. Typically, the vote occurred simultaneously as other legislatively elected roles such as auditor and treasurer. The vote had not been close to this point, and the legislature routinely reappointed Hunter's firm.

In the 1808-9 session opening days, the legislature authorized $1189.60 and 6 mils to the State Printer for work over above that required under the terms of his $825 annual salary. In the second to last day of the year, Gerard and Bledsoe communicated a blockbuster letter to the Speaker of the House, "Sir, as we conceive the public printer has charged the state more than he was justly entitled to for his services, and has not discharged his duty, we beg leave through you to submit the enclosed statements to the legislature, which we expect to substantiate." The Speaker made the letter and associated charges available to all members and referred the matter to the joint committee on public printing.

Blindsided, Hunter did not anticipate an unusually competitive fight for the printing contract. Initially, signally a friendly relationship between the printers, Gerard inserted in *The Argus* notes below public notices that newly published legal books were available in Hunter's bookstore. Later, in late fall, Hunter traveled to Philadelphia at least partially on the behest of the outgoing governor, Christopher Greenup. In a previous session, the legislature tasked the former governor to purchase a seven-hundred-dollar fire engine for the city of Frankfort. This request remained unfilled for almost two years. In the City of Brotherly Love, Hunter met the manufacturer and learned that yellow fever in the city had delayed production and conveyance. However, the manufacturer reported that the state-of-the-art engine left Philadelphia en route to Pittsburgh for transit down the Ohio River. Hunter realized that he faced a cunning and powerful rival upon returning to Frankfort, despite his competitors' young age and relative inexperience. The aspiring printers followed up their initial notice with four specific charges (see Figure 5 on page 152).

The first two charges relate to particular printing jobs completed at the legislature's specific direction by Hunter for the legislature over and above the standard work. Gerard and Bledsoe aver that Hunter charged for the printing these extra assignments at one dollar per one thousand ems (a square type) versus the prevailing rate of seventy-five cents. Hunter countered with examples of printers charging the state one and one-quarter dollars per one thousand ems. Further, he argued that nothing was amiss as he had notified the legislature in advance of his intended charges and provided consistent bills accordingly. The third charge is that Hunter failed to send six copies of the non-resident delinquent real estate tax lists to each of his subscribers as expressly required by law. Hunter responded that with the recent addition of *The Western World* and *Argus of Western America*, the post office could not distribute all six copies to each subscriber. As a result, he printed only the number of copies that the postmaster could deliver. The fourth charge is that Hunter inappropriately charged the state the higher "rule and figure" rate (twice the regular price of one dollar per one thousand ems) when he should have charged the lower book work rate of one dollar.

The house then took up the report of the joint committee, appointed to investigate certain charges exhibited by Messrs. Gerard and Bledsoe against Mr. W. Hunter as public printer: which was then read in the words and figures following, viz.

Charges against Wm. Hunter.

First—That he exacted more from the state for printing the Criminal Code, than he was entitled to, by the rules which he had stated to be customary in this country for printing.

Second—That he has charged the state, and actually received more for the printing of the decisions of the court of appeals than that work amounted to, by the rules of charging individuals as existed at that time, laid down by himself and others.

Third—That he has not complied with the requisitions of the law in the publication of the lists of non-residents lands.

Fourth—That he has not observed in his charges against the state even those rules laid down in his publication of the twenty-third of December 1808.

GERARD & BLEDSOE,

December 30th, 1808;

FIGURE 5. *Journal of the General Assembly, Session 17.*

A spirited debate ensued, with both parties offering written evidence from area printers, politicians, and public officials. In mid-January, each side sent formal depositions to the joint committee. The young aspirants gathered corroborating testimony from competitors and former Hunter apprentices. Exuding crocodile tears, Daniel Bradford stated, "Unpleasant as it is to be concerned in any way in the disputes between men of the same profession, yet to answer the queries you addressed to me yesterday, I answer plan work (book rate) is seventy-five cents per one thousand ems and rule and figure work double." Additional competitors and former state printer aspirants E.C. Berry, James H. Stewart, and Joseph M. Street all testified the going rate for book composition was seventy-five cents. Three of Hunter's employees stated that they printed only the number of lists that could be mailed but less than the legally mandated six lists per subscriber. The postmaster wrote that he sometimes received "more than he could send by mail, and they came more frequently than wished for." However, he believed that "they (all six legally mandated copies) might have been sent out over the space of a month."

In rebuttal, Hunter offered two prominent political leaders' testimony. The previous governor, Christopher Greenup, stated, "William Hunter never withheld information from the legislature," and he provided in advance "an estimate of his charges for printing the criminal law." The State Auditor (and future governor), George Madison, said: "he had a conversation with Mr. Bledsoe who observed that he did not intend to come forward with a view to lessen the price of printing and that he thought William Hunter had done the printing as low as it could be done."[65]

Playing catchup, Hunter charactered the charges as "so extraordinary" and offered an indignant and dismissive response. On the first charge, Hunter stated that he executed the work "in pursuance of an express and positive contract made with the legislature" and that his charge of one dollar per one thousand ems was reasonable, the exact amount that James M. Bradford had charged in the legislature in 1803. Hunter rejected the second charge by asserting that the committee received price estimates from him and approved the charges in advance. Hunter countered the third charge by stating that he complied with the law's spirit when the shortage of postal mail capacity limited him from complying with the letter of the law. "I endeavored to comply as near as circumstances admit." Lastly, "uncertain of what this charge means, Hunter stated that his invoices to the legislature were always consistent with his agreed-upon rates with the legislature. Attempting to show additional benefits over and above the minimum legislative requirements, Hunter concluded by describing several "things I do for no recompense." For example, I "often distribute more copies than the legislature orders" and "I have made great additions to my office to executive public work." Signally that his defenses needed strengthening, he said that he hopes "that the gentlemen who comprise the committee of enquiry will take a liberal and expanded view of the whole subject, and will do me all the justice I could wish or desire."

Amidst the state printer dispute, a raucous Kentucky legislature engaged in a wide range of topics, culminating in the less than decorous behaviors and breaches of legislative rules by two legislative members. While considering Gerard and Bledsoe's charges, Kentucky's most famous politician Henry Clay embroiled in a loud and physical dispute with Humphrey Marshall, a cousin of Supreme Court chief justice John Marshall. While one of the few Federalists remaining in the state, Marshall projected "a muscular voice in all the political controversies of Kentucky's early years."[66] Unbelievably, the two clashed over whether it was more appropriate to wear imported British or home-grown American clothes. Their legislative colleagues voted a formal censure after listening to the duos' vituperative insults. "Resolved, that the conduct of H [umphrey] Marshall and Henry Clay whilst in the service of the house of representatives on yesterday was an indignity offered to the same and highly reprehensible, but having made suitable acknowledgements, the house think proper to accept the same and proceed no further there in." The censure did not end the matter. An indignant Clay issued a formal challenge which his rancorous, longtime rival readily accepted. Marshall and their seconds traveled from Frankfort to Louisville, crossed the Ohio River into Indiana, and fought a pistol duel at the mouth of Silver Creek (modern-day New Albany, Indiana). At ten paces, each contestant fired two shots, resulting only in a slight wound in Marshall's belly. Clay received a flesh wound in his thigh in a third round, serious enough for the seconds to "pronounce their conduct on the occasion cool, determined and brave in the highest degree" and ended the gunfight.[67] While the duel may have assuaged the participants' public honor, the results did nothing to heal the enmity between the parties. They did not return to the legislature until early February. When the legislature got wind of the duel, the members issued a second censure and returned to considering next years' state printing contract.

Fractured on most issues, the legislature spoke with one mind when adjudicating the Gerard and Bledsoe charges against Hunter. In a written opinion, Edmund Bullock, chairman of the joint investigatory committee, concluded that Hunter made improper and exorbitant charges, billed the state more than individuals for the same work, and failed to comply with the legal requirement to publish six notices of non-resident taxes. As a result, the committee resolved that "he should be compelled to make reparations and refund the money so fraudulently drawn from the Treasury. Despite deep political divisions and distractions over dueling, the legislature voted an astounding fifty-nine votes to accept the committee's report and zero votes to reject.

How could this be? A confluence of events brought this about. First, Bledsoe's family connections, including the Secretary of State and two cousins in the legislature, Nudigate, and William Owsley, guaranteed that Gerard and Bledsoe received a fair hearing. The partners' charges placed the legislative members in an awkward position. Secondly, Gerard and Bledsoe signaled that they would drop the rate to an unheard of fifty cents per one thousand ems during the deliberations. However, two other printing firms, Daniel and Charles Bradford and William W. Worsley and Samuel W. Overton, publishers of the *Kentucky Reporter* in Lexington, confirmed the market rate by offering fifty-cent rates. To avoid the personal embarrassment of permitting the above-market one-dollar prices for many years, they had to vote against Hunter for the appearance that he had committed fraud on the state. Further, Hunter did not help his cause with a dismissive and indignant defense. He could have offered the legislature a more fulsome response, including proof of his assertions.

While fair prices and contract performance may have headlined the struggle over the state printing contract, another unstated factor may have more heavily influenced the legislators. Earlier in 1808, Hunter published a slavery abolitionist tract entitled "History of the Baptised Ministers and Churches in Kentucky, etc. Friends of Humanity." Written by the most prominent abolitionist Baptist minister in Kentucky, Carter Tarrant, who presided over the first Kentucky Abolitionist Society meeting on September 27, 1808. With widespread support for slavery, most Kentuckians viewed Tarrant as a "malcontent who fostered disharmony," and many Baptist churches closed their pulpits to his sermons.[68] While Hunter was not the author, the state's politicians would have taken notice of his willingness to publish unpopular criticisms of slavery and apparent support of the abolitionist movement. Henry Clay and Humphrey Marshall disagreed on everything but the need to continue and protect the right to hold people enslaved. Certainly, Hunter knew that the monograph would not be a best-seller, and he was putting his reputation for reliability and support of the state's leading politicians at risk. By printing abolitionist materials, Hunter continued his practice of courageously printing his views, despite their apparent unpopularity.

Sensing the handwriting was on the wall, Hunter withdrew his State Printer candidacy. On January 23, 1809, Gerard and Bledsoe were easily elected as State Printers. Garnering fifty-six votes, the insurgents prevailed over Worsley and Overton (twenty-three votes) and Daniel and Charles Bradford (seventeen votes).[69] However, the vote to change printers did not end Hunter's public printing responsibilities or controversy. The legislature ordered William Hunter to compose and print both the House and Senate Journals for the current session. To facilitate the preparation of the Journals, the legislature permitted Hunter to occupy the State Printer's office space in the capitol until ten days after the close of the legislative session. The newly minted partners deserve considerable credit as they navigated a complex political environment to create compelling arguments not to re-elect Hunter.

The financial resolution associated with the Gerard and Bledsoe charges and the payment amount to Hunter for his final year were left unresolved. It would be another three years until the legislature took up the matter of settling accounts with Hunter. In February 1812, the Kentucky House appointed a three-person committee to investigate Hunter's claim for payment for services performed during 1808-9. The committee members were George Madison (State Auditor), Christopher Greenup (former governor), and Martin D. Hardin (House member). The commissioners were charged with resolving the claim and determining a final settlement amount. It would appear that the choice of commissioners favored Hunter as both Greenup and Madison had offered supporting testimony. Curiously, the legislature allowed the commissioners two dollars a day for their efforts funded by William Hunter. Again, the matter went dormant. The only indication of a resolution was a cryptic notice on February 10, 1816, that ordered an eight-dollar payment to William Hunter per account rendered. If this refers to the 1808-9 controversy, the purported overcharge almost equaled the billings for additional services. The settlement made neither party happy, and the two sides just wanted closure, hence the lack of publicity.[70]

While the financial resolution went dormant in early 1809, a publicity swirl around the change in State Printer continued. Bledsoe left the newspaper partnership with Gerard after only a few short months in a peculiar change of affairs. Perhaps, Gerard and Bledsoe disagreed on editorial policy, or they principally formed the partnership to add political clout to replace Hunter as the State Printer. Whatever the reason, Bledsoe continued to use family connections to create employment. A few months later, he replaced his father-in-law as the agent for the penitentiary in Frankfort. Immediately after Bledsoe's departure, allegations of fraud and subterfuge by Hunter resumed in the pages of *The Argus* and were refuted in *The Palladium*. The editors re-hashed charges and counter-charges. Attempting to tell his side of the story, Hunter printed his "own justification for the delays in printing the House and Senate Journals. Evoking Thomas Paine, Gerard responded with a vengeance labeling *The Palladium* as established "at a time that tried men's principles." Further buttressing his point, Gerard reprinted the joint select committee findings that Hunter abused his office. Lastly, Gerard alleged Hunter left his office without completing the mandated legislative journals. This last charge turned out to be premature as copies of the 1808-9 legislative journals published by William Hunter exist today. Gerard sought to close off the debate by concluding, "We shall say no more on the subject now, nor hereafter, trusting that Mr. H's serious reflection and attention to his pursuits which he appears ostentatiously to admire, with a hope that he will let a life of future rectitude, atone for his past crimes."[71]

Hunter responded that he taught Gerard "all he knows." Smarting from this condescending remark, Gerard retorts, "No Mr. Hunter you have not yet taught me to be fraudulent." Gerard alleged that Hunter offered him twenty-five hundred dollars to transfer half of the public printing to *The Argus* or leave Frankfort. Bowing to Hunter's courageous Sedition Act editorials, Gerard recognized Hunter's republican political leanings and the "outstanding of this man once" as mitigating factors. He especially regarded Hunter's suppression of

"President Jefferson's proclamation against [Aaron] Burr is not to be forgotten." Gerard concludes that he will rise above the sordid affair by sarcastically concluding that "the editor yields to Hunter's omnipotence."[72] While the spirited debate created fury between the editors, it did not excite the general public. Quickly, *The Palladium* and *The Argus* returned to more pressing news.

Even before the loss of the public printing contract, Hunter began to dismantle his newspaper and publishing businesses. In the previous summer, Hunter sold his bindery business to Dave Niess, Jr. In an advertisement in *The Palladium*, Hunter offered a strongly positive recommendation, "Mr. Niess's qualifications, enable him to assure all who may have business in that line to execute, should they be disposed to entrust it to Mr. N. he will merit a continuance of their favors by executing their orders with fidelity and dispatch."[73] Niess continued to run the advertisement and endorsement for several years in *The Palladium* and the *Frankfort Argus*. Despite the highly publicized allegations of fraud, Hunter's character and recommendations carried lasting weight in the Frankfort community.

Hunter needed to move in a different direction. After ten years as the public printer and thirteen in the newspaper business, Hunter disposed of *The Palladium* and his remaining publishing and printing assets. Two former apprentices and current journeyman employees purchased the business. Robert Johnston and George W. Pleasants joined into a partnership to continue publishing *The Palladium*.[74] To provide the new editors/owners a boost, Hunter heartfully and unequivocally endorsed the new partners. Just as when he crossed the Atlantic Ocean to America fifteen years ago, Hunter needed to re-establish himself in a new career. However, now he had to reinvent himself into a new profession to provide for his financial well-being and repair his reputation. A modest nest egg garnered from the newspaper sale helped transition to new enterprises.

William turned his attention to worrisome overseas family concerns during the business turmoil. Separated for twenty-five years, he had not received correspondence (or any news) from his mother and sister for the last ten years. Uncertain why his letters were not answered and fearing for the worst, Hunter sent an inquiry to William Jarvis, the American trade consul in Lisbon, Portugal, seeking information on his mother and sister. Due to meager financial means, Margaret and William's sister moved to Lisbon to live with relatives in 1783 or 1784 after the death of John, his father. He described his mother as "Mrs. Margaret Hunter, an elderly Lady formerly residing with a Mr. Axtell who I imagine was once a Merchant of that place, but of this I am not certain." Perhaps his mother remarried, but it is unexplained why William thought that his mother would be living with a Mr. Axtell. As his mother would be at least sixty years in age, he went onto to ask about his sister. "Should my Mother be dead, I should wish your enquiries to extend to my Sister, who is probably married. Perhaps fortune may favor your enquiry; and I may yet have the happiness to find out through your friendly and benevolent assistance, a parent

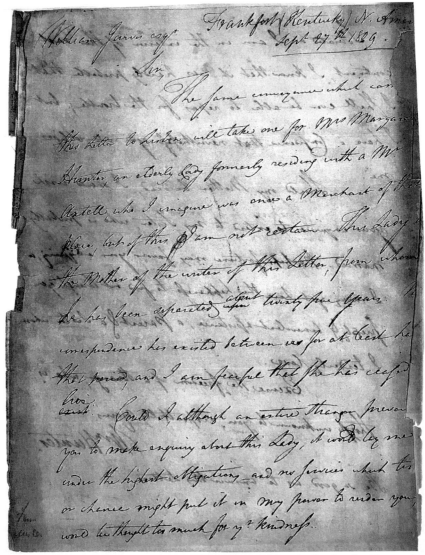

FIGURE 6. *William Hunter Letter to William Jarvis. Note similar handwriting to the journal.*

and a sister who I tenderly love." Hunter ended his letter with a plea for a response, "Situated as I am in the interior of the vast continent, I know that it is hardly probable that I shall ever be able to repay for this trouble; but I have a confidence that nevertheless you will oblige me . . . Be so good to answer this letter."[75] In the first decade of the 19th century, serving as an American trade consul served in a non-diplomatic, part-time role assumed by the largest American trading house in an overseas port. As such, the informally designated person did not serve in the Federal government and did not file documents pertinent to their trade consul dealings with the State Department. Deeply disappointing to Hunter, there is no record of any response from Jarvis among his surviving personal papers or anywhere in the historical record.

Losing the state printing contract and not connecting with his English family ended a difficult chapter of William's life in America. On the positive side, he received unwavering support from a nurturing wife and enjoyed raising two daughters and a son who would reach adulthood. However, his civic and business reputations required repair, and he sought new ways to support his loving family.

Part III

Building Businesses and Contributing to the Community

O ver the next ten years, an entrepreneurial-minded William Hunter opened and closed several retail and manufacturing businesses in the Frankfort area. Eschewing sole proprietorships, Hunter enlisted new and established business partners to obtain capital and share the risks. Hunter contributed his counting-house (accounting) skills and political connections to generate business and investments returns. Despite initial successes, Hunter never enjoyed the relative permanence of his printing career.

More importantly, Hunter regained his stature in the community, and his colleagues began to refer to him as Colonel Hunter, a purely honorific title connoting respect and admiration in the community.

During the second decade of the 1800s, the War of 1812 dominated the lives of Kentucky's citizens. Frankfort residents reacted to the late June news of the American declaration of war against the British with the firing of cannon and the "most decided evidence of approbation of the measure."[1] Support for the war emanated from the dominant presence of Revolutionary War veterans and their families in Kentucky. As a hotbed of anti-British sentiments, Kentucky furnished an outsized number of soldiers to the war effort. The state's militia act mandated each male between the ages of eighteen to forty-five to serve in the local militia. Requiring a significant, personal commitment, each militia company mustered four times a year with an annual battalion and regimental musters in the spring and fall, respectively. Marching north to battle sites in the Michigan and Ohio territories, militia and regular army units were familiar sights on Frankfort streets. Lacking discipline and effective leadership, the Kentucky volunteers suffered high casualty rates. After horrific initial losses in Michigan and Canada, Kentucky's soldiers would redeem themselves by participating in the overwhelming victories in the Battle of the Thames and under General Andrew Jackson in New Orleans.[2]

As required by law, Hunter served as a member of the local militia. He participated in the quarterly Frankfort militia musters and achieved the rank of a major in the 6th Regiment. Shortly after the declaration of war against Britain, Hunter resigned his militia commission and did not volunteer for service at the northern battlefronts, as did many of his war-minded neighbors. As might be expected, Hunter did not want to serve against his father's country and, fortuitously, exceeded the maximum age for mandatory service within a year. Later in life, political opponents would allege that he shirked his militia duty, a charge that he vehemently disputed.[3] While the war was immensely popular, Hunter was not the only Kentuckian with qualms about fighting the British. Protesters in two Kentucky towns burnt Hunter's political ally and friend, John Pope, in effigy for opposing the British conflict.

While Hunter did not serve in the military, the War of 1812 evoked memories of the American Revolution and his family's captivity. Frankfort became the site of a Trans-Atlantic prisoner of war controversy. When British forces sent twenty-three captured Americans across the Atlantic to be tried for treason as British subjects, President James Madison ordered twice that number of captured British Army officers to be incarcerated in Frankfort. The arriving prisoners generated quite the curiosity among local residents while marching to the local jail.[4] Viewing British prisoners parading through the town's streets sparked memories of his family's facing gaping on-lookers while en route to captivity in Lancaster and Le Havre. Although he lived in a land of opportunity with a wife and children, seeing the detainees also reinforced William's lifelong lament of being orphaned from his British family.

While the prisoners may have fueled melancholy feelings, the war triggered an unprecedented increase in military spending, generating a surge in Frankfort and Kentucky's economic activity. New manufacturing companies sprung up to supply the vitally needed clothing and food for the troops mustered in the western states. Also, Frankfort stood on vital supply routes generating both foot traffic and commercial distribution activity. Taking advantage of the wartime boom, Hunter shifted careers from printing to an interrelated mix of retailing and manufacturing businesses.

CHAPTER ELEVEN

Book Seller and Retailer

William Hunter started his business and reputational renaissance by leveraging his life-long love of books and reading. Before being ousted as the public printer, Hunter opened a bookstore on the Frankfort town square. In addition to purveying unsold self-published books, his shelves contained a wide variety of poetry, classical, and children's books. For historically minded adults, he featured a new biography of George Washington by David Humphrey and an American Revolution account by David Ramsey. Recognizing the increase in the residents' religiosity, the new bookseller purchased a prodigious twenty-four copies of the Reverend John Anderson's book, *Precious Truth or some points in Gospel Doctrine*. Only a Philadelphia retailer exceeded the number of books purchased by Hunter. Signaling that the copyright dispute over rights to the *Ohio Navigator* did not sever their relationship, Zadok Cramer, Hunter's former apprentice in Pennsylvania, wholesaled Anderson's book for sale in the Frankfort bookstore. On other occasions, Cramer did remotely compete with Hunter's bookstore by advertising books, primers, and dictionaries for sale in *The Palladium*. His advertisements featured testimonials from teachers at the Lexington Academy. Another competitor, the bookbinder David Neiss, offered novels such as *The Prisoners of Niagara or Evolution of Education* by Jesse Holman, a lively and romantic story at the end of the American Revolution. Demonstrating Neiss's ongoing cooperation on public and private printing, William Gerard published this book.

While many popular books generated foot traffic from the general public, lawyers, politicians, and judges would become the most valuable bookstore customers. Given intimate proximity to the legislature and Hunter's political relationships, legal books would be his most enduring sellers creating a profitable niche in the publishing business. The shop offered related products such as stationery, quills, ink, and writing paper in addition to books. This modest retail business would serve as the core to rebuilding his business career. However, by 1820 Hunter exited the retail business turning to legal publishing and other pursuits.

Despite the legislature's negative report on his character, Hunter expanded a valuable business and personal relationship with the official legislative reporter William Littell who had a legal mandate to edit the convoluted Kentucky legal statures. Similar to the modern publishing model, Hunter served as the publisher assuming sales and distribution responsibilities. His former employees Johnston and Pleasants performed the physical composition and printing. Hunter featured Littell's highly sought-after legal compendiums in his store and advertised copies for sale in the papers. Littell and Hunter received a very high-profile endorsement for *The Laws of Kentucky* from Henry Clay, the most notable person in Kentucky. In a written letter dated June 3, 1809, Clay averred that "I conceive the plan of the work a very good one." And "I have no hesitation in saying that it merits public patronage."[1] The strong recommendation by the highest-profile member of the Kentucky legislature indicates that Hunter did not inalterably damage his reputation. Clay provides further clues that the ousting of Hunter as State Printer served as a form of political payback. In the previous state printer election, John Allen, Clay's co-counsel in defending Aaron Burr, had strongly supported Hunter's re-election.[2] When but Allen ran against Charles Scott in the 1808 Gubernatorial election and lost, this opened Hunter up for removal as a supporter of the losing candidate. In the first legislative session after the election, Governor Scott sought a reliable advocate as State Printer. Gerard sensed this political opportunity and helped engender the transfer of state printing to his nascent but credible press. No one else besides Hunter made the connection, but Governor Scott led a Continental Army regiment against the British forces, including his father's unit at the 1778 Battle of Monmouth in New Jersey. While blame for the poor opening stages of the battle devolved to Major General Charles Lee, Brigadier General Scott's performance was less than exemplary. However, early nineteenth-century Kentuckians regarded Scott as a legendary war hero.

Littell's first volume covered the period from the commencement of Kentucky to 1797. With Clay's endorsement, the partners proclaimed, "It has so far, met the general and the unqualified approbation of every judge and gentleman of the bar to whom it has been shown." Hunter released the second volume, covering 1798 to 1801, during the summer of 1810 and the third volume in

1811. Hunter advertised, "No edition of laws yet published in any state of the Union, has been executed on a plan so expansive as this." Each volume sold for a healthy price of four dollars with payment on delivery. The publisher encouraged interested parties to purchase the books now as the price will rise when the series is complete.[3] The fourth volume would not be published until 1814. These groundbreaking statute compendiums provided Hunter with another way to augment his income.

Further enhancing Hunter's legal reputation, in 1810, the Frankfort court admitted Hunter to practice law. He joined sixteen accredited lawyers in the capital. One observer of the early Franklin County bar remarked, "Mr. Hunter was evidently a good business man but his standing as a lawyer must have been below the average."[4] Hunter's friend Harry Toulmin had a different view of his legal abilities and employed him to do the legal work around his Kentucky landholdings.[5] While the law would never become Hunter's primary profession, knowledge of the convoluted statutes helped him with many business ventures. And importantly, legal publishing and joining the Frankfort bar kept Hunter in touch with legislators, judges, and other government officials who came into his store to purchase this primary source required to perform their duties.

While the bookstore provided a modest living, Hunter worked hard over several years to collect debts from unpaid subscriptions and advertisements associated with his ownership of *The Palladium*. He noticed to the public that he retained Henry Armstrong as his debt collector and that delinquent customers could drop off payment to Peyton R. Pleasants at his bookstore. Hunter ran a series of ads requesting back payment. Most of his return from the sale of the printing business consisted of collecting these past due debts, and with little incentives, many customers never paid.

Hunter moved his store to a room in his home on the southwest corner of Montgomery (Main) and St. Clair streets.[6] Operating on Montgomery Street evoked bittersweet memories from his winter 1775 stay at Fort Chambly, whereas a child, he overheard British soldiers expressing lament at the death of the highly regarded Rebel General Richard Montgomery at the gates of Quebec City. Hunter also recalled the tension and stress in 1777, waiting for his father to return after the Hudson Highland campaign and the bloody assaults on Forts Clinton and Montgomery. However poignant, he kept these thoughts to himself and operated a retail establishment. Augmenting revenues from book sales, Hunter added a high-margin product line to his store shelves. An enterprising Hunter began retailing a wide variety of patent and family medicines from the well-known Michael Lee & Co. of Baltimore. While frowned upon today as shysters, patent medicines' manufacture and sale were among the fastest-growing industries in the early 19th century. With many ingredients and concoctions imported from Britain, the Lee family offered some of the best-known medicine in the United States. As typical with other patent medicine manufacturers of the era, the Lee family offered a wide range of products. The manufacturer provided a modicum of protection from fraud by enclosing the contents in a glass bottle encased in a paper wrapper. Purveyors advertised the unbroken seal as a testament to an untampered project. To aid in marketing the product, Michael Lee & Co. provided various user testimonials demonstrating

Lately received from Baltimore,

AND FOR SALE AT THE STORE OF

WILLIAM HUNTER & Co.

IN FRANKFORT,

(At the Baltimore prices,)

ORIGINAL
Patent & Family Medicines.

LEE'S ANTI-BILIOUS PILLS,

PREPARED BY

MICHAEL LEE & Co.

THE operation of these highly esteemed pills is perfectly mild, and the experience of thousands has proved they may be used in every situation in life, without the least inconvenience.

CASES OF CURES!

Selected from thousands, the authenticity of which can be ascertained by personal application to any of the subscribers—not being performed in Europe, (no one knows where) but in Baltimore:

Messrs. Michael Lee & Co.

Your Antibilious pills has had the desired effect in relieving me from head-ache, pains in the back, lassitude, &c. If you think proper, you are at liberty to use my name.   DANIEL CONN,

Balt. June 20, 1811.   Allquith street.

Messrs. Michael Lee & Co.

With pleasure I acknowledge the benefit received from your Antibilious Pills, in removing violent pains in the bowels, sickness and head-ache.

Balt. June 26, 1810.   RD. ROBINSON.
    Market street.

Messrs. Michael Lee & Co:

I have taken but two doses of your Antibilious Pills, and I am quite relieved from that sickness of the stomach, giddiness, &c. which has troubled me for some time. I shall recommend them to all my friends in similar cases.

Balt. July 13, 1810.   G. C. COLLINS.

Lee's Grand Restorative.

Lee's Essence and Extract of Mustard, for the Rheumatism, &c.

Lee's Ointment for the Itch.

Lee's Indian Vegetable Specific.

Lee's Eye-Water.

Lee's Tooth-Ache Drops.

Lee's Damask Lip Salve.

Lee's Persian Lotion.

Lee's Corn-Plaister.

Lee's Anodyne Elixir.

Lee's Restorative Powder, for the Teeth and Gums.

Sold, wholesale and retail, by the proprietors, No. 58, Prt street.

To country merchants and others who purchase to sell again, a liberal discount will be given, by the proprietors.

To detect counterfeits, observe each article has on the outside wrapper the signature of

MICHAEL LEE & Co.

FIGURE 7. The Palladium, *October 5, 1811, page 4.*

either relief or cures by using the products. Hunter purchased prominent, one-quarter-page ads in *The Palladium* to generate customer interest. The ad copy came from the manufacturer with a notation that Hunter offered these useful medicines at Baltimore prices, thereby intimating that Hunter subsidized the shipment cost to Frankfort.

Emphasizing choice assortments for the season, Hunter later added a wide variety of dry goods, groceries, and other products at his store. He advertised low prices and cash-only sales. While Hunter sought cash sales, he mostly settled for extending credit to regular customers and receiving barter goods. Typically, in early nineteenth-century Kentucky, store owners only received cash (specie) for ten to fifteen percent of sales. Credit sales accounted for eighty percent of sales, with the balance coming from barter. As a result, store owners offered two prices, a trade price for barter and credit and a lower cash price for immediate payment of specie. Hunter had two reasons for enticing cash sales. He obtained many books on credit and had to pay off his suppliers. Secondly, seeking to expand into other businesses and desperately cash-short, Hunter looked to his store as a method of generating capital.[7] He operated his store until late 1813, after which he moved into new businesses which he believed were more lucrative. However, the prospect of more profits came with the dangers of higher risks and required all the capital Hunter could muster.

CHAPTER TWELVE

Civic Prominence

Hand in hand with new business pursuits, Hunter performed high-profile civic duties reflecting his passion for education and politics. Despite the conflict over his services as the state printer, Hunter remained a member in good standing in the community and with government officials. Over the next five years, the state legislature appointed Hunter to manage civic institutions and overpublic works projects. Then, in 1812, the legislature reappointed Hunter trustee and a board member of the Kentucky Seminary. Along with the most prominent Frankfort civic leaders and state government officials, he had served on the legislature-appointed board of the predecessor Franklin Academy since 1803.[1] The secular secondary school educated young men and women from Frankfort and the surrounding region on the public square. Male students received instruction in Latin, Mathematics, and English with a maximum of thirty to thirty-five students per class. The Female Department consisted of two classes. The first taught orthography, reading, and writing, and the second arithmetic, geography, English grammar, composition history, and rhetoric. Tuition ranged from six dollars to ten dollars and twenty-five cents per class per quarter, with women charged a maximum of ten dollars. Hunter performed both mundane tasks for the committee, such as purchasing educational materials and supplies, and significant assignments such as procuring new land and managing construction projects.

Reflecting his life-long commitment to education and strong reputation in the community, Hunter served as a school trustee for most of his Frankfort life. In the over twenty years of his membership, Hunter served as a consistent and stabilizing force on the board as almost thirty prominent trustees rotated through the organization. In 1818, recognizing his commitment and expertise, the trustees elected William Hunter chairman. Further acknowledging his stature in the community, the trustees periodically met in Hunter's counting room. For a short time, he involved his son, Morrison as a clerk to the board with a salary of twenty-five dollars. Shortly thereafter, Amos Kendall, Frankfort's *The Argus* newspaper editor and rising politician, replaced Morrison as the board clerk. After the trustees learned more about his commitment to education, Amos Kendall joined the board as a trustee in 1820. Hunter formed a strong personal relationship and political connection with the twenty-one-year younger, though prematurely gray and frail Kendall that later proved pivotal in Hunter's life and would launch Gallaudet University in Washington City.[2]

On November 25, 1813, the state capitol complex on the public square burned to the ground. With other communities vying with Frankfort to host the state government, the legislature appointed a committee of five citizens to raise subscriptions among Frankfort residents to rebuild the capitol. However, the legislature made no guarantee that they would keep the capital in Frankfort or appropriate any money for reconstruction. As a result, if Frankfort citizens wanted to keep the capital, they must raise the rebuilding cost. Formally, on January 31, 1814, the legislature named William Hunter and four other community leaders commissioners to contract for and superintend the construction of a new Capitol building. As construction commenced, citizens amassed about half of the forty-thousand-dollar construction cost, with the Commonwealth eventually contributing the balance.

The impressive new brick capitol building measured one hundred feet by sixty-five feet. Legislators specified that the building was to be fire-proof, learning from history. Other design requirements included well-appointed interior spaces. The public rooms featured allegorical murals, including Themis, the god of justice, on the ceiling of the Assembly Hall. Legislators occupied a partially finished building in 1816. Two years later, the four commissioners petitioned the General Assembly. "Although the undersigned are fully aware that the conditions of the act under which they were appointed, do not enjoin it as a duty upon the legislature to make any appropriations . . . the commissioners have executed, for three years past, a laborious duty, without compensation, and have more over paid out of their own private funds . . . the sum of 8400 dollars."[3] Despite the legislature ignoring the commissioners' plea for additional funds, construction continued with final improvements completed in 1819. A year later, the legislature appropriated a symbolic two-hundred-dollar fee for William Hunter and the four other commissioners. Almost two decades later,

Hunter offered a petition to the Kentucky Senate to repay six hundred dollars that he paid out of his pocket to complete the project. Not surprising, given the tardiness of the request, senators referred the matter to committee, and the legislature never acted upon Hunter's petition. Though built to be fire-proof, the capitol building again burned in 1824, destroying many historic and valuable records. However, the legislature did not appoint Hunter to the commission to rebuild the capitol this time.[4]

When William returned to America as a young adult, he first sought opportunities in a counting-house to use his business and accounting expertise. His third civic contribution leveraged these interests and skills. A year after being appointed to overthe construction of the new capitol building, the legislature appointed Hunter with three other community leaders to a committee to review the accounts of the Kentucky Penitentiary. Since opening in 1800, the novel carceral institution suffered from management weaknesses and financial losses. Planned to be budgetary neutral with the prisoners earning the costs of the room and board, the jail never achieved fiscal equilibrium. Even changing keepers and purchasing agents did not improve the situation. Facing a large deficit and a convoluted financial reporting system, the legislature charged the penal investigation committee with unraveling the accounting and management weaknesses. Despite taking a year to investigate, the committee came back to the legislature with a less than satisfying conclusion. The committee uncovered an unexpected fifteen hundred- and fourteen-dollar deficit in the penitentiary's accounts. Even more importantly, the committee could not verify the revenues generated or the appropriate uses of funds. The committee opined, "no correct or even tolerable settlement of these accounts can now be made" due to "the want of original entries, vouchers and papers, and of a system by which the several accounts could be checked or substantiated." Perhaps not to the liking of the assembly, the commissioners posited that recent legislative changes would not be effective in rectifying the situation. The investigators recommended, "passage of an act containing such checks and provisions, as shall henceforth secure to the use of the state, the profits arising from the said institution."[5] As a result of the commissioners' report, the legislature instituted organizational changes, including a new prison keeper. However, new jail leadership did not immediately implement a more reliable system of accounting and controls, and jail operations resulted in further financial distress and accounting irregularities.[6]

Serving on legislatively mandated commissions facilitated Hunter's relationships with highly influential political and community leaders. A prime example is John Brown, a large man with an aristocratic demeanor, one of the most prominent politicians and wealthy planters in the state. Hunter served for many years with Brown on three high-profile boards and commissions, including the Kentucky Seminary, the commission to rebuild the capitol, and the committee to investigate the penitentiary. Hunter served on two boards with other prominent politicians and business leaders, including the state auditor George Madison, Daniel Weisiger, a leading businessman, and Richard Taylor, sergeant at arms for the legislature. Most importantly, Hunter developed deep-seated personal relationships that would greatly assist him during upcoming times of dire needs.

CHAPTER THIRTEEN

Manufacturer and Warehouse Owner

The Hunter's sale of *The Palladium* and the book store created investable capital. Like many famous Americans of the period, his spouse's inheritance provided a sizeable contribution to the family's investable capital. Before Hunter's marriage, Ann's father died intestate in 1791. When the executor legally divided the estate between Ann and her brothers, the Hunters received approximately three thousand dollars. Ann's father's residence, which the Hunters sold in 1813 for twenty-six hundred dollars, represented a significant portion of Ann's inheritance. Augmenting funds from the sale of *The Palladium* and his other business ventures, the Morrison estate produced seed money to invest in a new business.

Initially, Hunter focused on an entrepreneurial opportunity to use his newfound capital in the fast-growing Kentucky hempen manufacturing sector. Since their earliest entry, Euro-American settlers recognized the Blue Grass region's soil and climate as ideal for growing hemp. At first, a cottage industry, hemp farming supplied local users. However, the rise of the cotton economy and the disruption of European and American wars fostered a dramatic increase in hemp demand. Unfortunately, hemp cultivation was a dirty, smelly, labor-intensive process. After the growing season ended in September, enslaved laborers cut, treated, and left the hemp in the fields in a process called "rotting." The rotting process facilitated the considerable backbreaking labor required to separate the valuable fibers from the plant's outer shell to prepare shipment to a hempen factory.

A hempen factory consisted of a spinning facility, a weaving area, a rope-walk, and a warehouse. First, workers spun the cultivated hemp into industrial, rough yarns in the spinning facility. Then, in the weaving area, laborers weaved the threads into sailcloth or hempen bagging. Alternatively, workers twisted the fibers to make ropes in long, narrow buildings called rope walks. While sail cloth remained a minor portion of the business, bags and ropes dominated the Frankfort mills. A bag refers to hemp cloth bales primarily used to ship combed cotton to market. Often referred to as cotton bagging in favor of its principal use, a standard cotton bale weighed three hundred pounds consisting of two hundred and eighty-five pounds of cotton encased by fifteen pounds of hempen cloth and cordage.

The labor-intensive hempen (cotton) bags and rope manufacturing process required cheap manual labor, mainly consisting of enslaved men and boys. Workers endured noxious fumes and considerable grime performing arduous, monotonous labor. Due to its central location in the Blue Grass region, Lexington became the center of the bagging industry. Louisville rope walks enjoyed the advantage of not having to navigate the Falls of the Ohio at Louisville, providing easier access to southern tar and pitch, which were key ingredients for high-quality ropes. Without these advantages and much smaller in scope, Frankfort hempen manufacturing plants enjoyed year-round water access for shipment of finished products to market. Given high land transportation costs, only manufacturing facilities close to farms could be profitable. As a result, many northern Kentucky towns hosted competitive bagging plants and rope walks. Producers transported the finished products to port town on the Ohio River for shipment to customers via the Mississippi River and New Orleans. In the Crescent City, merchants resold the cotton bagging and bale rope to domestic cotton growers in the Mississippi Valley or shipped via ocean-going ships to international customers. Given its ideal growing climate and ease of transportation, Kentucky provided most of the cotton bagging and bale ropes to the burgeoning Mississippi Valley cotton producers.

On June 27, 1809, Frankfort's largest industrial concern, the Sproule and Hanna Cotton Bagging Factory, completely burned down. In his widely-read *Navigator*, Zadok Cramer alleged nefarious behavior on the part of the owners Charles Sproule and John H. Hanna. Cramer offered that "A bagging manufactory was burnt down at Frankfort about twelve months ago, by design it was conjectured." Worker arsonists were a common problem in the region's bagging factories. Often, enslaved laborers set blazes to protest working conditions and harsh treatment. While the fire's source is not known, subsequent events cast a long shadow on the business practices of this duo.[1] News reports estimated that

Charles Sproule and John Hanna lost five to six thousand dollars.[2] The business interruption provided an opening for a new, competitive mill and warehouse.

The demand for hemp products continued to grow, with the 1810 census indicating that Kentucky hump manufacturers produced over one million dollars of value or approximately twenty percent of products produced by Kentucky manufacturers. A high proportion of the over eighty-thousand enslaved people worked in the brutal, labor-intensive hemp business, which could not have operated without their labor.[3] Emboldened by this emerging boom in demand, a few months later, Hunter and a local entrepreneur and shipper, John Instone, entered into a partnership to build and operate a bagging manufactory. Also, an English immigrant and one of the richest men in town, Instone proved to be an excellent choice in partners due to his prominent political connections. President Jefferson appointed Instone as a Kentucky Commissioner of Bankruptcy based upon the recommendations of the state's senators. In addition to the partnership with Hunter, Instone served as cashier of the Bank of Kentucky, operated a ropewalk, and owned a fleet of keelboats for trade up and down the Kentucky and Ohio Rivers. Tax records indicate that he possessed at least thirty-five enslaved people employing the unfree labor both in the bagging business and in the operation of a farm in the Benson area outside of Frankfort.[4] The partners located their co-managed bagging plant near Brown's Ferry on the Kentucky River. This prime location offered convenient, all-year-round access to the river, no matter the water level.

Zadok Cramer described the company of Hunter and Instone as operating "an extensive bagging manufactory in which almost twenty-five hands, black-men and boys, are busily engaging, spinning, weaving, etc." As part of their bagging business, the partners built a warehouse on the river to ship and receive goods directly from docked boats. The partners advertised a fire-proof stone warehouse and wharf and boat slip designed to facilitate the year-round loading of boats in any stage of water. The partners boasted, "This situation equal, if not superior, to most places in the western country, for putting a cargo on board with expedition and in good order." The ad concludes with a promise of excellent service, "Every attention will be paid to meet the wishes of their customers, and punctual attendance at all times."[5]

Within a year of the disastrous fire, competition from a Sproule-led firm re-emerged. Hunter and Instone's partnership initially flourished and expanded its operations despite the newly invigorated local competition. Hunter advertised in the Lexington paper to "hire immediately, Seven Negro Men and

Fifteen Boys, to work in their bagging factory."[6] As only two percent of the blacks in Kentucky were free peoples, the partners sought to pay masters for the use of their slaves who would be compelled to work for the partnership.[7] The enslaved often worked in the masters' fields during planting and harvesting times and in the factories during the off-season. To hire an enslaved person, Hunter could expect to pay the owner between seventy-five and one hundred and fifty dollars per year (prorated for seasonal employment) plus the cost of boarding. Owners paid the property tax and contractually required renters to "properly" treat their slaves. Many Kentuckians believed (or rationalized) that they treated their enslaved peoples benevolently and certainly better than other parts of the country. However, slave ownership evoked no kindness, and proper treatment simply meant that renters had to return enslaved people at the end of the rental period "in working condition." The historical record is silent on how Hunter treated his enslaved employees, but we can assume that they, as other enslaved people, endured harsh treatment and brutal living conditions.[8]

Integrating his businesses, Hunter offered to barter hemp for bookstore customers. Seeking competitive advantages, the partners restructured their business arrangement, added capacity, and increased their geographic scope. John Instone opened a branch operation in Nashville under the firm name of John Instone & Co, and Hunter operated the Frankfort location as Hunter & Co. An over-arching partnership connected the two firms. Through the auspices of Instone's Nashville business, Hunter procured an assortment of bulk groceries, dry goods, and a wide variety of merchandise intended to be sold wholesale to area merchants. In early 1813, despite an innovative business structure and promising spin-off businesses, the partnership dissolved after just three years of operation.

For a while, John Instone, with a new partner, Thomas Garner, operated a brewery out of the former Frankfort cotton bagging plant and warehouse. The brewery also failed within a short time. In 1815, the state won a judgment against the business and conducted a sheriff's sale at Garner's farm on Henry's Mill Road near Lexington selling, "four hundred bushels of malt, two hundred weight of hops, one copper boiler and apparatus, about five hundred new tight barrels, three fermenting tuns, two steeping tuns, and one underback ditto."[9] Later in the year, William Hunter also won a judgment. The Franklin Circuit Court ordered a public sale on December 14 at noon. Two of Hunter's friends, John Brown and Achilles Sneed, served as commissioners overseeing the sale on behalf of the court. As an undivided moiety (undivided half share) sale, any purchaser would, by definition, become Hunter's partner. Unfortunately, the sale did not produce capital for Hunter to restart the business, and the enterprise lay vacant. Additionally, Hunter lost his partner's financial support. Restricting his professional aspirations, John Instone's health declined, and in 1818, he passed away at aged 64.

Just as Hunter and Instone ended their partnership, the Sproule-Hanna business also dissolved. After a substantial period of prosperity, disruptions due to the ongoing War of 1812 and other factors caused the hemp industry to enter a period of declining prices and volumes. Hunter thought he learned enough about the hemp milling business to continue in the hemp-based manufacturing business despite a setback in his first industrial foray. He partnered with Charles Sproule and a newcomer to the industry, Andrew Armstrong, to resume spinning rope and weaving cotton bagging. The new firm operated under Sproule, Armstrong & Co. Signaling that Hunter served the company more of an investor than an operator, his name did not appear on the firm's masthead.

In addition to hemp products, the partnership operated a merchant flour business purchasing wheat to be ground at P. G. Voorhies's flour mill. Sporting the accouterments of a successful business person, the lead partner Charles Sproule owned a large home in a prosperous section of town and enslaved four persons to perform household chores. Sproule married Margaret Humphrey a few years earlier, who bore him four children. Demonstrating an accumulation of wealth, Sproule even sat for portraiture by Matthew Harris Jouett, a talented student of Gilbert Stuart.[10] Also recently married, Armstrong owned farming properties outside of Lexington which produced raw hemp. Armstrong is best known as a veteran of the War of 1812. He kept a low profile with the Frankfort community. Armstrong did not significantly contribute to the partnership other than access to raw materials.

Seemingly successful, Hunter invested a significant financial, personal stake in the diversified milling company. As a recent Irish immigrant, Charles Sproule stood out from the multitude of American Revolutionary officers and soldiers who came to Kentucky after the war and dominated state politics and commerce. Partnering with a British immigrant became more comfortable for Hunter, who exhibited a propensity to associate with British natives. Following Colerick, Beaumont, and Instone, Sproule makes the fourth English or Irish-born business partner in succession. While investing with a partner who had ordinary life experiences worked well in the past, the partnership with Sproule would devastate him financially. More importantly, it would bring Hunter close to ruining his reputation and prominent standing in the community.

Placing too much trust in Sproule, who had successfully operated a hemp business for at least five years, Hunter regularly endorsed blank banknotes (essentially loan documents) used to procure raw materials and services for the milling business. Typically, the bank notes were paid off with proceeds from product sales at the end of the production process. In the interim, customarily, friends and political supporters became endorsees on the bank notes providing the bank extra security similar to a mortgage lien if the borrower defaulted on the loan.[11] Sproule took advantage of this situation and used a pre-signed note to procure a fifteen-thousand-dollar loan from the Bank of Kentucky. On December 1, 1815, the first loan had a one-year maturity and was also endorsed by John H. Hanna (Sproule's former business partner) and Edward Hardman. The bank extended the note for another year on December 2, 1816, but, for unknown reasons, this time, Henry F. Hume replaced former business partner Hanna as one of the three endorsees. Well-connected politically and well off by marriage, Hanna served as the United States District Court clerk in Frankfort. As an owner of an impressive, white brick colonial home situated across the street from the old capitol, Hanna would also have had the resources to pay off the Sproule, Armstrong & Co. debt.[12] Despite not paying down the principle, Sproule, Armstrong & Co. demonstrated a modest level of financial responsibility and resource. During 1816, the company made two interest payments of one thousand dollars and twelve hundred and twenty dollars to the bank.

In addition to unscrupulously using a signature without proper authorization, Sproule negotiated the loans with John P. Thomas, the state Treasurer who used Kentucky state government deposits at the Bank of Kentucky to fund the loans. Further demonstrating a nefarious circular intrigue, Thomas submitted, among six other individuals, the company of Sproule, Armstrong & Co. as securities for his faithful execution of the Treasurer's office. Suspicion of Thomas's activities grew, and the General Assembly commissioned a five-person select committee to investigate Thomas. Legislators chose first termer Joseph R. Underwood, a War of 1812 veteran, an accomplished orator, and up-and-coming politician to head the committee. In early 1817, the committee communicated its findings to the General Assembly. The committee found an extraordinary deficit of twenty-six thousand dollars, almost fifty percent of the money in the treasury account at the bank. Approximately two-thirds of the deficit occurred due to Thomas lending state funds to private individuals, including Sproule and Armstrong. The committee cited evidence that he had engaged in this illegal lending for a period of five or six years. Some of the loans had been repaid, such as advances to public printers, including William Hunter, and other loans to public officials. "Mr. Hunter acknowledged that he had once obtained a loan from Mr. Thomas of fifteen hundred dollars public money for a few days in a case where a bill of exchange was returned to him and was about to be protested for non-payment when every other prospect for getting the money failed."[13] Thomas used the public treasury as his personal "slush" fund to assist friends and political allies. Most damning, neither Thomas nor the committee could account for the remaining one-third.

Upon learning about the Sproule, Armstrong & Co. loan, Hunter immediately quizzed the other endorsees and found that neither knew about the loans or the use of public money to fund them. Alarmed, he "informed Mr. Thomas that a fraud had been practiced upon the endorsers of the note and that they would make no arrangement to pay it and the transaction should be exposed if he did not withdraw the note from the bank."[14] As the other endorsees did not testify, it is not clear whether they were aware of Thomas's funding of the loan from public sources. Deeply concerned with his personal credit at the bank, Hunter informed two bank directors (and political allies), John Brown and George M. Bibb, of the disputed loans. Brown and Bibb had already learned of the fraudulent loans by this time. Hunter fully cooperated with the Underwood's investigation providing detailed testimony. Neither Charles Sproule, Andrew Armstrong, nor the other co-endorsers offered evidence or testified in a usual turn of events. The demand for Hunter's testimony served to embarrass Bibb politically. Hunter maintained good relationships with Armstrong despite his absence from the legislative inquiry.

When the investigatory committee findings became public, Thomas resigned and began restitution. He sold his house, land, and other assets to refund sums of money to the state treasury. Losing his reputation and retiring from public life, Thomas did not face further criminal or civil proceedings. The committee found no fault on the part of William Hunter, but the association with Sproule did no good for his public reputation. Further, the operations of Sproule, Armstrong & Co. deteriorated. Still outstanding, the bank loan accumulated interest and represented an overwhelming threat to Hunter's financial position. Bagging factories struggled throughout Kentucky, with many closings due to falling hemp prices and an unfavorable business environment. Falling victim to the same economic pressures, the over-extended and debt-ridden operations of Sproule, Armstrong & Co. ceased. The company's demise left its owners and investors in dire financial straits.

The catastrophic impact on Charles Sproule's financial condition caused him to sell his valuable Frankfort house and lot on March 4, 1819. Despite generating cash from the sale, Sproule did not repay the bank and continued to experience economic distress. Unwisely, he wrote unfunded checks on the company, including a note to Samuel Carswell for nine hundred and twenty-one dollars. When the bank dishonored the note, Carswell sought legal remedy and had Sproule jailed for non-payment.

Recently, debtor laws changed in Kentucky, and delinquent borrowers received parole to remain within the town boundaries upon posting a bond. Absconding from these large debts, Charles Sproule, a recent widower, skipped town with his four young children moving out of state. Landing in Alabama, Sproule operated a river transport company. Armstrong followed Sproule's lead and also fled Frankfort and the state.

Sproule and Armstrong left Hunter "holding the bag." And clearly, Hunter made a poor decision to let Hanna remove his name from the endorlist for the second loan as he possessed sufficient financial resources to repay the loan. As none of the other endorsees had substantial assets to repay the loan, the law required Hunter to shoulder the entire principal and unpaid interest. In addition, to Sproule, Armstrong & Co. debt, Hunter owed the bank eight other loans. Hunter provided a lien on his city property as security for the $17,132 outstanding debt to satisfy the bank. Hunter and his family continued to live in the house. He sought ways to generate funds to pay down the bank, including providing a public room in the house for retail sales. However, with the failure of Sproule, Armstrong & Co., Hunter needed a new venture to redeem his financial footing.

Given his inability to repay the bank, Hunter did not have access to sufficient capital to re-enter the cotton bagging and rope businesses. However, in late 1818, Hunter entered into a partnership with John Armstrong to operate a warehouse in the former location of the Hunter & Instone Bagging Manufactory in Frankfort. Armstrong, a highly experienced shipper, operated a fleet of river and ocean-going ships from the Kentucky River, down the Ohio River to the Mississippi to New Orleans and beyond. His navigation skills were widely known to be reliable and safe. Hunter emphasized his counting house skills to prospective customers by asserting that "Bills of Lading and receipts taken with the utmost accuracy . . ." The partners promised "complete satisfaction to those who may favor them with their custom."[15]

The partners accepted for export all of the area's products except tobacco due to its odorous quality inhibiting the storage of other products. Hemp and spun yarn represented about half of the value of their transited goods. Other products in the warehouse awaiting shipment included flour, whiskey, tobacco, and bacon. With only a four percent market share in 1818, Hunter & Armstrong faced intense competition from two much larger warehouse businesses. The competitors dominated the high volume of flour and whiskey trades. Further, Hunter & Armstrong, contrary to their competitors, exported no candles, soap, paper, or powder. In total, the three warehouse companies handled $324,000 of exports and $312,000 of imports. In addition to storage, the partners also operated a consignment business "for a moderate commission."

Hunter continued to sell *Littell's Law* and other books using the new warehouse partnership. In the winter of 1818, the partners sold several hundreds of dollars of books to the Kentucky Senate and House. Additionally, they purveyed from their warehouse other products to the state government. Most notably, the partners charged the state $19.25 for gunpowder to fire a festive salute by militia Captain Robson.[16] While sales to the state were a minor portion of the partners' business, they demonstrated that Hunter retained a good measure of political support.

As economic conditions worsened, warehouse customers increasingly failed to pay storage charges. In those cases, the partners conducted a public sale to auction off the goods to settle the owner's charges. An example is the case of the firm of Charles St. Reno, which failed to pay storage charges on barrels of porter beer. Hunter & Armstrong offered the porter at auction. One has to wonder if there were any bidders for old beer![17] Hunter & Armstrong quietly closed down their business within a few months, which ended without disputes over unpaid debts and civil litigation.

CHAPTER FOURTEEN

Community Banker

The state government authorized and tightly controlled the early Kentucky banking industry. The politically active William Hunter had been involved with Kentucky banking since the inception of state-chartered banks.[1] In 1808, William Hunter, along with politically connected Daniel Weisiger, William Trigg, and John Brown, served on a commission to erect a brick bank building for the newly chartered Bank of Kentucky.[2] Soon thereafter, strong political associations helped Hunter secure a director's position in the state's hottest new investment opportunity. In 1813, the Kentucky legislature rechartered the Bank of Kentucky and named Hunter along with Henry Clay and six others as public directors. The bank's stockholders elected six additional directors, including Hunter's friends Daniel Weisiger and John Brown. The legislature named John Instone, one of Hunter's business partners, head cashier. Eventually, the legislature replaced Hunter with another director. However, Hunter gained valuable financial experience in lending, credit, and banking operations.

In 1818, many enterprising businesses could not obtain loans to finance their growth from either the Kentucky branches of the Bank of the United States or the Bank of Kentucky. To rectify the perceived dearth of lending facilities, the Kentucky legislator chartered forty-six new banks, including one in Frankfort. When the Frankfort Bank opened its doors in 1818, William Hunter became a director and an investor. Other directors were John H. Hanna, Henry Crittenden, Samuel Lewis, and George Adams. By charter, the legislature set capitalization at a modest one-half million dollars and offered investors five thousand shares priced at one hundred dollars each. Unlike the large Bank of Kentucky, the Frankfort Bank received no state monies. However, similar to the Bank of Kentucky, the state highly regulated the Frankfort Bank's lending practices and capitalization requirements.

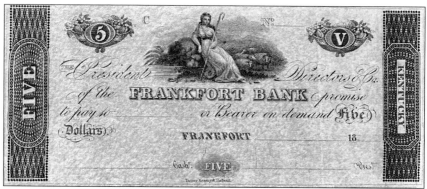

FIGURE 8. Uncirculated Frankfort Bank Note circa 1818–1820. Note the personal liability of the president and directors. Printed by the noted Tanner, Kearny and Tiebout engravers of Philadelphia.

The Frankfort Bank had a brief operating life. Within two years, the Frankfort and sister locally based banks issued twenty-six million in notes and loans, with most institutions quickly falling into insolvency. Derisively named "the forty thieves," in February 1820, the legislature revoked all of the licenses of the independent community banks, including the Frankfort Bank. While the Frankfort Bank ceased deposit and lending operations, the entity would continue to own and collect debts for several years. After its 1822 inception, the state government-sponsored Bank of the Commonwealth of Kentucky accepted the Frankfort banknotes for deposit at a high discount level. Bank investing further damaged Hunter's already teetering financial situation. For Hunter, banking proved to be no better than manufacturing for providing a source of financial means, especially in a deteriorating economy.

While Hunter attempted to create new and expand existing businesses, the national economy continually declined in the second half of the second decade of the nineteenth-century. Hunter's business enterprises faced an unprecedented economic maelstrom leading to the second major crisis in his life. In 1810, William Hunter "was an industrious, enterprising man in excellent credit." In 1817, "he met a disastrous blow in the failure of Sproule, Armstrong & Co. for whom he was endorser or surety for large amounts, and for whom he had to pay large sums."[3] By 1819, Hunter suffered a complete financial failure. Unfortunately, he was not alone as tens of thousands of businesses and people went bankrupt in the deep depression resulting from the Panic of 1819. During the height of the panic, the money supply dramatically shrank as specie became scarce, and people did not trust banknotes. As a result, the economy experienced a devastating contraction, the worst in the young republic's history.

Part IV

Turning to Politics

Starting in 1819 and continuing for the entire decade of the 1820s proved the most professionally difficult period in William Hunter's life. While over-charging allegations severely damaged his reputation ten years previously, Hunter now faced total economic collapse without sufficient means to repay large debts. Insolvency in the 1820s would prove even more challenging to resolve than restoring his community reputation in the last decade. Most other business leaders and investors faced similar financial situations as Hunter by endorsing bank loans that went into receivership. Perhaps this is why he retained a measure of respect in the community and that his stridently republican political voice continued to be heard and appreciated. As a result, admirably, Hunter turned to politics to improve the plight of Kentuckians. This course provided an outlet for his political ideals but kept William and his family on the edge of financial ruin. In the end, his investment in political capital paid off, but that would not become apparent for another decade.

CHAPTER FIFTEEN

Panic and Economic Devastation

Although historians refer to the monetary depression as the Panic of 1819, the economic decline started in 1815 after the War of 1812 and continued into the middle of the next decade. Agricultural prices plummeted, money became scarce, businesses folded, banks failed, and wealthy and poor people went bankrupt. Bank loans were next to impossible to obtain or renew. Population growth among free Kentuckians stagnated as hard times, and cheap enslaved labor drove many white people to Ohio or other points west. While there are several controversial theories about the cause of the panic, three causes stand out. First, the end of the Napoleonic wars caused a dramatic drop in demand and the prices of exports to Europe. The withdrawal of specie to pay down the loan used to finance the Louisiana Purchase further contributed to the unprecedented economic crisis. Sucking westerners' specie, eastern interests loaded wagons for a "line of march . . . to replenish the vaults of the mother bank in Philadelphia."[1] Lastly, the economy experienced overexpansion of the money supply due to increased bank credit lending without safe levels of specie conversion. As a result, riskier lending practices led to loans to businesses that were not sustainable in the long run and failed. Confidence in the banks plummeted with numerous devastating runs on banks to withdraw the remaining specie. Politicians scrambled to find scapegoats and solutions, splintering the state's Republican politicians into new factions. As the decade progressed, economic recovery occurred slowly, leading to sustained personal ruin for many families.

The Panic of 1819 particularly ravaged Kentucky's economy. Flour exports were a mainstay of the state's economy. When flour prices dropped from ten to six dollars a barrel, many farmers and mill owners could not pay principal or interest on their bank loans. Further, at renewal time, banks that needed species began calling loans leading to unforeseen foreclosures and forced asset sales at fire-sale prices. Increasingly, speculators and insiders employed spurious practices to purchase properties at well below market prices. For example, unscrupulous bidders at sheriff-managed bankruptcy sales conspired or stayed away so that debtors sold their property and businesses at distressed prices and did not receive the actual value of their property.

People felt swindled and agitated for solutions to their financial distress. Similar to the public discord around the 1798 Kentucky Resolutions, the citizens of Frankfort met *en masse* to publicly register their concerns and demand solutions. On May 13, 1819, debtors, farmers, and businessmen convened in the Franklin Church to discuss "the present state of the impending distresses." Prominent community leaders including George Adams, George M. Bibb, John Pope, and M. D. Hardin addressed the assembly. The meeting debated and then overwhelmingly approved a document consisting of fourteen resolutions. The first resolution below cogently and emotively summarizes the situation through the eyes of the Frankfort citizenry.

> Resolved, That the present scarcity of money, the pressure by the Banks upon those indebted to them, the pressure by creditors for their debts by suits and executions, the difficulty of raising very moderate sums of money even by enormous sacrifices of property, the heavy usury demanded for the use of money beyond what any useful employment and ordinary profit of regular business will justify the borrower in contracting to give, the general embarrassment which seems to encircle the commercial world, which is recoiling on the agricultural and mechanical classes, producing a smaller employment in the useful, industrious and sober callings, increasing the want of confidence between traders and dealers, employers and employed, is a public calamity which we acknowledge and deplore as hastening to a general suspension of payments, business and employment, and utterly destructive of social order and happiness.

The additional thirteen Frankfort Resolutions proposed solutions for debtor relief, economic stabilization, and business recovery. The resolutions conclude by imploring the Kentucky legislature to convene an emergency session "to save the country from the impending catastrophe." The town meeting selected William Hunter along with George Adams, George M. Bibb, John Pope, M. D. Hardin, James Hunter, and Jacob Creath as a committee of correspondence. Similar to the organizing concept employed by the thirteen colonies before the

War for Independence, the committee will "correspond with the people of the other counties in the state, and with such committees as may be appointed by them, receive the communications and answers from similar meetings in other counties and lay the result before the acting Governor."[2]

The governor and legislature did not call a special session but did act on several of the ideas presented in the Frankfort Resolves. On February 11, 1820, the legislature passed a moratorium preventing court orders on behalf of banks mandating payment of debts for one year. Further, in 1821, the legislature repealed the law, which imprisoned citizens who could not repay their debts.[3] The stay law and freedom from imprisonment for unpaid debts greatly benefited William Hunter in his dispute with the Bank of Kentucky. However, the legislative actions did not go far enough in the views of William Hunter and a large number of his fellow citizens. A weak economy fostered intense creditor/debtor tensions leading to a roiling political environment.

Hunter avoided the manufacturing and banking sectors and returned to retail ventures to generate income. In late 1818, he leased a room in his house to the Pearson and Hickman partnership, who offered "an elegant assortment of goods" for sale. This retail business did not prosper, and Hunter sought other opportunities in a downward sliding economy. Sensing an opportunity to assist people in raising cash immediately, he opened an auction house at his place on Montgomery Street. Hunter learned the auctioneering business and advertised the sale of books (of course), jewelry, watches, dry goods, and "fancy articles." Expanding his geographic reach, from November 1819 to March 1820, he ran a series of advertisements in the *Louisville Public Advertiser* soliciting to sell goods on commission. Hunter noted the approaching legislative session as an excellent opportunity to sell unwanted goods for cash. Remarkably, relatives of Hunter's erstwhile partner, George and John Sproule, set up a competing auction house. Ironically, the Sproules' first featured a sale of law books, a Hunter specialty, from the estate of Patrick Byrne. Bad debts and slow paying customers plagued the auction business like the newspaper business. Hunter regularly included in his ads warnings that he would be forced to resell winning bidder's merchandise if they did not come into the shop and pay for the items.[4]

Aggressively, the bankrupt Hunter pursued all avenues to restore his financial health. In a turnabout, Hunter used the courts to facilitate the collection of monies owed to him. In January 1821, he filed a suit against Charles B. King, an out-of-stater, in Frankfort to restore the property to satisfy the debts. In another attempt to raise funds, he petitioned the 1822 legislature to refund his contribution to re-build the state capital. The Senate passed a relief act to restore six hundred dollars to Hunter and two hundred dollars each to three other individuals. However, the House voted down the relief bill by a resounding margin of thirty-two yeas to fifty nays. Afterward, the House representative from Jefferson County, Craven P. Lockett, took up Hunter's cause and appealed to the legislature to reconsider. In an article in Kendall's *Argus of Western America*, he wrote, "Give the subscribers back their money, or sit not in the house." Both Lockett and Hunter had deep personal relationships with the former Governor Christopher Greenup. Lockett married one of Greenup's daughters, and Hunter served as an executor of Greenup's estate. Lockett ended his plea with, "The pride of the state is involved in this affair."[5] The effort to refund Hunter's contribution to building the state capitol came to naught. Lastly, Hunter sued Charles Sproule and Andrew Armstrong for the unpaid debts of Sproule, Armstrong & Co. As both defendants resided outside the state and had no in-state assets, any collections were a long shot. To bolster his position, Hunter initiated the suit to become the aggrieved party in the Bank of Kentucky dispute over his responsibility for the debts of Sproule, Armstrong & Co.

During this financially difficult period, William, Ann, and their children enjoyed several bright spots and joyous family moments. In the volunteer Frankfort Fire Department, William served as a "property man" who took charge of salvaged goods during and after a fire. This role leveraged Hunter's experience in the auction and consignment businesses. In addition, Hunter helped his son, Morrison, find employment as a clerk with the fire department. Previous to this role, Morrison had served as a clerk for the town of Frankfort. Morrison's fire department duties included setting up, advertising, and taking minutes at the departmental meetings. While providing minimal compensation, he contributed to family income and helped sustain the struggling family. Happily, for William and Ann, their eldest daughter found a suitor with bright prospects. Their eighteen-year-old daughter, Lavinia, married Leonard H. Lyne. Lyne served in the Kentucky House of Representatives from a prominent family in Henderson County and shared William's state and national politics. The wedding took place on February 20, 1821, in Frankfort. Lavinia's union with Leonard H. Lyne produced three children, Lavinia in 1825, Leonard H. in 1827, and William H. in 1829. Morrison moved to Mobile, Alabama, and married Ann Tremlett Toulmin, the daughter of Judge Harry Toulmin. His father published the first volumes of Kentucky laws drafted by Judge Toulmin. What makes this an odd coincidence is that Judge Toulmin moved from Frankfort before Morrison was born. Like many other Kentuckians, Morrison sought better opportunities in the rich cotton lands of the deep south and re-located, by chance, to Mobile, Alabama. Perhaps, their father's Kentucky connections offered a conversation starter, but their marriage occurred without familial intervention and is an interesting coincidence of history.

Despite positive family developments, Hunter continued to be dogged by disputes and litigation over the debts incurred by Sproule, Armstrong & Co. Finally, upon the expiration of the stay law, the Bank of Kentucky filed suit on July 9, 1821, to coerce collection of their debt against William Hunter and two days later served him with a subpoena. Notwithstanding the feeling that Sproule fraudulently deceived him, Hunter could not ignore the legally binding summons.

Seemingly the bank's court case was clear cut. Hunter granted the bank a lien on his property in 1819 as security for the outstanding $17,132 bank loan. However, Hunter failed to repay the loan, so the bank had the legal right to repossess his house and property. The bank had no prospects of repayments from Sproule, Armstrong & Co. as there was no functioning business to generate funds to pay down the debt. Further, Hunter did not have any other companies to create repayment funds. While seemingly cut and dried to the bank directors, Hunter would mount a significant legal challenge to their right to repossess the Montgomery Street house and property. Unbeknownst to the bank, in 1810, William Hunter, privately without public notice, transferred the home and property to two trustees to hold for the benefit of his wife. His motivations were to safeguard assets for the ongoing use of his wife and children in the event of his business failure. While the parties signed the trust documents, they did not duly record the trust agreement with the court.

One of the trustees, Achilles Sneed, had several conflicts of interest. First, in 1810, Sneed served as court clerk that should have filed the transfer deed, and secondly, in 1817, he served as a Bank of Kentucky director. Using the 1810 trust as controlling, Hunter fought back. On November 10, 1821, Hunter executed a deed of conveyance to Leonard H. Lyne, Hunter's son-in-law and member of the Kentucky House. Then, at a Frankfort town trustee meeting, Hunter presented the new duly signed deed denoting Lyne's trusteeship of the house and property, which the town's trustees formally accepted and entered into the town's record. Quite disingenuous, Achilles Sneed, a Frankfort town trustee, did not attend the town meeting so that he would not have to vote on the matter.

Bank management viewed this legal maneuver as a sham and continued prosecuting its case. In court, William Hunter argued that the bank, through the auspices of Sneed, consented to the title restrictions in 1817 when it accepted the property as security for the loan. As a single director (Achilles Sneed) cannot stand for the bank, the bank retorted that it did have no legally binding knowledge of the 1810 trust agreement and believed its claim to the property was free and clear of any encumbrances. The judge agreed with the bank, ordered the 1817 agreement to be controlling, and allowed the bank to continue the ejectment process to recover its debts. However, Hunter had further defenses again and tied the bank up in continued litigation. Courts considered the matter until 1830 when the Kentucky Court of Appeals made a final ruling. Judge Joseph R. Underwood affirmed the circuit court findings in a legally complex thirty-four-page opinion.

Dismissing Hunter's case as clear cut, the judge ordered the plaintiffs to pay the bank's legal fees and other costs. However, again, Hunter found himself in Underwood's crosshairs. Underwood drove the original Sproule, Armstrong & Co. legislative investigation with the political intention of harming rival George M. Bibb. Now again, Underwood had the final say that confirmed Hunter's bankruptcy.

At least Hunter's problems associated with Sproule, Armstrong & Co. were over, and he could move in other directions. Fortunately, the debtor laws had changed, and Hunter did not face incarceration, and he could pursue new ventures to reinstate his credit and recover financially.[6] Hunter tried one more time to become a successful manufacturer. While the Bank of Kentucky sought title to his home, Hunter retained ownership of his original cotton bagging factory. As the hemp business "has again become profitable," Hunter described his property's advantages in a *Frankfort Argus* advertisement, including a large building to accommodate fifty workers and year-round access to shipping on the Kentucky River. A capital poor but tenacious Hunter offered to renter the hempen business despite past failures. "Should any gentleman who can furnish the necessary capital, be desirous of embarking it in this line, they may rely upon its becoming a profitable investment . . . if he would prefer a partner, the advertiser, who has had several years' experience in it, would be willing to undertake the management of the concern for an equal share of the profits." No partner came forward, and the factory and the property continued dormant.[7] Frustrated commercially and fortunate to escape further prosecution, Hunter turned to politics to plead the plight of the state's debtors. His debtor experiences would propel Hunter to become a highly vocal spokesperson for a new political movement that would dominate Kentucky politics for the next four years. Hunter sought elected office and advocated enacting additional laws protecting debtors from his perception of the unreasonableness of commercial banks.

CHAPTER SIXTEEN

Ernest Legislator

A new divide emerged among Kentucky politicians replacing the Republican/Federalist party factions of the last twenty-five years. Advocates for debtors coalesced around the Relief (or Country) party while the banks and status quo proponents became the Anti-relief (or Court) party. In the period 1820-1, the Relief party successfully enacted laws to benefit debtors, including altering private contracts by fiat and harming the soundness of the banks. In addition to the stay laws, which helped Hunter for a short time, the legislature enacted laws requiring banks to accept new paper money from a new Bank of the Commonwealth, which had drastically depreciated. Banks and creditors fought back. They filed suit in court to overturn the debt relief laws. Unfortunately, a circuit court judge interpreting years of contractual laws rule in favor of the banks. Not deterred, the relief proponents appealed their case to the Kentucky Court of Appeals. Nevertheless, again, the banks prevailed. In an extraordinary move, the relief party sought to repeal the law enacting the Court of Appeals and replace the old court with a new court. The debt relief legislators would then appoint judges more favorable to debtors. However, this effort failed during the 1823-4 legislative session.

The controversy over the court of appeals dominated the 1824 electioneering activities. As a result, the election became a referendum for the public to choose between advocates of the relief (new courts) and anti-relief (old courts). Generally, Lexington and the Blue Grass portions of the state supported the old court, and the less prosperous sections supported the new court and advocated for relief from debt repayments. Realizing that his political influence lasted well beyond his editorship, William Hunter decided to seek election from

Frankfort to the statehouse. On March 31st, he announced his candidacy in the friendly and supportive pages of the *Frankfort Argus*. The four Relief Party and one Anti-Relief Party candidates made for a crowded field seeking two seats. On election day, Frankfort voters by a wide margin sent Hunter along with Anti-Relief Party candidate James MacBrayer to the General Assembly.[1]

After fifteen years of reporting on legislative activities, Hunter now had the opportunity to make the news. Riding a statewide electoral wave that included the governor and lieutenant governor, Hunter entered the General Assembly with a large majority of fellow Debt Relief Party representatives. In a reveling mood, the victors named a committee of arrangement which included the newly elected Hunter to plan and conduct a celebration following the new governor and lieutenant governor taking the oaths of office. "Exceedingly fine" weather on the appointed day livened the spirits of the victorious party. Celebratory firing from the town's artillery regiment signaled the start of the festivities. "After which, Governor Joseph Desha made a short address to the citizens present expressing" his "honor" at being elected and his "determination" to meet the citizen's needs and expectations. After the speech, William and the committee of arrangement adjourned to a festive dinner. They hosted over one hundred celebrants at Captain Weisiger's tavern and honored the incoming governor and many other politicians. The celebrants offered twenty-four toasts highlighting Founders, Revolutionary War generals, and veterans of the recent War of 1812. Interestingly, toasts were drunk to both Andrew Jackson and Henry Clay, whose paths soon diverged.[2]

Before the legislative session commenced, Hunter continued the book auction business. "The subscriber's Auction Room in Frankfort for the sale of Books, will, as usual, be open during the approaching session of the Legislature . . . Well worthy of the attention of purchasers . . ." Highlighting the auction is "The entire Law Library of the late William Littell and part of the valuable Library of the late James W. Forbes." Hunter warned purchasers to be early, as these valuable collections will be sold at the start of the auction. Typical of Hunter's auction businesses, he found it easier to sell books than collecting hard money for their purchase.[3]

Convening in mid-November, the General Assembly got right to work. The legislature assigned Hunter to the Committee on Public Claims and a special committee to investigate the State books and records after the recent fire in the Capitol Building, recognizing his counting-house and accounting skills. Other committee assignments quickly followed, including looking into publishing expenses and the books of the penitentiary. Finally, Hunter felt a bit of vindication of his integrity and reputation with one particular committee assignment. On November 17, 1824, the House voted to appoint Hunter to a committee to investigate the loss of money from the Treasury. Gratified at the respect and confidence of his fellow representative, the committee presented its report under Hunter's signature on January 5. Still raw from his Sproule, Armstrong & Co. disputes and maybe exacting payback, Hunter voted with the majority to reduce the authorized expense budget of the Bank of Kentucky.

In another emotional event a week later, Hunter voted with the majority to commission an oil painting of Lafayette by famed Frankfort artist Matthew Jouett to commemorate the former Continental Army General's visit to Frankfort in a few months. Curiously, given William's youthful association with Lafayette, the town leaders did not appoint William as a manager to plan the festivities and welcome the general to Frankfort. However, Ann provided food for the welcoming dinner, and the host committee reimbursed her three dollars for the cost of the ingredients. Any reflections by Hunter and Lafayette on their 1779 Brittany experiences are lost to history. Hunter shunned publicizing his family's Revolutionary War connection to Lafayette to avoid spotlighting his father's service in the British Army.

The legislature moved next to consider the most critical issue of the term. Believing that the Debt Relief Party received a voter mandate, proponents of the new court introduced legislation to establish its legitimacy. Just before Christmas 1824, and after several attempts, Hunter voted with the majority to create a new appeals court replacing the old court. The bill also provided provisions reorganizing the court of appeals. However, the bill would not be the last word on this issue. Debt relief and the old court/new court controversy would continue to roil Kentucky politics in the upcoming elections.

More important than any one vote, Hunter developed and strengthened many political and personal ties with rising politicians. He actively supported sending John Rowan, a gifted lawyer, to Washington as one of Kentucky's two senators. While not always agreeing on political issues, Hunter regarded the cerebral Rowan as a close personal friend who assisted him in times of need.[4] Signaling a new, important relationship, Hunter voted to affirm the legislature's support for Andrew Jackson presidential candidacy to the United States House of Representatives. Originally Kentucky's presidential electors named Henry Clay, but when no candidate received an electoral majority, the House of Representatives determined the outcome of the 1824 election. Jackson lost when Henry Clay entered into a supposedly "corrupt bargain" with the eventually Presidential winner John Quincy Adams. After this vote,

Hunter became a staunch and vocal Jackson supporter. And in turn, Jackson and Hunter's Kentucky political connections would positively impact future events in Hunter's life.

This frenzy of momentous activity quickly concluded, and the General Assembly closed its session on January 12, 1825. After sixty days of legislating, the Kentuckians enacted two hundred new laws, twenty-two of general importance to the entire estate.[5] After just two months of legislative service, William Hunter's electoral career concluded. Over the next year, the tide of public opinion shifted, and Debt Relief Party politicians, once an overwhelming majority, increasingly became unelectable. William Hunter returned to familiar pursuits.

CHAPTER SEVENTEEN

Partisan Editor

With the Old Court forces gaining popular support, the political battles intensified, leading to a fierce newspaper war in the run-up to the August 1826 state elections. Both sides started new politically driven newspapers to carry their messages to the public and increase their voter bases. While the papers carried a few advertisements, most of their pages were devoted to publishing articles supporting their positions or attacking the other side. The party newspapers commenced publication, first in Frankfort and then in other parts of the state. To disseminate the messages of the Relief Party, a new Frankfort newspaper under the editorship of William Tanner, a one-time Amos Kendall apprentice at *The Argus*, commenced in early 1826 called *The Patriot*.[1] An experienced but itinerant printer, Tanner is best known for being in the center of a firestorm dredged up from the last presidential election. In 1823, Tanner received one hundred dollars from Henry Clay to print a pamphlet penned by Amos Kendall attacking the stance of John Quincy Adams on the Treaty of Ghent. In the runup to the 1828 election, Jackson supporters pointed to this pamphlet as evidence that a corrupt bargain formed between John Quincy Adams and Henry Clay in Clay being named to Secretary of State after throwing his support to Adams in the House of Representatives, which assured his presidency. The ensuing political controversy ensured a wide and growing readership for *The Patriot*.[2]

Countering *The Patriot*, the Anti-Relief Party started a paper in Frankfort under the editorship of Jacob Holeman called the *Spirit of '76*. Until the start of the *Spirit of '76*, Holeman had partnered with James G. Dana to publish the Frankfort weekly *Commentator*. A celebrated veteran of the War of 1812 and a rough and tumble newspaper competitor, Holeman was best known for killing an unhappy reader alleging slander in an 1819 duel. Holeman's rough elbows and sharp wit made him an influential supporter of the Old Court and anti-debt relief party. Veteran editorialists provided a quick wit and keen eye for effective political attacks for both new "political party" news outlets.

Underemployed, Hunter evaluated his prospects. His retail store and auction business provided only modest income. As a result, he decided to rent out his Montgomery Street storeroom to retailers G. E. Russell and John L. Moore to sell groceries, dry goods, books, and stationery as well as other items on consignment.[3] Leasing his retail assets freed up Hunter to devote time supporting the Relief party campaign. After a seventeen-year absence and with the backing of Amos Kendall, he decided to return to newspaper printing, in which, previously, he had a measure of success. In addition to supporting his family, as an editor, he could keep his political connections current and advance the causes of the Relief Party members. His friend and political ally Amos Kendall continued to edit *The Argus,* and with the new Relief Party paper in Frankfort, Hunter sought a new printing location. As a growing commercial center, Louisville appeared to have good prospects. The town sported only one newspaper, the *Public Advertiser.* Its editor, Shadrack Penn, Jr., had been in business since 1818 and offered a bi-weekly paper. One observer described Penn as having the "dominant editorial voice in the state, an experienced politician, forcible writer, and a man of extraordinary tact." Penn sided with the anti-relief faction and denounced on the *Public Advertiser's* pages the New Court and the establishment of the Commonwealth Bank of Kentucky. With encouragement from Amos Kendall, Hunter perceived the political need for a rival paper espousing debtor relief policy in this politically important city.

Hunter hooked up with Joshua S. Russell, the printer and editor of the recently reestablished *Louisville Gazette,* to ease his market entry. The partnership with an existing paper avoided capital investment by the cash-strapped Hunter. Political enemies decried that Hunter received funding from unnamed political allies, tainting his editorial voice.[4] Dividing responsibilities, Hunter controlled the editorial content, and Russell focused on printing at the partner print shop at the corner of Third and Main Streets. Printed in modern type, the *Louisville Gazette* sported a lofty banner "Firm, Free and Temperate." Learning from past mistakes, the partners set the subscription price at three dollars per annum. Given Hunter's experience with notes and credit, subscriptions were to be paid in specie in advance. The partner promised the paper would provide the most current political and commercial information. Its editorials would support

Republican principles of 1798 (i.e., Kentucky Resolutions), advocate for states' rights, oppose extending the Federal judiciary and foster a spirit of Federalism. The partners believed that a single government would result in extensive corruption, and citizens must preserve the involatile rights of the states. The editorial policy ended with a promise, "We cannot command success—we will endeavor to deserve it."[5]

Characterized as "Decidedly New Court, but mild in character," Amos Kendall in the *Frankfort Argus* endorsed Hunter's new endeavor. "The experience of the editor promises to the public a highly useful and interesting paper." In a weak and not convincing attempt to provide political cover, Kendall characterized the *Louisville Gazette* as "much devoted to Commercial concerns." Kendall reported that A. G. Hodges had purchased Holeman's interest in the *Commentator* in the same issue. Now there were two independent editorial critics of Hunter and the Debt Relief Party published in Frankfort.[6]

After a few issues, Hunter became the sole owner of the *Louisville Gazette*. Immediately, a lively newspaper war ensued. In May, Hunter debated Old Court and New Court issues with J. G. Dana and A. G. Hodges, editors of the Frankfort *Commentator*. The *Commentator* took Hunter to task in the haughtiest tones for alleging that the people do not have confidence in the old court. Further, Dana criticized Hunter for voting for the new court, which caused "much disharmony and disruption" during its short existence. The Frankfort *Commentator* editorial concluded that "nothing can be more absurd, nothing in politics, we may say, can be more dishonest, than to disregard the obvious intent, and plain meaning of the constitution, and seek shelter under the allegation that the *very* letter is not violated."[7] While vituperatively sparring over current issues, both Hunter and Dana came from families that supported the British during the Revolution.

Later in the spring, the debate between Hunter's *Louisville Gazette* and The *Spirit of '76* intensified. Holeman derisively referred to William Hunter as "*the missionary editor* of the new court faction." More directly, Holeman called out his vanity for unsuccessfully seeking his party's nomination and charged him with "living in splendor on other people's property. Rehashing Hunter's battles over the Sproule, Armstrong & Co. debt, a *Spirit of '76* editorial concluded Hunter had been, "charged with dishonesty, and making secret deeds of trust for property, and afterwards mortgaging the same property to secure the payment of borrowed money, and when pay day come, making every fraudulent shift and contrivance, to defeat the mortgage and give a preference to a secret fraudulent deed of trust."[8] Clearly, Holeman omitted the fact that Charles Sproule perpetrated a fraud on an uninformed William Hunter and that Sproule and Armstrong fled the state and along with the other endorsers, leaving Hunter "holding the bag." Less knowledgeable Louisville readers must have questioned Hunter's integrity, which could not have done much for readership or advertising. In the pages of the *Louisville Gazette*, Hunter fought back by "calling the charges made in the last '76 of a contemptible nature." He alleged *The Spirit of '76* was "devoted to the destruction of private character" and was "at war with the principles of the revolution." The back and forth continued with Holeman calling Hunter "a small fry" and Hunter alleging that The *Spirit of '76* was really just a disguised mouthpiece for old-line Federalists Humphrey and J. J. Marshall.[9] Hunter continued attacking Holeman, the current state public printer, for not discharging his responsibilities and overcharging the state. Eagerly, Holeman fired back in the next issue that "Hunter well knows that the legislature in order to guard against such men as himself, regulated the prices . . . therefore, no printer can draw more than his just dues." While a turn of the tables on Hunter's allegations, Holeman descended into vituperative name-calling by referring to Hunter as "a petty scribbler" and a "pig."[10]

The war of words with another Frankfort newspaper, the *Commentator* became even more piquant over the reporting of the murder of the State's Attorney General. A Frankfort jury convicted Jereboam O. Beauchamp of killing Solomon P. Sharpe, an advocate of the New Court. Sharpe's wife alleged that an Old Court politician and lawyer, Patrick Henry Darby, conspired with Beauchamp to assassinate her husband for political reasons. Amos Kendall reported these allegations in *The Argus,* and William Hunter followed in turn. Darby issued a vitriolic rebuttal in the friendly *Commentator*, with which a few months prior, he merged his newspaper *The Constitutional Advocate*. "This is the second time that Mr. Hunter has prostituted the columns of his paper for other to a calumny which he never did himself believe." Darby states that Hunter ought to be "ashamed of such corruption of his press." Curiously, Darby ends his assessment of Hunter's reporting by asserting that his wife Ann controlled too much of his editorial perspectives. Darby asserts that William was "prompted to his cause (Relief Party) by the counsels of his pillow, which is rather his stronger, than his better part." While Ann may or may not have shared William's political beliefs, this is the first time her views were commented on publicly. Contrary to Darby's assertion, William had a solid track record of voting for relief measures in the state legislature and continued to advocate for debt relief well after this incident. Known for hotheadedness and exhibiting eccentricities, Darby's assertion that Ann inappropriately dominated William's political thinking fell on deaf ears.[11]

In a final summation on the eve of the election, *The Spirit of '76* reiterated its charge that Hunter squandered the bank's money "to give splendid parties and live at his ease." Holeman reprinted the entire legislative report accusing Hunter of defrauding the government as the State Printer noting unanimous acceptance even by senior members of the Relief Party today. In addition, the paper alleged that Hunter inappropriately attempted to shield his assets from bank repossession by transferring his household furniture to his son and deeding his house to his son-in-law. Hunter responded to the allegation by stating that "the last remnant of property was wrested from an unfortunate family, by a soul-less institution, to pay debts contracted as security for others." Holeman concludes concluded his election-eve edition with a final warning to voters that Hunter and by association the Debt Relief party had the demonstrated "capacity in defrauding justice, and staving off the payment of just debts."[12]

No matter how lively the debate, Hunter ceased publication of the *Louisville Gazette* after only eleven issues. With the increasing political ascendency of the Old Court advocates, his New Court messages did not resonate with the Louisville population. Further, the attacks on his character and integrity scared away subscribers in a town where he continued to be an outsider. People were not going to risk paying subscriptions in scarce specie in advance to a paper with political motivations on the losing side. Hunter did not plan to publish *The Louisville Gazette* beyond election day. Similarly, by election day, both *The Patriot* and *The Spirit of '76* also shut down (though the latter would resume publication for a short period).[13]

When the votes were tallied, Hunter and Kendall's side lost as the Old Court Party extended in majorities in the state legislature. The *Frankfort Argus* alleged a "trick and trap" by the opposition, including closing some polls early and re-opening others to add Old Court votes. In the end, a veto-proof margin of victory led the Old Court proponents to dissolve the New Court.[14] While, at the time, many interpreted the election as a bitter defeat and the New Court ceased operations, the results contained seeds of favorable change for the political allies of Hunter and Kendall. A new political divide fractured Kentucky politics. One of the most senior, well-respected Kentucky Old Court politicians, John Pope, became frustrated with the lack of compromise. While not changing his views on the court question, he aligned himself with New Court politicians. Following Pope's conversion to the debt relief faction, other well-respected state politicians such as Francis P. Blair, the talented editor of the *Frankfort Patriot*, and William T. Barry, who served as Kentucky's Secretary of State as well as other up and coming politicians, began to identify with the populist message of the Debt Relievers. This shift in politics would profoundly affect the 1828 presidential election.

While passionate about politics, Hunter needed a steady income to pay the bills and support his family. In an unlikely way, he chose to return to his auction business. He entered into an auction and commission business partnership with former newspaper competitor Daniel Bradford. During the first decade of the eighteenth-century, Hunter and the Bradford family were fierce competitors. Perhaps they had established a friendly rapport while serving together on a committee investigating the establishment of a Kentucky printer and bookseller association in 1805. Most recently, Bradford had a five-year run in publishing *The Lexington Public Advertiser* and served as the cashier of the Lexington Branch Bank of the Commonwealth of Kentucky. A score of years after being intense competitive rivals, these two former adversaries formed a partnership to operate a retail business together. The operating plan called for Hunter to conduct auctions in Frankfort during the annual legislative sessions and both partners to preside over the ongoing business in Lexington. In addition to retail sales, the auctioneers offered their services to sell real estate and other personal property in the surrounding areas. In addition, the duos also sold enslaved people.[15] As expected from two former editors, the partners widely advertised their services in local newspapers. They promised "to meet the wishes of their employers."[16]

While auctioneering and commissioned sales put food on the table, Hunter's heart lay in other areas. He regarded the forthcoming 1828 election as critical for western interests and began actively campaigning for Andrew Jackson to defeat President John Quincy Adams.

CHAPTER EIGHTEEN

Becoming a Jacksonian

Since their first association in 1818, the aging Hunter and the up-and-coming Amos Kendall intertwined an intense political relationship with a close, personal friendship. First, the two newspaper editors worked together as trustees of the Kentucky Seminary and then as fellow advocates for debtor relief in the 1819 to 1825 struggle. In another parallel, the two men unsuccessfully ventured into milling businesses with capital brought to their marriages by spouses. Both ventures became mired in debt, but Kendall's companies were more modest than Hunter's. He avoided bankruptcy through prudent caution, emergency loans from influential politicians, substantial assets acquired through marriage, and continual profits from his newspaper. Despite family experiences to the contrary, but similar to the prevailing sentiments of Jacksonians, both Kendall and Hunter willfully entered into the practice of buying and selling enslaved people.

A new political issue replaced the old court/recent court controversy, captivating Hunter and providing a newsworthy copy for Kendall's Argus. A political coalition of northern and western interests emerged to advocate increasing the 1824 statutory tariffs on imported goods to protect nascent American manufacturers further. Tariff protection for hemp, cotton bagging, and rope products resonated as a political issue with Kentucky citizens who regarded Hunter as an apparent hemp industry authority despite the failure of his manufacturing ventures a decade earlier.[1] The Pennsylvania Society for the promotion of Manufactures and the Mechanic Arts proposed a convention to meet on July 30, 1827, to address tariff law changes. As producers of grains, hemp, and cotton, Kentuckians generally advocated for high tariffs on competing raw materials and goods manufactured from these items. Northerners advocated for tariff protections, with Southerners generally opposing most tariffs.

On July 9th, at a meeting in Frankfort, two leading citizens, John J. Crittenden and Ishim Talbot, presented a plan and proposed delegates from Kentucky to attend the Harrisburg Convention. Both advocated the Old Court in the Debt Relief controversy and supported President Adams. Crittenden served as the United States District Attorney for Kentucky and famously fathered a Confederate general and a Union general during the Civil War.[2] Reputedly the wealthiest person in Frankfort, Talbot served two terms in the United States Senate. Crittenden proposed a platform supporting little change from the Tariff Bill of 1824. Four Kentucky representatives, all Old Court adherents, were named to communicate this message. Hunter spoke rose to speak at the meeting, but Crittenden supporters prevented him from speaking. Hunter complained that the "rudeness of your well-drilled flatterers prevented me" from giving [a reply] at the time." As a result, Hunter penned an open letter to Crittenden and Kendall published the message in the upcoming *Argus*. Sensitive to the lack of protection for his failed manufacturing businesses, Hunter disputed Crittenden's "steady as she goes" proposals. Hunter alleged that Crittenden underestimated the negative impact of imports on Kentucky manufacturing, stating "that while I was engaged in the manufacture of that article [cotton bagging], some years ago, I was much injured by the want of protection." He criticizes Crittenden for supporting additional duties on woolens, not advocating for more duties on imported spirits and rum. As a result, Crittenden supported tariffs which aided the New Englanders and harmed his fellow Kentuckians. Hunter wryly posits, "In short, sir your speech and project were better suited to the meridian of Boston than that of Kentucky, and would doubtless have received loud plaudits in Faneuil Hall." Playing to the patriotism of the many Kentucky veterans of the Wars of Independence and 1812, Hunter questioned why any Kentuckian would support tariff provisions that helped New England when the region did little to support the United States during the dark days of the War of 1812. When Crittenden retorted that there was no time to add unnecessary polish to Kentucky's input, any delay might cause the state's delegates to miss the convention's opening. To that, Hunter replied that if Kentucky's voice was unheard in Harrisburg, its citizens "have recourse to the old-fashioned mode of instructing our Representatives in Congress."

Both men could help themselves but insert personal barbs in their arguments. Crittenden first questioned why Kentuckians should listen to someone with so many financial difficulties. "The sarcastic sneers and allusions to my personal affairs and misfortunes in which you indulged yourself, I pass by as unworthy a great man." While Hunter might have thought he stood on high ground, he stooped to characterize Crittenden's wit as "pointless" and his jokes "as dull as those of Dutch Burgomaster."

All this banter made for good news, and Amos Kendall eagerly published an account of the Frankfort meeting and Hunter's letter in the *Argus*. Nationally, Jackson supporters picked up Hunter's article. Prominently, Duff Green's *United States' Telegraph* in Washington City republished Hunter's letter.

Despite Hunter's agitation, Kentucky sent four representatives to Harrisburg, all from the Old Court faction. The delegates were George Robertson (Kentucky State Legislature), James Cowan (Prominent Lexington attorney), Richard H. Chinn (US Attorney for the Kentucky District), and John Harvie (President of the Bank of Kentucky). All four men supported the anti-relief faction, emerging Whig political positions, and the Kentucky favorite son, Henry Clay. From Hunter's perspective, the chosen representatives did not represent Kentuckians' business and agricultural interests. As scheduled, the convention started on July 30th, with Matthew Carey opening the first session. After being geographically separated for over thirty-two years, Hunter would have enjoyed the opportunity to reconnect with his fellow printer, friend, and early sponsor. The convention met for the next four days and hammered out an exact position on a long list of tariffed items communicated to Congress. No southern states sent delegates, so the anti-tariff supporters did not have a voice in the final convention product. Instead, as Hunter suggested in his newspaper editorial, Kentuckians should approach their senators and representatives to influence the tariff legislation directly. As is its preference, Congress received the convention report but crafted a tariff law passed upon its considerations. In the end, the convention created copious newspaper copy but not implementable positions.

After considerable debate, Congress adopted a new tariff, formally called the Tariff of 1828 or cast by southern opponents as the Tariff of Abomination. Hunter and Kentuckians were pleased with the new law. Tariffs were raised on hemp, cotton bagging, and maintained at 1824 levels for cordage and yarns. Notably, for Kentuckians' whiskey trade, the Tariff of 1828 enacted a $10 per gallon on molasses, which helped compete against New England rum. The public squabble with Crittenden created awareness among both politicians and the community. As a result of active lobbying by Kentucky's elected representatives, Congress enacted Hunter's significant suggestions.

The tariff issues highlighted the ongoing changes in the Kentucky political alignment. Previously, Kendall and Hunter had been vocal Henry Clay supporters. However, Clay's service as Secretary of State in the John Quincy Adams administration changed the views of both men. Kendall, Hunter, and others switched their political allegiances to Andrew Jackson and openly campaigned for Jackson both on the stump and in the pages of the state's newspapers. The move to supporting Jackson fissured the Kentucky Republicans, with many, including Crittenden and the four Harrisburg delegates continuing to support Clay and by association Adams. The division over Old Court, New Court dissipated with the Old Court adherents generally backing Clay/Adams and the New Court proponents supporting Jackson.

The 1827 state elections demonstrated a very tight race between the two factions. The Clay/Adams or Administration faction received a two-vote majority in the Senate, with the House evenly divided. While the House elected a Jackson supporter to the speakership, other legislatively elected state positions went to Administration candidates. J. H. Holeman replaced Amos Kendall as the State's Public Printer. As with Hunter, the loss of the public printing contract presaged the end of Kendall's editorship at *The Argus*, but after the presidential elections. Separately, Adams and Jackson pre-campaign conventions in Kentucky whipped up support for their candidates. Each convention named candidates for governor and lieutenant governor. With little fanfare, Jackson supporters chose William T. Barry over John Pope. More drama occurred during the Administration party selection process. First, the convention selected John J. Crittenden, who promptly declined the nomination, and then named George Robinson, who also declined running for governor. The third choice, Thomas Metcalfe, accepted the candidacy. Joseph P. Underwood, who had driven much of the Sproule, Armstrong & Co. investigation, accepted the nomination for lieutenant governor.

As usual, Kentucky elections for state positions took place in advance of national elections. Campaigning started in the spring in advance of the early August elections. In July 1828, Hunter traveled with a like-minded political entourage to attend a rally in Shelbyville, a county seat of twelve hundred people twenty miles west of Frankfort. State Senator John Pope headlined a gathering of two hundred attendees and delivered a lengthy speech lasting into the evening. Other prominent attendees included a member of the US House of Representatives, Joseph LeCompte, State House Representative Lewis Sanders, and Amos Kendall. All of these politicians would receive a Federal appointment in the Jackson administration. An observer noted William Hunter among the speakers on the outdoor dais.[3]

Raising his political profile opened Hunter up to personal attacks. Writing under the title *Rattlesnake* on the pages of the *Western Citizen* (Paris, Kentucky), a writer alleged that Hunter was not an American but an Englishman by birth. This allegation touched a raw nerve. Despite being former competitors and on different sides of political issues, Shadrack Penn provided Hunter access to publish an open letter in the *Louisville Public Advertiser*. Hunter declared, "*I am not an Englishman by birth*, although I spent a few years of my early life in that country, which, by contrast it afforded, only confirmed my attachment to the republican institutions of this, the country of my birth." Noting that Benjamin Franklin spent more years in England than he and just as relevant today, so did the president and current candidate for re-election John Quincy Adams. Further, *Rattlesnake* alleged that Hunter supported the British during the War of 1812 and that senior military leaders had to remove him from the militia roster due to uncertain patriotism. Responding indignantly, "The war had not a more zealous advocate in the State than I was," and turning the tables stated, "I strongly suspect, that the charge originated with those who were themselves unfriendly to its prosecution." Highly sensitive about his background, Hunter said that he "would rather have the censure than the praise" from opponents of Andrew Jackson and William T. Barry. While strongly asserting his birthplace, Hunter continued to be attacked for being the son of a British sergeant who fought against the Americans during the Revolutionary War.[4]

In the August 4th through 6th electoral period, Kentuckians selected Metcalfe for governor by a narrow margin of seven hundred and nine votes. Andrew Jackson and other observers attributed Barry's defeat to his New Court background. However, demonstrating the electorate's close balance, the voters chose Jackson supporter John Breathitt for Lieutenant Governor by an equally slim one thousand and eighty-nine vote margin. Although defeated in the lieutenant governor race, Governor Metcalfe quickly nominated Underwood, Hunter's nemesis, to the Kentucky Court of Appeals, an appointment with considerable negative implications for Hunter. More important for the state's Jackson supporters, the Jacksonians gained a two-vote majority in the Senate and a forty-two-vote majority in the House. Fueled by Kendall and Hunter, Jackson's populist message resonated with Kentucky voters. However, Henry Clay remained popular, setting up a heated presidential campaign in the fall.

While Hunter's views on Andrew Jackson rankled Clay's Kentucky supporters, his views regarding enslaved people were in the state's mainstream. As a newly immigrated editor, Hunter and William Beaumont had published a series of anti-slavery articles in their first paper in the state and published an abolitionist monograph more recently. Despite lofty republican views expressed as a young man, later in life, Hunter used slavery as a newspaper owner and an industrialist. With an enormous rise in the black population, ownership of enslaved peoples predominated the culture of Blue Grass Kentucky. In fact, fifty-six percent of Frankfort households held enslaved people.[5] Almost all of Hunter's friends, political associates, and business partners owned or rented slaves. Only those without economic means, such as William Littell, did not retain enslaved people. Upon moving to Kentucky as an idealistic young immigrant, Hunter adopted the cultural norms of the predominant slave-holding society. Along with most who could afford the cost, he exploited enslaved peoples in all facets of his life, including purchasing slaves for his household. As with other period slave owners, he pursued runaways seeking escape from bondage. After closing his print shop in Louisville, Lorenzo, one of Hunter's enslaved employees, fled for freedom. Previously enslaved by Hunter, Lorenzo's mother received her freedom from slavery when purchased by Dr. John Mort Talbot of Louisville.[6] Together mother and son were last seen traveling "with a view of passing over to Indiana, or up the river." Hunter advertised a modest ten-dollar reward for Lorenzo's return, no matter where found. Most rewards for the recapture of runaway enslaved people ranged from twenty to fifty dollars, and in free states, rewards typically doubled the Kentucky amounts. Hunter's low reward signaled to the community that he did not want Lorenzo back.

The reward advertisement occurred at an auspicious time. Within two weeks of the ad, approximately seventy-five enslaved peoples passed through Louisville on the Ohio River to the Mississippi slave markets. One hundred miles downriver, the captives overpowered the five overseers and fled into Indiana. After an extensive search, fifty-six of the escapees were recaptured, with five hanging for the murders of the white overseers. At the very least, a wide-ranging alarm made Lucy's and Lorenzo's flight to freedom more perilous. An intriguing possibility is that Lucy and Lorenzo hooked with the nineteen escapees who disappeared on the underground railroad. There was no record of Lorenzo's recapture and return to bondage with Hunter in Frankfort.

The Hunters entered the 1820s with two enslaved women aged twenty-six to forty-four, two enslaved black men aged fourteen to twenty-five, one enslaved black man over forty-five years old in their household. Even through bankruptcy and economic hard times, Hunter exploited enslaved people. As demonstrated by his ad to recover Lorenzo, Hunter aggressively enforced his enslavement of blacks. Through his commercial and societal experiences in Kentucky, Hunter had modified his republican views developed as a young adult in England. He had become a Jacksonian in all regards. Through the state and increasingly on a national scale, political observers recognized Hunter's support of Andrew Jackson and mentioned him in the same breath as Kentucky's leading politicians. Although misidentifying the publication city of his newspaper, the Frankfort *Commentator* placed Hunter in the top ranks of Kentucky's political leaders, "The old republicans, Kendall and Penn, Barry and Rowan, Pickering, and our old friend Hunter of the *Kentucky Gazette*, Duff Green and that veteran democrat Coleman of New-York."[7]

Hunter's prospects appeared bleak despite enjoying a reputation as a locally prominent politician. His business career stood at a standstill, with no takers to partner in a new manufacturing business and little opportunity to return to printing and publishing. His ability to earn a living seemed permanently impaired. Adding to his troubles, Kentucky no longer served as a magnet for European enlightenment thinkers or offered the flywheel of economic growth and prosperity as it had when Hunter first entered the state thirty years ago. Alexis de Tocqueville keenly observed during his 1830 visit that although both banks of the Ohio River were lush, fertile lands, Ohio appeared significantly more prosperous. He perceived that Kentucky's "population is sparse," its "slaves tended half deserted fields," and its "society seemed asleep." Although twelve years younger as a state, de Tocqueville noted that Ohio's population had already exceeded Kentucky's by over a quarter of a million people. De Tocqueville attributed Kentucky's relative lack of economic activity solely to the ubiquitous practice of enslaving black workers.[8] He concluded, "Slavery, therefore, not merely prevents the whites from making money but even diverts them from any desire to do so."[9] While some observers found Kentucky to have notable strengths in childhood education, science, and artistry, other Kentuckians left the state searching for better opportunities.[10] Hunter personally experienced the outmigration of friends and former partners, including William Beaumont and Harry Toulmin, who left the state seeking greater financial security and finding governmental positions. It would be time for William Hunter to consider employment prospects outside of Kentucky.

Part V

❦

Protecting the Republic's Interests

Although born in Colonial America and the last president to personally fight in the American War of Independence, the Jacksonian Era represented a significant turning point for American society. Under Jackson's populous leadership, many American white citizens benefited from an unprecedented increase in the Federal government's power and size. His brutal, forced removal of Native Americans from east of the Mississippi River fueled an unprecedented cotton production boom leading to a massive demand for enslaved people to work the plantation economy. The cotton industry became an internal and export growth engine, driving even higher demand for enslaved people to tend to its production. African and Native Americans greatly suffered under Jackson's administration.

In Washington City, Jackson manipulated the Federal Government's resources as never before to cement his political power. Upon assuming presidential power, predecessors generally retained almost all government clerks and other minor officials regardless of political affiliation. Jackson instituted a new policy by firing many government officials and replacing them with his political supporters. Historians refer to his politically motivated governmental employment policies as the "Spoils System." Obtaining a much-needed rescue from financial distress, William Hunter became a beneficiary of this new policy. Working as a government official became the most stable and long-standing job in Hunter's life.

CHAPTER NINETEEN

Treasury Auditor

After the August Kentucky state elections, the 1828 presidential election campaigns heated up nationally and in Kentucky. Without a publishing platform, William Hunter's editorials did not appear in print, nor did opposing newspapers contest his views. Voters only heard Hunter's views at political rallies and other campaign events, not on the states' newspaper pages.

Assuming the editorial mantle, Kendall published a series of vituperative attacks in *The Argus* on John Quincy Adams for being a crooked President, including offering a "corrupt bargain" to Henry Clay. Allegedly, to break the deadlocked presidential race in the House of Representatives, Adams offered the Secretary of State position to Clay if he threw his support behind the New Englander. Later in Adam's presidency, Kendall waged an almost exclusively negative campaign asserting Adams personally profited from his presidency and made himself rich at the expense of taxpayers. Kendall painted Adams as an aristocrat, out-of-touch with the general populous and even a reckless gambling man. Sounding quaint today, Kendall devoted considerable space in the *Argus* to claiming that Adams installed a billiards table and chess set to facilitate his gambling vices at public expense. The backstory is that Congress appropriated fourteen thousand dollars to repair and replace White House furniture. Congressional overseers spotted the purchase of recreational equipment items that might be used for gambling. Kendall seized on this seemingly benign revelation and published a scathing article that concluded, "Let us put a stop to these things at once. Let us take up *Old Hickory*, drive Adams out of the President's Home and pitch his billiard tables after him."[1]

The Adams/Clay proponents vociferously fought back. In one September editorial, the Frankfort *Commentator* invoked a famous biblical allegory, "War,

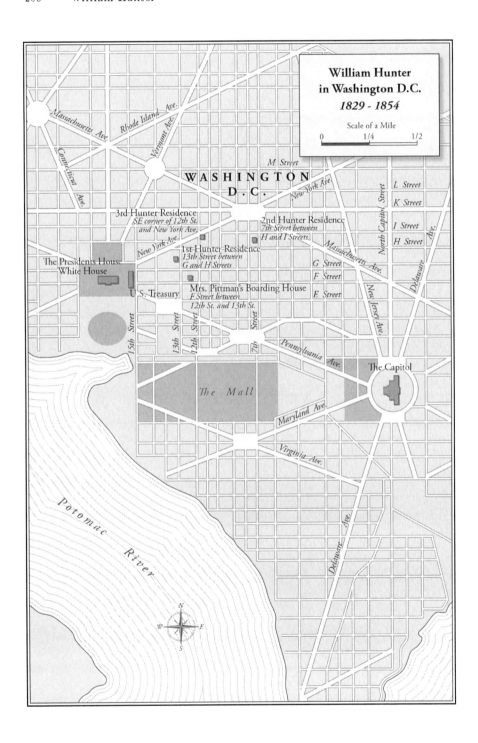

**William Hunter
in Washington D.C.**
1829 - 1854

Scale of a Mile

0   1/4   1/2

Pestilence and Famine; in front—General Jackson himself representing War; Amos Kendall upon his right representing Pestilence, and Francis Blair on his left, representing famine." The editorialist asserted the two newspaper editors misguided Jackson and left the impression that the fourth horse of the apocalypse, death, is represented by the readers under a Jackson administration. From a Kendall perspective, to be placed above other supporters on the right hand of the hero of New Orleans demonstrated how high his star had risen and how important his support of Jackson had become to garnering voters.

Kentucky held its presidential election on November 3, 4, and 5, and when the election officials tallied the votes, Andrew Jackson solidly won the state with fifty-five percent. Indicative of high voter interest and a lively campaign, voters cast forty-five thousand more ballots in 1828 than in 1824. Contrary to the recent state elections, neither side issued any allegations of voting fraud. The Middle Atlantic, Western, and Southern states voted for Jackson, giving him an overwhelming electoral college and raw vote victory. Only the New England states backed Adams. After a string of political losses since 1824, Hunter's political faction won, and he believed that the voters elected a true republican and man of the people. Such a leader had been his wish since first becoming politically aware young man in Walsall.

Shortly after the election, an emissary from the president-elect visited Frankfort, asking Amos Kendall if he had an interest in serving the Jackson administration. Naturally, Kendall leaped at the chance. Unfortunately, the newspaper business has not been prosperous since the loss of the public printing contract. While the newly elected legislators might restore the printing contact, Kendall, like Hunter two decades earlier, tired of scratching a living as a printer. Further, Kendall's grist mills failed to captivate his interest and provided little income. Nevertheless, Kendall knew there would be a long line of job seekers in Washington, so he secured a place in the Kentucky delegation to formally present the state's election results.

President-elect Jackson arrived in Washington City in mid-February and, signaling his job offer's sincerity, met with Kendall a few days later. Kendall recounted Jackson's assessment of his fitness to hold an administrative position in a letter to his wife. "He expressed his regard for me, and his disposition to serve me, in strong terms."[2] Jackson discussed appointing Kendall to a clerkship with a salary of two thousand dollars or an auditorship of three thousand. While Jackson would support the higher salaried appointment, he indicated that Congress might abolish the auditor position. Kendall responded that he preferred the higher salary and would risk the chance of Congressional elimination.

On March 22, 1829, President Jackson rewarded Amos Kendall with an appointment to the position of the Fourth Auditor in the Treasury Department, the largest agency in the Federal government. With more than a bit of hutzpah, he asked President Jackson for a special request before accepting the appointment. Usually, the Treasury Secretary had final authority over hires in the department. Kendall requested of Jackson that he, not the Secretary appoint the clerks in the Fourth Auditor's office, which inspected the Navy accounts. Jackson acceded to Kendall's request, and Kendall became the only auditor with the license to make clerkship appointments on their authority. The appointment mandate allowed Kendall to recognize and reward those who had politically helped him. Writing to fellow Kentuckian Frank Blair, Amos Kendall asked to "find places for some our poor kin (politically I mean) in Kentucky." Kendall practiced what he preached and recruited William Hunter to join him at Treasury, "satisfied of his integrity, appointed him, unsolicited to a clerkship in Washington . . ."[3] Despite Hunter's bankruptcy and legal problems, Kendall exhibited faith in his character, integrity, and judgment.

Struggling financially, Hunter went far beyond typical politicking in risking his meager resources in starting a Louisville newspaper to support the Jacksonians. Recognizing Hunter's solid, dependable political loyalty led Kendall to offer him a Federal appointment. Another reason for recruiting Hunter was Kendall's need to have clerks he could trust in a department dominated by Federalist appointees. By no means did Kendall have to offer Hunter a position. He could have just moved to Washington and left Hunter behind. There were copious up-and-coming party loyalists who were available and would jump at the opportunity. Kendall offered a clerkship to one of his *Argus* partners, Robert Johnston. Also, a former apprentice and journeyman in Hunter's print ship, Johnston readily accepted the appointment.

As an aging man in his sixties with a vexing debt load, Hunter had few other prospects for gainful employment. A clerkship offered a steady annual salary of fourteen hundred dollars without exposure to vagaries in competitive markets. The desk-bound job only required an easy six-hour workday given his advancing age. Further, Hunter would be at the center of national politics. From a personal perspective, Hunter's move became easy as he only possessed five hundred dollars of taxable property in Frankfort in 1829. It would be a fresh start in an exciting city. He decided to accept Kendall's job offer with few other prospects and come to Washington to serve as a Fourth Auditor's office clerk.

Although much larger than Frankfort, Washington City, as it was known in the 1830s, was still a small capital city and much smaller than the major American cities of Boston, New York, and Philadelphia. With the increasing size of government, Washington housed a permanent population of almost nineteen thousand residents. The city boasted three thousand homes, half brick and half wood, and over two hundred retail shops. Washington did not appear to be one integrated metropolis. Urban development occurred in patches, including the communities of Alexandria in the south, Georgetown in the west, and downtown around the government buildings. The undeveloped areas between these centers were heavily forested, with only narrow dirt roads connecting them. One visitor characterized the city as containing "a scattered box of toys" with "unusually wide," unlighted streets and "houses that are detached from one another."[4] Even the areas between the capitol and the President's House contained undeveloped open and forested spaces. The capital's most famous street, Pennsylvania Avenue, was a rough, dirt street prone to frequent flooding. The city did not grade and macadamize the prominent connection between the two branches of government until 1833.[5] One visitor characterized the houses and buildings around the Capitol building as "sordid." The same observer thought, "Washington is no place for persons of domestic tastes" but only attractive to those who "love dissipation."[6] However, dreary and unattractive to visitors, Hunter regarded Washington as significantly more impressive and better developed than Frankfort.

To start with the Treasury Department, Hunter traveled to Washington City, leaving his family in Kentucky. As with many government officials, William, along with fellow Frankfort associates Amos Kendall and Robert Johnston, took lodging in boarding houses. A staple of the Washington society, boarding houses offered temporary room and board to members of Congress and other government officials who resided in the city for parts of the year. While Kendall and Johnston boarded at Mrs. O. B. Brown's, Hunter found temporary lodging at Mrs. Pittman's boarding house. One of four boarding houses located on the north side of F Street between 12th and 13th streets, Mrs. Pittman's catered to clerks and other minor officials serving the government.[7] Her house could lodge approximately twenty people who would take their meals around a large table that extended from the dining room into the parlor when fully occupied. In subsequent years, she hosted two congressmen, Millard Fillmore and James Buchanan, who later would be elected president.[8] Across the street, William Gilbert operated a grocery store, and other innkeepers offered room and board to visitors. Hunter lived near other Fourth Auditor clerks. Samuel Grubb lived on F Street, a couple of blocks to the west. Two blocks to the east on F Street, the land lay nearly vacant. William's boss and chief clerk at the Fourth Auditors Office, Thomas Gilliss, resided in one of only three homes on the largely undeveloped block. In addition to his Treasury colleagues, Hunter could count on several influential Kentucky friends to show him the ropes in Washington and serve as political allies in his new role. These influential Frankfort political allies include Jackson's new postmaster William T. Barry and Kentucky's senators, John Rowan and George M. Bibb.

After the newly transplanted Kentuckian settled into his job, Hunter put his Frankfort affairs in order and moved Ann and their two adult daughters to Washington City. Unfortunately, Hunter did not completely put behind him all the debts incurred through his Frankfort business ventures. In 1832, the president and directors of Frankfort Bank sued Hunter, Instone, and several others for non-payment of debts.[9] The non-operating bank could not enforce collection as Hunter lived outside of Kentucky. By 1834, William and Ann moved into a house in a middle-class neighborhood between the President's House and the Capitol on 13th Street, a few blocks north of Pennsylvania Avenue. The affordable location offered a short, five-block commute to the Navy and Treasury Offices near the President's House. Another advantage is the higher elevation away from the unhealthy, swampy areas to the south. The Hunter's remained in this house for the next decade before moving to new quarters on the east side of 7th Street between H and I streets, northwest. Located across the street from the Patent Office (today's Smithsonian Portrait Gallery), Hunter's commute expanded by six blocks. Later in life, the Hunters moved to a larger property at the corner of 12th Street and New York Avenue northwest.

Clerks in five Treasury Department auditor offices reviewed expenditure warrants for proper authorization and appropriateness before passing on to one of two controllership offices for payment. The Fourth Auditor reviewed the accounts and disbursements of the United States Navy. In addition to the auditor, a chief clerk, fourteen clerks, and a messenger staffed the office. Hunter received a fourteen-hundred-dollar salary, the highest clerk pay level in the department. While a clerk's salary would not support an elegant lifestyle in Washington City, it provided a stable, dependable income impervious to the market vicissitudes.[10] Furthermore, Hunter's entrepreneurial and risk-taking days were over, and he would be content to live off his modest clerical income.

Kendall, Hunter, and Johnston were not the only newspaper editors, printers, and publishers brought to Washington by the new administration. Jackson believed that the press greatly assisted his election and sought to both reward those who helped as well as engendered favorable press during his administration. The opposition quickly caught wind of a prodigious number of offers of employment to the press. Castigating editorials appeared. First out of the blocks, the *National Journal* furnished a list of forty editors and publishers employed by the Jackson administration. *The Commentator* (Kentucky) noted the list did not include two hometown editors rewarded by Jackson. "We mean *Mr. Robert Johnston*, late of the firm of Amos Kendall & Co. publishers of the *Argus*, now a Clerk, at $1500 a year, in the Office of the Fourth Auditor at Washington, and *Mr. William Hunter*, long a printer in this town, and Editor of the *Kentucky Gazette* during the late presidential contest, also provided for in the same office." While making the list more complete, *The Commentator* misreported two key facts. Johnston earned a salary of $1150, not $1500, and Hunter edited the *Louisville Gazette*, not the *Kentucky Gazette,* during the last election. As well-versed, J. G. Dana would have known better; this is an odd set of errors.[11] In any event, upon reading, the Bradford family must have been miffed as they fiercely competed with Hunter in the newspaper industry for a long time. Errors and all, the story went national, republished over the next three months. Newspapers competed by offering lists of more and more rewarded printers and newspaper editors. By March 15, 1830, the list published in newspapers had grown to forty-nine and was still not complete.[12] Looking back over this period, modern scholars have identified at least seventy-four newspaper editors and printers rewarded with government positions. Even this list is not complete as the Federal government offered printing contracts to supportive editors throughout the country.[13] During the administration's first spring and summer, Jackson's department heads announced daily the removals of government officers and clerks and replacement by officials friendly to their politics. By the end of President Jackson's first term, Jackson supporters held one hundred and forty of the three hundred and thirteen federal positions, including twelve out of the seventeen positions in the Fourth Auditor's department.[14]

Immediately, the Fourth Auditor's office clerks anxiously felt Amos Kendall's presence. First, Kendall implemented new works rules. He enforced a six-hour per day work schedule and mandatory presence in the Treasury offices between nine to three. He insisted on clerks providing their full attention to government duty and prohibited outside employment. This ban did not extend to Kendall, who earned fifty dollars a speech/article to ghostwrite for members of Congress and the administration. Besides focusing the clerks on their jobs, Kendall embraced Jackson's desire to cut costs and improve government efficiency. He eliminated minor but publicly unpopular perks. Stating that "My office appeared more like an editor's than an auditor's," he canceled subscriptions to twenty newspapers purchased at government expense for Fourth Auditor clerks.[15] He even banned the reading of books and newspapers in the office. Additional cost savings included prohibiting personal use of government stationery and supplies and ending the clerks' franking privileges. Even more important, Kendall implemented better controls and checks on the integrity of the office. ". . . we learned that some of the pursers of the Navy and Navy agents were in the habit of making valuable presents to the clerks who examined their accounts, thereby creating advocates in the office. We forbade the clerks receiving any present of value from those whose accounts they had to settle, on pain of instant removal."[16] Kendall used these changes in office policies to demonstrate his cost cutting zeal, curry favor with President Jackson, and provide political ammunition for their supporters. Happy with his new auditor, Jackson began to rely more and more on Kendall's political acumen.

Kendall's improvements in office productivity, internal controls, and cost reductions impressed President Jackson. Armed with Kendall's information, Jackson personally investigated the Navy abuse allegations. "In a recent visit to the Navy Department, hearing that the books belonging to that branch of the public administration were very much behind, by the neglect of the late incumbents, he addressed himself to the clerks, told them there were a great many applicants for their places, and if they did not bring up the arrears for their places, he could soon find men that would."[17] To identify potential problem clerks, Jackson issued orders that department heads were to prepare monthly reports on the clerks' morals and report if the clerks paid their bills.[18] Kendall picked up on Jackson's goals of scrutinizing departmental operations and detecting fraud. He embraced Jackson's view that rotating new clerks into the department would shake things up and improve operational effectiveness and efficiency.

Kendall reviewed the activities of each clerk in succession. He found the clerk who oversaw the Navy Pension Fund less than forthcoming. After "so much reluctance" and "so little progress," the clerk produced an "unintelligible statement." Further, the Honorable Michael Hoffman, chair of the House Naval Committee, contacted Kendall to express his frustrations about getting clear answers to questions on the pension fund. On June 1st, he removed the pension fund clerk from office and assigned the fired clerk's responsibilities to William Hunter, someone he could trust to get to the bottom of the pension accounts. Hunter dove in and performed a thorough review of the pension fund. With little difficulty, Hunter concluded that no embezzlement occurred. However, the former clerk permitted reclaimed funds to be left in banks for extended periods, depriving the fund of sustaining interest income.[19] In reviewing departmental processes, Kendall identified six clerks that should be replaced for either questionable practices or inattention to their duties. On Saturday, May 24, 1829, Kendall fired these six clerks, despite lamenting the distress caused to several of the fired clerks. Kendall wrote in a letter to his wife, "Several of them have families and are poor. It was the most painful thing I ever did; but I could not well get along without it. Among them is a poor old man with a young wife and several children. I shall help to raise a contribution to get him back to Ohio, where he came from, and intend to give him $50 myself."[20] While Kendall emphasized needed improvements and replacing incompetent or self-serving clerks, the opposition newspapers characterized these firings as politically motivated. On the other hand, the administration press praised filling the auditor's office "with men of business, and not with babbling politicians."[21] By the end of 1829, Kendall had replaced seven of his clerks, kept Thomas H. Gilliss, the chief clerk, retained seven clerks, his messenger, and left one position unfilled.

Within the first few weeks, Kendall provided Jackson with a political bombshell to demonstrate his campaign commitments to clean up government and root out corruption. In a painstaking review of the office's accounts, Kendall discovered fraud of at least seven thousand dollars perpetrated by the former Fourth Auditor, Tobias Watkins. Appointed by President James Monroe in 1824, Watkins came from a well-respected Maryland family. Kendall identified a large number of irregular and falsified Navy disbursements. Contrary to past, more lenient practices, President Jackson ordered Watkins arrested, news that shocked Washington insiders and the clerks in Fourth Auditor's office. Although Watkins suspiciously left town before the Jackson inauguration, the opposition press labeled the arrest as "premature" and "based upon the ingenuity, the vindictiveness, and reckless malignity of Amos Kendall." Heretofore, Watkins lived an exemplary life with "unassailed and unsuspected honor," having served as an army physician during the War of 1812.[22] Laws that set a two-year statute of limitations for fraudulent acts limited the prosecution of Watkins to a few charges. A jury convicted Watkins of embezzlement of seven thousand dollars. The court imposed a three-month jail sentence and a seven thousand and fifty dollar fine. President Jackson ordered that Watkins remain in jail until he paid the large fine. A historic Supreme Court *habeas corpus* case freed Watkins due to unlawful imprisonment. However, the prosecution of Watkins greatly enhanced Kendall's stature with Andrew Jackson and started Kendall on the path to emerge as Jackson's most trusted member of his "kitchen cabinet."

Kendall identified additional malfeasance, including a Navy agent at Norfolk who accrued nine thousand dollars of governmental debt. By the end of 1829, reportedly, Kendall identified over three hundred thousand dollars missing from the Treasury department accounts. Elimination of waste and tightening expenditure controls had a material impact on the Navy's budget. In the first three years of the Jackson administration, Navy expenditures fell on average one-half million versus the final three years of the Adams administration.[23] Better management of the Navy's budget and the identification of substantial fraud dramatically increased Kendall's stature both within the administration and with the wider populous. While Hunter performed many investigations, his role remained in the background. Despite not receiving public acclaim, Hunter settled into his auditor responsibilities, finally performing the counting-house duties that he so eagerly sought when first landing in Philadelphia in 1793.

After the initial fury of upgrading the Fourth Auditors office, the professional lives of Hunter and Kendall diverged. Up to this point, the two men had common life experiences. Both moved to Kentucky with few financial resources and became prominent in the local community. Both tried but failed in commercial ventures. While both became notable newspaper editors, Kendall developed as the more incisive writer and clever politician. Office seekers eagerly sought Kendall's advice and help due to his particularly gifted crafting of negative political messages that resonated with voters. In particular, President Jackson began to rely heavily on Kendall for political communications and advice. In 1830, Kendall started a new Washington newspaper as a party mouthpiece to promote President Jackson. Passing over Hunter, he tapped the former clerk of the New Court, Francis P. Blair as editor. In addition, John C. Rives, a more junior clerk to Hunter in the Fourth Auditor's office, joined Blair as a partner. Rives enjoyed a very positive reputation in Washington circles. One newspaper described him as "a gentleman well known as one of the best accountants in the United States."[24] Seeking commercial viability, Kendall and Blair sought superior talent for their new venture and did not regard Hunter as up to the rigors of the highly competitive newspaper market. In his early sixties, Hunter agreed with Kendall and Blair as he highly valued the security of his government position. The choice of Rives proved to be a good decision as the partnership with Blair continued for the next seventeen years, only later dissolving over political differences.

With others providing pro-Jackson news media outlets, Hunter turned his attention to grassroots political organizing. To drum up support for the president's re-election, Kendall planned a series of strategically located Hickory Clubs to lead Jackson to victory in 1832. Organized in cities and towns throughout the nation, prominent citizens and influential politicians formed local Hickory Clubs. Local chapter activities included "get out the vote" rallies, direct campaigning, and placing pro-Jackson articles in local newspapers. Kendall instituted a Central Hickory Club in Washington City to coordinate efforts and provide consistent political messaging. Widely known, Kendall planned and implemented this new campaign strategy and provided the club's political platform. He stayed in the background devolving formal club leadership to local Washington City leaders. Serving as a national platform, Kendall published a series of political principles cloaking Jacksonian policies in an aura of democratic and republican ideals. The opposition press derisively referred to the re-election campaign organization as a "mongrel group" who "are united in their exertions to save themselves and the "spoils" which have been shared among them." Membership of the Central Hickory Club consisted of sixty-nine federal officeholders with combined salaries of $121,700, demonstrating Jackson's vast political patronage. Further, the opposition press likened club members to enslaved people bowing at the feet of President Jackson, who believed that he was "born to command slaves."[25]

Following Kendall's lead, Hunter and four other clerks in the Fourth Auditor's Office became club members and publicly served on its supporter roster of leading Jackson supporters. On behalf of the club, his activities consisted of direct campaigning and assisting Kendall with organizing activities. Consistent with Frankfort's political practices, Kendall, Hunter, and club leadership arranged a festive dinner at five o'clock in Carusi's Hall to hail Jackson's re-election. Located on C Street between 11th and 12th Streets (now the IRS headquarters building), the Carusi family operated a fashionable dancing academy, public ballroom, and dining room that regularly hosted political gatherings. "The hall was brilliantly illuminated, and decorated with national flags and appropriate paintings, for the occasion." The celebrants enjoyed a collation (a light informal meal) in the dining hall along with wine and other refreshments.[26]

President Jackson sent his written thanks to the assembly but declined to attend. In his place, Kendall and Senator Thomas Hart Benton addressed the celebrants and whipped them into a triumphant mood. The club members drank thirteen regular toasts. Interspersed between toasts, the United States Marine Band, with entertainment hall owner Gaetani Carusi, played patriotic tunes.[27] Continuing feting Jackson's victory, prominent members of the assemblage offered numerous volunteer toasts. Summing up his political philosophy, William Hunter offered a volunteer toast to "Thomas Jefferson and Andrew Jackson: Skilful [sic] pilots of our political ship. She has weathered many a storm; and, under the guidance of her able commander, will yet reach the port of safety, in despite of Northern rocks and Southern shoals." In Hunter's view, western interests were distinct from those of other sections of the country and needed to be protected by the new president.[28]

After a night of merriment and copious amounts of wine, the raucous revelry got out of hand. Henry Jackson, one of the club leaders and a manager of the night's festivities, stood up and toasted Senator Thomas Hart Benton. Another event manager and Federal Marshal for Washington City, Henry Ashton, took offense at Jackson's remarks believing that they indicated unanimous Hickory Club support for Martin Van Buren to succeed Andrew Jackson four years hence. Aspiring to his own presidential ambitions, Ashton took umbrage with Henry Jackson's remarks, and a brief tussle ensued. Nearby diners quickly calmed the two opponents, and the volunteer toasts continued late into the night. The next day, the opposition press characterized the celebration as a "second-rate affair" and reveled in the squabbles citing dissensions, quarrels, and jealousies among the Jackson supporters.[29] Ashton issued a written challenge to Henry Jackson, which might have elicited a duel of honor. However, there is no record of a duel, and little resulted from the overblown scuffle. Importantly for Hunter, his path would soon cross with Henry Jackson.[30]

The Jackson victory celebration would mark Hunter's last formal role in the Central Hickory Club. Over the next several months, the club conducted several events including, a dinner to honor Andrew Jackson on the anniversary of the "glorious victory of New Orleans," a celebration of Washington's birthday and Jackson's inaugural ball. Hunter did not publicly participate in any other these events and ended his participation in the club.

After Andrew Jackson's re-election, it became clear that Hunter's political influence had peaked and that Kendall's star began rising. Kendall developed an intimate, persuasive relationship with President Jackson by providing artful political advice and transforming the bureaucracy to assist the president politically. Calling him a lying machine, even vitriolic opponents recognized Kendall's closeness to the president. In a speech in the House, Congressman Henry A. Wise characterized Kendall as Jackson's "chief overseer, chief reporter, amanuensis, scribe, accountant-general, man of al work."

Wise concluded that "nothing was well done without the aid of his diabolical genius.[31] President Jackson rewarded Kendall with increasing responsibilities. In 1835, Jackson named Kendall as Postmaster General, one of the most critical Federal departments. Passing over Hunter and leaving him in the Fourth Auditor's office, Kendall took two of his best clerks, Robert Johnston and Joseph Perry, to the Post Office. Kendall remained Postmaster General throughout Jackson's second terms and through the four years of the Van Buren administration.

Kendall's enduring legacy is crafting the practice of a presidential "kitchen cabinet" that enjoyed unfettered access and significant influence with the President. Like Hunter, Kendall's business enterprises turned out unsuccessful, and he became mired in debt. For a while, a legal order confined Kendall to Washington City's boundaries for non-payment of debts. Unlike Hunter, Kendall experiences excellent prosperity at the end of his career by assisting Samuel Morse in promoting and expanding a national telegraph system. Harkening back to the days that Hunter and Kendall served together on the Kentucky Seminary board, Kendall becomes the President and major contributor of the educational institution that will become Gallaudet University. Unlike Hunter, in his last years of Kendall became deeply religious. He made a pilgrimage to the Christian Holy Lands and became an active member of the Calvary Baptist Church. Hunter never found religion.

From afar, it might appear that Kendall just was more talented and capable than Hunter. Indeed, he was more politically successful and enjoyed economic success later in life. However, the older, more experienced Hunter demonstrated to the younger Kendall what works and does not work in the newspaper business. Hunter taught him the "ropes" by showing the importance of taking sides as a newspaper editor, the need to become a government printer, and the need to have strong political advocates. On the other hand, Hunter greatly benefited, maybe even rescued, by receiving the clerk assignment in the US Treasury. Some historians have characterized Kendall's appointment as taking pity on the down and out Hunter. A more fulsome view indicated that Kendall needed reliable assistants. It recognized the contributions of a pathfinder whose life experiences helped the aspiring political leader identify opportunities and avoid political missteps. While a casual friendship may have endured, the former Frankfort newspaper editors parted ways. Like his experiences with Henry Clay and Francis Blair, Kendall had the habit of severing meaningful relationships after an associate no longer mattered to him. Likewise, Hunter may have been wary of Kendall's lightning rod reputation and distanced himself from his Kentucky friend. After the election of 1832, Hunter ended his active involvement in national politics. Given his advancing age, he needed his Treasury clerkship's stability to support his family and found himself without political mentors watching out for his interests. After the mid-1830s, Kentuckians sent to Washington politicians either hostile to Hunter or not known to him. To secure his modest Treasury position, he kept a lower profile by avoiding taking sides on controversial issues. Hunter's strategy worked. He retained the same clerkship through seven successive changes in presidential administrations.

William and Ann's two unmarried daughters Louisa and Lavinia moved with them to Washington City. Louisa never married and lived her entire life with her parents. Lavinia's husband, Leonard H. Lyne, died shortly after the birth of their third child. Without financial means, Lavinia and her children followed the Hunters to the Federal city. Shortly after her arrival, Lavinia met Henry Jackson, a former Pennsylvanian twenty-plus years older. William may have first met Jackson at the Central Hickory Club, as they were both members and introduced him to his daughter. In 1833, they married and moved into a home only a few blocks away from Lavinia's parents. Jackson also worked as a Treasury clerk in the Office of the Treasurer. Despite earning the same salary as William, the newlyweds did not live within their means. Perhaps Henry's continued association with the Central Hickory Club and its lavish events drained the couple's financial resources. As the couple's unpaid debts piled up, the Jacksons held a furniture sale to raise cash. George L. Douglass and William Hunter served as trustees for the public auction held on July 2, 1834, at the couple's home on 11th Street between F and G Streets. The trustees advertised for sale "a quantity of excellent household furniture . . . and a variety of other articles too numerous to mention."[32] While the auction may have generated cash to pay off or pay down the debt, the Hunters never again trusted Lavinia with money.

More dreadful news arrived as Ann and William's son, Morrison, passed away in Mobile, Alabama. During the 1820s, Morrison and his wife Ann brought four children into the world. Shortly after the birth of the last child, Morrison died. His wife continued to live in Mobile and served as a nurse during the American Civil War. Adding to the terrible news, William and Ann experienced the loss of a fourth child. On December 23, 1839, Louisa, William's and Ann's youngest daughter, died. A single woman, she passed away at the age of thirty-two. The Hunters remembered her life with a simple service at their 13th Street home. The *Daily National Intelligencer* carried a one-line mortuary notice without an obituary.[33] Of the Hunter's five children, only Lavinia survived.

The Hunters did not bring enslaved people to Washington as their sale likely financed the family's move to Washington. Similar to Kentucky's daily life, the nation's capital depended upon the institution of slavery. Slave auction houses and slave pens operated in sight of the Capitol. Although the capital city's residents employed enslaved people similar to residents in Frankfort, Washington City's racial situation appeared strikingly different. When the Hunters arrived, the city's free African Americans outnumbered enslaved residents, and as time went by, the number and percentage of free blacks dramatically increased. Conflicts increased between newly arrived European immigrants and free blacks, exacerbating racial tensions. In 1835, the city experienced its first race riot. The attempted murder of a white woman by Arthur Bowen, a free African American, sparked a violent uprising. Immigrant shipbuilders from the Navy yard descended upon the predominantly free black neighborhoods in a wantonly destructive rage. The mass violence is referred to as the Snow Riot and started as an out-of-control rage centered at an African American-owned restaurant named Mr. Beverly Snow's Epicurean Eating House. At the corner of 6th and Pennsylvania Avenue, rioters destroyed the prominent eating establishment. The mob ransacked John F. Cook's house and school for black children at the intersection of 14th and F Streets within a few blocks of Hunter's home. In the end, Washington District Attorney Francis Scott Key, author of "The Star-Spangled Banner," tried, convicted, and sentenced Bowen to death by hanging. As the result of fervent pleadings from the intended victim, Anna Maria Thornton, President Jackson pardoned Bowen. Tragically, the story does not end well as Thornton sold Bowen to a steamship operator, and Bowen endured slavery for the rest of his life.

While the District of Columbia's Emancipation Day would not occur until after William's death, many free African Americans in Washington City found employment as household servants. Economic necessity probably limited Hunter's ability to purchase slaves as housing expenses consumed most of their limited financial means. Therefore, the Hunters switched from owning enslaved peoples to offering free Blacks employment. The Hunters employed one or two free black female servants to perform household chores throughout their stay. Surviving servant names include Lucinda Parker and her daughter Jane and Mary Taylor, the last servant employed by Ann. These African-American servants lived in the Hunters' household. Free employment more closely aligned with William's early thoughts on slavery, but there is no evidence that he advocated for slavery abolition or believed in racial equality. Later in life, Ann brought an Irish immigrant by the name of Ann Black into the household as a servant. Economy, not a racial decision, drove Ann's choice of servants.

On January 5, 1836, John C. Pickett assumed the position of Fourth Auditor, followed by Aaron O. Dayton in 1838. Dayton would serve as William's boss for the remainder of his career. William settled into his low-profile life in the department. He principally served as the auditor of the Navy pension accounts and a separate pension fund for those officers and seamen who served on privateer ships.[34] Hunter audited the work of nineteen pension agents who reviewed and approved sailor applications for pensions. Since Hunter's arrival in the Federal city, pensioners grew from five hundred and ninety-six to nine hundred and forty-six in 1842. Annually, William watched over the disbursements of over two hundred and twenty-thousand dollars to these annuitants. Each quarter he prepared accounts of the Navy and Privateer pension agents as well as an account of pension stock purchased by the Secretary of the Navy. Further, he audited claims by pensioners for arrearages and other improperly paid pensions. At the end of the year, Hunter prepared reports of receipts and disbursements and summaries of the Navy and Privateer pension funds for use by the Secretaries of Treasury and Navy as well as Congress. Other duties included the registering of Naval requisitions and the preparation of annual statements of contingent expenses of the Navy.

While not politically active, Hunter pursued his lifelong interests in books and reading. He became active in the operations of the Library Company of Washington. Loosely modeled after the more famous Library Company of Philadelphia, leading residents of the Federal city started their own version in 1797. While never achieving the stature of Philadelphia, the Washington City Company annually added three to four hundred books to its five thousand volumes in its collection. Interested citizens purchased a share for around thirty-five dollars to access the collection. The library occupied a room in the Old Masonic Building on the west side of 11th Street, just opposite of Carusi's Hall. In 1836, Hunter served as an appointed judge to oversee the annual election of library directors.

In 1850, William and Ann purchased a larger property at the corner of 12th Street New York Avenue Northwest. Subdivided into three lots, the Hunters constructed a brick home for themselves and a wood structure for their daughter Lavinia and her husband, Henry. However, during this period, Henry died, leaving Lavinia without sufficient supporting funds. William and Ann assumed the financial responsibility to support Lavinia.

In 1853, the Federal government embarked upon a project to reclassify clerks to improve the consistency of compensation given various levels of responsibilities. William's pay had remained constant at fourteen-hundred dollars per year for twenty-three years. The reclassification process downgraded Hunter to a second-class clerk and reduced his annual salary to twelve hundred dollars. The reduction provided a blow to his ego as nine other clerks in his office were rated higher. His only compensation adjustment was a two-hundred-dollar reduction throughout twenty-five years of government service![35] However, Hunter could take pride in his government service. Hunter remained fruitfully employed while serving under eight presidents by being productive into his eighties. Without the protection of civil service regulations, he remained in office despite several changes in political parties. Of the fourteen clerks in the office when he started, only George M. Head enjoyed as much seniority as Hunter. He did not benefit from political sponsorship for most of his government service and remained in office due to his industrious and faithful performance.

Hunter served the Treasury Department in "those official duties which were congenial to his declining days" until his death on October 22, 1854. A notice of his death and the funeral arrangements appeared in the local papers. As expected from a highly proficient newspaper editor, the family offered for publication an eloquent obituary highlighting his contributions as a newspaper publisher, politician, and civic-minded citizen. A well-written, detailed obituary appeared two days later in Washington's *National Intelligencer*. Other newspapers, such as the *Buffalo Commercial Advertiser,* picked up the story and published it in its entirety for their readers. The news filtered back to Frankfort despite Hunter's twenty-five-year absence. In its November 4th edition, a Frankfort newspaper, the *Tri-weekly Kentucky Yeoman*, remembered Hunter as a "gentleman" who, when leaving for Frankfort for Washington, "was an old man then, although his movements indicated a good degree of muscular activity." Hunter's notable muscles are a reminder that the business of printing still required manual labor. Additionally, the *Yeoman* republished Hunter's entire obituary from the *National Intelligencer*.[36]

Hunter's obituary described him "having lived an irreproachable life, employed in honorable and useful pursuit" which "acquired for him extensive influence in the earlier days of the Republic. However, the otherwise comprehensive obituaries contained one telling exception. The eulogies omitted his family origin as the son of a British soldier who fought against the Americans during the Revolutionary War. Hunter lived his whole life in America, hiding or obscuring this fact from American contemporaries. Hunter's memoir fills this gap for his family. The memoir recounts his revolutionary war and family life until his 1793 return to the United States and then abruptly ends. No reason existed in Hunter's mind to continue his memoir to document the remainder of his life. Hunter's family, friends, and political colleagues knew the rest of the story. Further, he left a rich historical record on the pages of his newspapers *The Western Telegraphe*, *The Mirror*, and *The Palladium*. Legal statutes and legislative journals memorialize his contributions to Kentucky's political institutions and Frankfort's civic affairs. The National Archives preserves Hunter's impact on the Navy's pension accounting and controls. He knew that all of these contributions were well preserved. He also knew that he needed to prepare a journal of his early days so that his family and posterity would know the complete story.

CHAPTER TWENTY

Legacy

P oignantly, William's last will started, "Having jointly labored with me through a long eventful life, and in all the various changes in my pecuniary affairs, discharging her duty as a good and faithful wife, she richly merits all that I give, and ten times more, were it in my power to give it." Only a property containing several homes at the corner of 12th Street and New York Avenue remained in Hunter's estate. While modest at that time, these properties would provide a stable financial base and residence for his wife and surviving daughter. In addition to the family, one or two Black servants lived with Ann. Unlike their earlier slave-holding time in Kentucky, these African-American servants were free workers. Besides census records, little is known about these workers, except they assisted Ann with household work.

Ann continued to reside in Washington City, earning a modest income by opening her home to boarders, a common occurrence in the politically itinerant city. During the height of the Civil War, Ann traveled with her daughter, Lavinia Hunter Jackson, to Granville County, North Carolina. The purpose of their visit is not known; however, it is possible that they traveled to be with a wounded or sick relative. In the summer of 1863, the two women applied to the War Department for a pass to return home. The Secretary of War referred their case to President Abraham Lincoln for final adjudication. Writing back to Edward Stanton, Lincoln concluded the "old Lady might come but not the daughter."[1] It's unknown how the mother and daughter dealt with this travel dilemma, but after the war, both lived at the family houses located on adjacent lots at the corner of 12th Street and New York Avenue in Northwest DC.

Ann did not survive the end of the Civil War, passing away October 9, 1864, ten years to the month after William. Ann divided her property at the corner of New York Avenue and 12th Street into three parcels in her highly prescriptive will. First, to pay off debts to Robert C. Murphy, husband of her granddaughter Livonia Lyne Murphy, Ann left the vacant corner lot. The lot transfer came with the stipulation that Murphy erect a "pyramidical or obelisk marble monument" to William at his gravesite in the iconic Congressional Cemetery in Southeast DC. Apparently, Ann did not trust her remaining child, Lavinia Hunter Jackson, to be responsible with the real estate, so she stipulated that she could live in Ann's brick house fronting 12th Street for the rest of her life, so long as she properly maintained the house with due care and kept fire insurance in an amount no less than three thousand dollars. Upon Lavinia's death, the 12th Street brick house and property would pass in fifty-fifty shares to a grandchild, Harry Hunter (Morrison Hunter's child), and grandchild Lavinia Murphy, wife of Robert Murphy. The third parcel, a house fronting New York Avenue, was left to Anne Morrison Murphy, her great-granddaughter. Unfortunately, Anne Morrison Murphy became incapacitated, and her mother assumed guardianship in 1874. Ann's last will provision recognized "the fidelity of my serving woman, Mary Taylor" she bequeathed "the mahogany bureau in my back bedroom and . . . also, the furniture and bedding in the room she now occupies."

Unfortunately, Harry did not survive to receive his inheritance. In the early stages of the Civil War, he traveled to New Orleans to enlist in the 8th Texas Infantry as a first sergeant. After exhibiting excellent leadership capabilities through considerable combat, the Confederacy promoted Harry Hunter several times, reaching the rank of captain. In 1864, Hunter received severe wounds and died at a hospital in Uniontown, Alabama. After the war, Harry's siblings won a court judgment to receive Harry's share of his inheritance in the form of a lot and house at the 12th Street address.

Robert Murphy kept up his end of the bargain with Ann and erected a seven-foot-tall marble obelisk over William's burial site in Washington DC's Congressional Cemetery. Inscribed on the base are Hunter's name and life span. Curiously, the marker also states that his wife, E. Hunter erected the monument. Why this mistake occurred is lost to history. Possibly Ann requested the "E" to emphasize that during most of her life, contemporaries knew her as Ann and wanted posterity to know that there should have been an E added at the end of her name! What is known is that the Hunters had a loving and enduring marriage. While William lamented in his last will that he did not better generate financial resources for this wife and family, Ann spent much of their limited life savings to commemorate the enduring love of her life physically. Further, Ann stipulated a simple, flat stone slab to mark her grave, giving prominence to her husband. Her less prominent marker did not reflect false modesty but pride in her husband's accomplishments that she wanted history to recognize.

The Hunters purchased a six-person burial plot to provide spaces for other family members. William and Ann's daughter, Lavinia Jackson Hunter, passed

FIGURE 9. William Hunter's grave obelisk and Ann Hunter's flat slab in foreground at the Congressional Cemetery in Washington, DC.

in 1874 at age seventy-one and is interred in the family plot. Their second daughter to survive to adulthood, Louisa Mary Ann Hunter, who died in 1839 at thirty-two, is buried next to them. The last occupant in the plot is grandson-in-law Robert C. Murphy who died in 1888 at age sixty-two. There is one unfilled grave spot in the burial plot; perhaps a Hunter descendent will come forward to claim this unused space.

Fittingly, famous Kentuckians and friends' burial sites surrounded William Hunter's Congressional Cemetery grave. Not far away, cenotaphs were commemorating Senators Henry Clay and George M. Bibb. Also buried in the Congressional Cemetery are two governmental colleagues and the cemetery's large mausoleum houses John C. Rives's remains, a former fellow Treasury clerk. One year before William's death, his former apprentice and fellow Treasury clerk, Robert Johnston, passed away with his remains buried in Congressional Cemetery. In 1844, Johnston and two other men attested to the preparation of Hunter's last will.

Part VI

◡ ✻ ◡

Reflecting on a Remarkable Life

Over eighty-six years, William Hunter amassed a prodigious number of extraordinary life experiences, spanning from the American War of Independence almost to the American Civil War. He resided in England, the United States, Canada, and France and extensively traveled through these countries. William worked all of his teen and adult life in several diverse occupations, including printer, publisher, retailer, auctioneer, lawyer, industrialist, real estate agent, and government auditor. He served on numerous civic commissions, boards, and councils. His neighbors elected him to the Kentucky legislator and a Frankfort Town Trustee. Moreover, most importantly, he overcame young children's loss, remained devoted to his wife (and she to him), and raised three children to adulthood.

For the vast majority of his life, William lived without the benefits of his parents and siblings. After 1793, he never returned to Britain nor traveled to Lisbon, Portugal, to see his mother or sister. Conversely, William never sent travel funds to his mother and sister in Lisbon to join him in America. Poignantly, he lost track of his mother and sister for long periods. He did not know when they passed. The lack of connections with his British family is probably why contemporary accounts describe him as an orphan.

Unfortunately, there are no paintings or physical descriptions of William and his family. From the historical record, we do know that historians regarded Hunter as "a man of considerable prominence" who became "a quite noted publisher in his day."[1] Other contemporaries describe William as "enterprising" and "genteel." The best description of his life is that Hunter represented an example of a respected and successful community leader, including the strengths and flaws of the period. He found an opportunity in Early America and furthered building the new republic's media and political institutions.

In his memoir, William Hunter offered his contemplative thoughts on his life:

> But for the kind feelings of a beloved Mother, so effectively brought into action at this critical period of my life, I might long since have fallen in battle, or perished in some insalubrious climate, the victim and mere mercenary instrument of the British government instead of enjoying at this day, the rights and privileges of an independent Citizen in the United States of America. What a contrast! And what a crowd of reflections does it force upon the mind!

We know considerably less about Ann other than she worked anonymously in Hunter's businesses and employed, along with William, enslaved and free labor in household duties. As typical in the time, Ann's life occurred mostly lived outside the public sphere.

CHAPTER TWENTY-ONE

Taking Stock

Today, biographies of individuals living in Revolutionary Era America generally fall into two categories—those that venerate the lives of the elite founding white males who fought for independence and shaped America and those that chronicle the everyday lives of the populous, including oft-neglected women, children, Blacks, and Native Americans. The Founders' legacies are well-known and sometimes over-emphasized and exaggerated. On the other end, it has become increasingly common to chronicle the lives of everyday people and their important contributions to Early America. The legacies of common people are reflected in common rather than individual legacy. While the stories of people in these categories are important, there is a third important archetype. Although his contributions did not rise to those of a noted Founder, Hunter left a lasting mark in early America. He made a societal impact greater than most. America's early development rested upon the shoulders of thousands of such enterprising citizens. Hunter spoke his mind as a journalist, took risks to set up new businesses, helped start educational institutions, and aided civic projects. Understanding the people who made contributions beyond the small number of Founders is essential to interpret Early America's history fully.

Born to British parents, he switched his allegiance to the enemy he witnessed his father fight against so ferociously. He became an ardent nineteenth-century American in every sense. William believed America provided a better political system and more opportunities than Britain. Further, he could freely espouse his views advocating equality of mankind, freedom of religion, and the supremacy of reason.

Similar to the more famous Founders and common people of the era, William had what people may judge today as character flaws. Most egregiously from a modern perspective, and even though he was a self-proclaimed man of the Enlightenment, Hunter owned and hired slaves. Early on, his newspapers advocated the abolition of slavery in a courageous series of editorials. However, societal and economic pressures changed William's behaviors, and he joined the majority of his Kentucky neighbors and embraced slavery. While not exculpatory, William's inconsistencies on slavery represented the predominant views of the community during this period. Even members of abolitionist societies and those who intellectually opposed slavery owned and hired enslaved peoples. Besides enslaving African Americans, William exhibited many harsh racial prejudices prevalent during his lifetime. He particularly expressed disdain for Native Americans and did nothing to point out the many atrocities committed towards these native people. Kentuckians generally sought to exterminate or deport all Native Americans from their borders, a policy which William silently acquiesced.

William's interests in literature, philosophy, and politics and his general love of reading aided in becoming an accomplished and noted book publisher and newspaper editor despite a disjointed and limited formal education. Principally he became educated through copious reading and self-learning. One can imagine Hunter sitting in his bookstore reading a book for sale while waiting for the next customer to arrive. His journal indicates a high level of literacy, including familiarity with various historical texts, novels, and fiction. His writing style reflects a highly practiced writer with a broad range of historical, philosophical, and political understanding.

Today, Hunter's distinctive contributions are the books and articles that he penned and published during his life. His previously unattributed and unevaluated memoir is the only known extant journal written by the son or daughter of a British soldier serving in the American Rebellion. With elegantly composed prose, William described the trials and tribulations of soldiers and their families on campaign with the British Army. The fact that families endured the same hardships and prisoner of war incarceration as soldiers is generally under-reported. Typically, accounts of soldiers, battles, and army movements fail to include information on soldiers' families. This omission can be rectified by referring to and interpreting William's journal. Similarly, Hunter's legal publishing has withstood the test of time. Remarkably, surviving copies of Hunter's published compendium of Kentucky statute laws command as much as eighty-five hundred dollars from booksellers today. This compares to the five dollars a copy that Hunter received from the Commonwealth of Kentucky in 1819.

Despite consistently entering into business partnerships, Hunter never achieved long-term business success. He was particularly bad at judging the character and capabilities of industrial business partners. The Charles Sproule business venture almost sank him financially, personally, and professionally. More successful, Hunter's newspaper partnerships endured longer than his commercial ventures and broke big stories on the Alien and Sedition Acts and the return of Lewis and Clark to a local and national audience.

His most significant business and newspaper partners did not achieve noteworthy successes later in life. After fleeing Frankfort, Charles Sproule operated a transportation company in the Mississippi Territory before fading into obscuring. John Colerick died suddenly in 1804 from natural causes. His obituary in the *Philadelphia Evening Post* cited John as "a man of great industry and assiduous in business and will be long remembered for his gentle, charitable and friendly disposition."[1] Numerous New England and east coast newspapers reprinted his death notice, particularly papers devoted to the Federalist cause. With the print shop journeymen and apprentices, his wife, Ann, continued to publish the paper for several years before the business fell into bankruptcy. William Beaumont migrated to Natchez in the booming Mississippi Territory, where he opened a tavern and coffee house at the corner of Second and First North Streets. While he entertained thoughts of starting a newspaper, Beaumont merely offered a wide selection of newspapers from all parts of the states for reading "in the Genteelest stile."[2] As with other Beaumont ventures, the public house proved commercially unsuccessful. Beaumont continued to be plagued by straying horses, and he turned to the government for employment. Like his early days in Pittsburgh, he became Natchez town clerk while desperately seeking more lucrative Federal employment. Referring to Beaumont as a "martyr to republicanism," notable western Pennsylvania political friends such as Albert Gallatin continued to support him for a Federal position.[3] Finally, in 1809, he received a Senate-confirmed appointment as a Surveyor and Inspector of Revenue for Natchez.[4] Beaumont died in 1814. One of his daughters, Mary, indirectly helped memorialize the family name. Her husband, Henry Millard, fought for Texas against the Mexicans and settled in the newly independent territory. Millard named Beaumont, Texas, in honor of Mary, who passed away two years prior.[5]

Hunter outlived all of his partners. Further, he contributed valuable governmental services for the last twenty-five years of his life. While he did not make good partner choices, Hunter made lasting contributions to the communities and governments he served.

CHAPTER TWENTY-TWO

Why William Hunter's Life Is Relevant Today

It is easy to dismiss the youthful remembrances of a pre-teen boy as inadequate to thoroughly understand the American Revolution's complexities. Likewise, the experiences of one of the many thousands of westward migrating immigrants might seem pedestrian. And finally, on first blush, William's twenty-five years as an obscure government auditor might appear unremarkable. While race and family background benefited him, there are compelling reasons why the life of William Hunter is highly relevant today.

For those interested in the American Revolution, William's "one of a kind" journal represents a more balanced view of British soldiers than most revolutionary war accounts written from an American perspective. His memoir uniquely portrays the daily lives of soldiers who performed their duties with a strong sense of patriotism and professionalism. He dispels the predominant depiction in American texts that the British "lobster backs" were brutal, cruel automatons who pillaged throughout North America. Like the Rebels, the Britishers' prime goals were to do their duty, survive brutal combat, and protect their families.

On a personal level, William's life is an example of overcoming adversity, taking risks, and capitalizing on opportunities. Tenaciously, he cheerfully faced considerable setbacks and difficulties. These included enduring several years of tightly confined wartime captivity, suffering through dangerous ocean voyages, surmounting limited economic means, and experiencing premature separation from his family. In the face of these substantial obstacles, he did not complain. His positive attitude in the face of these setbacks is an inspiration to those today. Overcoming these setbacks, William sought ways to capitalize on his talents.

As an immigrant, William embodies the experiences of those who have relocated to the United States and who have made substantial contributions to and helped mold the American story. While technically, he received citizenship under the Constitution as born on American soil, his parents raised him to be British with the prospect of living his entire life in England. He typifies a non-native American who endured dangerous risks to pursue better opportunities to build a more free and prosperous life. While not a Horatio Alger "rags to riches" story, William is an example of many eighteenth-century and now twenty-first-century immigrants who added intellectual and economic capital to build new communities and businesses.

Besides economic opportunities, William is an example of citizens seeking a republican form of government built upon freedom of thought and freedom to practice or not practice religion. Hunter's interest in republicanism is a reminder that most immigrants have come to the United States for its democratic institutions and its commitment to the rule of law. Many today might argue that Hunter entered the United States with many privileges as white-skinned and English speaking. If he were here today, William would soundly disagree, citing the widespread prejudice he endured for being the son of a British soldier and having his loyalty doubted. While he enjoyed privileges over enslaved and native peoples, William's life story is a positive example for today's immigrants and those longer-tenured citizens.

William's fifteen-year career as a newspaper publisher and editor demonstrates the early American media industry's demanding, risky, and mostly unprofitable nature. Currently, we face a similar situation with polarized newspapers eking out modest existences espousing articulated ideological and party lines. Just as today, William learned that papers without ideological, governmental, or party backing and those purported to be in the middle of the spectrum were not economically sustainable.

William's unequivocal and resolute stand against the 1798 Alien and Sedition Acts demonstrated considerable courage and fortitude. By being the first newspaper editor to oppose the anti-free speech legislation publicly and criticizing the Adams administration, he took sizeable personal risks and opened his family to potential economic disaster. Hunter had no assurances that he would avoid prosecution and conviction leading to jail time and bankrupting fines. Hunter's principled stand and taking positions unpopular with government officials remind us of the need to have the courage of our convictions in the face of oppression.

Often, today's citizens dismiss the efforts of government officials as unduly bureaucratic, ineffective, and wasteful. William's service as a Treasury auditor is a reminder that government service is a worthy career and essential to the operation of our democracy. He uncovered and exposed fraud and official malfeasance by several naval officers with a discerning eye. William's service highlights that the Federal government workers provide valuable checks and balances. Dedicated government officials help maintain the rule of law, keep an effective government in operation, and ensure fairness for all citizens.

Lastly, William's life story is a remarkable example of embracing adventure, overcoming challenges, and taking prudent risks. He gleaned valuable life lessons from his varied, non-traditional background. Everyone might not get to grow up on two continents, to reside in three national capitals, and to learn multiple languages, but his experiences in adapting to and thriving in numerous cultures are a potent reminder that these skills are critical to succeeding in the increasingly tight-knit twenty-first-century global community.

APPENDIX I

Discovery of the Journal and Identifying the Author

I discovered the William Hunter journal through a chance encounter at a dinner party. That exchange sparked the identification of the only extant journal or diary written by a child of a British soldier during the American Revolution. Initial examination of the treasured journal indicated a well-written, two-sided document in excellent penmanship that covered the Revolutionary period. Not recorded as a contemporaneous diary but written years afterward by a well-versed author, the journal is a remembrance for family and friends of the author's childhood and young adult experiences. Remarkably, the diary is written from an American perspective, espousing sympathy for the Rebel cause.

However exciting to read a newly uncovered primary source, a glaring roadblock stood in the way of historically interpreting the document—the author's name is not found in the document, and no one in the living family knew the writer's name. Other issues include missing the first page(s), several cut-out portions, and missing pages in the middle sections. Over the years, it appears that family members added edits or comments in pencil and different handwritings. Finally, the journal abruptly ended in 1794.

Only left with clues from the 35-page, 12,000-word journal, the next steps were to assess the document's veracity, identify the author, and fill in the missing sections. From the pronouns that the author uses, one can reason that the author is a male. His father is a member of the British Army in the 26th Regiment of Foot. I consulted with Don Hagist, an expert on the British Army in North America, who assisted with investigating the journalist's name. As no officer in this regiment had a family accompanying him, his father must have been enlisted. Later in the diary, the journalist mentions that his father served in recruiting efforts indicating that he was likely a non-commissioned officer

(NCO). We identified several sergeants who had family members consistent with the author's journal through reviews of muster rolls. Given this information, Sergeant John Hunter lines up as a good possibility. Hunter's service dates line up with the journal entries, except that he did not serve with the famous Benedict Arnold conspirator Captain John Andre, nor in a flank or grenadier company. However, consistent with the journal, Sergeant John Hunter left on recruiting mission to Britain per regimental muster rolls and received a discharge in 1783 and Chelsea pension on August 15, 1783.

From the journal, we know the author moved to Philadelphia in 1793 and worked in the printing business. However, we still didn't know the son's name even with this information. An electronic search of accessible digital archives and books identified a list of Hunters who were printers and had immigrated to the United States. Further investigation found the following brief biography of a resident of Kentucky.

> Col. Wm. Hunter was a native of New Brunswick, New Jersey; captured, when quite young, by a French man-of-war, and with his parents taken to France; left an orphan in a foreign land, he learned the printing business; returned in 1793, to Philadelphia, where he established a French and American paper, with which Matthew Carey (afterwards one of the most useful and remarkable men in the world) became associated . . .[1]

The basic life story of the Kentuckian William Hunter lines up with the journalist. Interestingly, the biographical account omits his father's role in the Revolution and glosses over why a French privateer would capture an American during the War of Independence.

A second source corroborates William Hunter as the journalist. Hunter wrote a letter to the United States Counsel William Jarvis seeking the whereabouts and status of his mother and sister. This letter identifies his mother's name as Margaret but does not identify his sister. Further establishing William Hunter as the author of the Revolutionary War journal, the handwriting of the two documents are similar.

The final piece of the puzzle is the burial records for William Hunter in the Congressional Cemetery in Washington, DC. In these prestigious final resting grounds, a large stone obelisk marks the grave of William Hunter, born in 1768 and died in 1854. An accompanying obituary in the Washington, DC paper, *The National Intelligencer* on October 24, 1854, confirms the basic facts contained in the journal. Buried next to William is his oldest surviving offspring,

Lavenia Hunter Jackson. The current journal owner can trace her family linage back to Lavenia, thereby establishing a solid reason for possessing the eighteenth-century journal among family papers.

The journal is unique among Revolutionary era works. Some passages recount both major events not previously known to historians and interesting passages detailing the daily lives of British Army soldiers and their families. However, one of the most interesting facets is that the author "turned" from supporting his father's loyalty to the British Crown to sympathizing with American independence. By the journal's date, the author had become a loyal American with anti-British and pro-French sentiments. Like most men and women of the time, the journalist espoused racist views and offered derogatory descriptions of Native Peoples.

Not a contemporaneously written diary, an aging man proudly wrote the journal to memorialize his untold and disguised early life. Given the references to a French King living in an Edinburgh Castle, the journal had to be written after 1830.[2] Despite being in the sixties, the author possessed a remarkable memory as his story is factually correct with only a few minute errors. It's possible that he kept notes or a diary from these early years, which aided his recall. William Hunter's remembrance hopes have been satisfied as a proud family has well preserved the highly readable journal. For successive generations, William's early life experiences created an indelible impact as he lived through an eventful time, survived many dangerous experiences, and contributed to the societies in which he lived.

Unfortunately, we don't have an image of William, as no portrait or likeness of William has survived. Despite a fulsome written record, we also lack a physical description of William Hunter. All that is recorded is that he remained remarkably muscular for an older man. Further, we don't know much about his personality and how he spoke and sounded. The only clue is that contemporaries describe him as "genteel."[3] Lastly, we know just a few biographical facts about his wife and family and their lives. We know that William remained married for over fifty years, and the marriage produced three children who lived into adulthood.

Short Bios of notable people in William Hunter's Life

ALEXANDER ADDISON

Born in Morayshire, Scotland, Addison (1758 or 59—1807) completed a religious education at Edinburgh and began a clerical career. He immigrated to the United States in 1785, seeking preaching opportunities in rural Pennsylvania. When becoming a religious leader did not materialize, Addison moved to Washington, PA, studied law, and passed the bar examination in 1788. With his high intellect, he made a strong impression on his neighbors. In setting up the first Federal courts, President Washington commissioned Addison as the President-Judge of the Fifth District Court in Pennsylvania. In this role, Addison was pivotal in prosecuting Whiskey Rebels. During this time, William Beaumont fervently believed that Addison developed a life-long hatred of him due to his Republican political beliefs and his association with moderate rebels. Beaumont referenced persecution by Addison in his many letters to political leaders to secure a public appointment in the new Mississippi Territory. In January 1799, Addison wrote one of the most intellectually complete essays supporting the Federalist-passed Alien and Sedition Acts entitled *Liberty of speech, and of the press: a charge to the grand juries of the county courts of the fifth circuit of the state of Pennsylvania*. Many political critics emerged due to the region's increasing support of Democratic-Republican politics. In 1800, political opponents wrote an anonymous letter to the *Herald of Freedom*, alleging that Addison used five hundred dollars of public money to purchase William Hunter's and William Beaumont's partnership interests in *The Western Telegraphe and Advertiser*. With the change in administration to Thomas Jefferson, Addison the Jeffersonians impeached Addison on spurious charges and removed him from office.

CHRISTOPHER GREENUP

A resident of Frankfort from 1792, Greenup (c. 1750-1818) became friends with William Hunter. A career politician, Greenup served in the Kentucky Senate and House, as a Representative in the United States House, and importantly for Hunter, the third governor of Kentucky. Hunter lost his state government printing contract in 1808 when Greenup completed his constitutionally mandated one term. Greenup continued to serve as a presidential elector, justice of the peace, Kentucky Secretary of State. He died in 1818. Greenup named William Hunter as one of his three executors to carry out his last will and testament.

HARRY INNES

A Virginian by birth, Innes (1752-1816) staunchly advocated for the separation of Kentucky into a new state. After the formation of Kentucky, President George Washington appointed Innes to be the Federal judge in the Kentucky district court, a position that he held until his death. Hunter and Innes shared an intense love of books.

AMOS KENDELL

Perhaps Hunter's most important friendship, Amos Kendall (1789-1869) also published a newspaper in Frankfort, the *Argus of Western America*. Finding politics more rewarding, Kendall came to Washington, DC, with the election of President Andrew Jackson. A staunch Democratic Party supporter, Jackson appointed Kendall to serve as the fourth auditor of the Treasury. In this role, he lobbied Jackson to select his own clerks and, with his permission, named William Hunter as a clerk in his office. This pivotable appointment provided a much-needed job for Hunter after his failed Louisville newspaper. He started a Democratic newspaper in Washington City (DC) from behind the scenes. However, he did not involve Hunter in this venture. Kendall's star continued to rise. He received an appointment to Postmaster General and served as an intimate member of Jackson's "Kitchen Cabinet." Again, Kendall did not bring Hunter along to help with these new responsibilities. After his government service, Kendall invested heavily in Samuel Morse's telegraph and became independently wealthy. He used earnings from this wildly successful business to fund the founding of Gallaudet University to educate blind people.

WILLIAM LITTELL

Like William Hunter, Littell (1768–1824) was born in New Jersey and grew up in Pennsylvania. He studied divinity, physics, and medicine before moving to Kentucky in 1801. In Frankfort, he became interested in the scholarly aspects of law and began to compile and edit the Kentucky State laws. Recognizing the need to disseminate concise and accurate copies of laws, the legislature retained Littell's services to edit the laws back to the state's beginning in 1792. William Hunter published the first set of Littell's legal books. After Hunter sold his printing business, he continued to publish Littell's work for a few years before Littell turned to other printers and publishers. Despite not publishing together, they remained friends. Littell included references to Hunter in his 1814 satiric and witty book *Festoons of Fancy*, in which Hunter may have provided some of the prose. Scholarly prolific, but eccentric, Littell passed in 1824.

GEORGE NICHOLAS

A Lieutenant Colonel in the Eleventh Regiment of the Virginia Line during the Revolutionary War, George Nicholas (1754?–1798) moved to Kentucky to employ his considerable skills as a lawyer and political theorist. As Kentucky was formally part of Virginia, he worked alongside James Madison on political speech issues and attended the Virginia Convention to ratify the Federal Constitution in 1788. This experience provided a background for his seminal efforts to craft Kentucky's first commonwealth constitution in 1792. Demonstrating his patriotism and integrity, Nicholas turned down a $100,000 bribe from the Spanish government to detach the western country from the United States. His political stock continued to rise, and he was appointed Kentucky's first attorney general. As the populous desired changes, Nicholas led the efforts to influence the second Kentucky constitutional convention. Unfortunately, Nicholas's health declined as the convention neared, and he passed while the convention remained in session. At his death, Nicholas enjoyed the finest reputation of any Kentucky leader. It's unclear how much personal interaction existed between Nicholas and William Hunter, but Nicholas's writings were prominently featured on the pages of *The Mirror* and *The Palladium*.

JOHN ROWAN

Rowan (1773–1843) started his career as a legal partner of George Nicholas in Lexington, KY. After a deadly drunken brawl, Governor Christopher Greenup gave Rowan a chance at a political career by appointing him Secretary of State in 1804. Over the next twenty years, Rowan served in the Kentucky Legislature and courts. William Hunter allied himself with Rowan, who Kentuckians recognized as the informal, but powerful leader of the Debt Relief party in the 1820s. After the 1824 sweep, the Debt Relief party sent Rowan to the US Senate, where he served one term. Important for overdue debtors such as Hunter, Rowan made a speech in the Senate advocating the end of imprisonment for unpaid and delinquent debts. Like Hunter, Rowan enjoyed a life-long interest in education and served as the first president of Louisville Medical Institute and the Kentucky Historical Society.

HARRY TOULMIN

Much like William Hunter, Toulmin (1766–1823) fled England due to differences in religious beliefs and political views. He arrived in the United States in the same year as Hunter (1793). With a recommendation from Thomas Jefferson, the university trustees, selected Toulmin as the president of the new Transylvania University in Lexington, Kentucky. However, his religious views clashed with the trustees, and he resigned to become the Secretary of State under Governor James Garrard for eight years. After Garrard's second term expired in 1804, Thomas Jefferson appointed Toulmin to a Federal courtship in the new Mississippi Territory. In 1822, Hunter's son, Morrison, married Toulmin's daughter, Ann, in Mobile, Alabama. This marriage produced four children, including Harry Hunter, who inherited Washington, DC property from Ann Hunter upon her death.

JOSEPH ROGERS UNDERWOOD

A long-time William Hunter nemesis, Kentuckians elected Joseph R. Underwood (1791–1876) to numerous positions over a political life that stretched from the War of 1812 to the end of Reconstruction after the Civil War. Underwood served in the state legislature, as a state appellate judge, and in the US House and Senate. He became life-long friends with Henry Clay, opposed Andrew Jackson, and helped build the new Whig Party to oppose the Jacksonians. Although he owned slaves, he never reconciled his religious and ethical beliefs with their bondage and shipped his able-bodied enslaved people to Liberia.

APPENDIX III

William Hunter Publications

Philadelphia

1795   *A New Spanish Grammar* Philadelphia: Colerick & Hunter

Washington, PA

1795   *An Address to the Citizens of Philadelphia Respecting the Better Government of Youth* by Matthew Clarkson, Mayor, first published in the *Philadelphia Gazette* Saturday June 6, 1795. Published by Colerick, Hunter & Beaumont

1795   Almanack for the year of 1796 being Bissextile or Leap Year Washington, PA: Colerick, Hunter & Beaumont

1796   *Dilworth's Spelling Book, Improved. A Book Well Adapted to the Forwarding of Youth in the English Language* Washington, PA: Colerick, Hunter & Beaumont

1796   "Mrs. Barbauld's Lessons." by Colerick, Hunter & Beaumont, January 1796

1796   "The New England Primer." October 8

1796   Almanack for the year of 1797

1797   Beveridge's Private Thoughts."

1797   "The Gentleman's Pocket Farrier, Price 20 cents."

Washington, KY

1797   *A Sermon on Sacred Music Preached Before a Public Concert in Washington,* by Rev. John Poage Campbell, published by request Washington, PA: Hunter and Beaumont, 38 pages, Early American Imprints.

1798   *The Ohio Navigator,* attributed in Charles Evans Bibliography to William Hunter, Washington, KY: Hunter and Beaumont (Two Editions)

1798   *The Kentucky Spelling Book* Washington, KY: Hunter & Beaumont

1798   *The Kentucky Primer* Washington, KY: Hunter & Beaumont

1798   *A View of the Administration of the Federal Government* Washington, KY: Hunter & Beaumont

1798   *Speeches of Erskine and Kidd in the trial for Publishing Paine's The Age of Reason*—a politician and lawyer who defended radicals and reformers including Thomas Paine, for publishing the Rights of Man.

1798   *A Summary of the Declaration of Faith and Practice of the Baptist Church*

1798   *The Several Acts Relative to the Stamp Duties*

1798   *A Sermon on Sacred Music* by Rev. John A. Campbell

1798   Steuben's Manual Exercises

Frankfort

1799   *The Constitution or form of Government for the State of Kentucky Published by order of the Constitutional Convention*, Frankfort, Printers to the Commonwealth Hunter and Beaumont.

1799   *Acts Passed at the First Session of the Seventh General Assembly for the Commonwealth of Kentucky*, Frankfort: Hunter & Beaumont, Printers to the Commonwealth.

1799   *The History of the Independents, or Congregationalists, a Very Numerous Sect in the Eastern States*, Collected and Published with Observations by Gabriel Nourse, Frankfort: Hunter & Beaumont, Printers to the Commonwealth, 12 pages.

1800   Acts *passed by the first session of the Eighth General Assembly for the Commonwealth of Kentucky*, Frankfort: Printed by William Hunter

1800   *The Almanack for the year 1801* Frankfort, KY: William Hunter

1801   *Kentucky Laws, Statutes, etc. The Militia Laws, Frankfort, KY*, printed by William Hunter.

1801   Acts *passed by the first session of the Ninth General Assembly for the Commonwealth of Kentucky*, Frankfort: Printed by William Hunter

1802   *A Collection of all the Public and Permanent Acts of the General Assembly of Kentucky which are now in Force.* by Harry Toulmin Frankfort, KY: William Hunter.

1802   Acts *passed by the first session of the Tenth General Assembly for the Commonwealth of Kentucky*, Frankfort: Printed by William Hunter

1802   *Laws Adopted by the Governor and Judges of the Indiana Territory at Their First Session Held at Saint Vincennes, January 12, 1801*, Published by Authority, Frankfort, KY, by William Hunter.

1803   *Kentucky Laws, Statutes, etc. by Authority, An Act to Amend the Act Entitled an Act Concerning the Militia, February 24, 1803*, Frankfort, KY, printed by William Hunter.

1803   Acts *passed by the first session of the Eleventh General Assembly for the Commonwealth of Kentucky*, Frankfort: Printed by William Hunter

1803   *The Law of Kentucky on I. Mayhem, II. Assaults, especially circumstanced, III. Treason: Intended as a specimen of the revision of the criminal law of this commonwealth.* By Harry Toulmin and James Blair, from the press of William Hunter, printer to the state.

1804   *Acts Passed at the First Session of the Twelfth General Assembly for the Commonwealth of Kentucky*, Frankfort, KY: William Hunter

1804   *A Review of Criminal Law of the Commonwealth of* Kentucky by Harry Toulmin and James Blair Frankfort, KY, William Hunter. From James D. Birchfield, Fall 1987, Volume 7 number 3, The Kentucky Review—UK page 73.

1805   Acts *passed by the first session of the Thirteenth General Assembly for the Commonwealth of Kentucky*, Frankfort: Printed by William Hunter

1806   An *Epistle from William surnamed Littell to the People of the Realm of Kentucky*, Frankfort, KY Printed by William Hunter.

1806   Acts *passed by the first session of the Fouteenth General Assembly for the Commonwealth of Kentucky*, Frankfort: Printed by William Hunter

1806   *Political Transactions in and Concerning Kentucky from the First Settlement Thereof Until it Became an Independent State in June, 1792* by William Littrell, Esq. i2mo., 147 pages. Printed by William Hunter, Printer to the Commonwealth, Frankfor, Ky., 1806.

1806   *A Review of the Criminal Law of Kentucky* by Harry Toulmin and James Blair printed by William Hunter, State Printer

1806   *A View of the President's Conduct* by Joseph Hamilton Daveiss

1806   *The American public prosecutor's assistant: being a collection of precedents in criminal prosecutions, more immediately founded on the Common Law, and of the statues of Kentucky, but generally applicable to the awls of the several states of America.* By Harry Toulmin, Frankfort, KY from the press of William Hunter.

1807   Kentucky. *Laws for regulating the militia. To which is added, an act for establishing rules and articles for the government of the armies of the United States.* Frankfort, Ky.: Printed by W. Hunter, 1807.

1807   Acts *passed by the first session of the Fifteenth General Assembly for the Commonwealth of Kentucky*, Frankfort: Printed by William Hunter

1808   *Principles of Laws and Equity* by William Littrell

1808   Acts *passed by the first session of the Sixteenth General Assembly for the Commonwealth of Kentucky*, Frankfort: Printed by William Hunter

1808   *History of the Baptised Ministers and Churches in Kentucky, & Friends to Humanity* by Carter Tarrant

1810-11 *The Statute Law of Kentucky* Volumes 2 and 3 Printed for William Hunter by Johnston and Pleasants

1814   *The Statute Law of Kentucky* Volume 4 Printed for William Hunter by Robert Johnston

Published by Hunter, printed by others

1809-19 *The Statute Law of Kentucky*, Printed by Johnston and Pleasants for William Hunter, Five volumes.

Notes

Prologue

1. Washington City is used throughout the text as it is the period name for the District of Columbia.

Part I: Discerning Revolutionary Journalist

1. Introducing mystery at the outset, the first pages of William's journal are missing. Likely, a weakened binding allowed the pages to come loose and become lost to history.

2. S.H.F Johnston, *The History of the Cameronians (Scottish Rifles) 26th and 90th*, vol. 1, 1689–1910 (Aldershot: Gale & Polden Limited, 1957), 137.

3. Johnston, 1, 1689–1910:137–38.

4. There is no relationship between Lisburn, Ireland and Lisbon, Portugal. No marriage records have been located for William's parents. A marriage date just prior to the 26th Regiment's overseas deployment is assumed as children began to appear in the historical record in North America.

Chapter 1: Garrison Duty in British North American Colonies

1. *Oxford Journal*, Saturday, May 30, 1767, 3.

2. *Pennsylvania Gazette*, Thursday July 2, 1767, Issue 2010, 2 and *New-York Gazette or Weekly Post-Boy*, Thursday July 9. 1767, Issue 1279, 3.

3. Further augmenting the regiment's authorized complement of women and children, women from North America joined the regiment through marriage or as single women seeking employment. The number of women accompanying the 26th Regiment approximated a quarter of the total number of soldiers in the regiment. The particularly high number of spouses and single women reflected the 26th Regiment's peace time garrison duty in North America. Assuming matching last names, the number of wives varied significantly by rank with non-commissioned officers having the highest percentage of wives at 66% while none of the officers had a spouse accompany them. In addition, there were approximately two children per woman with fourteen women with no children and three women with five children. Kenneth Baumgardt, "The Royal Army in America During the Revolutionary War The American Prisoner Records" (Christiana Delaware: Department of Defense, US Army Corps of Engineers, 2008), http://www.dtic.mil/dtic/tr/fulltext/u2/a491107.pdf.

4. Don N. Hagist, "The Women of the British Army in America," *RevWar 75* (blog), 2002, http://revwar75.com/library/hagist/britwomen.htm.

5. Brunswick is named New Brunswick today, which is in central New Jersey, located 27 miles southwest of Manhattan, NYC. French and Indian War era residents constructed a large barracks to house British troops in the town. Today, the site of the barracks is covered with modern development.

6. For example, *World Catalog* cites William Hunter's birthyear as 1770 with a question mark. https://www.worldcat.org/wcidentities/lccn-n88126502.

7. W. Nelson and A. Van Doren Honeyman, *Extracts from American Newspapers: Relating to New Jersey. 1704-1775*, Documents Relating to the Colonial History of the State of New Jersey, 1905, 162, https://books.google.com/books?id=geB4AAAAMAAJ.

8. Johnston, *The History of the Cameronians (Scottish Rifles) 26th and 90th*.

9. Great Britain, K. G. Davies, and Great Britain, eds., *Documents of the American Revolution, 1770-1783: Colonial Office Series* (Shannon: Irish University Press, 1972), Vol. I, 394.

10. Nelson and Van Doren Honeyman, *Extracts from American Newspapers: Relating to New Jersey. 1704-1775*, 161–62.

11. *God and a Soldier All Men Doth Adore, In Time of War and Not before: When the War Is over, and All Things Righted, God Is Forgotten, and the Soldier Slighted. : Whereas an Uncommon and Riottous* [sic]

Disturbance Prevails throughout This City, by Some of Its Inhabitants, Who Stile Themselves the S--s of L-----y, but Rather May More Properly Be Called Real Enemies to Society . . . (New York, N.Y.: s.n., 1770).

12. For a fulsome account of the Battle of Golden Hill see Bob Ruppert, "The Battle of Golden Hill - Six Weeks before the Boston Massacre," *Journal of the American Revolution*, October 24, 2014, https://allthings-liberty.com/2014/10/the-battle-of-golden-hill-six-weeks-before-the-boston-massacre/.

13. *Pennsylvania Packet*, Thursday June 13, 1771, Issue 2216, 2.

14. New Jersey Historical Society, *Documents Relating to the Revolutionary History of the State of New Jersey*, Documents Relating to the Revolutionary History of the State of New Jersey, v. 1 (John L. Murphy Publishing Company, 1901), 158–59, https://books.google.com/books?id=TFtKAQAAMAAJ.

15. *Pennsylvania Journal or Weekly Advertiser*, Thursday, September 6, 1770, Issue 1448, 4.

16. Davies, K. C., ed., *Documents of the American Revolution, 1770-1783*, Vol. V, 71.

17. *New Hampshire Gazette*, Friday, May 15, 1772, Vol. XVII, Issue 812, 1.

18. *Connecticut Journal*, Friday, May 29, 1772, Issue 241, 1.

19. Lieutenant General Thomas Gage to Earl of Hillsborough, 366, *Documents of the American Revolution*, Colonial Office Series, Volume IV, 97.

20. *Pennsylvania Packet*, Monday, June 15, 1772, Issue 34, 3.

21. John Gilbert McCurdy, *Quarters: The Accommodation of the British Army and the Coming of the American Revolution* (Ithaca: Cornell University Press, 2019).

22. *Newport Mercury*, Monday, June 11, 1773, Issue 749, 2.

23. Don N. Hagist, *British Soldiers, American War: Voices of the American Revolution* (Yardley, PA: Westholme, 2012), 99.

Chapter 2: Defense of Canada in the War for American Independence

1. Both British and American Rebel forces sought the support of native groups. While most American Indians sided with the British, several tribes actively fought on the Rebel side.

2. As business partners, Moses Hazen and Gabriel Christie jointly owned the land upon which Fort Saint-Jean stood. During the American invasion, Christie served in the King's Rifles in the West Indies. After equivocating for a period, Hazen joined the American cause and led a Canadian regiment for rest of the war. After peace in 1783, the partners fought a long and bitter legal battle over the Saint-Jean property. Settling in upstate New York, Hazen never returned to live in Canada and Christie resided in Montreal as an absentee seigneur.

3. Charles Carroll and Brantz Mayer, *Journal of Charles Carroll of Carrollton During His Visit to Canada in 1776* (Baltimore, MD: Printed by John Murphy for the Maryland Historical Society, 1876), 89, https://ia800303.us.archive.org/26/items/carrollofcarrollton00charrich/carrollofcarrollton00charrich.pdf.

4. Possibly the author's father was injured on October 14, 1775 as the British Commander recorded in his diary that a barrel of gunpowder blew up in the Fort's South Redoubt. Diary is located at the Canada Library and Archives, Charles Preston fonds 1775-1776. Fonds/Collection MG23-B10, R7098-0-2-E. For a description of the siege, see Charles C. Maconochie, "From the Outposts 1775, The Defense of St. John's," *Blackwell's Magazine*, April 1914, 563–72.

5. Benjamin Trumbull, "Journal or Minutes of the Principal Movements towards St. John's of the Siege and Surrender of the Forts There in 1775," in *Collection of the Connecticut Historical Society*, vol. VII (Hartford: Connecticut Historical Society, 1899), 162.

6. *American Archives: Containing a Documentary History of the English Colonies in North America, from the King's Message to Parliament of March 7, 1774, to the Declaration of Independence by the United States. Fourth Series*, American Archives: Containing a Documentary History of the English Colonies in North America, from the King's Message to Parliament of March 7, 1774, to the Declaration of Independence by the United States. Fourth Series, vol. 4, 1843, 816, https://books.google.com/books?id=IEwMAQAAMAAJ.

7. Six miles in the author's journal, page 3.

8. Two cannon in some sources.

9. *Carroll and Mayer, Journal of Charles Carroll of Carrollton During His Visit to Canada in 1776*, 89.

10. Carroll and Mayer, 95.

11. Thomas Hughes, *A Journal by Thos. Hughes: For His Amusement, & Designed Only for His Perusal by the Time He Attains the Age of 50 If He Lives So Long, (1778-1789)*, ed. E. A. Benians (Cambridge: The University Press, 1947), 67.

12. Walter F Ayars III, ed., *Lancaster Diary 1776* (Lancaster, PA: Printed by Lancaster Press, Inc. for the Greater Lancaster Chapter, Lancaster County Bicentennial Committee, 1975), 33.

13. Ayars III, 33.

14. Ayars III, 39.

15. Ayars III, 37.

16. Later in the war a higher percentage of the POW's found job opportunities, especially the German speaking Hessians who were granted extended freedom of movement and found employment with the many farmers and businesspeople of German heritage in the local community. This provided a much higher living standard and helped alleviate the labor shortage caused by the Rebel need for soldiers and sailors.

17. Ken Miller, "A Dangerous Set of People: Briiish Captives and the Making of Revolutionary Identity in the Mid-Atlantic Interior," *Journal of the Early Republic* 32, no. 4 (2012): 591.

18. In the 1760s, Dr. James Sutton and his son David developed the Suttonian system of inoculation (a variolation technique). The process started with abstaining from meat and alcohol for two weeks prior to the inoculation. A charged lancet is held slantwise to create a one sixteenth of an inch-deep incision in the skin. Afterwards, regular purges, exercise in the open air, bland diet and cold water were ordered. With a bit of mystery, a secret remedy was also administered. No one is sure of its ingredients, but later physicians believe Sutton mixed mercury and antimony, two common medical components of the period.

19. Barbara Tunis, "Dr. James Latham (c. 1734-1790): Pioneer Inoculator in Canada," *University of Toronto Press Journals*, Canadian Bureau of Medical History, vol. 1, no. 1 (Spring 1984): 1–3, https://doi.org/10.3138.

20. Miller, "A Dangerous Set of People: Briiish Captives and the Making of Revolutionary Identity in the Mid-Atlantic Interior," 593.

21. "Proceedings of the Lancaster, Pennsylvania, Committee | American Archives," Northern Illinois University, At a meeting of the Committee of Observation, Inspection and Correspondence at the house of Adam Reigart, August 5, 1776, Volume I, 759-760, http://amarch.lib.niu.edu/islandora/object/niu-amarch%3A94840.

22. Baumgardt, "The Royal Army in America During the Revolutionary War: The American Prisoner Records."

23. Miller, "A Dangerous Set of People: British Captives and the Making of Revolutionary Identity in the Mid-Atlantic Interior," 598.

24. Extract of a Letter from a Field Officer in the King's Army: Dated New-York, December 2, 1776, Pennsylvania Evening Post, Saturday, April 19, 1777, Vol. III, Issue 341, 219.

Chapter 3: War through the Eyes of a Child with a Father in Combat

1. Barnet Schecter, *The Battle for New York: The City at the Heart of the American Revolution* (New York: Walker & Co, 2002), 204.

2. Oscar Theodore Barck, Jr., *New York City during the War for Independence with Special Reference to the Period of British Occupation* (New York: Columbia University Press, 1931), 84.

3. Arthur R. Bowler, *Logisitics and the Failure of the British Army in America* (Princeton, N.J: Princeton University Press, 1975), 68–69.

4. For an account of the highly kinetic forage wars, see the diary of a British officer, Archibald Robertson, *Archibald Robertson: His Diaries and Sketches in America, 1762-1780.*, Archibald Robertson, Lieutenant-General, Royal Engineers, ([New York]: New York Public Library, 1971), 122–27, //catalog.hathitrust.org/Record/000363536.

5. Bowler, *Logistics and the Failure of the British Army in America*, 69.

6. Spelled Neversink in some accounts.

7. Society, *Documents Relating to the Revolutionary History of the State of New Jersey*, 202–3.

8. Banastre Tarleton to his mother, 18 December 1776, Princeton, New Jersey James J. Barnes and Patience P. Barnes, eds., *The American Revolution through British Eyes: A Documentary Collection* (Kent, Ohio: Kent State University Press, 2013), 291–93.

9. From Captain John Bowater January 9, 1777 Marion Balderston and David Syrett, eds., *The Lost War: Letters from British Officers during the American Revolution* (New York: Horizon Press, 1975), 118.

10. Phillip Papas, *Renegade Revolutionary: The Life of General Charles Lee* (New York: New York University Press, 2014), 222.

11. Dandridge estimates that 1900 of the 2600 Fort Washington Rebel captives died within two months of imprisonment. Danske Dandridge, *American Prisoners of the Revolution*, originally published 1910 (Echo Library, 2017), 34.

12. Bowman identifies seven churches used as prisons, all non-Anglican ministries, Larry G. Bowman, *Captive Americans: Prisoners During the American Revolution* (Athens, Ohio: Ohio University Press, 1976), 13.

13. Bowman, 18–19.

14. Johann Conrad Döhla and Bruce E. Burgoyne, *A Hessian Diary of the American Revolution*, 1. paperback printing (Norman: University of Oklahoma Press, 1990), 47–50.

15. *New-York Gazette and Weekly Mercury*, Monday October 20, 1777, Issue 1356, 1 and *Pennsylvania Ledger*, Wednesday October 29, 1777, Issue CI, 1.

16. Modern day Kingston, New York which is located sixty miles south of Albany and at least 90 miles from British General John Burgoyne's trapped army.

17. Döhla and Burgoyne, *A Hessian Diary of the American Revolution*, 58.

18. Döhla and Burgoyne, 60.

19. Carl Baurmeister, Bernhard A. Uhlendorf, and Edna Vosper, "Letters of Major Baurmeister during the Philadelphia Campaign, 1777-1778. II," *The Pennsylvania Magazine of History and Biography* 60, no. 1 (1936): 46.

20. G. D. Scull, James Gabriel Montrésor, and John Montrésor, *The Montresor Journals*, Collections of the New-York Historical Society . . . 1881. Publication Fund Series. vol. 14 xiv, 578 p. (New York: Printed for the Society, 1882), 494, //catalog.hathitrust.org/Record/000012843.

21. John W. Jackson, *With the British Army in Philadelphia 1777–1778* (San Rafael, CA and London, England: Presidio Press, 1979), 176.

22. The Canadian and Hudson valley campaigns significantly depleted the 26th Regiments' troop strength requiring the addition of two hundred new recruits prior to sailing to Philadelphia. Likely, British officers sought to train these new troops before relying on them in combat.

23. Troyer Steele Anderson, *The Command of the Howe Brothers during the American Revolution* (Cranbury, NJ: Scholar's Bookshelf, 2005), 301.

24. Ira D Gruber, *The Howe Brothers and the American Revolution* (Chapel Hill, N.C: The University of North Carolina Press, 1972), 260, https://muse.jhu.edu/books/9781469611303/.

25. Johann von Ewald, *Diary of the American War: A Hessian Journal* (New Haven: Yale University Press, 1979), 117.

26. Ewald Gustav Schaukirk, "Occupation of New York City by the British," *The Pennsylvania Magazine of History and Biography* 10, no. 4 (1887): 425.

27. Willard O. Mishoff, "Business in Philadelphia during the British Occupation, 1777-1778," *The Pennsylvania Magazine of History and Biography* 61, no. 2 (1937): 174.

28. For a current assessment of battle casualties, see Mark Edward Lender and Garry Wheeler Stone, *Fatal Sunday: George Washington, the Monmouth Campaign, and the Politics of Battle*, Campaigns and Commanders, vol. 54 (Norman: University of Oklahoma Press, 2016), 366–67.

29. Jonathan R. Dull, *The French Navy and American Independence: A Study of Arms and Diplomacy, 1774–1787* (Princeton, NJ: Princeton University Press, 1975), 123.

30. Henry Clinton, *The American Rebellion Sir Henry Clinton's Narrative of His Campaigns, 1775-1782 with an Appendix of Original Documents*, ed. William D Wilcox (New Haven: Yale University Press, 1954), 111.

31. Piers Mackesy, *The War for America: 1775–1783* (Lincoln: University of Nebraska Press, 1992), 217. Montresor in his Journal listed fifteen French ships of the Toulon squadron with 878 cannon versus the 830 guns cited by Mackesy. G. D. Scull, James Gabriel Montrésor, and John Montrésor, *The Montresor Journals*, Collections of the New-York Historical Society . . . 1881. Publication Fund Series.[v. 14] xiv, 578 p. ([New York: Printed for the Society, 1882], //catalog.hathitrust.org/Record/000012843, 504.

32. Karl Bauer, Bruce E. Burgoyne, and Marie E. Burgoyne, *Journal of a Hessian Grenadier Battalion* (Westminster, Md: Heritage Books, 2005), 84.

33. A British resupply fleet arrived in New York Harbor a month after William Hunter sailed with his family to Britain. Schaukirk, "Occupation of New York City by the British," 426.

34. At this point in the journal, the bottom portion of the page is cut out, omitting approximately ten lines of text. It is uncertain whether the author or a later reader/relative decided to remove the three inches of prose from the journal. There are no clues on either side of the existing pages indicating any sensitivities

or embarrassing events. Perhaps, the missing section describes more fully Sergeant Hunter's recall to England.

Chapter 4: Captive Again!

1. Typically, ships had between five and five and half feet of space between decks, Stephen Russell Berry, *A Path in the Mighty Waters: Shipboard Life and Atlantic Crossings to the New World* (New Haven: Yale University Press, 2015), 21.

2. David Syrett, *Shipping and the American War 1775–83: A Study of British Transport Organization*, University of London Historical Studies 27 (London: University of London, Athlone Press, 1970), 185.

3. Stephen Russell Berry, *A Path in the Mighty Waters: Shipboard Life and Atlantic Crossings to the New World* (New Haven: Yale University Press, 2015), 236.

4. Patrick Villiers, "Le Havre, port de guerre au XVIIIe siècle," Presses universitaires de Rouen et du Havre, 1999, https://books.openedition.org/purh/7835?lang=en.

5. Villiers.

6. For a description of soldier's use of free time, see Hagist, *British Soldiers, American War*, 125.

7. Haythem Bastawy, "Translations of A Thousand and One Nights," *Leeds Trinity University* (blog), April 22, 2015, http://www.leedstrinity.ac.uk/blogs/Translations-of-A-Thousand-and-One-Nights.

8. Villiers, "Le Havre, port de guerre au XVIIIe siècle."

9. C. Hippeau, *Le Gouvernement de Normandie Au XVIIe et Au XVIIIe Siècle d'après La Correspondance Des Marquis de Beuvron et Des Ducs d'Harcourt, Lieutenants Généraux et Gouverneurs de La Province*, 9 volumes (Caen: G. de Laporte, 1863), Vol. I, 447, //catalog.hathitrust.org/Record/000368654.

10. Possibly referring to an inspection visit by the French Minister of War Louis Gottschalk, *Lafayette In America—1777–1783*, 1st ed. (Arveyres, France: L'Esprit de Lafayette Society, 1975), 37.

11. William's journal is silent on any relationship or contact between his father and the English gentleman. Gentlemen and officers did not fraternize with enlisted private soldiers but may have some personal relationships with senior non-commissioned officers, especially in a prisoner of war situation.

12. Marie Joseph Paul Yves Roch Gilbert Du Motier Lafayette, Stanley J. Idzerda, and Marie Joseph Paul Yves Roch Gilbert Du Motier Lafayette, *Lafayette in the Age of the American Revolution: Selected Letters and Papers, 1776–1790*, The Papers of the Marquis de Lafayette (Ithaca, N.Y: Cornell University Press, 1977), Vol. 2, 299.

13. *Gil Blas* (In French *L'Histoire de Gil Blas de Santillane*) is a novel by Alain-Rene Lesage published between in the early 18th Century. "Gil Blas," accessed April 14, 2018, http://www.exclassics.com/gilblas/gbintro.htm.

14. St. Malo is a port city 164 miles across the Normandy peninsula from Le Havre.

15. Possibly referring to a counter-revolutionary guerilla war called Chouannerie named for its leader Jean Chouan.

Chapter 5: Gaining an Education and Trade in Britain

1. "Extract of a Letter from Swansea," *Hampshire Chronicle*, April 3, 1780, 398 ed., sec. three, The British Newspaper Archive, https://www.britishnewspaperarchive.co.uk/viewer/BL/0000230/17800403/009/0001?browse=true.

2. "Letter from Jersey," *Northampton Mercury*, February 28, 1780.

3. The Recruiting Act of 1779 set the maximum bounty at 3 pounds, 3 shillings.

4. Thomas Simes, *The Military Guide for Young Officers, Containing a System of the Art of War*, Second Edition (Uckfield, East Sussex, England: The Naval & Millitary Press Ltd., 1776), 205–10.

5. Sylvia R. Frey, *The British Soldier in America: A Social History of Military Life in the Revolutionary Period* (Austin: University of Texas Press, 1981), 13.

6. Linda Colley, *Britons: Forging the Nation, 1707–1837* (New Haven: Yale University Press, 1992), 332.

7. Frank O'Gorman, "Coventry Electoral Broadsides, 1780," *The Yale University Library Gazette* 67, no. 3/4 (1993): 161.

8. Thomas Carter, "Historical Record of the Twenty-Sixth, or Cameronian Regiment [Microform] : Carter, Thomas, d. 1867 : Free Download, Borrow, and Streaming : Internet Archive," accessed April 15, 2018, https://archive.org/details/cihm_03214.

9. *Hereford Journal*, Thursday, July 19, 1781.

10. Born Yorkshire 1748, William Myers rose through various command culminating in a Major General in 1796. Myers died in the West Indies in 1803. https://www.napoleon-series.org/military/organization/Britain/Infantry/Regiments/c_15thFoot.html

11. *Newcastle Courant*, Saturday, October 19, 1782, 3.

12. Johnston, *The History of the Cameronians (Scottish Rifles) 26th and 90th*.

13. A.P. Baggs, G.C. Baugh, and D.A. Johnston, "History of the County of Stafford: Volume 17, "Offlow Hundred," *British History On-Line* (blog), 1976, https://www.british-history.ac.uk/vch/staffs/vol17/pp143-146.

14. Thomas Carter, ed., *Historical Record of the Twenty-Sixth, or Cameronian Regiment* (London: W. O. Mitchell, Military Publisher, 1867), 93.

15. Colonel Erskine commanded the 80th Regiment, the Royal Edinburgh Volunteers in which one source reports that there were no soldiers of English descent. However, the June 1778 inspection indicates the regiment had 682 Scottish lowlanders, 111 English and 82 Irish men. Johnston, *The History of the Cameronians (Scottish Rifles) 26th and 90th*, 1, 1689–1910:154.

16. *Caledonian Mercury*, Monday, July 7, 1783.

17. Exiled, the French King Charles X (on the throne from 1824 to 1830) lived in Holyrood Castle from 1830 until 1834. This is strong evidence that the journal was written after 1830, probably during the first few years Hunter lived in Washington, DC.

18. The six towns of Tunstall, Burslem, Hanley, Stoke, Fenton and Longton comprise modern day Stoke-on-Trent. One of the largest pottery producers in eighteenth-century Britain, the area was well-known for its pottery and ceramics.

19. *The Universal British Directory of Trade, Commerce*, and Manufacture, vol. 4 (London: British Directory Office, 1791), 665.

20. Frederick Milward operated a printing and book business on High Street, Walsall. "Exeter Working Papers in Book History: Staffordshire," accessed April 13, 2018, http://bookhistory.blogspot.com/2013/01/staffordshire.html.

21. James Raven, *Publishing Business in Eighteenth-Century England*, People, Markets, Goods: Economies and Societies in History, vol. 3 (Woodbridge: The Boydell Press, 2014).

22. Caroline Louise Nielsen, "The Chelsea Out-Pensioners: Image and Reality in Eighteenth-Century and Early Nineteenth-Century Social Care" (Newcastle, England, Newcastle University, 2014), 146.

23. "Exeter Working Papers in Book History: Staffordshire," accessed April 13, 2018, http://bookhistory.blogspot.com/2013/01/staffordshire.html.

24. L. Hussakof, "Benjamin Franklin and Erasmus Darwin: With Some Unpublished Correspondence.," *Science* 43, no. 1118 (1916): 773–75.

25. Raven, *Publishing Business in Eighteenth-Century England*, 39.

26. John Darwall, *Discourse on Spiritual Improvement from Affliction*, Fourth (Walsall, England: Frederick Milward, 1790).

27. Mary Darwall, *Poems on Several Occaisons*, two vols. (Walsall, England: Frederick Milward, 1794).

28. In the late eighteenth-century, it was common to list on the title page not only the publisher/printer, but also the shops where the book maybe purchased.

29. At this point in the narrative, a second section of the journal has been cut out for no apparent reason.

30. The thirty-nine articles outline the basic tenants of Protestantism as defined by the Church of England and adopted in whole or part by many other Protestant religions today. The articles start with the holy trinity and cover topics such as free will, sacraments, marriage of clergy, idols and oaths.

31. Hill Cox was born on August 4, 1771 and died on April 3, 1833. He lived his whole life in Staffordshire.

32. The Journal does not reference that Frederick Milward had a son, but he would have been too young to be the author's fried.

33. Colley, *Britons*, 284.

34. Leaving no clues for its omission, a section of the journal is missing.

35. Joseph Priestley and Joseph Priestley, Jr., *Memoirs of Dr. Jospeh Priestley* (Mechanicsburg, PA: Sunbury Press, Inc., 2021), 70.

36. Henry St. John, First Viscount Bolingbroke (1678-1751), Anthony Ashley-Cooper, 3rd Earl Shaftesbury (1671-713), David Hume (1711-1776), and Thomas Hobbes (1588-1679).

37. In addition to base pay, Sergeant Hunter recieved a portion of the bounty for enlisting recruits. Don N. Hagist, *Noble Volunteers: The British Soldiers Who Fought the American Revolution.* (Yardley, PA: Westholme Publishing, 2020), 43.

38. George Gitton, "Last Will and Testament - George Gitton," February 1823, Reference PROB 11/1703/313, The National Archives - United Kingdom.

Chapter 6: Returning to America

1. Joseph Priestley quoted in Jennifer S. Uglow, *The Lunar Men: Five Friends Whose Curiosity Changed the World*, 1st American ed (New York: Farrar, Straus, and Giroux, 2002), 456.

2. Don Arnel, "List of Printers, American Print History," Georgia State University, *Digital Commons at Georgia Southern* (blog), Summer 2014, https://digitalcommons.georgiasouthern.edu/cgi/viewcontent.cgi?referer=https://www.google.com/&httpsredir=1&article=1001&context=amer_print_history_data.

3. William's journal does not mention the name of the ship or the captain. *The Federal Gazette*, November 18, 1793, notes the arrival of the Brig *Diana*, Captained by Elisha Turner 63 days out from Liverpool. There is only one other arrival in Philadelphia from Liverpool in the month of November 1793, the *Aerial*. However, William did not sail on the *Aerial* as it was detained by an English Privateer for 30 days, a remarkable event that William would have noted in his journal. Ship building records in Bath report a brig with the name of *Diana* under the command of Elisha Turner was built in 1793. W.A. Baker and Marine Research Society of Bath, A Maritime History of Bath, Maine and the Kennebec River Region, *A Maritime History of Bath, Maine and the Kennebec River Region* (Marine Research Society of Bath, 1973), https://books.google.com/books?id=P44TAAAAYAAJ, 815. With William noting the ship to be from Kennebec, the Diana is most certainly the ship upon which he transited the Atlantic.

4. W.A. Baker and Marine Research Society of Bath, *A Maritime History of Bath, Maine and the Kennebec River Region, A Maritime History of Bath, Maine and the Kennebec River Region* (Marine Research Society of Bath, 1973), 815, https://books.google.com/books?id=P44TAAAAYAAJ.

5. The *Aerial* with 30 passengers arrived in Philadelphia on November 18, 1793 after a 49-day passage from Liverpool after a 3 month internment. *Federal Gazette*, November 20, 1793,3.

6. The American trade embargo lasted between March 1794 to June 1795 with the implementation of *Jay's Treaty* between the United States and Great Britain.

7. Gardner W. Allen, *A Naval History of the American Revolution*, vol. 1 (Williamstown, MA: Corner House Publishers, 1970), 309.

8. St. Andrew's Society of Philadelphia and R.B. Beath, *An Historical Catalogue of the St. Andrew's Society of Philadelphia with Biographical Sketches of Deceased Members*, 1749-1913, An Historical Catalogue of the St. Andrew's Society of Philadelphia with Biographical Sketches of Deceased Members, 1749-1913 (Society, 1907), 346, https://books.google.com/books?id=q9pS4mIGrjsC.

9. During the 1790s, 23,340 people immigrated to Philadelphia including 3350 from Great Britain and 10,420 from Ireland, Hans-Jürgen Grabbe, "European Immigration to the United States in the Early National Period, 1783-1820," *Proceedings of the American Philosophical Society* 133, no. 2 (1989): 190–214.

10. On North Second Street between High and Chestnut, which dates back to at least 1785, see Fred. Perry Powers, "Tales of Old Taverns" (The Site and Relic Society of Germantown, March 17, 1911), http://www.morrisarboretum.org/archives/HistoricPDF/2006-3-008cTaverns.pdf.

11. Edmund Hogan, *The Prospect and Check on the Next Directory of Philadelphia* (Philadelphia: Francis and Robert Bailey, 1795), 66.

12. This street intersection does not exist today, but would have been 0.6 miles from the house where the Yellow Fever epidemic was thought to have begun.

13. Dr. Benjamin Rush first recognized the 1793 Philadelphia Yellow Fever epidemic when treating Mrs. Le Maigre and learning from Dr. Hugh Hodge of nearby residents suffering similar symptoms. Physicians noticed similar disease conditions in other areas of the city, but Rush's warnings of a raging epidemic placed the epidemic's start in people's minds at the Le Maigre's home on Water Street. For an overview of the epidemic and its impact on various economic classes and social groups see, Katherine Polak, "Perspectives on Epidemic: The Yellow Fever in 1793 Philadelphia," *Constructing the Past* Vol. 5, no. 1 (2004): Article 9.

14. William's salary was not as favorable as he claims in his journal. Apprentices could $6 to $7 dollar per week and supervisors $8 per week, R. Remer, *Printers and Men of Capital: Philadelphia Book Publishers in the New Republic*, Early American Studies (University of Pennsylvania Press, Incorporated, 2000), 44,

https://books.google.com/books?id=75_rNcHsW1kC. Another source indicates that journeymen printers earned between $5 and $10 dollars a week in the middle Atlantic States. Henry Lemoine, *Present State of Printing and Bookselling in America* [1796] (Chicago: Privately Printed, 1929), 17.

15. Don Hagist, Muster Rolls of the 47th Regiment of Foot.

16. Francis B. Heitman, *Historical Register of Officers of the Continental Army During the War of the Revolution* (Clearfield, 1932), 123.

17. Quoted from *Federal Gazette* (Philadelphia) July 1791 Nancy Isenberg and Andrew Burstein, *The Problem of Democracy: The Presidents Adams Confront the Cult of Personality* (New York, NY: Viking, 2019), 122.

18. Remer, *Printers and Men of Capital: Philadelphia* Book Publishers in the New Republic, 171n.

19. Rosalind Remer, "A Scottish Printer in Late-Eighteenth-Century Philadelphia: Robert Simpson's Journey from Apprentice to Entrepreneur," *The Pennsylvania Magazine of History and Biography* 121, no. 1/2 (1997): 10.

20. David G. McCullough, *John Adams* (New York: Simon & Schuster, 2001), 471.

Chapter 7: Nascent Printers

1. Robert Simpson, "Narrative of a Scottish Adventurer: From the Memoirs of Robert Simpson, Esq., Edinburgh, 1827," *Journal of the Presbyterian Historical Society*, no. 27 (1949): 41–67.

2. Remer, "A Scottish Printer in Late-Eighteenth-Century Philadelphia: Robert Simpson's Journey from Apprentice to Entrepreneur," 10.

3. For example, John Colerick printed the first American Edition of *The History of Greece from the Earliest State to the Death of Alexander the Great* by Oliver Goldsmith (1728-1774) in 1800. Likely, Matthew Carey outsourced the book's printing to Colerick as production costs in rural areas were cheaper than charged in Philadelphia.

4. James Hardie, *The Philadelphia Directory and Register*, Second (Philadelphia: Jacob Johnson & Co., 1974).

5. Rollo G. Silver, *The American Printer 1787–1825* (Charlottesville, Va.: Bibliographical Society of the University of Virginia, 1967), 28–46.

6. September 30, 1794 Advertisement *Philadelphia Gazette*, Page 3.

7. October 4, 1794 Advertisement *Philadelphia Gazette*.

8. Sturgis E. Leavitt, "The Teaching of Spanish in the United States," *Hispania*, Published by: American Association of Teachers of Spanish and Portuguese Stable, 44, no. 4 (December 1961): 591–625.

9. The first Spanish Grammar book in British North America is attributed to Garret Noel, Garret Noel, *A Short Introduction to the Spanish Language*, New York Printed by James Parker, 1751.

10. Hipólito San Joseph. Giral del Pino and Real Academia Española., "A New Spanish Grammar; or, The Elements of the Spanish Language: Containing an Easy and Compendious Method to Speak and Write It Correctly: With Several Useful Remarks on the Most Particular Idioms & Fundamental Rules, Shewing How to Make Use of Them, as Well in Speaking as in Writing: The Whole Extracted from the Best Observations of Spanish Grammarians, and Particularly of the Royal Spanish Academy of Madrid," 1795, http://opac.newsbank.com/select/evans/47435.

11. An example of a French American newspaper is the "*Courrier Français Philadelphia, PA*," Libary of Congress, n.d., https://lccn.loc.gov/sn87052031.

12. Catherine Hebert, "French Publications in Philadelphia in the Age of the French Revolution: A Bibliographic Essay," *Pennsylvania History: A Journal of Mid-Atlantic Studies* 58, no. 1 (January 1991): 37–61.

13. Remer, *Printers and Men of Capital: Philadelphia Book Publishers in the New Republic*, 25.

14. *Philadelphia Gazette*, Monday, May 25, 1795, Page 2.

Chapter 8: Impartial Printers

1. Reuben Gold Thwaites, *Early Western Travels, 1748–1846; a Series of Annotated Reprints of Some of the Best and Rarest Contemporary Volumes of Travel, Descriptive of the Aborigines and Social and Economic Conditions in the Middle and Far West, during the Period of Early American Settlement*, 32 v. (Cleveland, O.: The A. H. Clark company, 1904), 347, //catalog.hathitrust.org/Record/000277487.

2. Alexis de Tocqueville believed that the burgeoning number of local newspapers had more to do with the American political system than town pride in a local paper. He stated, "This bizarre multiplication of American newspapers has more to do with the extraordinary subdivision of administrative power than the extensive freedom of the politics or the absolute independence of the press." Alexis de Tocqueville et al., *Democracy in America: And Two Essays on America*, Penguin Classics (London: Penguin, 2003), 602.

3. Peter Gilmore, *Irish Presbyterians and the Shaping of Western Pennsylvania, 1770–1830* (Pittsburgh, PA: University of Pittsburgh Press, 2018), 62–63.

4. "Examination of Hugh Henry Brackenridge, [18-19 November 1794]," Founders Online, National Archives, accessed April 11, 2019. https://founders.archives.gov/documents/Hamilton/01-17-02-0361. [Original source: *The Papers of Alexander Hamilton*, vol. 17, August 1794- December 1794, ed. Harold C. Syrett. New York: Columbia University Press, 1972, pp 382-287.]

5. Later, Beaumont campaigned for and became personally acquainted with Albert Gallatin, a politically active Swiss immigrant living in Pennsylvania's Fayette County along the border with Maryland. Gallatin would rise to national prominence. Pennsylvania voters sent him to Congress as both a senator and member of the House and he became Secretary of Treasury under President Thomas Jefferson. In this position, he helped Beaumont secure a Federal tax collector position.

6. Henry Lemoine, *Present State of Printing and Bookselling in America [1796]* (Chicago: Privately Printed, 1929), 18.

7. Reiteration of original publishing philosophy as published in the inaugural edition, *Western Telegraphe & Washington Advertiser*, August 16, 1796.

8. British writer William Cowper placed a slight variation of this quote in the preface to his translation of Homer's Iliad, "free, but so free to be licentious." W. Cowper, R. Southey, and W. Harvey, *The Works of William Cowper: Translation of Homer's Iliad*, The Works of William Cowper: Comprising His Poems, Correspondence, and Translations. With a Life of the Author (Baldwin and Cradock, 1837), https://books.google.com/books?id=MnA4AAAAYAAJ, X. He also penned this slight variation in his published letter of December 17, 1794 to William Hayley. W. Cowper and J.S. Memes, *The Letters of William Cowper.* Edited by Rev. J. S. Memes. [With a Portrait.] (W. R. M'Phun, 1861), https://books.google.com/books?id=p-5pcAAAAcAAJ, 587-8.

9. Examples of newspapers with the same motto include: Cincinnati's second paper, *Freeman's Journal* established July 12, 1795, Beaver County, PA the Beaver Gazette, started June 8, 2013, the first paper in the southern tier of New York State *The American Constellation* from 1800 to 1803, *Miami Herald* established September 12, 1817.

10. Boyd Crumrine, Franklin Ellis, and Austin N. Hungerford, *History of Washington County, Pennsylvania with Biographical Sketches of Many of Its Prominent Pioneers and Men* (Philadelphia: H.L. Everts & Co., 1882), 476–564.

11. Charles Williamson served as an officer of the British Army 25th Regiment of Foot between 1775 and 1781 when he resigned his Captaincy. While crossing the Atlantic on his way to see Lord Charles Cornwallis with letters of introduction, a French privateer captured Williamson. Detained as a private citizen who might assist the enemy (not a combatant), Rebel commanders quartered Williamson with a private family in Boston. Falling in love, Williamson married the daughter of the family who lodged him. After a few months Williamson and his new bride sailed for Britain. Ten years later, Williamson would return to the United States and become a citizen.

12. For more information on the life of Charles Williamson see, Rev. William Main, ed., *Charles Williamson—A Review of His Life* (Perth: Cowan & Co. Limited, 1899), https://archive.org/stream/charleswilliamso00main/charleswilliamso00main_djvu.txt.

13. *Western Telegraphe*, Tuesday, December 6, 1796, 3.

14. *Western Telegraphe*, Tuesday, April 4, 1797, 4.

15. "Walsall: Social Life," *British History On-Line* (blog), n.d., https://www.british-history.ac.uk/vch/staffs/vol17/pp249-254.

16. *Western Telegraphe*, Tuesday, November 8, 1796, 3.

17. *Western Telegraphe*, Tuesday, October 20, 1796, 4.

18. *Western Telegraphe*, Tuesday, February 16, 1796, 1.

19. "The African Complain" was originally published in the April 30, 1796 edition of the *Western Telegraphe*. It was republished in the Bennington, *Vermont Tablet of the Times* on April 4, 1797, the Philadelphia *Minerva* on April 29, 1797 and the *Philadelphia Independent Gazetteer* on April 30, 1797.

20. *Western Telegraphe*, Tuesday, October 25, 1796, 4.

21. Brackenridge, Hugh Henry, *Incidents of the Insurrection in the Western Parts of Pennsylvania, in the year 1794* (Philadelphia: John McCullough, 1795).

22. *Western Telegraphe*, Monday, August 25, 1795, 4.

23. *Western Telegraphe*, Tuesday, November 24, 1795, 4.

24. Although attributed to Matthew Clarkson, Rev. Ashbel Green, a Presbyterian minister and later President of Princeton College was likely the author, John Hall, Geradus Clarkson, and Samuel Clarkson, *Memoirs of Matthew Clarkson of Philadelphia 1735–1800* (Philadelphia: Thompson Printing Company, 1890), 78.

25. *Western Telegraphe*, Monday, September 17, 1795, 2.

26. *Western Telegraphe*, Tuesday, Sept. 1, 1795, p. 8. Readex: America's Historical Newspapers, infoweb. newsbank.com/apps/readex/doc?p=EANX&docref=image/v2:14B7BC0F6518D6D3@EANX-14FD75B-F50E3E210@2376914-14FD2B7F018826A0@7. Accessed 20 Sept. 2019.

27. *Western Telegraphe*, Tuesday, February 16, 1796, 4.

28. Previously published almanacs west of the Appalachian Mountains include a John Bradford 1788 edition in Lexington, Kentucky.

29. Copied from an original publication by William Burdon, *The gentleman's pocket-farrier; shewing how to use your horse on a journey; and what remedies are proper for common accidents, that may befall him on the road. : The remedies this little tract prescribes, are simple, and easily obtained; and never fail of a cure, where the disorder is curable; therefore no man who values his horse should presume to travel without it.*

30. Crumrine, Ellis, and Hungerford, *History of Washington County, Pennsylvania with Biographical Sketches of Many of Its Prominent Pioneers and Men*, 490.

31. 1800 United States Federal Census, Washington Township included the Town of Washington, Pennsylvania, 115.

32. *Western Telegraphe*, Tuesday, August 16, 1797, 3.

33. *Western Telegraphe*, Tuesday, April 11, 1797, 3.

34. *Herald of Liberty*, Monday, September 30, 1799.

35. *Western Telegraphe*, Tuesday, May 16, 1797, 3.

36. *The Pittsburgh Gazette*, Saturday, July 8, 1797, 4.

37. "To Thomas Jefferson from William H. Beaumont, 25 January 1803," *Founders Online*, National Archives, accessed April 11, 2019, https://founders.archives.gov/documents/Jefferson/01-39-02-0338. [Original source: *The Papers of Thomas Jefferson*, vol. 39, *13 November 1802–3 March 1803*, ed. Barbara B. Oberg. Princeton: Princeton University Press, 2012, pp. 389–390.]

38. Over this life, William Beaumont's actions continually invited litigation. Another example is a lawsuit between Beaumont and Isaac Leet, Jr., during October 1796 court term.

39. William Beaumont, "Letter Form William Beaumont to Thomas Jefferson," January 25, 1803, On-line, United States Archives, https://founders.archives.gov/documnts/Jerfferson/01-39-02-0338.

40. *The Herald of Liberty*, Monday, December 22, 1800, 3.

41. *The Pittsburgh Gazette*, Saturday, June 11, 1796, 1. *Aurora General Advertiser* (Philadelphia, PA), Friday, June 24, 1796, 3. *Kline's Carlisle Weekly Gazette*, Wednesday, October 5, 1796, Vol. XII, No. 581, 1.

42. "A list of the causes for Trial at the August Term, 1798" *The Herald of Liberty* (Washington, PA), Monday, August 20, 1798, Page 4.

43. *Philadelphia Evening Post*, Saturday, March 10, 1804, 3.

Chapter 9: Republican Printers

1. The use of a Royal page size does not comport to common 18th century usage. The actual size of *The Mirror* is 22.625 by 36.875 inches. Royal is 20 by 25 inches and Super Royal is 19 by 27 inches. The closest approximation is a Double Demy which is 22.5 by 35.5 inches.

2. *Western Telegraphe*, Tuesday, July 4, 1797, 4.

3. Dr. Joseph Priestley and Harry Toulmin are two examples of British Enlightenment thinkers who favored Kentucky immigration. Toulmin went so far as to draft and publish a book describing Kentucky's agricultural, economic, and religious strengths aimed to attract British immigrants. Toulmin, Harry. *Thoughts on Emigration*, 1792. https://books.google.com/books?id=nILDzQEACAAJ.

4. Eighteenth-century travelers arriving in Washington left the river at a small hamlet called Limestone, climbed a steep hill and journeyed four miles south of the river to Washington. Early European settlers

located Washington atop these bluffs to help protect against river-borne Native American attacks. Today Limestone and Washington are part of a town called Maysville, named by the Virginia legislature after an early land speculator John May. Washington's original town center has been preserved as a living and working historic village. A private residence today, Hunter's and Beaumont's print shop is located at 2014 Main Street. For information on Historic Washington, KY http://www.cityofmaysville.com/old-washington-historic-district/.

5. Harry Toulmin, *A Description of Kentucky*, ed. Thomas D. Clark, Reprint of 1792 Edition with editorial notes (Lexington, KY: University of Kentucky, 1945), 76.

6. John Filson, *The Discovery, Settlement and Present State of Kentucke (1784): An Online Electronic Text Edition*, ed. Paul Royster, Digital Commons@University of Nebraska - Lincoln (Wilmington: John Adams, 1784), 19, https://digitalcommons.unl.edu/cgi/viewcontent.cgi?article=1002&context=etas.

7. Georges Henri Victor Cullot, *A Journey in North America, Containing a Survey of the Countries Watered by the Mississippi, Ohio, Missouri, and Other Affluing Rivers, With Exact Observations on the Course and Soundings of These Rivers; and on the Towns, Villages, Hamlets and Farms of That Part of the New-World; Followed by Philosophical, Political, Military and Commercial Remarks and by a Projected Line of Frontiers and General Limits* (Paris: Arthur Bertrand, 1826), 98.

8. Paul C. Pappas, "Stewart's Kentucky Herald, 1795-1803: A Portrait of Early American Journalism West of the Alleghenies," *The Register of the Kentucky Historical Society* 67, no. 4 (1969): 337.

9. *Kentucky Gazette*, Wednesday, January 4, 1797, 1.

10. Samuel M. Wilson, "The 'Kentucky Gazette' and John Bradford its Founder," *The Papers of the Bibliographical Society of America* 31, no. 2 (1937): 132.

11. Samuel Vail started The Farmers' Library and Ohio Intelligencer in Louisville, KY on January 7, 1801. As the population moved south and west of the Ohio Rivers, three additional newspapers started in 1803 and two in 1804.

12. "Old Washington Historic District," *City of Maysville Kentucky* (blog), n.d., http://www.cityofmaysville.com/old-washington-historic-district/.

13. *The Palladium*, Tuesday, February 17, 1801, 4.

14. In addition to American dollars and British shillings, the partners received a myriad of coins from other countries. "There was scarcely a civilized country on the globe with a mint whose coins did not circulate in Kentucky. R. T. Durrett Early Banking in Kentucky quoted in General Bash W. Duke, *History of the Bank of Kentucky 1792-1895 Including an Interesting Account of Early Banking from Official Records and Other Sources at the Request of the Directors* (Louisville, KY: John P. Morton & Company, 1895), 6.

15. While "Fryday" appears in articles and as a person's name, competitor newspapers did not use the less frequent spelling to denote the publication date.

16. Leland D. Baldwin, *The Keelboat Age on Western Waters* (Pittsburgh, PA: University of Pittsburgh Press, 1980), 61.

17. *The Palladium*, Tuesday, January 6, 1801, 3.

18. Donald E. Roy, *Selected Pittsburgh Imprints, 1807–1860, In the Library of the Historical Society of Western Pennsylvania*, 179. In addition, rare book seller purveying copies of the Cramer's *Ohio Navigator* cite it as the first Ohio River guide to be published.

19. In addition to the Sedition Act, the Federalist enacted three other laws to inhibit dissent and reduce the influence of French sympathizers in the United States. The first of these acts raised the residency requirement for naturalization from five to fourteen years. The Alien Enemies Act allowed for the arrest and deportation of male enemy foreign nationals in time of war. Both of these acts were not the main source of controversy. The fourth act, The Alien and Friends Act delegated authority to the president to deport non-citizens plotting against the government. Representing a threat to the party, this act permitted the President to deport many recent immigrants who sided with the Democratic-Republicans. Collectively, historians generally refer to these four acts collectively as the Alien and Sedition Acts.

20. *The Mirror*, Saturday, Saturday, July 21, 1798, 1.

21. "Abigail Adams to William Cranch, 15 November 1797," *Founders Online*, National Archives, https://founders.archives.gov/documents/Adams/04-12-02-0167. [Original source: *The Adams Papers*, Adams Family Correspondence, vol. 12, *March 1797–April 1798*, ed. Sara Martin, C. James Taylor, Neal E. Millikan, Amanda A. Mathews, Hobson Woodward, Sara B. Sikes, Gregg L. Lint, and Sara Georgini. Cambridge, MA: Harvard University Press, 2015, pp. 290–293.] "A series of five articles signed Aristides was printed in the Lexington *Kentucky Gazette*, 6, 9, 13, 16, 20 Sept., and republished in the *Washington Gazette*, 14–21 Oct., 21–28 Oct., 28 Oct.–4 November. Addressed "to the Citizens of Western America,"

the articles commented on the differences between the eastern seaboard and the western states, arguing that the East was too closely aligned with British-inspired ideas about debt and taxation."

22. Subsequent to the debates over the Alien and Sedition Acts, the use of the pseudonym expanded to both factions. Federalist John Marshall published articles under the pseudonym Aristides and Democratic-Republican William P. Van Ness defended Aaron Burr under the same byline. Most famously, William Lloyd Garrison used the pseudonym in his abolitionist writings.

23. W. Bird and W.R. Bird, *Press and Speech Under Assault: The Early Supreme Court Justices, the Sedition Act of 1798, and the Campaign Against Dissent* (Oxford University Press, 2016), 375, https://books.google.com/books?id=hKnnCwAAQBAJ.

24. Bruce A. Ragsdale, "The Sedition Act Trials," *Federal Trials and Great Debates in the United States History*, Federal Judicial History Office, 2005, 1.

25. Wendell Bird, "New Light on the Sedition Act of 1798: The Missing Half of the Prosecutions," *Law and History Review* 34, no. 3 (2016): 584.

26. "I do not think it wise to execute the Alien Law against poor Priestley, at present. He is as weak as water as unstable as Reuben or the Wind. His Influence is not an Atom in the World." "From John Adams to Timothy Pickering, 13 August 1799," *Founders Online*, National Archives, https://founders.archives.gov/documents/Adams/99-02-02-3877.

27. *Louisville Public Advertiser*, Saturday, August 2, 1828.

28. Lewis Collins and R.H. Collins, *Collins' Historical Sketches of Kentucky: History of Kentucky*, Collins' Historical Sketches of Kentucky, v. 2 (Covington, KY: Collins & Company, 1882), 407, https://books.google.com/books?id=gZFQAQAAIAAJ.

29. Douglas C. McMurtrie, "Notes on Printing in Kentucky in the Eighteenth Eentury," *Filson Historical Quarterly* 10, no. 4 (October 1936): 270–71.

30. *The Palladium*, Tuesday, August 14, 1798, 1. The Palladium measured eleven by eighteen inches in size consisting of four pages each with four columns.

31. *Kentucky Gazette*, Wednesday, May 2, 1798, 1.

32. G. S. Rowe, "The Disillusionment of a 'Republican Schoolmaster,'" *Western Pennsylvania History*, n.d., 247, hppts://journals.psu.wph/article/download/3597/3428/.

33. Alexander Addison, "Liberty of Speech, and of the Press. A Charge to the Grand Juries of the County Courts of the Fifth Circuit of the State of Pennsylvania. / By Alexander Addison, President of Those Courts." (Washington [Pa.]: :: Printed by John Colerick, for the author. Ann Arbor, MI :: Text Creation Partnership, 1798), /z-wcorg/, http://name.umdl.umich.edu/N25101.0001.001.

34. *The Mirror* Friday, December 7, 1798, Vol. II, No 65.

35. Carl Wilhelm Scheele and Antoine Lavoisier also have claims to the identification of oxygen. More clearly, Priestley is credited with the invention of carbonated water and the rubber eraser.

36. *The Mirror* Friday, January 11, 1799, Vol. II, No. 70, Friday, January 25, 1799, Vol. II, No. 72, and Friday, February 15, 1799, Vol II, No. 75.

37. *The Mirror* Saturday, December 9, 1797, 4.

38. Lowell H. Harrison, "John Breckenridge and the Kentucky Constitution of 1799," *The Register of the Kentucky Historical Society* 57, no. 3 (1959): 228–29.

39. *The Palladium*, Thursday, March 6, 1800, 2.

40. *The Mirror*, June 21, 1799, 3.

41. http://www.cityofmaysville.com/old-washington-historic-district/

Chapter 10: Government Printers

1. Anderson Chenault Quisenberry compiled an analysis of Revolutionary soldiers who lived in Kentucky during the war or moved to the state after the war. He reports that 72 of 89 Kentucky Counties are named after prominent Revolutionary War officers, soldiers, and politicians. He believes that almost all of the early European settlers in Kentucky served in the Revolution. He compiled a list of over three thousand veterans living in the state which received Federal and State pensions for their war service. Hunter's new home county of Washington County, contained 49 of these pensioners. Quisenberry, Anderson Chenault. *Revolutionary Soldiers in Kentucky: Containing a Roll of the Officers of Virginia Line Who Received Land Bounties, A Roll of the Revolutionary Pensioners in Kentucky, a List of the Illinois Regiment Who Served under George Rogers Clark in the Northwest Campaign, Also a Roster of the Virginia Navy*. Baltimore, Maryland: Clearfield Company/Genealogical Pub. Co., 2003.

2. Perrin William Henry, *The Pioneer Press of Kentucky: From the Printing of the First Paper West of the Alleghanies, August 11, 1787, to the Establishment of the Daily Press in 1830.* (The Filson Club: John V. Morten and Company, 1888), 24.

3. W. Draper, *Junius: Stat Nominis Umbra*, Junius: Stat Nominis Umbra (Printed for Henry Sampson Woodfall, 1772), vii and x, https://books.google.com/books?id=D70uAAAAMAAJ.

4. A. Ellegård, *Who Was Junius?* (Almquist & Wiksell, 1962), 118–19, https://books.google.com/books?id=bFwzAAAAIAAJ.

5. *The Palladium*, Tuesday, December 25, 1798, 2.

6. There were 19 ads in The Mirror's November 10, 1798 edition to only 7 ads in the Palladium's November 13, 1798 edition.

7. *The Palladium*, Tuesday, August 14, 1798, 3.

8. *The Palladium*, Tuesday, August 28, 1798, 2.

9. "III. Resolutions Adopted by the Kentucky General Assembly, 10 November 1798," *Founders Online*, National Archives, accessed September 29, 2019, https://founders.archives.gov/documents/Jefferson/01-30-02-0370-0004. [Original source: *The Papers of Thomas Jefferson*, vol. 30, *1 January 1798–31 January 1799*, ed. Barbara B. Oberg. Princeton: Princeton University Press, 2003, pp. 550–556.]

10. Humphrey Marshall, *The History of Kentucky: Exhibiting an Account of the Modern Discovery; Settlement; Progressive Improvement; Civil and Military Transactions; and the Present State of the Country,* Volume 2, (Frankfort, KY: Geo. S. Robinson, Printer, 1824), 277.

11. A Lexington based printer and newspaper publisher James H. Stewart held the state printing contract in 1796.

12. "To Thomas Jefferson from Henry R. Graham, 10 July 1802," Founders Online, National Archives, accessed April 11, 2019, https://founder.archives.gov/documents/jefferson/01-38-02-0042. [Original source: *The Papers of Thomas Jefferson*, vol. 38, 1 July-12 November 1802, ed. Barbara B. Oberg, Princeton: Princeton University Press, 2011, pp44-45.]

13. J.A. Bear and L.C. Stanton, *Jefferson's Memorandum Books, Volume 2: Accounts, with Legal Records and Miscellany, 1767–1826*, Princeton Legacy Library (Princeton, N.J: Princeton University Press, 2017), 1018, https://books.google.com/books?id=5Ao1DgAAQBAJ.

14. "To James Madison from Zachariah Lewis, 7 January 1804 (Abstract)," Founders Online, National Archives, last modified June 13, 2018, http://founders.archives.gov/documents/Madison/02-06-02-0275. [Original source: The Papers of James Madison, Secretary of State Series, vol. 6, 1 November 1803–31 March 1804, ed. Mary A. Hackett, J. C. A. Stagg, Ellen J. Barber, Anne Mandeville Colony, and Angela Kreider. Charlottesville: University of Virginia Press, 2002, p. 315.]

15. *The Palladium*, Thursday, June 19, 1800, 3.

16. *The Palladium*, Saturday, October 29, 1803, 1.

17. *The Palladium*, Saturday, October 8, 1803, 3.

18. In addition to his physician practice, Dr. Isaac Gano (1766 or 1770–1811) served as a Franklin County tax collector and Quarter Session Judge. When Thomas Jefferson sought a tax collector for the Indiana Territory, Christopher Greenup provided a strong recommendation while Albert Gallatin described Gano as "liable to intoxication." In the end, Gano remained in Frankfort. "To Thomas Jefferson from Albert Gallatin, 28 March 1804," *Founders Online*, National Archives, https://founders.archives.gov/documents/Jefferson/01-43-02-0116. [Original source: *The Papers of Thomas Jefferson, vol. 43, 11 March–30 June 1804*, ed. James P. McClure. Princeton: Princeton University Press, 2017, pp. 120–123.]. There is no other evidence that Gano was a drunkard. He ably served as a surgeon in St. Clair and Anthony Wayne's campaigns against the northwest Indians in the 1790s. His obituary indicates he acted as a "Good Samaritan" and "relied on the atoning merits of Jesus Christ, *Essex Register*, Salem, MA, November 23, 1811.

19. *The Palladium*, Thursday, March 27, 1806, 1, including the reprint of slave sale ads from the *Charlestown Courier*, March 4, 1806.

20. "To Thomas Jefferson from John Bradford, 29 November 1803," *Founders Online*, National Archives, accessed April 11, 2019, https://founders.archives.gov/documents/Jefferson/01-42-02-0050. [Original source: The Papers of Thomas Jefferson, vol. 42, 16 November 1803–10 March 1804, ed. James P. McClure. Princeton: Princeton University Press, 2016, pp. 54-55.]

21. *The Palladium*, Saturday, May 26, 1804, 4.

22. *The Palladium*, Saturday, February 9, 1805, 1.

23. "To Thomas Jefferson from James Garrard, 4 November 1803," *Founders Online*, National Archives, https://founders.archives.gov/documents/Jefferson/01-41-02-0493. [Original source: *The Papers of Thomas*

Jefferson, vol. 41, 11 July–15 November 1803, ed. Barbara B. Oberg. Princeton: Princeton University Press, 2014, pp. 664-665.]

24. B.B. Williams, *A Literary History of Alabama: The Nineteenth Century* (Fairleigh Dickinson University Press, 1979), 24, https://books.google.com/books?id=OKvwAtysmYcC.

25. *The Palladium*, Saturday, January 25, 1806, Vol. VIII, No. 24.

26. *The Palladium*, Monday, September 16, 1805, 2.

27. *The Palladium*, Friday, December 4, 1801, 4. *The Palladium* Thursday, September 29, 1803, 4.

28. *The Palladium*, Thursday, March 10, 1803, 3.

29. E. C. Berry published the *Guardian of Freedom* starting from February 8, 1804 until at least March 25, 1805 which is the last issue located. Copies of the *Guardian of Freedom* are incomplete and scattered among several archives, see "Proceedings of the American Antiquarian Society - American Antiquarian Society - Google Books," accessed July 22, 2018, https://books.google.com/books?id=RXUrAQAAIAA-J&printsec=frontcover&source=gbs_ge_summary_r&cad=0#v=onepage&q=hunter&f=false., 371-2.

30. *The Palladium*, Saturday, October 29, 1803, 1.

31. *The Palladium*, Saturday, October 29, 1803, 1.

32. *Western World*, Monday, July 7, 1806, 4.

33. Ronald Rayman, "Frontier Journalism in Kentucky: Joseph Montfort Street and the Western World, 1806-1809," *The Register of the Kentucky Historical Society* 76, no. 2 (1978): 101.

34. John Wood to William S. Hunter, June 22, 1807, folder 1807, box 2, Harry Innes Papers 1754-1900, Manuscript Division, Library of Congress, Washington, D.C. Note William S. Hunter lived in Versailles, Kentucky and is not related to William Hunter of Frankfort.

35. *Western World*, Saturday, July 19, 1806, 4.

36. *Western World*, Monday, July 7, 1806, 2-3.

37. *Western World*, Saturday, August 23, 1806, 2.

38. Hunter published *The Palladium* on Thursdays and printed the *Western World* on Saturdays to even the work load in his print shop. The off-set printing schedule gave each paper several days to generate interest in their news and permitted the editors to criticize and attack each other. *Western World*, Saturday, August 23, 1806, 2.

39. *Western World*, Saturday, August 16, 1806, 4.

40. *The Palladium*, September 11, 1806.

41. Joseph M. Street to the People, *Western World*, August 16, 1806, 4.

42. *The Palladium*, Thursday, December 11, 1806, Vol IX, No. 17.

43. Willard Rouse Jillson, "Aaron Burr's 'Trial' for Treason, at Frankfort, Kentucky, 1806," *The Filson Club Historical Quarterly* 17 (1943): 224.

44. *The Palladium*, December 5, 1806, quoted in the *Wilmington Gazette* (Wilmington, NC), Tuesday, February 3, 1807, 4.

45. For additional information the Burr's Frankfort trials see, Willard Rouse Jillson, "Aaron Burr's 'Trial' for Treason, at Frankfort, Kentucky, 1806," *The Filson Club Historical Quarterly* 17 (1943): 202–29.

46. "To Thomas Jefferson from Christopher Greenup, 22 December 1806," *Founders Online*, National Archives, https://founders.archives.gov/documents/Jefferson/99-01-02-4732.[This is an Early Access document from the Papers of Thomas Jefferson. It is not an authoritative final version.]

47. The Report of the Select Committee to whom was Referred the Information Communicated to the House of Representatives, charging Benjamin Sebastian, 1806, folder Law Practice – Burr, Aaron Conspiracy, box 6, Harry Innes Papers 1754-1900, Manuscript Division, Library of Congress, Washington, D.C.

48. Two other Kentucky Court of Appeals judges, George Muter and Caleb Wallace resigned under pressure for being associated with negotiations with the Spanish government in the 1790s.

49. *The Palladium*, Thursday, February 5, 1807, 1.

50. Extract of a letter from a Gentleman in Lexington to the Editor of the Enquirer, dated February 15, 1807, *Enquirer* (Richmond, VA), Tuesday, March 17, 1807, 3.

51. *The Palladium*, Thursday, November 13, 1806, 2.

52. *Western World*, Thursday, December 18, 1806, 3.

53. *The Palladium*, Thursday, December 25, 1806 Vol. IX, No. 19.

54. For a full account of President Thomas Jefferson's message to Congress, Thomas Jefferson to Congress, January 22, 1807, Message on Aaron Burr, from The Works of Thomas Jefferson in Twelve

Volumes. Federal Edition. Collected and Edited by Paul. Leicester Ford. http://www.loc.gov/resource/mtj1.037_0538_0546.

55. *Western World*, Thursday, July 8, 1807, Vol. II, No. 54, 2, *Western World*, Thursday, July 23, 1807, 2, *Western World*, Thursday, August 6, 1807, 3, *Western World*, Thursday, October 22, 1807, , 2-3.

56. *Western World*, Thursday, September 24, 1807, 2-3.

57. "To the people of Franklin," Joseph M. Street, Frankfort, August 4, 1807, folder Innes versus Street, box 8, Harry Innes Papers 1754-1900, Manuscript Division, Library of Congress, Washington, D.C.

58. As there were few assets, likely the sale to Henry Gore and Troilus Barnes yielded little for Street. Street moved to the Illinois Territory where he was appointed agent for the Winnebago Indians. When the tribe was forcibly relocated, Street followed the Native Americans to Iowa where Street died in 1840. For more information on Joseph Street see, Rayman, Ronald. "Frontier Journalism in Kentucky: Joseph Montfort Street and the Western World, 1806-1809." *The Register of the Kentucky Historical Society* 76, no. 2 (1978): 98–111.

59. For the most current assessment of Burr's intent and actions, James E. Lewis, *The Burr Conspiracy: Uncovering the Story of an Early American Crisis* (Princeton: Princeton University Press, 2017), 457.

60. Harry Toulmin, To the Editor of the *Kentucky Palladium, The Palladium*, Wednesday, December 12, 1804.

61. *The Palladium*, Thursday, October 9, 1806, Vol. IX, No. 8.

62. Despite the lack of evidence from the Lewis and Clark Expedition, several authors continued to promote the idea of White, Welsh speaking Indians living on the Upper Missouri River. For an overview of this historiography and a thorough debunking of the Welsh myth, see James D. McLaird, "Legend of the White Mandan," *South Dakota State Historical Society*, South Dakota History, n.d., 245–73.

63. *The Palladium*, Thursday, January 1, 1807, 2.

64. *The Argus of Western America*, Wednesday, November 16, 1808, 561.

65. Kentucky. General Assembly. House of Representatives, *Journal*, 1808, 173–74, https://books.google.com/books?id=8VdBAQAAMAAJ.

66. Kurt X. Metzmeier, *Writing the Legal Record: Law Reporters in Nineteenth-Century Kentucky* (Lexington, Kentucky: University Press of Kentucky, 2017), 108.

67. *The Reporter* (Lexington) published a letter from the seconds of Clay/Marshall which disclosed Clay's written challenge, Marshall's acceptance, presents the rules observed and describes in detail the duel's outcome. *Reporter* (Lexington), Thursday, January 26, 1809, 3.

68. Charles Tarrants, "Carter Tarrant (1765-1816): Baptist and Emancipationist," *The Register of the Kentucky Historical Society* 88, no. 2 (1990): 121–47, 145.

69. Kentucky. General Assembly. House of Representatives, 220.

70. Kentucky. General Assembly. House of Representative, Journal, 1816, 652.

71. *The Argus of Western America* (Frankfort), April 15, 1809, 2.

72. *The Argus of Western America* (Frankfort), April 22, 1809, 2-3.

73. *The Palladium*, Saturday, July 14, 1810, 4.

74. George Washington Pleasants' ownership ended within three years as he died April 15, 1812 young from consumption. His obituary states the he "was a worthy, promising young man—he was highly esteemed by his acquaintances." *American Statesman* (Lexington, KY), Saturday, April 1812, 3.

75. William Hunter, "To William Jarvis, Esq., American Consul, Lisbon, Portugal," September 27, 1809, Special Collections, Kentucky Historical Society.

Part III: Building Businesses and Contributing to the Community

1. Reprinted from the *Kentucky Gazette, Reporter* (Lexington, KY), Wednesday, July 1, 1812, Vol. 5, Issue 38.

2. For an account of Kentucky in the War of 1812, see David Kirkpatrick, *The War of 1812 in the West: From Fort Detroit to New Orleans* (Yardley, Pennsylvania: Westholme, 2019).

3. Kentucky. Adjutant General P. Butler. *State of Kentucky, Adjutant-general's office – Frankfort, May 5th, General Orders*, Frankfort, 1812. Pdf. https://www.loc.gov/item/rbpe02103600/.

4. The British captives would eventually be released in 1814 and no executions took place in Britain. Kirkpatrick, 146.

Chapter 11: Book Seller and Retailer

1. Henry Clay, *The Papers of Henry Clay - Supplement 1793–1852*, ed. Melba Porter (Lexington, KY: Kentucky Historical Society, 1992), 11–12.

2. Henry Clay, *The Papers of Henry Clay - The Rising Statesman 1797–1814*, ed. James F. Hopkins and Mary W. M. Hargreaves, vol. I (Lexington, KY: University Press of Kentucky, 1959), 330.

3. *The Palladium*, Saturday, July, 14, 1810, 4.

4. L.F. Johnson and F.K. Kavanaugh, *History of Franklin County Bar, 1786–1931* (F.K. Kavanaugh, 1932), 29, https://books.google.com/books?id=c_g-AAAAIAAJ.

5. Harry Toulmin, "Harry Toulmin Papers, 1809-1815.," *Social Networks and Archival Context* (blog), n.d., https://snaccooperative.org/vocab_administrator/resources/7492847.

6. Mary Willis Woodson, "My Recollections of Frankfort," *The Register of the Kentucky Historical Society* 61, no. 3 (July 1963): 205, https://www.jstor.org/stable/23375966.

7. Craig Friend, "Merchants and Markethouses: Reflections on Moral Economy in Early Kentucky," *Society for Historians of the Early American Republic* 17, no. 4 (Winter 1997): 564.

Chapter 12: Civic Prominence

1. *The Palladium*, Thursday, July 28, 1803, 4.

2. For a transcription of the trustee meeting minutes see, J. J. Crittenden and William S. Waller, "Minutes of the Board of Trustees of the Kentucky Seminary from January 1812 to January 1830 Frankfort Kentucky," *The Register of the Kentucky Historical Society* 48, no. 162 (January 1950): 3–24.

3. Kentucky. General Assembly. House, *Journal of the House of the General Assembly of the Commonwealth of Kentucky . . .*, 26th Assembly (Frankfort, KY: Gerard and Kendall, 1818), 333.

4. For a complete description of the construction of Kentucky's Capitol buildings see, Bayless E. Hardin, "The Capitols of Kentucky," *The Register of the Kentucky Historical Society*, 1945, 43, no. 144 (July): 173–200.

5. *Journal of the House of the General Assembly of the Commonwealth of Kentucky*, January 25, 1816, 193.

6. For an overview of the management issues see, Paul Knepper, "The Kentucky Pennitentiary at Frankfort and the Origins of America's Firt Convict Lease System 1798-1843," *The Filson Club Quarterly* 69, no. 1 (January 1995): 41–66.

Chapter 13: Manufacturer and Warehouse Owner

1. Z. Cramer, *The Navigator: Containing Directions for Navigating the Monongahela, Allegheny, Ohio and Mississippi Rivers; with an Ample Account of These Much Admired Waters, from the Head of the Former to the Mouth of the Latter ; and a Concise Description of Their Towns, Villages, Harbors, Settlements, &c. with Maps of the Ohio and Mississippi; to Which Is Added an Appendix, Containing an Account of Louisiana, and of the Missouri and Columbia Rivers, as Discovered by the Voyage Under Capts. Lewis and Clark* (Cramer & Spear, 1821), 215, https://books.google.com/books?id=DQkyAQAAMAAJ.

2. *Kentucky Gazette*, Tuesday, June 27, 1809, 3.

3. Kentucky total 1810 population is listed at 406, 511 which includes 80, 561 enslaved people and 1713 free persons of color. 1810 Census data as reported in the *Reporter* (Lexington), Saturday, February 16, 1811, 2.

4. Wapping Street in Frankfort was named by John Instone after his boyhood home on Wapping Street, London. Woodson, "My Recollections of Frankfort," 201.

5. *Kentucky Gazette*, Tuesday, January 16, 1810, 1.

6. *Reporter* (Lexington, KY), Saturday, June 27, 1812, 4.

7. The percentage of African Americans who were free in Kentucky at only two percent of the population was the lowest in the nation. In 1810, the free black percentage in the Upper South was 10% and in 74% in the North.

8. James A. Ramage and Andrea S. Watkins, *Kentucky Rising: Democracy, Slavery, and Culture from the Early Republic to the Civil War* (Lexington: University Press of Kentucky: Kentucky Historical Society, 2011), 241.

9. *Kentucky Gazette*, Monday, May 15, 1815, 3.

10. Filson Club and S.W. Price, Filson Club Publications, *Filson Club Publications*, No. 17 (Filson Club, 1902), 51, https://books.google.com/books?id=x1EMAQAAMAAJ.

11. Kurt X. Metzmeier, *Writing the Legal Record: Law Reporters in Nineteenth-Century Kentucky* (Lexington, Kentucky: University Press of Kentucky, 2017), 22.

12. "The Hanna House on Second Street: From History of Second Street, South Frankfort Published in the Register, Vol. II., September 1913," *Register of Kentucky State Historical Society* 15, no. 44 (May 1917): 47.

13. Kentucky. General Assembly. House of Representatives, *Journal*, 289.

14. Kentucky. General Assembly. House, *Journal of the House of the General Assembly of the Commonwealth of Kentucky . . .*, 289.

15. *Argus of Western America*, Friday, December 11, 1818, 3.

16. Kentucky. General Assembly. House, *Journal of the House of the General Assembly of the Commonwealth of Kentucky . . .*, 572–73.

17. *Argus of Western America*, Friday, April 20, 1820, 3.

Chapter 14: Community Banker

1. "The bank was made a political instead of a financial insitution." Duke, *History of the Bank of Kentucky 1792-1895 Including an Interesting Account of Early Banking from Official Records and Other Sources at the Request of the Directors*, 14.

2. *The Palladium*, Friday, April 29, 1808, 3.

3. Kentucky. Court of Appeals et al., *Reports of Civil and Criminal Cases Decided by the Court of Appeals of Kentucky, 1785–1951* (J. Bradford, 1832), 548, https://books.google.com/books?id=jTkEAAAAYAAJ.

Chapter 15: Panic and Economic Devastation

1. *Kentucky Gazette*, Friday, November 27, 1818, 3.

2. Language such as the inclusion of journeyman and apprentices in the list of disaffected citizens provide hints that William Hunter drafted or edited the *Frankfort Resolves* which were first published in *The Argus of Western America*, May 14, 1819, 3.

3. While Kentucky became the first state to end imprisonment for non-payment of debts, the law was poorly written leading to confusion and uncertainty. Not all provisions were favorable to debtors as the new law allowed some seizures of debtor properties without a final court order.

4. *The Commentator* (Frankfort), Saturday, December 6, 1823, 4.

5. Reprinted from the *Argus of Western America* in the *Louisville Public Advertiser*, Saturday, January 5, 1822, 2.

6. In 1821, Kentucky became the first state in the union to abolish imprisoning debtors.

7. *Frankfort Argus*, Wednesday, February 18, 1824, Volume XVI, No. 52.

Chapter 16: Ernest Legislator

1. Hunter finished second in a 5 candidate field to claim one of the two seats. The vote count for the Relief Party James MacBrayer (859), William Hunter (705), James Hunter (209), and Allen F. Macurdy (195) and for the Anti-Relief faction John H. Todd (487).

2. *Frankfort Argus*, Wednesday, August 25, 1824, 3.

3. *Frankfort Argus*, Wednesday, October 20, 1824, 3.

4. *Louisville Public Advertiser*, Saturday, August 2, 1828, 3.

5. Arndt Stickles M., *The Critical Court Struggle in Kentucky 1819–1829* (Graduate Council, Indiana University, n.d.), 22.

Chapter 17: Partisan Editor

1. William Tanner edited at least three other Kentucky newspapers including the *Harrodsburg Central Watchtower* (1829), *Maysville Monitor* (1833-7) and the *Frankfort Yeoman* (1843-52) before death in 1864.

2. H. Clay, *The Papers of Henry Clay. Volume 7: Secretary of State, January 1, 1828–March 4, 1829* (University Press of Kentucky, n.d.), 76, https://books.google.com/books?id=bPG15jXbWC4C.

3. *Frankfort Argus*, Wednesday, February 1, 1826, 4.
4. *The Spirit of '76*, Friday, March 24, 1826, 48.
5. Re-printed editorial policy dated February 20, 1826, *Louisville Gazette*, March 24, 1826, 4.
6. *Frankfort Argus*, Wednesday, April 12, 1826, 3.
7. *The Commentator* (Frankfort), Saturday, May 6, 1826, 2.
8. *The Spirit of '76* (Frankfort), Friday, June 24, 1826, 255-6.
9. *The Spirit of '76* (Frankfort), Friday, July 7, 1826, 285 and Friday July 14,1826, 304.
10. *The Spirit of '76* (Frankfort), Friday, July 21, 1826, 314-6.
11. *The Commentator* (Frankfort), Saturday, July 29, 1826, 3.
12. *The Spirit of '76* (Frankfort), Friday, August 4, 1826, 350-1.
13. Jacob H. Holeman (1793-1857) continued with an edition called *The Spirit of '76* extra which published lists of non-resident tax sales. He did so in an unsuccessful attempt to retain the state's public printing contract.
14. *The Commentator* (Frankfort), Saturday, August 26, 1826, 3.
15. *The Commentator* (Frankfort), Saturday, December 15, 1827, 3.
16. *Kentucky Gazette*, November 30, 1827, 2.

Chapter 18: Becoming a Jacksonian

1. *Frankfort Argus*, Wednesday, May 5, 1824, 3.
2. John J. Crittenden remained loyal to the Union during the Civil War. His oldest son George Bibb Crittenden served as a Brigadier General in the Confederate Army, and a younger son, Thomas Leonidas Crittenden, served as a Major General in the Union Army.
3. Thomas Sanders, "Thomas Sanders Letter to Mrs. Jane Sanders, Harrodsburgh" (Letter, Shelbyville, July 27, 1828), Sanders Family Papers, Filson Historical Society.
4. *Louisville Public Advertiser*, Saturday, August 2, 1828, 1.
5. Based upon 1810 census data prestned in A. C. QUISENBERRY, "'Heads of Families' in Franklin County: Census of 1810," *Register of Kentucky State Historical Society* 13, no. 39 (1915): 79–95.
6. Dr. John Mort Talbot served the Louisville community as a highly respected physician. He received an honorary degree from the University of Louisville before moving to Huntsville, Alabama where he died in 1867. Intriguing, he survived Mrs. Eliza Caroline, described as a consort of Talbots who died on September 28, 1818. Likely a consort is another name for an intimate relationship with an enslaved woman. While in Alabama a second woman, referred to as his wife, Sarah Payne passed away on November 16, 1863. Possibly Talbot entered into a romantic relationship with Lucy in between these two relationships. In any event, there are no records pertaining to Lucy after the reward advertisement for her son Lorenzo.
7. Quoting an undated editorial in the *Louisville Focus*, *Frankfort Commentator*, Saturday, September 1, 1827, 2.
8. Alexis de Tocqueville et al., *Democracy in America: And Two Essays on America*, Penguin Classics (London: Penguin, 2003), 405–6.
9. Tocqueville et al., 408.
10. Ramage and Watkins, *Kentucky Rising*.

Chapter 19: Treasury Auditor

1. *Frankfort Argus*, November 29, 1826, 2.
2. Amos Kendall, *Autobiography of Amos Kendall*, ed. W. Stickney (Boston: Lee and Shepard, 1872), 284, https://books.google.com/books?id=6KrSAjBaXKEC.
3. Kendall, 236.
4. Basil Hall, *Travels in North America in the Years 1827 and 1828*, 3 v. (Edinburgh, London: Cadell and Co.; Simpkin and Marshall, 1829), Volume III, 1, //catalog.hathitrust.org/Record/000292062.
5. For a unique statistical view of life in Washington during William Hunter's time see, J. Elliot, *Historical Sketches of the Ten Miles Square Forming the District of Columbia: With a Picture of Washington, Describing Objects of General Interest Or Curiosity at the Metropolis of the Union . . .* (J. Elliot, Jr., 1830), 294–354, https://books.google.com/books?id=cfsLHcNlHCMC.
6. Harriett Martineau, *Retrospect of Western Travel*, vol. I (New York: Harper & Brothers, 1838), 143–45.

7. *The Sunday Star* (Washington, DC), Sunday, March 17, 1918, Part 4, 3.

8. "Illustrated Letter, Amasa J. Parker to Harriet Parker Describing the Boardinghouse Where He and Two Future Presidents Resided, 31 December. 31 December, 1837," Manuscript/Mixed Material, *Library of Congress* (blog), n.d., https://www.loc.gov/item/mcc.084/.

9. *Frankfort Argus*, Wednesday, August 29, 1832, 4.

10. Bare bone annual expenses for a family of three with a nurse amounted to $839 per year W.B. Bryan, *A History of the National Capital from Its Foundation Through the Period of the Adoption of the Organic Act*, A History of the National Capital from Its Foundation Through the Period of the Adoption of the Organic Act (Macmillan, 1916), 75, https://books.google.com/books?id=CkgOAAAAIAAJ.

11. In addition to noting the omission of William Hunter and Robert Johnston from the *National Journal* article, *The Commentator* also identified Shadrack Penn, Hunter's fierce competitor in Louisville as receiving a valuable contract from the Jackson-led Post Office worth a profit of two thousand dollars per year. Given these known omissions, the editor believed that the list in the *National Journal* is far from complete. *The Commentator* (Kentucky), Tuesday, December 22, 1829, Vol. XIII, Issue 261, 3.

12. *Daily National Journal*, March 15, 1830, 3.

13. Jeffrey L. Paisley, "President Jackson's Editorial Appointees," *The Tyranny of Printers* (blog), accessed May 8, 2020, http://pasleybrothers.com/newspols/Jackson_appointees.htm.

14. *Extra Globe*, Thursday, May 10, 1832, 3.

15. Kendall, *Autobiography of Amos Kendall*, 311.

16. Kendall, 463.

17. *Frankfort Argus*, Wednesday, June 10, 1829, 3.

18. Bryan, *A History of the National Capital from Its Foundation Through the Period of the Adoption of the Organic Act*, 75.

19. Kendall, *Autobiography of Amos Kendall*, 310.

20. Kendall, 292.

21. *United States Telegraph*, Saturday, September 15, 1832.

22. *Columbian Centinel* [*sic*], Saturday, May 9, 1829, 2.

23. *Extra Globe*, Thursday, May 17, 1832, 3.

24. *United States Telegraph*, Volume IV, Issue 16, 3.

25. The four clerks supporting the Central Hickory Club are Richard Bennett, Hampton C. Williams, George M. Head and Joseph Perry. *United States Telegraph*, Saturday October, 27, 1832, 3.

26. *Daily Globe*, Thursday, December 13, 1832, 2

27. During his presidency, Jefferson, recruited the entertainment hall owner Gaetani Carusi along with several other Italian musicians to join the Marine Band.

28. *Daily Globe*, Thursday, December 13, 1832, 2.

29. *Daily National Intelligencer*, Volume XX, Issue 6190, 3.

30. *United States Telegraph*, Friday, December 14, 1832, 3.

31. Mr. Wise and Mr. Duncan, ed. H. S. Legaré, *The North American Review* 52, no. 110 (1841): 119–20.

32. *Daily National Intelligencer*, Volume XXII, Issue 6670, 3.

33. *Daily National Intelligencer*, Volume XXVII, Issue 8380, 3.

34. By law, 2% of prize money raised by the sale of captured ships and their cargos was placed in a fund to provide old age pensions to the participants. The Navy pension plan was funded by the government's share of captured ships and cargoes. The accounting for the two funds were segregated as they had separate funding streams.

35. Classification of Clerks in the Treasury Department, *Baltimore Sun*, Volume XXXIII, Issue 43, 1.

36. *The National Intelligencer*, October 24, 1854.

Chapter 20: Legacy

1. Letter from Abraham Lincoln to Edward Stanton, August 20, 1863, Abraham Lincoln, *Collected Works of Abraham Lincoln*, ed. Roy P. Basler, Marion Delores Pratt, and Lloyd A. Dunlap, vol. 8 (New Brunswick, N.J: Rutgers University Press, 1953), 521, http://name.umdl.umich.edu/lincoln8.

Part VI: Reflecting on a Remarkable Life

1. J.A. Bear and L.C. Stanton, *Jefferson's Memorandum Books, Volume 2: Accounts, with Legal Records and Miscellany, 1767–1826*, Princeton Legacy Library (Princeton, N.J: Princeton University Press, 2017), 1018, https://books.google.com/books?id=5Ao1DgAAQBAJ.

Chapter 21: Taking Stock

1. *Philadelphia Evening Post*, Saturday, March 10, 1804, 3, and reprinted in numerous newspapers including *The Maryland Herald* and *Hagerstown Weekly Advertiser*, March 14, 1804,3, *Colombian Centenal* and *Massachusetts Federalists*, March 21, 1804, *National Aegis*, March 21, 1804 and the *Columbian Minerva* March 27, 1804.

2. *Mississippi Herald* and *Natchez Gazette*, Friday, December 21, 1804, 4.

3. For "martyr to republicanism," see "To Thomas Jefferson from Henry R. Graham, 10 July 1802," Founders Online, National Archives, accessed April 11, 2019, https://founder.archives.gov/documents/jefferson/01-38-02-0042. [Original source: *The Papers of Thomas Jefferson*, vol. 38, 1 July-12 November 1802, ed. Barbara B. Oberg, Princeton: Princeton University Press, 2011, pp44-45.] For Albert Gallatin's letter supporting Beaumont's appointment see, "To Thomas Jefferson from Albert Gallatin, 25 February 1805," Founders Online, National Archives, accessed September 29, 2019, https://founders.archives.gov/documents/Jefferson/99-01-02-1233. [This is an Early Access document from the Papers of Thomas Jefferson. It is not an authoritative final version.]

4. Congressional Record, December 18, 1809 nominated by James Madison.

5. Likewise, William Beaumont's wife, Elizabeth's legacy can be seen today. She lived thirty-eight more years than William, passing in what is now New Orleans. Her portrait hangs in the Tyrell Historical Library in Beaumont, Texas.

Appendix I: Discovery of the Journal and Identifying the Author

1. Lewis Collins, *Collins' Historical Sketches of Kentucky: History of Kentucky*, Volume 2, n.d., 560.

2. Exiled, the French King Charles X (on the throne from 1824 to 1830) live in Holyrood Castle in Edinburgh, Scotland until 1834.

3. F. Cuming, *Sketcher of a Tour to the Western Country Through the States of Ohio and Kentucky: A Voyage down the Ohio and Mississippi Rivers, and a Trip Through the Mississippi Territory, and Park of West Florida. Commenced at Philadelphia in the Winter of 1807 and Concluded in 1809*. (Pittsburgh: Cramer, Spear and Eichbaum, 1810), 193.

Bibliography

Primary Sources

Manuscripts

American Archives, Northern Illinois University Digital Library
  Peter Force Collection
Frankfort, Kentucky, Kentucky Historical Society
  Special Collections
Lexington, Kentucky, University of Kentucky Archives
  Marquis de Lafayette, Records,1825
London, United Kingdom, the National Archives
  Army Records, Chelsea Pensioners Records, Muster Rolls
  Estate Records, George Gitton Last Will and Testament
Louisville, Kentucky, Filson Historical Society
  Sanders Family Papers.
Ottawa, Ontario, Canada Library and Archives,
  Charles Preston fonds 1775-1776.
Philadelphia, Library Company of Philadelphia
  Western Telegraphe
Privately Held Family Records
  William Hunter Journal
University of Chicago, Rare Manuscripts
  Reuben T. Durrett Collection
Washington, DC, District of Columbia Archives
  Estate Records, Last Will and Testaments
Washington, DC, Library of Congress
  Courrier Français, Philadelphia, PA,
  Peter Force Collection
  Words and Deeds in American History
Washington, DC, National Archives
  26th Regiment of Foot records

Newspapers

William Hunter Published Newspapers

The Western Telegraphe
The Mirror
The Palladium
Louisville Gazette

British Newspapers

Blackwood's Magazine
Caledonian Mercury
Hampshire Chronicle
Newcastle Courant
Northampton Mercury

American Newspapers

The American Constellation (Western New York State)
The Argus of Western America (Frankfort, Kentucky)
Aurora General Advertiser (Philadelphia, Pennsylvania)
Beaver Gazette (Beaver County, Pennsylvania)
The Commentator (Frankfort, Kentucky)
Colombian Centenal [*sic*] *and Massachusetts Federalists*
Columbian Minerva (Dedham, Massachusetts)
Connecticut Journal
Daily National Journal (Washington, DC)
Extra Globe (Washington, DC)
Federal Gazette (Philadelphia)
Freeman's Journal (Cincinnati)
Guardian of Freedom (Frankfort, Kentucky)
Kentucky Gazette (Lexington, Kentucky)
Kline's Carlisle Weekly Gazette
Herald of Liberty (Washington, Pennsylvania)
Louisville Public Advertiser
The Maryland Herald and Hagerstown Weekly Advertiser
Mississippi Herald and Natchez Gazette
National Aegis (Worcester, Massachusetts)
Newport Mercury
New-York Gazette or Weekly Post-Boy
New-York Gazette and Weekly Mercury
Pennsylvania Gazette
Pennsylvania Journal or Weekly Advertiser
Pennsylvania Ledger
Pennsylvania Packet
Philadelphia Evening Post
The Pittsburgh Gazette
Reporter (Lexington, Kentucky)
The Spirit of '76 (Frankfort, Kentucky)
The Sunday Star (Washington, DC),
Tablet of the Times (Bennington, Vermont)
United States Telegraph (Washington, DC)
Washington Gazette
The Western World (Frankfort, Kentucky)

Published Materials

Adams, S., and H.A. Cushing. *The Writings of Samuel Adams: 1778-1802*. Vol. IV. The Writings of Samuel Adams. New York: G.P. Putnam's Sons, 1908. https://books.google.com/books?id=6pILAAAAIAAJ.

Addison, Alexander. "Liberty of Speech, and of the Press. A Charge to the Grand Juries of the County Courts of the Fifth Circuit of the State of Pennsylvania. / By Alexander Addison, President of Those Courts." Washington [Pa.]: Printed by John Colerick, for the author. Ann Arbor, MI: Text Creation Partnership, 1798. /z-wcorg/. http://name.umdl.umich.edu/N25101.0001.001.

Allanson, C. *The Necessity of Social Love and Charity: A Sermon, Preached on Sunday, August 5, 1770, in the Cathedral at York, . . . By the Reverend Mr. Allanson. . . .* Eighteenth Century Collections Online. A. Ward, 1770. https://books.google.com/books?id=66UuihepL7YC.

Assembly, Kentucky. *Acts Passed at the First Session of the Twelfth General Assembly of the Commonwealth of Kentucky*. Session Laws of American States and Territories Prior to 1900. Frankfort, KY: William Hunter, 1804. https://books.google.com/books?id=f1FNAQAAMAAJ.

Beaumont, William. "Letter Form William Beaumont to Thomas Jefferson," January 25, 1803. On-line. United States Archives. https://founders.archives.gov/documnts/Jerfferson/01-39-02-0338.

Baurmeister, Carl, Bernhard A. Uhlendorf, and Edna Vosper. "Letters of Major Baurmeister during the Philadelphia Campaign, 1777-1778. II." *The Pennsylvania Magazine of History and Biography* 60, no. 1 (1936): 34–52.

Carroll, Charles, and Brantz Mayer. *Journal of Charles Carool of Carrollton During His Visit to Canada in 1776.* Baltimore, MD: Printed by John Murphy for the Maryland Historical Society, 1876. https://ia800303.us.archive.org/26/items/carrollofcarrollton00charrich/carrollofcarrollton00charrich.pdf.

Clay, H. *The Papers of Henry Clay. Volume 7: Secretary of State, January 1, 1828-March 4, 1829.* University Press of Kentucky, n.d. https://books.google.com/books?id=bPG15jXbWC4C.

Clay, Henry. *The Papers of Henry Clay - Supplement 1793-1852.* Edited by Melba Porter. Lexington, KY: Kentucky Historical Society, 1992.

Clay, Henry. *The Papers of Henry Clay - The Rising Statesman 1797-1814.* Edited by James F. Hopkins and Mary W. M. Hargreaves. Vol. I. Lexington, KY: University Press of Kentucky, 1959.

Cowper, W., and J.S. MEMES. *The Letters of William Cowper. Edited by Rev. J. S. Memes. [With a Portrait.].* W. R. M'Phun, 1861. https://books.google.com/books?id=p5pcAAAAcAAJ.

Cowper, W., R. Southey, and W. Harvey. *The Works of William Cowper: Translation of Homer's Iliad.* The Works of William Cowper: Comprising His Poems, Correspondence, and Translations. With a Life of the Author. Baldwin and Cradock, 1837. https://books.google.com/books?id=MnA4AAAAYAAJ.

Cullot, Georges Henri Victor. *A Journey in North America, Containing a Survey of the Countries Watered by the Mississippi, Ohio, Missouri, and Other Affluing Rivers, With Exact Observations on the Course and Soundings of These Rivers; and on the Towns, Villages, Hamlets and Farms of That Part of the New-World; Followed by Philosophical, Political, Military and Commercial Remarks and by a Projected Line of Frontiers and General Limits.* Paris: Arthur Bertrand, 1826.

Cuming, F. *Sketcher of a Tour to the Western Country Through the States of Ohio and Kentucky: A Voyage down the Ohio and Mississippi Rivers, and a Trip Through the Mississippi Territory, and Park of West Florida. Commenced at Philadelphia in the Winter of 1807 and Concluded in 1809.* Pittsburgh: Cramer, Spear and Eichbaum, 1810.

"Extract of a Letter from Swansea." *Hampshire Chronicle.* April 3, 1780, No. 398, sec. 3. The British Newspaper Archive. https://www.britishnewspaperarchive.co.uk/viewer/BL/0000230/17800403/009/0001?browse=true.

Hall, Basil. *Travels in North America in the Years 1827 and 1828.* 3 v. Edinburgh, London: Cadell and Co.; Simpkin and Marshall, 1829. //catalog.hathitrust.org/Record/000292062.

Hall, John, Geradus Clarkson, and Samuel Clarkson. *Memoirs of Matthew Clarkson of Philadelphia 1735-1800.* Philadelphia: Thompson Printing Company, 1890.

Hardie, James. *The Philadelphia Directory and Register.* Second. Philadelphia: Jacob Johnson & Co., 1974.

Journal of the House of Representatives of the Commonwealth of Kentucky Begun and Held in the Town of Frankfort on the First Day November 1824 and of the Commonwealth in the Thirty-Third Year. Frankfort, KY: J. H. Holman, 1824.

Kendall, Amos. *Autobiography of Amos Kendall.* Edited by W. Stickney. Boston: Lee and Shepard, 1872. https://books.google.com/books?id=6KtSAjBaXKEC.

Kentucky. Court of Appeals, J. Hughes, A. Sneed, M.D. Hardin, G.M. Bibb, A.K. Marshall, W. Littell, and Kentucky (District). Supreme Court. *Reports of Civil and Criminal Cases Decided by the Court of Appeals of Kentucky, 1785-1951.* J. Bradford, 1832. https://books.google.com/books?id=jTkEAAAAYAAJ.

Kentucky. General Assembly. House. *Journal of the House of the General Assembly of the Commonwealth of Kentucky* . . . State Journal Company, 1817. https://books.google.com/books?id=vKc1AQAAMAAJ.

———. *Journal of the House of the General Assembly of the Commonwealth of Kentucky* . . . 26th Assembly. Frankfort, KY: Gerard and Kendall, 1818.

Kentucky. General Assembly. House of Representatives. *Journal,* 1808. https://books.google.com/books?id=8VdBAQAAMAAJ.

Kentucky and Kentucky. General Assembly. *Acts of the General Assembly of the Commonwealth of Kentucky.* Session Laws of American States and Territories Prior to 1900, 1804. https://books.google.com/books?id=f1FNAQAAMAAJ.

———. *Acts of the General Assembly of the Commonwealth of Kentucky.* Session Laws of American States and Territories Prior to 1900, 1820.

Lincoln, Abraham. *Collected Works of Abraham Lincoln.* Edited by Roy P. Basler, Marion Delores Pratt, and Lloyd A. Dunlap. Vol. 8. New Brunswick, N.J: Rutgers University Press, 1953. http://name.umdl.umich.edu/lincoln8.

Mayo, Robert M.D. *The Affidavit of Andrew Jackson: Taken by the Defendants in the Suit of Robert Mayo Vs. Blair & Rives for a Libel, Analysed and Refuted.* American History Pamphlets, v. 525. Washington City, DC: Printed by the Plaintiff, 1840. https://books.google.com/books?id=dDBCAAAAIAAJ.

Nelson, W., and A. Van Doren Honeyman. *Extracts from American Newspapers: Relating to New Jersey. 1704-1775.* Documents Relating to the Colonial History of the State of New Jersey, 1905. https://books.google.com/books?id=geB4AAAAMAAJ.

New Jersey Historical Society. *Documents Relating to the Colonial, Revolutionary and Post-Revolutionary History of the State of New Jersey.* Documents Relating to the Colonial, Revolutionary and Post-Revolutionary History of the State of New Jersey, 1894. https://books.google.com/books?id=D31JAAAAYAAJ.

Pearce, Thomas. "Population of the Township of the Borough of Walsall, Taken May 1801 by One Thomas Pearce, on the Overseers of the Poor." Borogh of Walsall: Walsall Local History Centre. Accessed October 15, 2018. https://go.walsall.gov.uk/Portals/0/images/importeddocuments/walsall_census_1801_transcript.pdf.

Priestley, Joseph, and Joseph Priestley, Jr. *Memoirs of Dr. Joseph Priestley.* Mechanicsburg, PA: Sunbury Press, Inc., 2021.

Quisenberry, Anderson Chenault. *Revolutionary Soldiers in Kentucky: Containing a Roll of the Officers of Virginia Line Who Received Land Bounties, A Roll of the Revolutionary Pensioners in Kentucky, a List of the Illinois Regiment Who Served under George Rogers Clark in the Northwest Campaign, Also a Roster of the Virginia Navy.* Baltimore, Maryland: Clearfield Company/Genealogical Pub. Co., 2003.

Scull, G. D., James Gabriel Montrésor, and John Montrésor. *The Montresor Journals.* Collections of the New-York Historical Society . . . 1881. Publication Fund Series [v. 14] xiv, 578 p. [New York: Printed for the Society, 1882. //catalog.hathitrust.org/Record/000012843.

Smith, W. T. *A Complete Index to The Names of Persons, Places and Subjects Mentioned in Littell's Laws of Kentucky - A Genealogy and Historical Guide.* Lexington, KY: The Bradford Club Press, 1931.

Society, New Jersey Historical. *Documents Relating to the Revolutionary History of the State of New Jersey.* Documents Relating to the Revolutionary History of the State of New Jersey, v. 1. John L. Murphy Publishing Company, 1901. https://books.google.com/books?id=TFtKAQAAMAAJ.

The Universal British Directory of Trade, Commerce, and Manufacture. Vol. 4. 5 vols. London: British Directory Office, 1791.

Thwaites, Reuben Gold. *Early Western Travels, 1748-1846; a Series of Annotated Reprints of Some of the Best and Rarest Contemporary Volumes of Travel, Descriptive of the Aborigines and Social and Economic Conditions in the Middle and Far West, during the Period of Early American Settlement.* 32 v. Cleveland, O.: The A. H. Clark company, 1904. //catalog.hathitrust.org/Record/000277487.

———. *The Ohio Valley Press Before the War of 1812-15.* Reprinted from the Proceedings of the American Antiquarian Society for April 1909. Worcester, MA: The Davis Press, 1909. http://scans.library.utoronto.ca/pdf/2/41/pennsylvaniaser214harruoft/pennsylvaniaser214harruoft_bw.pdf.

United States. Congress. Senate. *Journal of the Executive Proceedings of the Senate of the United States of America.* S. Prt. order of the Senate of the United States, 1828. https://books.google.ca/books?id=amAUAAAAYAAJ.

United States. Department of the Treasury. *An Account of the Receipts and Expenditures of the U.S.,* 1837. https://books.google.com/books?id=rnNEAQAAMAAJ.

Secondary Sources

Arnel, Don. "List of Printers, American Print History." Georgia State University. *Digital Commons at Georgia Southern* (blog), Summer 2014. https://digitalcommons.georgiasouthern.edu/cgi/viewcontent.cgi?referer=https://www.google.com/&httpsredir=1&article=1001&context=amer_print_history_data.

Arthur, T.S., and W. H. Carpenter. *History of Kentucky from the Earliest Settlement to the Present Time.* Philadelphia: Claxton, Remsen & Haffelfinger, 1869.

Ayars III, Walter F, ed. *Lancaster Diary 1776.* Lancaster, PA: Printed by Lancaster Press, Inc. for the Greater Lancaster Chapter, Lancaster County Bicentennial Committee, 1975.

Baggs, A.P., G.C. Baugh, and D.A. Johnston. "History of the County of Stafford: Volume 17, (." *British History On-Line* (blog), 1976. https://www.british-history.ac.uk/vch/staffs/vol17/pp143-146.

Baker, Thomas N. "John Wood Weighs In: Making Sense of the Burr Conspiracy in the Western World." *Ohio Valley History,* Published by The Filson Historical Society and Cincinnati Museum Center, 14, no. 4 (Winter 2014): 3–22.

Baker, W.A. and Marine Research Society of Bath. *A Maritime History of Bath, Maine and the Kennebec River Region*. A Maritime History of Bath, Maine and the Kennebec River Region. Marine Research Society of Bath, 1973. https://books.google.com/books?id=P44TAAAAYAAJ.

Baldwin, Leland D. *The Keelboat Age on Western Waters*. Pittsburgh, PA: University of Pittsburgh Press, 1980.

Bastawy, Haythem. "Translations of A Thousand and One Nights." *Leeds Trinity University* (blog), April 22, 2015. http://www.leedstrinity.ac.uk/blogs/Translations-of-A-Thousand-and-One-Nights.

Baule, S.M. *Protecting the Empire's Frontier: Officers of the 18th (Royal Irish) Regiment of Foot during Its North American Service, 1767–1776*. War and Society in North America. Ohio University Press, 2014. https://books.google.com/books?id=KmmoAgAAQBAJ.

Baumgardt, Kenneth. "The Royal Army in America During the Revolutionary War: The American Prisoner Records." Christiana Delaware: Department of Defense, US Army Corps of Engineers, 2008. http://www.dtic.mil/dtic/tr/fulltext/u2/a491107.pdf.

Berry, Stephen Russell. *A Path in the Mighty Waters: Shipboard Life and Atlantic Crossings to the New World*. New Haven: Yale University Press, 2015.

Bird, Wendell. *Criminal Dissent: Prosecutions under the Alien and Sedition Acts of 1798*. Harvard University Press, 2020. https://books.google.com/books?id=gze6DwAAQBAJ.

———. "New Light on the Sedition Act of 1798: The Missing Half of the Prosecutions." *Law and History Review* 34, no. 3 (2016): 541–614.

Bird, Wendell, and W.R. Bird. *Press and Speech Under Assault: The Early Supreme Court Justices, the Sedition Act of 1798, and the Campaign Against Dissent*. Oxford University Press, 2016. https://books.google.com/books?id=hKnnCwAAQBAJ.

Blumenthal, Walter Hart. *Women Camp Followers of the American Revolution*. Women in America: From Colonial Times to the 20th Century. New York: Arno Press, 1974.

Brooke, Esq., F.S.A., Richard. *Liverpool as It Was during the Last Quarter of the 18th Century 1775-1800*. Liverpool, England: J. Maudsley & Son, 1853.

Bryan, W.B. *A History of the National Capital from Its Foundation Through the Period of the Adoption of the Organic Act*. A History of the National Capital from Its Foundation Through the Period of the Adoption of the Organic Act. Macmillan, 1916. https://books.google.com/books?id=CkgOAAAAIAAJ.

Carter, Thomas. "Historical Record of the Twenty-Sixth, or Cameronians Regiment [Microform]: Carter, Thomas, d. 1867: Internet Archive." Accessed April 15, 2018. https://archive.org/details/cihm_03214.

Chabot, C., and E.T.B. Twisleton. *The Handwriting of Junius Professionally Investigated*. J. Murray, 1871. https://books.google.com/books?id=FXogAQAAMAAJ.

Cole, Donald B. *A Jackson Man: Amos Kendall and the Rise of American Democracy*. Southern Biography Series. Baton Rouge: Louisiana State University Press, 2004.

Colley, Linda. *Britons: Forging the Nation, 1707-1837*. New Haven: Yale University Press, 1992.

"Collins' Historical Sketches of Kentucky: History of Kentucky - Lewis Collins - Google Books." Accessed June 3, 2018. https://books.google.com/books?id=gZFQAQAAIAAJ&printsec=frontcover&dq=collins+history&hl=en&sa=X&ved=0ahUKEwiD0pPzkLjbAhXtuFkKHZWgCGcQ6AEITzAG#v=onepage&q=hunter&f=false.

Collot, G.H.V., and J.C. Bay. *A Journey in North America, Containing a Survey of the Countries Watered by the Mississippi, Ohio, Missouri, and Other Affluing Rivers: With Exact Observations on the Course and Soundings of These Rivers; and on the Towns, Villages, Hamlets and Farms of That Part of the New-World; Followed by Philosophical, Political, Military and Commercial Remarks and by a Projected Line of Frontiers and General Limits*. A Journey in North America. O. Lange, 1826. https://books.google.com/books?id=ouVDAQAAMAAJ.

Columbia Historical Society (Washington, D.C.). *Records*, 1908. https://books.google.com/books?id=SgI8AAAAIAAJ.

Conway, Stephen. *The British Isles and the War of American Independence*. Oxford: Oxford Univ. Press, 2002.

Cramer, Z. *The Navigator: Containing Directions for Navigating the Monongahela, Allegheny, Ohio and Mississippi Rivers; with an Ample Account of These Much Admired Waters, from the Head of the Former to the Mouth of the Latter; and a Concise Description of Their Towns, Villages, Harbors, Settlements, &c. with Maps of the Ohio and Mississippi ; to Which Is Added an Appendix, Containing an Account of Louisiana, and of the Missouri and Columbia Rivers, as Discovered by the Voyage Under Capts. Lewis and Clark*. Cramer & Spear, 1821. https://books.google.com/books?id=DQkyAQAAMAAJ.

Crittenden, J. J., and William S. Waller. "Minutes of the Board of Trustees of the Kentucky Seminary from January 1812 to January 1830 Frankfort Kentucky." *The Register of the Kentucky Historical Society* 48, no. 162 (January 1950): 3–24.

Crumrine, Boyd, Franklin Ellis, and Austin N. Hungerford. *History of Washington County, Pennsylvania with Biographical Sketches of Many of Its Prominent Pioneers and Men.* Philadelphia: H.L. Everts & Co., 1882.

Curry, Leonard P. "Election Year — Kentucky, 1828." *The Register of the Kentucky Historical Society* 55, no. 3 (1957): 196–212.

Dagenais, Maxime, Julien Mauduit, and Amy S. Greenberg. *Revolutions across Borders: Jacksonian America and the Canadian Rebellion,* 2019.

Darwall, John. *Discourse on Spiritual Improvement from Affliction.* Fourth Ed. Walsall, England: Frederick Milward, 1790.

Darwall, Mary. *Poems on Several Occasions.* First. two vols. Walsall, England: Frederick Milward, 1794.

Draper, W. *Junius: Stat Nominis Umbra.* Printed for Henry Sampson Woodfall, 1772. https://books.google.com/books?id=D70uAAAAMAAJ.

Duke, General Bash W. *History of the Bank of Kentucky 1792-1895 Including an Interesting Account of Early Banking from Official Records and Other Sources at the Request of the Directors.* Louisville, KY: John P. Morton & Company, 1895.

Dupre, Huntley. "The Political Ideas of George Nicholas." *Register of Kentucky State Historical Society* 39, no. 128 (1941): 201–23.

Ellegård, A. *Who Was Junius?* Almquist & Wiksell, 1962. https://books.google.com/books?id=bFwzAAAAIAAJ.

Elliot, J. *Historical Sketches of the Ten Miles Square Forming the District of Columbia: With a Picture of Washington, Describing Objects of General Interest Or Curiosity at the Metropolis of the Union . . .* J. Elliot, Jr., 1830. https://books.google.com/books?id=cfsLHcNlHCMC.

"Exeter Working Papers in Book History: Staffordshire." Accessed April 13, 2018. http://bookhistory.blogspot.com/2013/01/staffordshire.html.

Field, Alston G. "The Press in Western Pennsylvania to 1812." *The Western Pennsylvania Historical Magazine* 20, no. 4 (December 1937): 231–64.

Filson Club, and S.W. Price. *Filson Club Publications.* Filson Club Publications, No. 17. Filson Club, 1902. https://books.google.com/books?id=x1EMAQAAMAAJ.

Filson, John. *The Discovery, Settlement and Present State of Kentucke (1784): An Online Electronic Text Edition.* Edited by Paul Royster. Digital Commons@University of Nebraska - Lincoln. Wilmington: John Adams, 1784. https://digitalcommons.unl.edu/cgi/viewcontent.cgi?article=1002&context=etas.

Fleming, C. *The Palladium of Great Britain and Ireland. Or Historical Strictures of Liberty, from Before the Reformation Down to the Present Times. Which Prove, to Whom and to What It Has Chiefly Owed Its Origin and Preservation, in These Islands.* Eighteenth Century. C. Henderson; and T. Becket and P. A. de Hondt, 1762. https://books.google.com/books?id=8uhbAAAAQAAJ.

Fleming, G.T. and American Historical Society. *History of Pittsburgh and Environs, from Prehistoric Days to the Beginning of the American Revolution . . .* History of Pittsburgh and Environs: From Prehistoric Days to the Beginning of the American Revolution. American Historical Society, Incorporated, 1922. https://books.google.com/books?id=TPUMAAAAYAAJ.

"Fourth Estate: A Weekly Newspaper for Publishers, Advertisers, Advertising . . . - Google Books," 1921. https://books.google.com/books?id=uTZJAQAAMAAJ&pg=RA12-PA16&lpg=RA12-PA16&dq=colonel+william+hunter+washington+ky&source=bl&ots=FOjwIGc4xC&sig=NahjW-B87U8bDnzjfl_xWMVjoSUA&hl=en&sa=X&ved=0ahUKEwjQyaDppZPcAhWRo1k-KHWYVBcYQ6AEIWDAL#v=onepage&q=colonel%20william%20hunter%20washington%20ky&f=false.

Frazier, Thomas R., and John Morton Blum. *The Underside of American History: Other Readings.* New York: Harcourt Brace Jovanovich, 1971.

Frey, Sylvia R. *The British Soldier in America: A Social History of Military Life in the Revolutionary Period.* Austin: University of Texas Press, 1981.

Friend, Craig. "Merchants and Market Houses: Reflections on Moral Economy in Early Kentucky." *Society for Historians of the Early American Republic* 17, no. 4 (Winter 1997): 553–74.

Genealogical Society of Pennsylvania. *The Pennsylvania Genealogical Magazine,* 1917. https://books.google.com/books?id=ScIxAQAAMAAJ.

"Gil Blas." Accessed April 14, 2018. http://www.exclassics.com/gilblas/gbintro.htm.

Gilmore, Peter. *Irish Presbyterians and the Shaping of Western Pennsylvania, 1770-1830.* Pittsburgh, PA: University of Pittsburgh Press, 2018.

Giral del Pino, Hipólito San Joseph. and Real Academia Española. "A New Spanish Grammar; or, The Elements of the Spanish Language: Containing an Easy and Compendious Method to Speak and Write It

Correctly: With Several Useful Remarks on the Most Particular Idioms & Fundamental Rules, Shewing How to Make Use of Them, as Well in Speaking as in Writing: The Whole Extracted from the Best Observations of Spanish Grammarians, and Particularly of the Royal Spanish Academy of Madrid," 1795. http://opac.newsbank.com/select/evans/47435.

Gleen, Netti Henry. *Early Frankfort Kentucky 1786-1861,* n.d.

God and a Soldier All Men Doth Adore, In Time of War and Not before: When the War Is over, and All Things Righted, God Is Forgotten, and the Soldier Slighted. : Whereas an Uncommon and Riottous [sic] Disturbance Prevails throughout This City, by Some of Its Inhabitants, Who Stile Themselves the S--s of L-----y, but Rather May More Properly Be Called Real Enemies to Society . . . New York, N.Y.: s.n., 1770.

Grabbe, Hans-Jürgen. "European Immigration to the United States in the Early National Period, 1783-1820." *Proceedings of the American Philosophical Society* 133, no. 2 (1989): 190–214.

Greenwood, Emma L. "Work, Identity and Letterpress Printers in Britain, 1750–1850." A thesis submitted to The University of Manchester for the degree of Doctor of Philosophy in the Faculty of Humanities, 2015. https://www.research.manchester.ac.uk/portal/files/54576325/FULL_TEXT.PDF.

Hadsell, Richard Miller. "John Bradford and His Contributions to the Culture and the Life of Early Lexington and Kentucky." *The Register of the Kentucky Historical Society* 62, no. 4 (1964): 265–77.

Hagist, Don N. *Noble Volunteers: The British Soldiers Who Fought the American Revolution.* Yardley, PA: Westholme Publishing, 2020.

———. "The Women of the British Army in America." *RevWar 75* (blog), 2002. http://revwar75.com/library/hagist/britwomen.htm.

Hardin, Bayless E. "The Capitols of Kentucky." *The Register of the Kentucky Historical Society,* 1945, 43, no. 144 (July): 173–200.

Harrison, Lowell H. "John Breckenridge and the Kentucky Constitution of 1799." *The Register of the Kentucky Historical Society* 57, no. 3 (1959): 209–33.

———. *John Breckinridge Jeffersonian Republican.* 1st ed. Louisville, KY: The Filson Club, 1969.

Hay, Thomas Robson. "Charles Williamson and the Burr Conspiracy." *The Journal of Southern History* 2, no. 2 (1936): 175–210. https://doi.org/10.2307/2191694.

Hazard, Samuel, John Blair Linn, William Henry Egle, George Edward Reed, Thomas Lynch Montgomery, Gertrude MacKinney, and Charles Francis Hoban. *Pennsylvania Archives.* J. Severns & Company, 1906.

Hebert, Catherine. "French Publications in Philadelphia in the Age of the French Revolution: A Bibliographic Essay." *Pennsylvania History: A Journal of Mid-Atlantic Studies* 58, no. 1 (January 1991): 37–61.

Hippeau, C. *Le Gouvernement de Normandie Au XVIIe et Au XVIIIe Siècle d'après La Correspondance Des Marquis de Beuvron et Des Ducs d'Harcourt, Lieutenants Généraux et Gouverneurs de La Province.* 9 volumes. Caen: G. de Laporte, 1863. //catalog.hathitrust.org/Record/000368654.

Hogan, Edmund. *The Prospect and Check on the Next Directory of Philadelphia.* Philadelphia: Francis and Robert Bailey, 1795.

Hopkins, J.F. *A History of the Hemp Industry in Kentucky.* University Press of Kentucky, 2015. https://books.google.com/books?id=eKggBgAAQBAJ.

Hough, Granville. "Granville Hough's Ship Listings H-I." Accessed September 19, 2018. http://www.awiatsea.com/Other/Hough%20List%20H-I.html.

Hughes, Thomas. *A Journal by Thos. Hughes: For His Amusement, & Designed Only for His Perusal by the Time He Attains the Age of 50 If He Lives so Long, (1778-1789).* Edited by E. A. Benians. Cambridge: The University Press, 1947.

Hussakof, L. "Benjamin Franklin and Erasmus Darwin: With Some Unpublished Correspondence." *Science* 43, no. 1118 (1916): 773–75.

"I. The Constituencies | History of Parliament Online." Accessed April 14, 2018. http://www.historyofparliamentonline.org/volume/1754-1790/survey/i-constituencies.

Iacone, Audrey Abbott. "Early Printing In Pittsburgh, 1786-1856." *Pittsburgh History,* no. Summer 1990 (n.d.): 66–69.

Isenberg, Nancy, and Andrew Burstein. *The Problem of Democracy: The Presidents Adams Confront the Cult of Personality.* New York, NY: Viking, 2019.

Jackson, John W. *With the British Army in Philadelphia 1777-1778.* San Rafael, CA and London, England: Presidio Press, 1979.

Jillson, Willard House. *Early Frankfort and Franklin County Kentucky—A Chronology of Historical Sketches Covering the Century 1750 to 1850.* Louisville, KY: The Standard Printing Company, 1936.

———. *The Newspapers and Periodicals of Frankfort, Kentucky 1795-1945*. Frankfort, KY: The Kentucky State Historical Society, 1945.

———. "Aaron Burr's 'Trial' for Treason, at Frankfort, Kentucky, 1806." *The Filson Club Historical Quarterly* 17 (1943): 202–29.

———. *Old Kentucky Entries and Deeds: A Complete Index to All of the Earliest Land Entries, Military Warrants, Deeds and Wills of the Commonwealth of Kentucky*. Filson Club Publications. Genealogical Publishing Company, 2012. https://books.google.com/books?id=3lSEj5FZ_MYC.

Johnson, Lewis Franklin. *The History of Franklin County, Kentucky*. Franklin, KY: Roberts Printing Company, 1912.

Johnson, L.F., and F.K. Kavanaugh. *History of Franklin County Bar, 1786-1931*. F.K. Kavanaugh, 1932. https://books.google.com/books?id=c_g-AAAAIAAJ.

Johnston, S.H.F. *The History of the Cameronians (Scottish Rifles) 26th and 90th*. Vol. 1, 1689–1910. 2 vols. Aldershot: Gale & Polden Limited, 1957.

Katz, W. A. "An Episode in Patronage: Federal Laws Published in Newspapers." *The American Journal of Legal History* 10, no. 3 (1966): 214–23. https://doi.org/10.2307/844293.

Kessler, Charles H. *Lancaster in the Revolution*. Lititz, PA: Sutter House, 1975.

King, John P. *Highland, New Jersey*. Charleston, S.C.: Arcadia Publishing Co., 2001.

Knepper, Paul. "The Kentucky Penitentiary at Frankfort and the Origins of America's First Convict Lease System 1798-1843." *The Filson Club Quarterly* 69, no. 1 (January 1995): 41–66.

Kramer, Carl E. *Capitol on the Kentucky - A Two Hundred Year History of Frankfort & Franklin County*. Frankfort, KY: Historic Frankfort, Inc., 1986.

Leavitt, Sturgis E. "The Teaching of Spanish in the United States." *Hispania*, Published by: American Association of Teachers of Spanish and Portuguese Stable, 44, no. 4 (December 1961): 591–625.

Lemoine, Henry. *Present State of Printing and Bookselling in America [1796]*. Chicago: Privately Printed, 1929.

Lewis, James E. *The Burr Conspiracy: Uncovering the Story of an Early American Crisis*. Princeton: Princeton University Press, 2017.

Main, Rev. William, ed. *Charles Williamson - A Review of His Life*. Perth: Cowan & Co. Limited, 1899. https://archive.org/stream/charleswilliamso00main/charleswilliamso00main_djvu.txt.

Mann, Frank Paul. "The British Occupation of Southern New York during the American Revolution and the Failure to Restore Civilian Government." Syracuse University, 2013. https://surface.syr.edu/cgi/viewcontent.cgi?article=1099&context=hst_etd.

Marshall, Humphrey. *The History of Kentucky: Exhibiting an Account of the Modern Discovery; Settlement; Progressive Improvement; Civil and Military Transactions; and the Present State of the Country*, First ed. 2 vols. Frankfort, KY: Geo. S. Robinson, Printer, 1824.

Martineau, Harriett. *Retrospect of Western Travel*. Vol. I. Two vols. New York: Harper & Brothers, 1838.

Mayo, R. *A Chapter of Sketches on Finance: With an Appendix, Showing the Train of Insidious Causes by Which the Removal of the Deposites Was Effected; Being Detached from a Book Now in Preparation for the Press, Entitled, Sketches of Eight Years in Washington, &c., &c*. Goldsmiths'-Kress Library of Economic Literature 1450-1850. F. Lucas, jr., 1837. https://books.google.com/books?id=mwxBAAAAYAAJ.

Mayo, Robert M.D. *The Treasury Department and Its Various Fiscal Bureaus, Their Origin, Organization, and Practical Operations, Illustrated: Being a Supplement to the Synopsis of Treasury Instructions for the Administration of the Revenue Laws Affecting the Commercial and Revenue System of the U.S.: In Fourteen Chapters . . . Extra Edition*, 1847. https://books.google.com/books?id=NUdVAAAAcAAJ.

McLaird, James D. "Legend of the White Mandan." *South Dakota State Historical Society*, South Dakota History, n.d., 245–73.

McMurtrie, Douglas C. "A Check-list of Kentucky Almanacs, 1789-1830." *Register of Kentucky State Historical Society* 30, no. 92 (1932): 237–59.

———. "Notes on Printing in Kentucky in the Eighteenth Century." *Filson Historical Quarterly* 10, no. 4 (October 1936): 261–80.

Metzmeier, Kurt X. *Writing the Legal Record: Law Reporters in Nineteenth-Century Kentucky*. Lexington, Kentucky: University Press of Kentucky, 2017.

Miller, James McDonald, and Harlowe Lindley. *The Genesis of Western Culture The Upper Ohio Valley, 1800-1825*. Columbus, OH: The Ohio State Archeological and Historical Society, 1938.

Miller, Ken. "A Dangerous Set of People: British Captives and the Making of Revolutionary Identity in the Mid-Atlantic Interior." *Journal of the Early Republic* 32, no. 4 (2012): 565–601.

Mishoff, Willard O. "Business in Philadelphia during the British Occupation, 1777-1778." *The Pennsylvania Magazine of History and Biography* 61, no. 2 (1937): 165–81.

Morison, Stanley. *John Bell, 1745-1831: Bookseller, Printer, Publisher, Typefounder, Journalist, Etc. ; Founder or Part-Proprietor of The Morning Post . . .* Cambridge: Cambridge Univ. Press, 2009.

Mr. Wise and Mr. Duncan. Edited by H. S. Legaré. *The North American Review* 52, no. 110 (1841): 109–48.

Nash, Gary B. *First City: Philadelphia and the Forging of Historical Memory.* Early American Studies. Philadelphia: University of Pennsylvania Press, 2002.

Nielsen, Caroline Louise. "The Chelsea Out-Pensioners: Image and Reality in Eighteenth-Century and Early Nineteenth-Century Social Care." Newcastle University, 2014.

O'Gorman, Frank. "Coventry Electoral Broadsides, 1780." *The Yale University Library Gazette* 67, no. 3/4 (1993): 161–69.

Paisley, Jeffrey L. "President Jackson's Editorial Appointees." *The Tyranny of Printers* (blog). Accessed May 8, 2020. http://pasleybrothers.com/newspols/Jackson_appointees.htm.

Pappas, Paul C. "Stewart's Kentucky Herald, 1795-1803: A Portrait of Early American Journalism West of the Alleghenies." *The Register of the Kentucky Historical Society* 67, no. 4 (1969): 335–49.

Perrin William Henry. *The Pioneer Press of Kentucky: From the Printing of the First Paper West of the Alleghanies, August 11, 1787, to the Establishment of the Daily Press in 1830.* The Filson Club: John V. Morten and Company, 1888.

Polak, Katherine. "Perspectives on Epidemic: The Yellow Fever in 1793 Philadelphia." Constructing the Past Five, no. One (2004): Article 9.

Powers, Fred. Perry. "Tales of Old Taverns." The Site and Relic Society of Germantown, March 17, 1911. http://www.morrisarboretum.org/archives/HistoricPDF/2006-3-008cTaverns.pdf.

Pruitt, P.M., and G.W. Hubbs. *Taming Alabama: Lawyers and Reformers, 1804-1929.* University of Alabama Press, 2010. https://books.google.com/books?id=2l7o4Dyr9nkC.

Quisenberry, A. C. "'Heads of Families' in Franklin County: Census of 1810." *Register of Kentucky State Historical Society* 13, no. 39 (1915): 77–95.

Ragsdale, Bruce A. "The Sedition Act Trials." *Federal Trials and Great Debates in the United States History,* Federal Judicial History Office, 2005.

Ramage, J.A. *John Wesley Hunt: Pioneer Merchant, Manufacturer and Financier.* Kentucky Bicentennial Bookshelf. University Press of Kentucky, 2015. https://books.google.com/books?id=lZYfBgAAQBAJ.

Ramage, James A., and Andrea S. Watkins. *Kentucky Rising: Democracy, Slavery, and Culture from the Early Republic to the Civil War.* Lexington: University Press of Kentucky : Kentucky Historical Society, 2011.

Raven, James. *Publishing Business in Eighteenth-Century England.* People, Markets, Goods: Economies and Societies in History, volume 3. Woodbridge: The Boydell Press, 2014.

———. *The Business of Books: Booksellers and the English Book Trade 1450 - 1850.* New Haven: Yale Univ. Press, 2007.

Rayman, Ronald. "Frontier Journalism in Kentucky: Joseph Montfort Street and the Western World, 1806-1809." *The Register of the Kentucky Historical Society* 76, no. 2 (1978): 98–111.

Remer, Rosalind. *Printers and Men of Capital: Philadelphia Book Publishers in the New Republic.* Early American Studies. Philadelphia: University of Pennsylvania Press, 2000. https://books.google.com/books?id=75_rNcHsW1kC.

———. "A Scottish Printer in Late-Eighteenth-Century Philadelphia: Robert Simpson's Journey from Apprentice to Entrepreneur." *The Pennsylvania Magazine of History and Biography* 121, no. 1/2 (1997): 3–25.

Robertson, Archibald. *Archibald Robertson: His Diaries and Sketches in America, 1762-1780.* Archibald Robertson, Lieutenant-General, Royal Engineers, New York: New York Public Library, 1971. //catalog.hathitrust.org/Record/000363536.

Rosenberg, Norman L. "Alexander Addison and the Pennsylvania Origins of Federalist First-Amendment Thought." *The Pennsylvania Magazine of History and Biography* 108, no. 4 (1984): 399–417.

Rowe, G. S. "The Disillusionment of a 'Republican Schoolmaster.'" *Western Pennsylvania History,* n.d. hppts://journals.psu.wph/article/download/3597/3428/.

Royle, Trevor. *The Cameronians: A Concise History.* Random House (Digital), 2011.

Ruppert, Bob. "The Battle of Golden Hill - Six Weeks before the Boston Massacre." *Journal of the American Revolution,* October 24, 2014. https://allthingsliberty.com/2014/10/the-battle-of-golden-hill-six-weeks-before-the-boston-massacre/.

Sachs, Honor. *Home Rule: Households, Manhood, and National Expansion on the Eighteenth-Century Kentucky Frontier.* The Lamar Series in Western History. New Haven: Yale University Press, 2015.

Schaukirk, Ewald Gustav. "Occupation of New York City by the British." *The Pennsylvania Magazine of History and Biography* 10, no. 4 (1887): 418–45.

———. "Occupation of New York City by the British." *The Pennsylvania Magazine of History and Biography* 10, no. 4 (1887): 418–45.

Schofield, Robert E. *The Enlightened Joseph Priestley: A Study of His Life and Work from 1773 to 1804.* University Park, Pennsylvania: Pennsylvania State University Press, 2004.

Scroggins, W.G. *Leaves of a Stunted Shrub: A Genealogy of the Scrogin-Scroggin-Scroggins Family.* Nativa, LLC, 2009. https://books.google.com/books?id=AnkEAwAAQBAJ.

Sener, Samuel Miller. *The Lancaster Barracks: Where the British and Hessian Prisoners Were Detained During the Revolution.* Harrisburg Publishing Company, 1895.

Seymour, C. B. "The Recall: From the Standpoint of Kentucky Legal History." *The Yale Law Journal* 21, no. 5 (1912): 372–82. https://doi.org/10.2307/784294.

Sheppard, S. *The Partisan Press: A History of Media Bias in the United States.* McFarland Publishers, 2007. https://books.google.com/books?id=2COfBQAAQBAJ.

Shoptaugh, Terry L. "Amos Kendall: A Political Biography." Exeter, NH: University of New Hampshire, 1984.

Silver, Rollo G. *The American Printer 1787-1825.* Charlottesville, Va.: Bibliographical Society of the University of Virginia, 1967.

Simpson, Robert. "Narrative of a Scottish Adventurer: From the Memoirs of Robert Simpson, Esq., Edinburgh, 1827`." *Journal of the Presbyterian Historical Society,* no. 27 (1949): 41–67.

Smith, Alice E. "Caleb Cushing's Investments in the St. Croix Valley." *The Wisconsin Magazine of History* 28, no. 1 (1944): 7–19.

Smith, Billy G., ed. *Life in Early Philadelphia: Documents from the Revolutionary and Early National Periods.* University Park, Pa: Pennsylvania State University Press, 1995.

Smith, Culver H. *The Press, Politics, and Patronage: The American Government's Use of Newspapers, 1789-1875.* Athens, GA: University of Georgia Press, 1977.

Smith, James Morton. "The Grass Roots Origins of the Kentucky Resolutions." *The William and Mary Quarterly* 27, no. 2 (1970): 221–45. https://doi.org/10.2307/1918651.

Sneed, W.C. *A Report on the History and Mode of Management of the Kentucky Penitentiary from Its Origin, in 1798, to March 1, 1860.* Kentucky. Penitentiary. Senate of Kentucky, 1860. https://books.google.com/books?id=7IyaDoWOAQwC.

St. Andrew's Society of Philadelphia, and R.B. Beath. *An Historical Catalogue of the St. Andrew's Society of Philadelphia with Biographical Sketches of Deceased Members, 1749-1913.* An Historical Catalogue of the St. Andrew's Society of Philadelphia with Biographical Sketches of Deceased Members, 1749-1913. Society, 1907. https://books.google.com/books?id=q9pS4mIGrjsC.

Stevens, John Austin, B.F. DeCosta, H.P. Johnston, M.J. Lamb, N.G. Pond, and W. Abbatt. *The Magazine of American History with Notes and Queries.* A. S. Barnes., 1877. https://books.google.com/books?id=8Zk_AQAAMAAJ.

———. *The Magazine of American History with Notes and Queries.* A.S. Barnes, 1890. https://books.google.com/books?id=CEpIAAAAYAAJ.

Stewart, Donald H. *The Opposition Press of the Federalist Period.* Albany, NY: State University of New York Press, 1969.

Stickles, Arndt, M. *The Critical Court Struggle in Kentucky 1819-1829.* Graduate Council, Bloomington, IN: Indiana University, 1929.

Sullivan, Aaron. *The Disaffected: Britain's Occupation of Philadelphia during the American Revolution.* 1st edition. Early American Studies. Philadelphia: University of Pennsylvania Press, 2019.

The American Almanac and Repository of Useful Knowledge for 1834. Vol. Five and Six. Gray and Brown, 1834.

"The Hanna House on Second Street: From History of Second Street, South Frankfort Published in the Register, Vol. II., September 1913." *Register of Kentucky State Historical Society* 15, no. 44 (May 1917): 45, 47–48.

"The Life and Times of Robert B. McAfee and His Family Connections, Part 5." *Kentucky Ancestors - Genealogical Quarterly of the Kentucky Historical Society* 43, no. 2 (Winter 2007): 81–94.

Tarrants, Charles. "Carter Tarrant (1765-1816): Baptist and Emancipationist." *The Register of the Kentucky Historical Society* 88, no. 2 (1990): 121–47.

Tiedemann, Joseph S. *Reluctant Revolutionaries: New York City and the Road to Independence, 1763–1776.* 1. print., Cornell paperbacks. Ithaca, NY: Cornell University Press, 2008.

Tocqueville, Alexis de, Gerald E. Bevan, Isaac Kramnick, Alexis de Tocqueville, and Alexis de Tocqueville. *Democracy in America: And Two Essays on America.* Penguin Classics. London: Penguin, 2003.

Toulmin, Harry. *A Description of Kentucky.* Edited by Thomas D. Clark. Reprint of 1792 Edition with editorial notes. Lexington, KY: University of Kentucky, 1945.

———. "Harry Toulmin Papers, 1809-1815." *Social Networks and Archival Context* (blog), n.d. https://snaccooperative.org/vocab_administrator/resources/7492847.

Trumbull, Benjamin. "Journal or Minutes of the Principal Movements towards St. John's of the Siege and Surrender of the Forts There in 1775." In *Collection of the Connecticut Historical Society*, Vol. VII. Hartford: Connecticut Historical Society, 1899.

Tunis, Barbara. "Dr. James Latham (c. 1734-1790): Pioneer Inoculator in Canada." *University of Toronto Press Journals*, Canadian Bureau of Medical History, 1, no. 1 (Spring 1984): 1–11. https://doi.org/10.3138.

Uglow, Jennifer S. *The Lunar Men: Five Friends Whose Curiosity Changed the World.* 1st American ed. New York: Farrar, Straus, and Giroux, 2002.

VanBurkleo, Sandra F. "'The Paws of Banks': The Origins and Significance of Kentucky's Decision to Tax Federal Bankers, 1818 - 1820." *Journal of the Early Republic* 9, no. 4 (1989): 457–87. https://doi.org/10.2307/3123752.

Venable, W.H. *Beginnings of Literary Culture in the Ohio Valley: Historical and Biographical Sketches.* R. Clarke & Company, 1891. https://books.google.com/books?id=Kl-z4SMemksC.

Villiers, Patrick. "Le Havre, port de guerre au XVIIIe siècle." Presses universitaires de Rouen et du Havre, 1999. https://books.openedition.org/purh/7835?lang=en.

British History On-line. "Walsall: Social Life," n.d. https://www.british-history.ac.uk/vch/staffs/vol17/pp249-254.

Warfield, E.D. *The Kentucky Resolutions of 1798: An Historical Study.* G. P. Putnam's Sons, 1887. https://books.google.com/books?id=WNxGcSz3kakC.

Williams, B.B. *A Literary History of Alabama: The Nineteenth Century.* Fairleigh Dickinson University Press, 1979. https://books.google.com/books?id=OKvwAtysmYcC.

Wilson, Samuel M. "The 'Kentucky Gazette' and John Bradford its Founder." *The Papers of the Bibliographical Society of America* 31, no. 2 (1937): 102–32.

Winters-Ibrahim, Rachelle, ed. *Excerpts from the Earliest Mason County, Kentucky Newspapers: The Mirror 1799 . . . and The Maysville Eagle, 1818 . . . and 1825.* Westminster, Md: Heritage Books, 2006.

Woodson, Mary Willis. "My Recollections of Frankfort." *The Register of the Kentucky Historical Society* 61, no. 3 (July 1963). https://www.jstor.org/stable/23375966.

Index

Israel, John, 118

J

Jackson, Andrew, 161, 190–93, 198, 202–203, 206, 209–10, 212, 213–16, 218, 221, 224–25, 238, 240, 242, 250, 265
Jackson, Henry, 217–18, 220, 222
Jarvis, William, 157–59, 237, 261
Jay Treaty, 140
Jefferson County, Kentucky, 186
Jefferson, Thomas, 82, 94, 98, 106, 117, 119–20, 122, 129, 134, 137, 139, 141, 146, 157, 173, 217, 239, 242, 255–56, 259–60, 265–66
Jockey Hollow, New Jersey, 35
Johnson, Joseph, 60
Johnston, Robert, 157, 163, 211–13, 218, 227, 247, 252
Jordan, Mark, 9
Jouett, Matthew, 175, 191
Junius, 131, 259

K

Kendall, Amos, 168, 186, 193–97, 199–203, 205, 207, 209–19, 240, 262, 264–65
Kentucky Abolitionist Society, 155
Kentucky Gazette, 111, 113–14, 117, 121, 123, 133–34, 205, 213, 257–58, 261–64
Kentucky Penitentiary, 169
Kentucky Reporter, 154
Kentucky Resolutions, 119–20, 125, 132, 184, 195
Kentucky River, 136, 173, 178, 188
Kentucky Seminary, 167, 170, 199, 219, 262
Key, Francis Scott, 221
King, Charles B., 185
King George III, 1, 7, 11, 55, 117, 131
King Louis XVI, 41, 43, 62
Knyphausen, Major General Wilhelm von, 30

L

Lady Godiva, 51
Lafayette, Marquis de, 31, 44–45, 48, 191, 251
Lake Champlain, 14, 17
Lake George, New York, 17
Lake Ontario, 96
Lancaster, Pennsylvania, 15, 17–21, 31, 41, 43, 161, 249
Leeds, England, 54
Lee, Henry, 119
Lee, Major General Charles, 23–24, 33, 163, 249
Le Havre, France, 40–41, 43, 45, 161
Leslie, General Alexander, 33
Lewis and Clark, 148–49, 232, 261–62
Lewis, Samuel, 180
Lexington, Battle of, 13, 81

Lexington, Kentucky, 110–12, 114, 121–22, 133, 136, 154, 162, 172–75, 189, 198, 201, 241–42, 256–57, 259–63
Library Company of Philadelphia, 222
Library Company of Washington, 222
Linnaeus, Carl, 59
Lipseed, James, 10
Lisbon, Portugal, 4, 58, 69, 157, 228, 247, 261
Lisburn, Ireland, 1
Littell, William, 139, 144, 163, 190, 204, 241, 269–70
Liverpool, England, 70–73, 253
Lockett, Craven P., 186
London, 14, 33, 42, 48–50, 57–58, 60–61, 65, 68, 70, 87, 131, 250–51, 252, 255, 262, 264
Longueuil, Quebec, 13
Lorenzo, 204, 264
Louisiana Purchase, 141, 183
Louisville Gazette, 194–97, 213, 264
Louisville, Kentucky, 113, 125, 148, 154, 172, 194, 196–97, 204, 210, 213, 240, 242, 257–58, 263–65
Louisville Public Advertiser, 185, 203, 258, 263–64
Lucy (enslaved person), 204
Lyne Jr., Leonard H., 186
Lyne, Leonard H., 186–87, 219, 225
Lyne, William H., 186

M

Mackworth, 48
Madison, George, 153, 155–56, 170
Madison, James, 120, 122, 134, 161, 241, 259, 266
Manhattan, New York, 9, 18, 25–26, 35, 247
Marshall, Humphrey, 132, 142, 153, 155, 196, 259
Marshall, J. J., 196
Marshall, John, 107, 153, 258
Marshall, Thomas, 107
Mason County, Kentucky, 113, 119, 124, 127
Maurice, William, 61–62, 66
McCarty, James, 19
McDonell, Lt. Donald, 27
McGaghey, John, 132
McKee, John, 106
McKee's Port, Pennsylvania, 101
Mercer County, Kentucky, 119
Metcalfe, Thomas, 202–203
Michael Lee & Co., 164, 165
Middletown, Kentucky, 129
Millard, Henry, 232
Milward, Frederick, 57–62, 252
Milward (Possibly), George, 60
Mingo Creek, Pennsylvania, 92
Mischianza, 32–33
Mississippi River, 96, 115–16, 120, 129, 140–41, 144, 146, 148, 172, 206
Mississippi Valley, 172

Acknowledgments

This book would not have been written without the inspiration and valuable assistance of my family, and numerous friends, professional archivists, and historian colleagues. Thank you.

Don Hagist, an expert on the British Revolutionary War soldiers and their families, helped ascertain that William Hunter authored the unsigned and unattributed journal. Don aided in understanding the social dynamics of British Army families on deployment in 1770s North America. He graciously shared extensive research and provided valuable guidance and support. Thanks to Vermont Historian Gary Shattuck and noted Revolutionary Era writer John Knight for reading an early draft and providing valuable suggestions. Gary's legal background and John's sense of history helped sharpen my arguments and improve the narrative.

Many archivists and librarians aided and facilitated my research. The University of Chicago provided access through its Rare Book room to William Hunter's personal copies of his *Palladium* newspaper. Numerous librarians at the Library of Congress, The Library Company of Philadelphia, American University Library, and the American University Law Library responded to dozens of research and access requests in the rare book, periodicals, and general collection rooms.

I appreciate the expert map making skills of George Stoll (http://www.georgestollmaps.com) who produced the five maps in the book and his coaching on place name standardization. Special thanks to the Knox College Library and Maryjo McAndrew, the Senior Archive Assistant, for providing high-resolution copies from the Special Collections & Archives of William Hunter's *The Western Telegraphe* newspaper. Additionally, thank you to the archivists at the Washington County, Pennsylvania Historical Society, Kentucky Historical Society, the District of Columbia Library, and the Kentucky Filson Society for access to primary sources records.

I am blessed with a family interested in history. My wife, Mary, read successive drafts and served as a sounding board throughout the book's research and drafting. Thank you for your encouragement and support. Additionally, my brother, Chuck, and sons Evan and Alan read various drafts and offered valuable assistance formulating my narrative.

Finally, thank you to Publisher Lawrence Knorr and the people at Sunbury Press for seeing the opportunity to bring William Hunter's story to the reading public. Their professionalism greatly aided in the book production. Of course, any errors and omissions are mine.

Diaries and memories provide a special window into our past. I hope that readers will be inspired to better understand their ancestors and make other untold family stories available to scholars and readers of the Revolutionary and Early American Eras.

About the Author

A former management consultant with one of the largest global consulting firms, Gene established a second career as a writer and a historian of the American Revolution.

Since 2013, he has authored 20 scholarly articles for the prestigious, peer-reviewed *Journal of the American Revolution*, a leading source for information on the American Revolution and the nation's founding. Gene is well-known for his writings on Revolutionary War generals, Ethan Allen, and Vermont history, as well as taking a unique look at Revolutionary events. For example, his article entitled "How the British Won the American Revolution" ignited considerable interest and new thinking, a theme in newly issued books. For six consecutive years running, at least one of Gene's essays has been selected for the print edition of the Annual Volume of the *Journal of the American Revolution*.

While pursuing his scholarship, Gene has frequently been asked to write book reviews and assist other authors. Over ten reviews have been published in the *Washington Independent Review of Books* and the *Journal of the American Revolution*. As a follow-up to one review, Gene gave the keynote address at a book launch for *Strong Ground: Mount Independence and the American Revolution* in Vermont. Increasingly, authors seek Gene's assistance, with five citing his assistance in their newly published books in the past year.

In addition, he has interviewed for podcasts and newspaper articles. Gene has been a guest speaker on the *Dispatches* podcast devoted to American Revolution topics. For the past three years, he has been interviewed by the *Charleston Patriot-Bridge* newspaper for its annual Bunker Hill remembrance edition. A frequent public speaker, he has addressed commemorative Revolutionary War events in Boston, Vermont, and Washington, DC. In Brooklyn, New York, he gave the keynote address to a several thousand-person audience assembled to commemorate the Battle of Brooklyn.

Lastly, Gene hosts and curates a website providing a historiographic compilation of primary and secondary sources at www.researchingtheamerican revolution.com. The website helps casual and professional researchers locate primary and secondary sources on a comprehensive range of American Revolution topics. Presaging readership interest in a Hunter biography, the most visited web pages are those devoted to Revolutionary War diaries and memoirs.

Made in United States
North Haven, CT
23 April 2022

18509581R00178